THE COURAGE
TO BE IMPERFECT

THE COURAGE
TO BE IMPERFECT

The Life and Work of
Rudolf Dreikurs

JANET TERNER
and
W. L. PEW

WITH THE EDITORIAL ASSISTANCE OF
Robert A. Aird

HAWTHORN BOOKS, INC.
PUBLISHERS/NEW YORK
A Howard & Wyndham Company

To Ben, Jessica, and Michele
with gratitude and love
—Janet Terner

To Mim, Barby, Becky, Debby, Bill, and Mike
for their patience and encouragement
—W. L. Pew

Whatever you can do, or dream you can, begin it.
Boldness has genius, power and magic in it.

Goethe

Contents

ix

PART III

A Movement Is Born

Acknowledgments

Deep appreciation is expressed to Sadie "Tee" Dreikurs for her continued cooperation and support from the book's conception in 1972 to its completion in 1977. Dr. Eva Dreikurs Ferguson, the daughter of Rudolf Dreikurs, carefully read the entire manuscript and her many helpful suggestions are gratefully acknowledged. Special appreciation goes to Eva Kirschner of Israel, who conducted numerous interviews there and assembled important materials with great devotion for the chapter on Israel; to John Feulner for his careful translation from German to English of Dreikurs's student notebooks, and early papers and letters; and to Robert Aird for his dedicated editorial assistance. Appreciation is also expressed to the following people, whose advice, technical assistance, and encouragement helped bring this book to fruition: William McKelvie, Weltha Logan, Manford Sonstegard, Melba McIntyre, Eliora Margalit, Andrea Williams, Robert Powers, Jane Collins, Audrey Cenedella, Nancy Catlin, Cary Binney, Ray Corsini, Marianne Beith, Inge Scott, Lee N. Fryer, Phyllis Pantell, and Pamela Swardson. The many people—family, friends, and colleagues of Rudolf Dreikurs, both in the United States and abroad, who generously shared their personal experiences of Dreikurs, made the preparation of this book especially rewarding and helped bring "Dr. D." to life on the printed page. The genial cooperation and helpfulness of the staffs of the Manuscript Division and the Science and Technology Division of the Library of Congress are also acknowledged.

JANET TERNER

Introduction

We are living in an age of social upheaval and revolution in which our cherished traditional values regarding sex, marriage, family life, and work are increasingly being challenged and frequently being abandoned. Few realize that what we are witnessing in society today was accurately predicted by Alfred Adler more than fifty years ago, including the demand for equality by minority groups and the feminist revolution. These predictions were not random speculations but clear consequences of his socially based, holistic, teleological, self-determining view of mankind. In this view, life is seen as movement, growth, and change, an evolutionary process that becomes increasingly intolerant of the rankings and degrees of domination and subordination that have characterized civilization, with local variation, for thousands of years. Only in a democratic society could all people begin to experience their potentialities, and Adler and Dreikurs both saw the United States, with its complex, imperfect, yet throbbing democratic structures as the logical setting for that realization. They were not alone in that vision. Long before, when setting the tenets for democracy in America, the Founding Fathers presaged the same view. And more recently, Jean-François Revel, in his *Without Marx or Jesus*, envisioned that, "The revolution of the twentieth century will take place in the United States. It is only there that it can happen. And it has already begun. Whether or not that revolution spreads to the rest of the world depends on whether or not it succeeds first in America."

Today more than ever, in response to the breakdown and uncertainty of our traditional social conventions, thoughtful people are actively seeking to reach a better understanding of themselves and to rediscover a central purpose and meaning to their lives. They seek to overcome the loneliness, anomie, and despair of powerlessness that has come to characterize much of urban-suburban American life. Increasingly skeptical of the lofty exhortations of the "experts," they insist on experiencing directly and learning for themselves more effective modes of being in this world and of relating to others. This explains the tremendous appeal of books like *I'm OK, You're OK* and *Parent Effectiveness Training*, which skillfully translate valid psychological constructs into understandable and usable modes for improving interpersonal transactions. Both books rest upon an inherent assumption, enunciated much earlier by Adler and Dreikurs, that most maladaptive, antisocial behavior stems from faulty training and that the only practical solution is greatly to increase the psychological understanding and skill of the citizenry, particularly parents and teachers. It is, after all, the people who will ultimately decide whether we ameliorate or exacerbate the social problems and uncertainties we face.

It was Rudolf Dreikurs, however, who played a major role in setting this whole trend in motion. What he began in the late 1930s as an unpretentious mother's discussion group has evolved into a movement of significant proportions in communities all across the nation, where concerned adults come together in small groups to study, discuss, and experience Dreikurs's teachings. With remarkable clarity of thought and an economy of words, he conveyed in lectures, demonstrations, and books to thousands of groping parents, educators, and counselors an understanding of what is evolving in our homes, schools, and society. Briefly, it is an ever-quickening revolution from traditional autocratic social structures to democratic ones. What was central to Dreikurs in this evolution was the change in the underlying psychological dynamics of human interactions that had to follow from it. More importantly, he pointed out effective new techniques of interacting that anyone can easily learn and that are compatible with a democratic structure and its requirements of mutual respect, freedom of choice, and self-determination. It is estimated that today, at any given time, twenty thousand people are engaged in Dreikurs's study groups. The basic text for these groups, *Children: The Challenge*, a brilliant book in its genre, has never received the benefit of publicity from TV talk shows, massive publisher's advertising, or book-club backing, and yet it continues to be a strong seller since its publication in 1964.

Today there is a growing recognition that the main thrust of psychology is moving more in directions proposed by Adler than in those set out by Freud. A psychological system, to be useful, must fit the social structure in which it exists. Freud's pessimistic view of man as a victim of biological urges beyond his control and as a being inherently in conflict with himself, his fellowman, and society is incompatible with democratic theory. The behaviorists, by denying the centrality of man's beliefs and values and sense of purpose in all his actions, have disemboweled him of his humanity, and they have fallen back on outdated autocratic techniques to make him behave.

It is by means of the sweeping, unified, yet simple constructs of the Adlerian view of human development and functioning that we can encompass the evolving social structures of democratic societies. The Adlerian view is congruent with most of the significant psychological schools that are flourishing today—Existentialist, Gestalt, Learning Theory, Reality Therapy, Transactional Analysis, Logotherapy, Client-centered Therapy, and so on, to name some of the major ones. All, explicitly or implicitly, are based on a similar concept of man as purposive, ever striving for growth, value, and meaning in this world, and self-determining in his movement through life. As Viktor E. Frankl put it, "What he [Adler] . . . achieved and accomplished was no less than a Copernican switch." But just as Copernicus needed a Galileo to convey to the world the meaning and significance of his revolutionary discovery, so Adler needed Dreikurs, who transplanted his ideas to the fertile soil of America and developed and refined them into a clear-cut, teachable system with practical applications for family life, education, preventive mental health, and every form of human interaction. The story of Dreikurs's life is both an inspiration and an opportunity for conveying the vitally important and timely concept of life he offered to us all.

JANET TERNER

PART I

THE VIENNA YEARS
1897-1937

1

Childhood: A Power Struggle with Authority

> The individual is the picture and the artist. He is the artist of his own personality.
>
> Alfred Adler
> *The Education of the Child,* 1930

In a stately section of Vienna, overshadowed by her great university and medical centers, joy filled the small but well-appointed apartment at No. 4, Pfluggasse. It was February 8, 1897. That day Sigmund and Fanny Dreikurs's first child, Rudolf, was born. With exhilaration, Sigmund embraced his older brother, the physician who had attended Fanny through the delivery. After stealing a glance at his new son and his resting wife, he rushed off, beaming with pride, to carry the news to his awaiting family. The birth of a son was another sign that life in recent years had turned favorably for him.

Although slight in build, Sigmund was an imposing figure. His piercing eyes, accentuated by his balding pate and handlebar moustache, his impeccable attire and ramrod stance, gave credence to his arrogant self-assurance. He looked and felt older than his twenty-seven years, perhaps because he had struggled so to achieve his present status. He epitomized the self-made man, and the fruits of his driving ambition were already evident. His import-export firm, *Weiss und Dreikurs,* whose tradings reached to the far corners of the Austro-Hungarian Empire, was succeeding beyond his dreams. His meteoric rise in the business world won the admiration of family and friends alike, which gave him particular satisfaction.

Sigmund was the youngest of four brothers and a sister, all born in Vienna. His parents came from Poland and migrated to Vienna like many poor Jewish families in search of a new and better life. In Vienna's rich

3

environment, their hopes soared, and they struggled to provide the finest education for their children. Indeed, Sigmund's three older brothers acquired doctorates, the first two in medicine and the third in economics. Even his sister was formally educated for a teaching career, but she gave it up when she married. As the family assimilated into Vienna's middle class, they shed their Jewish ties and largely converted to Catholicism, the state religion.

When it came time for Sigmund to enter the university, the family funds had run out. He was bitterly disappointed. Typical of the youngest child in many large families, he was inordinately ambitious to surpass his accomplished older siblings. He therefore turned his driving energy and talents to art. But his hopes for becoming a great painter were dashed by his poor eyesight. Twice frustrated, he turned his driving ambition to the business world.

"My father," Rudolf Dreikurs recalled years later, "often told me that his ambition was to show his older, more educated brothers that he could make money and outstrip them all. And he did. Actually, money became the key factor in our family. In the long run, it was his weak spot. While my father was relatively well off, he was so concerned not to spend money that he was very stingy. My mother always complained that she did not get enough to dress us properly because he didn't want to spend money for clothing. Later, he lost his life for his money."[1]

Sigmund felt fortunate in his marriage to Fanny Cohn. He had made one of the best matches of anyone in his family. They had met a few years earlier at the wedding of his older brother, which she happened to attend as a close friend of the bride. He was immediately attracted by her beauty and warmth. Her cultured, wealthy background fit perfectly with his own ambitions, and they were married in 1895.

Fanny had grown up under different circumstances from Sigmund. Raised in Gutentag, a small town in Posen, Prussia, she was the second of five daughters and one son born to an aristocratic Jewish family. Rudolf described his mother as "a half orphan [her mother died when she was a child], who was exceedingly beautiful. She was not formally educated, but she was even more intelligent and intellectually ambitious than my father. She was an idealist. She was warm. It was quite obvious that I was her favorite."

Her pictures reveal a tall, beautiful woman of proud bearing, but she was friendly, talkative, and generous. Idealistic in her outlook, which no doubt reflected the liberal tradition of her Germanic family, Fanny devoted herself to various worthy causes throughout her life. In contrast to

Sigmund, she maintained her close ties to Judaism and became actively involved in the Zionist movement that arose in Vienna. Her hard work and dedication to these organizational activities led her family to teasingly dub her "the original club woman."

Both Sigmund and Fanny had great expectations for their son. Emphasis was placed on education, the cultural arts, and the importance of proper manners, behavior, and dress. The proud father now had a namesake to teach, to share his dreams, and to fulfill his own ambitions. Fanny, too, wanted only the best for her son.

They gave their son a popular Germanic name reminiscent of the great Rudolfs in Austria's past. Their choice expressed an identification with and assimilation into Austrian culture, which was so typical of rising Viennese Jewish families.

The family atmosphere—the attitudes, values, and relationships within the immediate family—as Rudolf Dreikurs later claimed, provides the initial, critical medium through which the child's personality takes shape. From his experience of it, the child creates a picture of himself, of others, and of the world at large. It shapes his values and provides the testing ground for actions that will give him a sense of belonging and significance.

Rudolf's family background, his parents' cultural and economic position, and their hopes and ambitions would appear to provide all the necessary ingredients for a content childhood. But to the sandy-haired, freckled young boy it seemed quite different. As an only child for his first five years, he felt bewildered, inadequate, and like a clumsy dwarf surrounded by the giant, accomplished adults who peopled his entire world. His stern father impatiently demanded perfection of him, his mother indulged and pampered him, and nursemaids, aunts, and uncles all made Rudi the focus of attention. He was a little prince who quickly grasped that to be important and to have a place in the family, he must be the center of attention. The rub was that he also had to live up to all the demands placed upon him. A photograph of him at age four reveals a frail, sensitive child with eyes full of wonder—truly the wistful prince.

Suddenly, when he was five, Rudolf's world was torn asunder, his throne toppled, and his sovereignty destroyed by the arrival of a baby sister, Bertha. His earliest childhood recollection stemmed from this event:

> I remember when I woke up in the morning, I was told to get up by the governess. We went down into the garden, and I remember the

window on the third floor opened. My uncle, who was the physician, called out, "Come up, your sister is born!"

The governess hurried me up the stairs, but I didn't quite believe the story, and said to her, "Don't run, it's baloney." When I came up, I remember seeing a little baby.

Then I remember my father took me to his office. While I was there, I remember seeing a military funeral at the military church across the way. I was quite impressed by the uniforms and all that. Then my favorite aunt, my father's sister, met me and took me to lunch. It was a very good lunch, and I enjoyed it very much. After that, my uncle picked me up and brought me to his family. I remember that evening. I was still so excited, I could not sleep.

Dreikurs described this recollection several times in later years and could not resist giving his interpretation of its meaning. "I turned this obvious dethronement, and actually being thrown out of the house, into a tremendous asset. In these early years I somewhat replaced my family with the world . . . I suddenly became a man of the world."

In the psychological theory of Alfred Adler (of which Dreikurs later became a chief exponent), early recollections—the sparse, fragmentary memories of childhood incidents—provide a valuable clue to the adult personality. Out of the myriad experiences in the first decade of life, only a few, generally less than a dozen, remain vivid into adulthood. Adler discovered that these early recollections are commentaries on life, retained as concrete reminders of the individual's basic beliefs and outlook.

With his sovereign position in his immediate family toppled by his sister's arrival, young Rudi, enlisting the aid of others, turned adversity into adventure and managed to find ways to remain special—the center of attention. The optimistic determination not to let obstacles stand in his way, revealed in this recollection, would become the most persistent characteristic of Rudolf Dreikurs's personality.

Adler wrote, "Every oldest child has experienced for some time the situation of an only child and has been compelled to adapt himself when another child is born and he is no longer unique. . . . The change always makes a great impression and generally, he is not prepared. The new baby really takes away from him attention, love and appreciation. He begins trying to pull his mother back to him and thinking how he can regain attention using force and . . . new tricks."[2]

"I felt quite dethroned by my sister," Dreikurs recalled. "I was told my resentment over this came out pretty strongly in my becoming such a severe feeding problem that for many months I could not keep any food down, regardless of how everybody tried to cater to my taste.

"I felt very unfairly treated. She, in my mind, always got people against me. She always got everything. Particularly, she was the favorite of my father. I probably got quite a few beatings because of her."

Rudi struggled to adapt himself to his new position. Sensing his father's greater affection for his "good" little sister, he felt hopelessly defeated. "I never could live up to his expectations," he later reflected. "I was withdrawn and convinced of my inadequacy and stupidity."

Deeply resenting the "unfairness" of his situation, Rudi went on strike, passively rebelling against authority—a strike that endured throughout his childhood and early adolescence. It invoked the wrath of his domineering father, a man who did not believe in sparing the rod. "My mother," he remarked, "a soft and idealistic woman, somehow supported me in my rebellion against my father."

Rudi's feelings of inadequacy were expressed in his physical bearing. "I didn't walk properly, I had bad posture, for which I was beaten."

Sigmund's harshness and brutality left a lasting impression on Rudolf. In this connection, he wrote:

> I remember an incident which took place years later in the large ornamental hall of the University of Bratislava, Czechoslovakia. Alfred Adler had been invited to give a lecture there, but he became sick and asked me to substitute for him. It was a most impressive formal setting with hundreds of dignified academicians in attendance. I spoke about education. In the discussion I was asked whether I believed in spanking. Quite impulsively I answered, "Yes, I believe that everyone who abuses children should be spanked." I certainly evoked a shock reaction, because at that time spanking was still an accepted educational method. In that moment I recognized the reason for my outburst: My identification with children—with all suppressed groups—was an effort to get back at my father who spanked me frequently.

However, not everything in the relationship between Sigmund and Rudolf was negative. "One of our greatest pleasures," Dreikurs recalled, "was to wrestle. It was in the living room, and we'd move the chairs away and everything. Of course, he always wrestled me down, but I liked it very much and always went back for more. It was the only form of physical contact between us that was warm."

Another positive memory was their train trips together. "I always stood at the window. I loved to ride and watch the scenery go by. Father often stood by me and answered my questions. That was a tremendous source of information and pleasure to me."

Geography and travel remained lifelong avocations for Dreikurs. His travels sharpened his perceptual skills, and geography was the only subject he found intellectually stimulating in his grammar school years. Travel was both a route to adventure and an escape. "As a boy, no matter who the relation, if I was invited, I was delighted to go there and stay away. I was always glad to be somewhere else. Later, I was one of the few who left Europe, not with the feeling that I had to leave, but that I had a chance to leave."

Rudi was poorly prepared for the give-and-take of peer relationships. As the sole child in his earliest years, he was isolated from other children by an overprotective family atmosphere. This was further aggravated by the fact that his family moved several times before he was six. By the time Rudi was about to enter school, the family had settled into a large, single-family dwelling in the "Cottagegasse," an elegant section of suburban Döbling.

Rudi yearned for companionship and to escape the unrelenting pressures of the home:

> When I was six years old . . . I had some playmates, but it was rather traumatic for me. The neighboring landlord had a son about my age—unruly, wild, and rough. He always beat me up. I was not prepared for this—I was overprotected and had no way to fight back. His bullying intensified my feeling of utter helplessness.
>
> But there was another boy, older than I, who was very gentle. We three played together, and later on the bully came to like me. I really admired him, and the rough stuff ended.

His mother usually managed to intrude upon his early efforts to make his way in the outside world: "The first day I went to school, I was seated next to a boy from a very poor family. He treated me with great respect, in contrast to the neighbor boy, who beat me up. I immediately brought the schoolmate home, declaring proudly, 'Mom, I have a friend.' I could not understand why my mother disapproved. She gave him something to eat, sent him home, and didn't permit me to bring him home again. That was the end of that friendship."

From his early years on, Dreikurs demonstrated a tendency to react vigorously whenever his integrity was challenged: "One instance I remember very well that is characteristic of my development: We three boys were walking to school. The biggest boy showed a rare stamp from Mexico to the other boy, who admired it. I had just begun collecting stamps, and I meekly said I had the same stamp. They both looked at me, and one said, 'You are much too stupid to know anything about it.' Consequently I became an avid philatelist."

From an Adlerian standpoint, school poses an important challenge to a young child. It is the testing ground for his ability to function in the community. For the pampered child who has little faith in his abilities, it is a trying period. So long as he can gain the attention of the teacher, he may be successful. But if he loses special consideration, trouble is bound to follow. So it was for Rudi:

> Like all middle-class children, we had a governess. In first grade, while out walking with her, we met my teacher. Apparently these two hit it off, and my teacher began to join us on these walks. I then had a special role in the class.
>
> My first three years were spent in public school. I don't remember anything outstanding about them, but I did like my first-grade teacher, who was an admirer of my governess.
>
> When I was nine, and in the fourth grade, I was sent to a private school in order to skip a grade. My parents wanted me to take the exams for entrance into the *gymnasium*[3] a year early. I felt quite inferior to the wealthy children, as I was not particularly well dressed, because my father was so stingy. I had a tough time.
>
> It all started when I made an appointment to meet my mother, but there was some misunderstanding, and she did not come. I went home and cried, feeling unfairly treated and abandoned.
>
> The woman teacher I had there was very nice, but for some reason I felt inferior. No doubt it had to do with my earliest relationships with girls. My first contact with girls in this coeducational school was pretty crushing for me. I was not well dressed, I was not very good-looking, and I was rather clumsy. A number of the boys hit it off real well with the girls. I felt attracted to one of the girls, the biggest show-off of the whole class. All the boys were after her. I felt badly

that neither she nor anyone else really paid any attention to me whatsoever. I felt especially [inadequate] because there was one boy—exceedingly gifted, tall, flamboyant—who really hit it off with the girls, even though he was a mischief maker and always got bad marks.

In sum, Dreikurs remarked, "I wasn't too good in school, or at play. I was inhibited. School was more or less torture."

The unyielding demand for discipline and obedience plus the rigorous academic requirements of the *gymnasium* were unbearably reminiscent of his father's demands. He balked and went on strike, just as he had at home:

> When I entered the *gymnasium* at age ten, trouble really began. For some reason, I couldn't learn the grammar or verbs in Latin, and I almost flunked. Mother and father sat down with me and literally tried to blow it into me. The more they tried, the more discouraged I became. I just couldn't grasp it and became convinced I had no talent for language.
>
> School was not a challenge—a threat, yes—but not a challenge. I wasn't interested and didn't do the work. I knew that if I studied, I wouldn't remember anyhow, so what was the use. I went through the whole eight years never studying, barely able to keep up, and always in the bottom third of my class.
>
> In the last years, a friend and I made a pact to see what would happen if we deliberately left our books at school, preventing us from doing the homework. We figured we could get by without it, and we managed pretty well. . . . It was one of my major achievements that I got through school without ever becoming interested. Actually, I was interested in so many other things.

One can easily imagine Sigmund's frustration and anger toward his son's insubordinate behavior, his backwardness, and his laziness. Rudi too was convinced that he was lazy and could never measure up. Neither of them understood how desperately Rudi wanted to please his father, nor that laziness is a curious by-product of ambition mixed with discouragement—ambition so high that the individual has no hope of realizing it.[4] Perhaps, Rudi reasoned, if he appeared incapable of learning, they would see no use in demanding work from him, and leave him alone.

Nevertheless, this perceptive and sensitive lad was growing and learning. Even the dry grammar, facts, and theorems that poured from the educational system he so despised inadvertently filtered into his curious mind.

Rudi's earliest awakening to his own potential came through his "other interests"—stamps, travel, and most important of all, music:

> Music was an important element in our family. My father had musical interests—he was a member of Vienna's leading choirs, which regularly performed in the largest concert halls. A cousin of mine, a half year younger than I, was a musical genius. He had a brilliant future ahead of him as a virtuoso violinist and composer that was tragically ended years later when he was killed in the war at age eighteen.
>
> We were the only two boys in the family, and my father decided that I had to play the violin too. I was not delighted over the prospect, because now I had to study even more, and I had a poor teacher. After a few years I wanted to stop, but since my parents had invested so much money, I had to continue. The longer I took lessons, the less I learned. Violin never interested me. But I was interested in the piano, probably because my cousin didn't play it and because my parents refused to let me have a piano.
>
> Finally, I worked out a deal with my parents. They promised that if I performed satisfactorily at my teacher's next recital, I could switch to piano. This I did.
>
> My father—always pinching pennies—economized by finding a governess who could teach me both piano and French. She was a very practical and vital person, and I fell in love with her more or less. She was understanding and did not make practicing unpleasant, and I appreciated her very much. She only complained that I did not practice enough. I was very close to her, and later, when she died, I gave the eulogy.
>
> In the meantime, stimulated by my best friend's mother, who invited me to play duets with her, I discovered the pleasure of sight reading. After that, I played whatever music came into my hands, and I began to improvise, to "play around." This had the expected results. Now my parents objected to the time spent at the piano instead of doing my homework. Their objection became rather vociferous when I discovered Wagner and not only played the score

but sang with it. Distressing as it was to other members of the family, in consequence, I became a rather good pianist, even accompanying my father when he sang. Later, I began to study composition and almost became a professional musician.

Music became Dreikurs's most cherished avocation. Whether in Europe or in America, he was an enthusiastic concertgoer, regularly playing in amateur chamber music groups, and jumping at every opportunity to play duo-pianos. Besides the piano, he also became competent with guitar, cello, viola, and violin.

Notes for Chapter 1

1. The direct quotations of Rudolf Dreikurs are a composite derived from two sources: (1) the magnetic-tape recordings of an oral interview conducted with Rudolf Dreikurs by William H. Mackaness in 1961 as background material for his doctoral dissertation, *A Biographical Study of the Life of Rudolf Dreikurs, M.D., with Emphasis Placed upon His Work Relating the Theoretical Principles of Individual Psychology to the Modern Classroom Setting.* (Ann Arbor, Mich.: University Microfilms, 1963) and (2) Rudolf Dreikurs, "Guiding, Teaching, and Demonstrating: An Adlerian Autobiography," *Journal of Individual Psychology* 23 (1967): 145–157.

2. Alfred Adler, *What Life Should Mean to You,* ed. Alan Porter (New York: Capricorn Books, 1958), pp. 144–145.

3. The rigorous German secondary school designed as a preparatory program for university-bound students.

4. Adler, *What Life Should Mean to You,* pp. 144–145.

2

From Youth to Manhood

I do have the feeling the world is waiting for me.
Rudolf Dreikurs,
"Mein Beruf," 1915

"For almost every child," Adler asserted,

adolescence means one thing above all else: he must prove that he is
no longer a child. . . . The approach of adult responsibilities is an
especial strain to the children who have been accustomed to [hav-
ing] everything done for them; . . . they have been brought up in an
artificially warm atmosphere and the air outside feels bitterly cold.
[Yet] at this time we find apparent reversals of progress. . . . [Some]
children who had previously seemed less gifted begin to . . . reveal
unsuspected abilities. [They] are stimulated by their new freedom,
see the road toward fulfillment of their ambitions clear before them,
and are full of new ideas. . . . The children who had previously felt
slighted . . . now, perhaps, when they are more widely connected
with their fellows, conceive the hope that they can find appreciation.
Many of them are completely hypnotized by this craving for appreciation.[1]

"In my second decade," Dreikurs recalled, "I came into my own, and
found my place in society in a positive way. Yet the earlier perceptions I
had of myself prevented me from grasping this until much later in my
life."[2]

The critical turning point came when he was sixteen:

It happened on vacation. I went on a bike trip to see my friend, who
lived on the other side of the lake. The next morning I awoke with a
temperature and feeling ill. Of course, my father got after me: "See
how irresponsible you are! You got all sweated up, overexcited about

13

this trip! You had to ride your bike there! So now as a consequence you are sick!"

But when my neck got stiff, he became frightened and called the doctor. To remove any uncertainty, they sent back across the lake to get another doctor, who diagnosed my illness as polio. Still, my father railed on that if I had not made that bicycle trip, I would never have gotten polio.

When the acute fever lapsed, Rudi was shocked to discover that the use of his legs, particularly his left one, was seriously impaired, and that his abdominal muscles were severely weakened. Little was then known about this dread disease, and the prospect of lasting paralysis was frighteningly real. Rudolf's physician uncle wisely urged his parents to send him to Silesia to use the mineral baths and to recuperate as much as possible under his care. Rudi stayed there nearly three months. Although faced with the most critical challenge thus far in his life, he was at last freed from the parental shackles—his mother's relentless fussing, his father's endless carping. Now it was up to him. Slowly, the healing waters soothed and strengthened his muscles, the restful environment invigorated his body, and his uncle's patient encouragement fired his courage to overcome the illness. He succeeded, through the force of his own determination, training other muscles to take over for the weakened ones. By the time he returned to Vienna in the fall of 1915, only a slight, temporary limp remained. Though left with certain muscles permanently weakened, he knew he had won the battle.

WYNEKEN AND THE AUSTRIAN YOUTH MOVEMENT

Hastening Rudi's recovery was a sudden desire to return to Vienna, where the German youth movement had arrived in Austria with revolutionary fervor. Robert Fraenkel, the close friend with whom he had made the no-homework pact, had written him enthusiastic reports about a strange event on Mount Höhe Meissner, where the spellbinding ideas of Gustav Wyneken had captivated Vienna's youth.

The event on Höhe Meissner marked the spiritual highpoint of the German youth movement. Hundreds of youths from Germany and Austria had gathered that misty Sunday in October 1913. Youth had been organized before—in religious, social, political, or athletically oriented groups—but always under adult direction whose aim was to channel young people into established patterns set by the older generation. But the German youth movement was different. It claimed that youth had an existence of its own and a right to determine its own values and directions that would transcend the artificial boundaries of social class or nationality imposed by the older order.

The movement's roots lay in the earlier *Wandervoegel* ("wandering bird") movement that embraced a mixture of resurrected German romanticism with insurrection against the beer-hall conventionality. Dressed in traditional garb, with backpacks and guitars slung over their backs, the *Wandervoegel* boys roamed through fields and woods and gathered around old castles, there to revive old hiking songs and circle dances. From these amorphous origins rose not only the intellectual and liberal branch of the youth movement in Austria but also the embryonic notions of Aryan supremacy and racial anti-Semitism of the Nazi *bunde*. It was big enough to nurture both.

Gustav Wyneken, who inspired the Austrian youth movement, was a radical progressive educator. In 1906, he founded the Free School Community (Frei Schulgemeinde) in Wickersdorf, Germany, a genuinely democratic school where students participated as full partners. One of the first coeducational schools in Germany, it was a radical departure from the authoritarian imperial schools. Although he admired the *Wandervoegel* movement, Wyneken believed that it was superficial. He resolved to create a comprehensive program combining academic training with agricultural work, spiritual awareness, physical education, and community living. All students, except the very youngest, exercised an equal vote in community decisions. Wyneken's central idea was "youth culture," and his goal was to develop, through education, a new type of man and woman. He asserted that youth had been denied the realization of the latent superiority that lay in its inherent intellectual and ethical naturalness and enthusiasm.[3]

In 1910, Wyneken was removed from the school over conflicts with local authorities, and he then began championing his cause through books and the youth movement. His appearance at Höhe Meissner captured the imagination of a group of Viennese university students, who returned home to propagate his ideas. The Austrian youth movement differed from its German forerunner because in liberal Vienna it became a predominantly Jewish-intellectual phenomenon. It appealed to those children of the liberal bourgeois establishment who decried the materialistic preoc-

cupation and satisfaction of their elders. The Viennese Youth Movement
presented a united front against the adult generation and searched for a
more relevant existence.

"When I returned to Vienna in the fall of 1913," Dreikurs remarked, "I
was drawn immediately into this exciting movement and became an active member. Probably the youth movement shaped my life more than
any other single factor. . . . Wyneken, whom I never met personally, . . .
and Alfred Adler were the two personalities who, with their ideologies,
had the greatest influence on me."

In Vienna, Wyneken's deputy was Siegfried Bernfeld, then a medical
student in his early twenties who later became a leading psychoanalyst.
In a rented room near the old church *Marie am Gestade,* he and George
Barbizon organized discussion groups for youths. They called it a
Sprechsaal, a room for speaking out. Here the young people found an
unprecedented opportunity to express themselves, to discuss problems,
and to explore all manner of intellectual and social issues. The unsatisfied,
rebellious, willful, brooding yet gifted youth of the city came. It was here
that these young people planned their cherished Sunday excursions—
hiking and camping in the meadows and mountains in the style of the
Wandervoegel.[4]

The tone of the movement was definitely intellectual, and much of the
discussion centered on school reform. "We discussed our parents, we discussed our teachers," Dreikurs commented, "and we discussed ourselves.
The highlight of the development came when Bernfeld organized weekly
lectures for our parents. We dragged them downtown to hear Bernfeld
tell them how they abused us, how they lacked respect for us, and that we
had certain rights. We were very concerned with moral issues in regard to
sex and behavior in general. We became conscious of our rights, and
didn't mind at all teaching our parents and teachers what they should do.
In this period of life when we became integrated into society we took a
stand as a group for higher intellectual, moral, and spiritual values."

If educational issues were foremost in the movement, not far behind
was the question of relations between the sexes. The movement was
revolutionary in its commitment to equality between the sexes, and the
girls participated fully in its activities. This was remarkable considering
the highly protective, chauvinistic attitudes that prevailed generally. The
movement therefore provided an exciting new testing ground for the
meeting of the sexes. Their discussions ranged from premarital sex to
monogamy versus free love, and included social problems such as prosti-

tution and even such taboo subjects as masturbation. Through his leadership, Bernfeld brought his enthusiastic interest in Freud's new science to the attention of the group.

Within the organization, the youth formed small groups of friends who pursued special interests, such as art, poetry, politics, and hiking. Off they went, hatless and coatless in winter and summer, the boys easily recognized by their blowing manes, open shirts, shorts, and sandals; the girls by their simply styled belted frocks with lutes slung over the shoulder. Though too liberal in their attitude to hark back to German romanticism, they did mimic the country excursions, the singing, and the dancing.

Mitzi Deutsch, "the sportswoman who climbed the tallest trees, swam the Danube, and mastered Nietzsche and modern philosophy better than all the others,"[5] led the Grüne Wandervoegel Hiking Club in which young Dreikurs participated. "I was rather a tomboy," she recalled, "and did not spare them. We walked up to eight hours per day. This suited Rudi, who wore enormous mountaineering boots and, despite his round-shouldered deportment, walked well. We had our special recipes, and he was quite good at barbecue cooking. I would not say that he was very forthright, but if challenged, he defended his points with tenacity."[6]

As the youth movement grew, so did the doubts and suspicions in the minds of parents and local authorities, as Dreikurs soon discovered. "I started one of these discussion centers—a *Sprechsaal*—in my own community and was almost expelled from school because of my 'subversive' activities," he remembered. "Called by the director of our school, I was asked to explain the peculiar things we were doing and was threatened with expulsion. I told him we met weekly and admitted that we freely discussed our parents and teachers. Because we were not a secret organization, I invited them to come and see for themselves, to hear what we thought of them. They accepted that, and no bad consequences took place."

With that the opposition melted away. For Dreikurs the incident was an important lesson. Later he saw the open, public setting of Adler's child guidance clinics as a most valuable quality. Openness became for him a crucial ingredient of democratic functioning, a cornerstone of his training technique, and an effective means of dissipating opposition wherever it arose.

Reflecting on the meaning of the youth movement, Dreikurs commented, "It had a lasting effect on most of us. I owe my leadership ability to it. Of the approximately one hundred boys and girls in the movement, I could count twenty who became internationally known, which is a high percentage for any group of young people." Among those who went on to make important contributions in their field, besides Dreikurs, were psychoanalysts Bernfeld and Otto Fenichel (who was Dreikurs's close friend in those days), anthropologist Dr. Maria Glas (formerly Mitzi Deutsch), mathematician Dr. Hilda Geiringer, poet Theodor Kramer, composer Hans Eisler, and sociologist Dr. Paul Lazarsfeld. Many others played an active role in European political developments after the war, and a number of the girls were early proponents of womens' rights.

During those expansive years, Dreikurs reflected, "I had a very interesting love affair, if you can call it that. She was six years older than I and already engaged, which prevented her from falling in love with me. But she was the most encouraging female I ever met. We talked about everything. She was impressed with my knowledge of chemistry, astronomy, and such things. I looked about six years older than I was and was surprised to be recognized as an older man. I felt very encouraged by it."

Zdenka Pollack—"Mimi"—was an attractive, refreshing young woman, aptly nicknamed after the famed heroine of *La Bohème*. Bright yet fun loving, Mimi was in her early twenties when they met. She had completed school and was employed as a bank clerk. She was one of the first girls to join the youth movement. Having both an older and a younger brother, Mimi felt at ease in the company of young men. Her naturalness ruled out coyness or reliance on classic feminine wiles. Rudi found her especially appealing; she was attractive yet unthreatening and seemed to enjoy debating all manner of subjects as deeply as he.

Mimi's first impressions of Rudi were not very flattering. "He wasn't popular, maybe because he was kind of bullish or clumsy. He was a nice fellow, but not very gracious—like a teddy bear." Common interests drew them together. "We both liked music and went to lectures, concerts, and the opera together."[7]

Despite her seeming independence, Mimi had her own insecurities and found Rudi's attentiveness reassuring. When her previous engagement ended, the two became close companions and were soon identified as a couple within the movement. What began as shared interests evolved over the next four years into a love that, in reality, was more platonic than physical. While free love and sexuality were openly discussed in the movement, most of the youths had been raised with strict middle-class morals, and the gap between their ideas and actions was often great. "If you compare us to the youth of today, it is impossible to think that we were of the same age," Mimi later mused. "We were such innocent, naïve little lambs. There was nothing much going on all those years. Oh, we held hands and things like that, but it was mostly idealistic and platonic."

The gap between appearance and reality led to a scandalous incident that ironically brought about Dreikurs's first link to Alfred Adler. It occurred when Rudolf, Mimi, and Paul Stein, who later practiced medicine in New York, went on a hiking excursion to Rax Mountain. They misjudged the time, and it turned dark before they could get back. So they wound up staying overnight together in an alpine hut.

"Of course, it was so cold, you couldn't possibly take off your clothes," Mimi laughed. "Besides, we never thought of doing such a thing anyway!"

A great scandal followed. Mimi's beloved grandfather, who took a special interest in her, was mortified. He was already troubled by her unorthodox and unladylike behavior and feared her "ruination." "After this happened," Mimi related, "he wrapped me around his little finger and made me promise never to see Rudolf Dreikurs again. I promised. But it was a promise I knew I couldn't keep and didn't want to keep. Yet I didn't know how to extricate myself." Trapped in a conflict over pleasing her family or pleasing Rudolf and being true to her own beliefs, Mimi experienced a mild breakdown.

Mimi's alarmed parents took her to a psychiatrist, one of Freud's close disciples. "He was a rough fellow," she recalled. "I couldn't stand him, and refused to see him again after that one session. He committed suicide very shortly thereafter," she added.

> After that, I went to Adler, who treated me for about two weeks. I went every day, during which he analyzed my dreams and we talked. He was always so nice, like a good old daddy. I wasn't nervous about going, just curious, which is one of my main characteristics.
>
> His manner was kindly, very good-natured, and reassuring. We sat in comfortable club chairs, and the session always began with a dream, which Adler would analyze. He would ask me, "What would it be like if the events in the dream were taking place right now?" He tried to get me to relate my dreams to my daily life. Then he would make comments which were revelations to me—how he could come up with such knowledge about me! He inspired confidence so that you felt free to tell him everything, even things you thought you'd never dare tell. It's hard to describe—he was so tolerant and understanding.

Once I came to see him and said, "Today you have no luck. I didn't dream at all."

In a soft voice, he replied, "Oh, sit down. You concentrate. I'm sure you dreamed. We dream every night."

And sure enough, I remembered some dream. I don't know whether he had a hypnotic power or what, but I was certain I hadn't dreamed, and then, all of a sudden, the dream came to me.

After two weeks, he told me that I was O.K. and didn't need to come back anymore. And I didn't experience any further trouble.

I think Adler had a conference with my grandfather, and that was really the turning point. He told me, "Your grandfather understands very well what is going on." I think Adler might have called Rudolf in and talked to him about my problem because it involved him too, but I'm not certain.

Adler's talk with Mimi's grandfather placated him, and Mimi was free to resume seeing Rudolf. Whether Dreikurs actually met Adler at the time is not now known, but his concern and curiosity led him to follow Mimi's account of her therapy with great interest. Her description of Adler perhaps made him wistful, for he saw the warmth, cheerfulness, and encouragement he had sorely missed in his own father. Thus, Adler first entered the impressionable young Dreikurs's life.

The years 1913–1915, ranging from his sixteenth to eighteenth years of age, were crucial to Dreikurs. In conquering polio, he found courage and a new faith in himself. In the youth movement he found acceptance and friendship and discovered his leadership abilities. He embraced the democratic philosophy of Wyneken and recognized the potentiality of youth. His faith in both never waivered in the years that followed. He also learned how rebellion can be turned into useful and productive activity.

War Intrudes—A Man Emerges

The days of Dreikurs's glorious youth quickly drew to a close. The assassination of Archduke Franz Ferdinand, on a peaceful Sunday in 1914, triggered World War I. Initially the incident created barely a stir in Vienna, but within two months the great powers of Europe were embroiled in a war of unprecedented dimensions.

Seventeen years old and still in school when war broke out, Dreikurs felt its effects immediately as he watched his older friends depart for the army and sensed the irretrievable changes within the youth movement. The war had a sobering effect, and he pondered the meaning and direction of his life. When he graduated from the *gymnasium*, with military service looming immediately before him, he wrote a long diary entry, *"Mein Beruf"*[8] ("My Profession"). Philosophical, speculative, ambitious, and personal, it reveals his earliest views on what he planned to accomplish in life:

September 14, 1915

Until three days ago, I had no idea what was to be "my" profession. I did not know which direction to go, what I was actually capable of doing or what should become of me. Possibilities, though none of which seemed really exciting, were: music, psychology, or as a fill-in, banking. I rejected music since I had the feeling I lacked sufficient technical skill. As to psychology, I had an aversion to its purely scientific aspect. Such was my situation when on Saturday, September 11, suddenly, like a bolt of lightning, everything within me that was confused and irreconcilable took shape.

Mankind has two ways of expressing what goes beyond the personal realm: Art and Science. They proceed from opposite standpoints. "Artistic" to me means a way of experiencing life and somehow expressing it in some form; "scientific" means to study form, shapes, appearances—to find the basis of life through observations, analysis, and logical thinking. We can now discern that science and art are working toward each other. Science is no longer satisfied in merely describing external forms and its laws, but it is breaking things down into its basic elements. The biggest step is being taken in psychology inasmuch as it comes nearer to the nucleus of life, the psyche or soul. . . .

Science does everything through the five senses, whatever can be observed and understood with these belong in its sphere, whatever does not is omitted. Wherever there is "awareness" it belongs in the artistic sphere which includes art itself, hypnosis, expressions of the will, empathy, intuition, etc. Science cannot use these since they are not tangible.

Does man differ from other animals? To a certain degree, the animal thinks just as the human does, but it is not conscious of doing so. So one difference is consciousness or recognition. But there is something else. The animal has no art, and it lacks all those things previously assigned to "artistic tendencies," and above all, *spirit,* the expression of will. This "willing," and analagous to it, the *"lifesense,"* are still beyond our five senses. The human being has not yet reached the highest form of development possible, because there are certain things for which we do not yet have the "sense," which we cannot comprehend or create. While one of these "senses" is being noted here or there, it is imperative for the continued development of the species man, that this sense be discovered and raised to consciousness. After that, man will recognize it, utilize it, observe with it, and see much that he cannot now fathom. This development was left to our time because we are now witnessing the birth of this sense. Through this sense, art and science become one. . . .

How this should be accomplished—developed beyond being a mere idealistic concept—shall be my task. I am convinced within myself that I can do it, and that this goal is an expression of my whole life up to now.

I stand on the foundation of art, but I shall never be an artist because I master none of its media well enough. My friends tried to persuade me to study music. If I had had the right inclination and calling I would have worked harder at it; its theoretical aspects would not be such a horror. What was it then that I spent my time with? Only now can I give the answer, with art as such.

My striving to comprehend other people, myself and the world, my concern with music, poetry, metaphysics, conversation—is an expression of the artistic tendency. Hence my aversion to all theory, to all science.

But I can also reason, and I have sufficient talent for logic. I have always sensed a division within me, of being torn between abandonment to feelings and their analysis. I am an expression of modern mankind which is suffering from this conflict. All this comes together in me and I live in *my* time. That is the greatest joy man can experience. I therefore believe in my destiny!

My whole development points to this new idea. At first I was a sensitive person of many moods, to a degree that almost destroyed me. Through the survival instinct I learned to conquer my moods and feelings. Thus, last winter I was a sober, rational person. But that was unsatisfying—without feeling I was impoverished. Art was finished—no piano, no poem. I wanted to come down again. It went slowly—Mimi supported my intentions. Until now—this summer—such turmoil arose within me, the greatest I had ever experienced. Then everything fell into place. I became more natural. I abandoned myself to feelings, but I stayed strong since I had learned to control myself. The conflict within me was solved. So, my idea is an expression and result of this. . . . My whole being has now found its expression, and the searching period of my life is over!

Now to my practical plans. I have to master the sciences: medicine, biology, psychology—else all will be idle talk and mere utopia. Because of my studies I will neglect art. But I will keep in mind what my ultimate goal will be and will mark the places for attack later on. When my studies are finished I shall first become a neurologist. This field as it is being practiced today already holds sufficient interest for me. But I can also do it my way. This will help me progress and gain new experiences.

There will come a point in time when science, which up to then will have been substance to me, through the power of my being, of my art, will become pure form which I will then dominate. Then my actual work will begin and I shall achieve everything. I do have the feeling the world is waiting for me. There cannot be many who possess precisely those attributes that I have. I have written all this down to keep it before my eyes and always help orient my way toward my goal. *Glück auf, Kamerad!*

But Dreikurs found that he was in no position to pursue his heady plan. Within weeks he was slogging through the muddy trenches that crisscrossed Europe in a stalemated, purposeless, and brutal war. The Austrian Imperial Army drew upon the German-speaking *gymnasium* graduates to fill its officer ranks. Dreikurs was sent for officer's training and emerged at age eighteen, a young and green lieutenant.

He first saw duty with a regiment stationed near Russia, then with a Polish-Slovakian regiment in Galicia, and toward the end, served on the Western Front in Italy.

"I had a most amazing history," Dreikurs recalled. "I spent twenty-seven months on the front, many months as commander of a scout unit, and led many patrols—but never came into a situation where I had to shoot at anyone. The only time I used my gun was to shoot some crows—

which I missed. I was under heavy bombardment in the trenches, but mostly waiting passively for what would happen next. The big fights always occurred either shortly before I arrived or soon after I had left."

When Dreikurs returned to Vienna on furloughs, he found political unrest and deep undercurrents sweeping the city. The growing strength of the working class, only enfranchised in 1907, posed an increasing threat to the shaky government long dominated by the aristocracy, wealthy landowners, and the Catholic church. Once war broke out, Parliament was suspended, and Count Karl von Stürgkh assumed dictatorial power under the aging Emperor Franz Josef. Industries were placed under military control to prevent strikes, and the labor party (Social Democrats) was regularly harassed. Antiwar sentiment and open rebellion against the government grew. When Stürgkh was assassinated, followed a month later by the death of Franz Josef, the empire was on the brink of collapse.

The repressive atmosphere touched Dreikurs directly. The youth movement, always a subject of suspicion, was closely scrutinized. While on furlough, he attended a meeting of the youth group in his home district, which was now under the leadership of Otto Fenichel. Suddenly, police stormed in, arrested Dreikurs and Fenichel as "subversives," and threw them into jail. Through the intervention of some influential friends, they were released and the charges against them dropped. As the war dragged on, the youth movement fell apart, and many of its members became actively involved in the uprising of labor against the war. Everyone suffered from lack of food. As starvation became widespread, the social order began to break down; army supply trucks were attacked, overturned, and ransacked in food riots. News from the war front became less important as conditions steadily worsened in Vienna.

In the fall of 1917, Dreikurs was wounded in the leg while serving on the Western Front in northern Italy. He managed to scramble into a huge bomb crater, where he remained trapped the entire day. The fury of gunfire raged all around him, and his leg throbbed with pain. He recalled:

I waited. I figured that if the Austrians continued advancing as they had all morning, it would be wonderful, because I sustained an easy shot and could go home to my family. But if the Italians advanced and I was captured, I would spend the rest of the war away from my family. Yet, if I stayed here any longer, in the midst of the cross fire, a bomb might hit, and I'd be gone altogether.

It was a matter of extreme possibilities. I waited the whole day long in the hole and couldn't look out. . . . So I got bored and looked in my knapsack for something to do. The only thing I was able to find was a children's book with nice little designs which Mimi had sent to me for amusement. It was the only thing that I had to occupy myself. I joked to myself: Here I was with a children's book—confronted with the destiny of my life. . . . Only after darkness did my men come and get me.

At the hospital Dreikurs learned that the bullet had pierced his leg a fraction of an inch from a main artery and that he had narrowly escaped bleeding to death. Fortunately, his wound would leave no permanent damage. Granted medical leave, he returned to Vienna to complete his recovery, burdened by a slight limp, but happy to rejoin his family and friends.

When fully recovered, Dreikurs prepared to return to the front once again. By that time, the army was desperately short of physicians, and announced that educational leave would be granted to military personnel who qualified for admission to medical school. Early in 1918 he was granted combat deferment to study medicine.

Sigmund Dreikurs's relief that Rudolf was safely home from the war was matched by a new pride in his son who had served Austria with honor and had chosen a noble career. Now, he assumed, Rudolf would settle down, give up his foolish idealism, and approach life in a hard-headed, businesslike fashion. After all, it had worked for him, and what else makes the man but the success he achieves? The elder Dreikurs still believed he could control the direction of his son's life.

But the "boy" he and Fanny apprehensively sent off to war twenty-seven months earlier was no more. He had become a man. Given the awesome task of leading other men in war, he had met the challenge responsibly. He had seen comrades die and witnessed the brutality of war. His youthful ideals were not discarded, but instead tempered by the lessons of war. Now his father's despotic demands were no longer something he could stomach in passive silence. Instead, he reacted directly, angrily challenging his father's demands.

The change is evident in Dreikurs's portraits from this period. The forlorn, insecure look of the young lieutenant about to go off to war had vanished two years later. His filled-out face and receded hairline made him appear older, and there was a resoluteness in his eyes and a confidence in his easy smile.

During the long, lonely months on the battlefield, Rudolf corresponded with Mimi daily and began to give serious thought to marriage. Their families even got together and began to discuss arrangements. But there were problems, one of which was that Mimi was six years older than he. The biggest obstacles, however, were that he had his entire university career before him and that financially he was in no position to support a household. So the marriage was continually postponed.

Dreikurs grew impatient. At one point, while on furlough from the front and weary of the turmoil in Vienna, he pleaded with Mimi to join him on a peaceful retreat to the mountains. But her sense of propriety took the upper hand, and she refused, saying she could not get away. Rudolf was disappointed. Present at the time was Stefanie Koch, who shared an apartment with Mimi. She enthusiastically interjected that she would love to get away for a few days.

Much later, Mimi recalled how she thought this would be perfectly "safe," since Steffi claimed to be madly in love with some young poet. When Steffi's own sister admonished Mimi: "For heaven's sake, are you going to allow that? Don't you know what she's doing?" Mimi reacted strongly, "If he is not to be trusted, then he's not my bag!" Blind to Steffi's clever designs on Rudolf, Mimi also underestimated his susceptibility to the ardent wooing of another woman.

Stefanie Koch was the sister of Dreikurs's closest friend in the army, and he first met her when he brought greetings to their family while on leave sometime earlier. Later he introduced her to his own circle of friends, and Mimi and Steffi, both employed as bank clerks and living alone, decided to save money by rooming together.

Steffi was a petite, fragile-looking woman. She came from a traditional Jewish family that was rather rigid in its attitudes. Inordinately bright and clever, she was ambitious and had a knack for getting what she wanted. She found Dreikurs attractive and admired his enthusiasm, his intellectual bent, and his ambition to be a doctor. She pursued him, and following a whirlwind courtship, they eloped in August 1918. The ceremony was performed at the armory by a Jewish chaplain, since Rudolf was still in uniform. The only witness was his sister, Bertha. Afterward, Rudolf sent her home to break the news to his parents, who were shocked and displeased that he had acted without consulting with them, but especially because they were genuinely fond of Mimi. His financial status had not changed one iota, and they didn't even have a roof over their heads. That wedding night Rudolf called his parents and asked if he and his bride could come home.

Dreikurs's marriage to Steffi was to prove both inspiring and tragic. And he never forgot Mimi. For years he carried around the burden of having hurt her deeply. Indeed, she was badly shaken by the ironic turn of events and even wrote to Adler of her pain. Adler responded with an encouraging letter, which he poignantly signed, "Your fatherly friend." Mimi got over the hurt and married not long afterward.

Nearly fifty years later, while Rudolf and Tee Dreikurs were on a round-the-world trip in 1963, he met Mimi once again in Hawaii. Mimi recalled that it was a little like seeing a ghost, the real person before you a total stranger, the one you knew and remembered now dead. Dreikurs tried to explain to her what had happened in that distant past. "I felt kind of sorry for him," she remarked, "because for fifty years he carried the burdensome thought that he had done a terrible wrong to me."

Notes for Chapter 2

1. Adler, *What Life Should Mean to You*, pp. 182, 187–188.

2. The direct quotations of Rudolf Dreikurs are a composite derived from two sources: (1) the Dreikurs-Mackaness interview; and (2) Dreikurs, "Guiding, Teaching, and Demonstrating."

3. Walter Z. Laqueur, *Young Germany: A History of the German Youth Movement* (London: Routledge & Kegan Paul, 1962), pp. 53–65.

4. Herbert Steiner, ed., *Käthe Leichter: Leben und Werk* (Vienna: Europa Verlag, 1973).

5. Ibid.

6. Dr. Maria Glas (formerly Mitzi Deutsch), personal communication, April 1974.

7. Zdenka (Mimi) Pollack Orenstein, personal communication, June 1973.

8. Rudolf Dreikurs, "Mein Beruf," September 14, 1915, from his student notebooks, Rudolf Dreikurs Papers, Manuscript Division, Library of Congress, Washington, D.C.

3

Background to a Career:
The Freud-Adler Debate

The main difference between Freud and Adler was that
Freud wanted knowledge and Adler looked for truth.

Phyllis Bottome
Alfred Adler: a Portrait from Life, 1958

Dreikurs entered medical school in 1918, intent upon exploring the "mysteries of the mind." To pursue his goal, he wrote, "two avenues were open: through psychology which was part of philosophy, or through medicine and psychiatry. Knowing my tendency to go far afield, I thought that medicine and psychiatry would keep my feet on the ground, which philosophy would not. But actually, I was not interested in medicine as such."[1]

Dreikurs never explained what incidents or experiences led to his commitment to study the psyche. But it was a reasonable, almost self-evident choice for an adventurous mind that developed in Vienna's psychologically charged atmosphere.

For beneath the surface of Vienna's *gemütlichkeit* charm, a psychiatric revolution was unfolding that would reverberate throughout the century. Sigmund Freud and Alfred Adler were among its chief architects. Typically Viennese yet totally different in outlook and temperament, each was determined to unravel the riddles of human behavior. For a time, their lives and work had intertwined; then they separated, each to forge a vastly different conception of human nature. The revolutionary ideas they set in motion and the controversy they generated made the study of the psyche seem exciting, full of mystery, and ripe for exploration. That appealed to Dreikurs's pioneering spirit. He had been aware of these two giants of modern psychology since his youth movement days, when Bernfeld vigorously injected Freudian ideas into the discussions. Moreover,

Dreikurs's close friend, Otto Fenichel, was an enthusiastic proponent of the psychoanalytic viewpoint. Because of Mimi, Dreikurs was also familiar with Adler.

The great controversy touched off by Freud's and Adler's contrasting views of human nature, which continues in varying form even today, played a central role in shaping the direction of Dreikurs's career. Transplanted to America, it enlisted him in an uphill struggle against the psychoanalytic stranglehold that gripped the mental health professions. Acknowledgment of Dreikurs's contributions and their meaning to contemporary thinking would be incomplete without an understanding of the great controversy that roared through Vienna in those first decades of this century.

The Life Style as a Historical Tool

The many historical accounts of the Freud-Adler encounter have been written mostly by Freud's followers and admirers and have created a distorted picture that has only recently been challenged. No effort will be made here to resolve these historical issues. However, by using Adler's concept of the life style, it is hoped that a fresh perspective of Freud's and Adler's personalities and the contrasting theories they generated will emerge.

The concept of the "life style," a phrase so popular that it has become a common idiom, was one of Adler's most brilliant discoveries. Yet few are aware of its origin, psychological meaning, or concrete usefulness for understanding the individual personality. "The concept of the life style," Dreikurs would later teach, "is the unique configuration of an individual, indicating his pattern of concepts about himself and others and his movement through life. It is based on the ideas, convictions, and goals that each person develops in his formative years."[2]

Because man is a social animal, the child's social environment is a crucial ingredient in forming the life style. In earliest childhood, that social environment is created by the dynamic interpersonal relationships within the family constellation of siblings and parents. As the child attempts to find his place and take part in the activities of that dynamic constellation, he develops a set of convictions, based upon his perceptions, to help him interpret, predict, and control experience. But, as Dreikurs pointed out, while the child is a keen *observer*, he is a poor *interpreter* of the meaning of what goes on around him, and his convictions reflect his subjective, and therefore biased, perception of those events. From these early, biased—often faulty—judgments, created by the child to organize and direct his actions, emerge the basic convictions of the adult life style.

The concept of the life style can be useful in explaining the biased convictions an individual brings to the study of psychology as a science. Adler was particularly aware that the investigator cannot divorce himself from his own personal convictions:

> That every individual's conception of life is determined by, and is part of, the person's style of life, has thrown light upon the rather bewildering fact that philosophers and psychologists differ widely in their interpretation of the inner world. It is plain that each of them regards mind and body from a viewpoint that is determined by his philosophy of life. Thus an author whose wrong conception of life is like that of a pampered child will inevitably declare that all trouble arises because the individual is unable to "get" what he wants. And he will take it for granted that all failures, neuroses, psychoses, delinquencies, suicides, [and] perversions are due to the fact that these people have suppressed their wishes. These authors will also find that the real world is hostile and destined to perish.[3]

The divergent theories of human nature developed by Freud and Adler are remarkably consistent with the convictions—the life style—each developed about himself and the world in his formative years. By briefly describing their lives and the controversy generated by them, the historical background for Dreikurs's important contributions in this generation will be more easily understood and appreciated.

FREUD AND HIS QUEST FOR IMMORTALITY

From the many accounts of Sigmund Freud's early years, important clues emerge concerning the basic outlook he developed toward life. Born in Freiburg, Moravia, in 1856, to Jewish parents, Freud's family migrated to Vienna when he was three.

He was the eldest of eight children, and his young mother lavished great love upon him and pampered him. Freud yearned to be famous even as a child. His boyhood heroes were Hannibal and Napoleon's General Massena, and he devoured the story of Napoleon's meteoric career, searching for the secret of "power over men."[4] He had often been told that when his mother was carrying him in her womb, it had been prophesied that her son would be a great man, which led him to remark: "A man who has been the indisputable favorite of his mother keeps the feeling of the conqueror, that confidence of success often induces real success."[5] By his middle years, however, a gnawing fear had grown inside him that his lifelong dreams and ambitions might not be fulfilled.

As his mother's favorite, he never liked or forgave his sister Anna for "dethroning" him and forcing him to share the warmth and love of his mother. Anna later reminisced that Sigmund was the privileged eldest, a tyrant who forbade her to read Balzac and Dumas, and was the only sibling to have a room and an oil lamp to himself.[6] While his mother indulged him, his stern father, an older man with patriarchal, authoritarian views, did the disciplining. Freud often expressed great hostility and resentment toward him.

The pampered child, according to Adler, often adopts a meaning in life commensurate with his experiencing a mother who "smothers her child in caresses and [who] constantly acts, thinks and speaks for him . . . [thereby] accustoming the child often to regard himself as the center of events and to feel all other situations and persons are hostile to him."[7]

As a student, Freud did excellent work and graduated *summa cum laude* from the *gymnasium*. Intellectual endeavors were his forte. "He was his mother's first-born and darling, his father's spoiled 'scholar' and pride, [and] the pet of his teachers,"[8] so it is not surprising that he developed a view of himself as special, one who must be in the center of the arena and who feels justified in his hostile antagonism to those who do not cater to his demands and "rights." Events that followed later in his life conform in many respects to such a picture.

Searching for a career suitable to fulfill his destiny, Freud chose medicine. Yet the choice was made "without great enthusiasm," and at no time did he "feel any particular predilection for the career of a physician." He was moved, he wrote, "rather by a sort of curiosity . . . directed more toward human concerns than toward natural objects."[9]

ADLER—TO BE A BETTER DOCTOR

Alfred Adler also came from Jewish parentage. Fourteen years younger than Freud, he was born in 1870, in Penzing, a far suburb of Vienna where his father, a grain merchant, could maintain close ties with the countryside.

The Adlers were a happy, independent, and relatively comfortable family. Alfred was the second son, two years younger than his older brother, whose name, ironically, was Sigmund. As the second-born, he never experienced the privilege of being the sole center of attention. Instead, he "felt himself put in the shade by a model eldest brother, a true 'first-born' who always seemed to Alfred to be soaring far beyond him."[10]

"The impressions under which the second child outlines his self-created [life style]," Adler later wrote, "are mainly to be found in his having constantly in front of him another child who is not only more advanced in his development, but who also . . . disputes his claim to equality by keeping the upper hand. . . . In almost every case. . . one can observe in the second child a vigorous onward struggle, which shows itself either in his greater energy or in his more impetuous temperament."[11]

His frustrated ambition to catch up to his elusive brother made him unhappy as a child. Because he suffered from rickets in childhood, every move was a strain for him, while his envied brother ran and jumped effortlessly. Consequently, he adopted a "steam engine" approach to life.

Believing that Sigmund was his mother's favorite child, young Alfred emulated his father, a self-assured, free-spirited businessman of considerable humor. From his father he acquired independence of mind, skepticism, and a love of paradox—best expressed by his favorite motto, *"Omnia ad opinionem suspensa sunt"* ("Everything can be different" —Seneca).

To overcome his physical weaknesses, Adler spent whatever time he could outdoors. In nearby fields where the local children gathered to play, Adler joined in the games and became part of a wide social milieu. It was unusual for a middle-class Jewish lad of that period to spend most of his time with his Gentile peers. Because he was lively and friendly, he was popular among them. These experiences influenced his later ideas about man's social nature and his feeling of being "at home" among his fellowmen.

He chose medicine as a career following an early confrontation with death. When he was five, he had become so seriously ill with pneumonia that the doctor told his father—in Alfred's presence—that there was no hope for his survival. He recalled, "At once a frightful terror came over me and a few days later when I was well, I decided definitely to become a doctor so that I should have a better defense against the danger of death and weapons to combat it superior to my doctor's."[12] He never veered from this goal.

Overcoming his physical weaknesses and ills, Adler emerged as a passionate, persistent, and ambitious youngster, full of adventure and a fighting spirit. As a student he rebelled against the authoritarian school system and did only average work, appearing to be more interested in his numerous friendships and in having fun. But as he approached the study of medicine, he took to his books in earnest.

FREUD'S EDUCATION AND EARLY CAREER

The University of Vienna Medical School was a trend-setting, world-renowned institution when Freud attended it, from 1873 to 1881, intent on making a career in medical research. Its faculty reflected the dominant outlook of the nineteenth century—a reverence for science and its methods that derived ultimately from the impact of Newton's discoveries. In this mechanistic view, living things, like inanimate matter, were equated with matter and energy, to be explained by chemical and physical forces, subject to exact laws. While a medical student, Freud did research on brain physiology for six years in the laboratory of Ernst Brücke, a leading proponent of mechanistic physiology.[13] This approach rejected any a priori metaphysical notions and discredited teleological or vitalistic concepts as unscientific.

Freud adopted Brücke as his venerated teacher and emulated the "scientist" image.[14] Suddenly, after six years of research, Freud gave up his research career and decided to become a practicing physician, but, again, without visible enthusiasm.

With more years of training ahead, Freud sought to sweeten the arduous process with a brilliant discovery that would bring rapid fame and prestige.[15] He embarked on experiments with cocaine, praising the virtues of the new drug with eloquence. Yet this effort resulted in bitterness when a colleague robbed him of credit for discovering cocaine's anesthetic quality. Moreover, a storm of criticism fell upon Freud when a friend whom he treated with cocaine became severely addicted. This was a blow to his childhood vision of greatness.

Freud then traveled to Paris, in 1885, to study with the famous Jean Martin Charcot, who had bravely introduced hypnosis and the concept of unconscious psychic energies into academic medicine. Charcot "impressed him not only by the boldness of his conceptions of hypnosis, hysteria and traumatic neuroses, but also by the immense prestige and sumptuous life of the Prince of Science."[16]

Freud returned to Vienna as an outspoken champion of Charcot's ideas but was greatly disappointed by his skeptical reception. He thought he was bringing them great discoveries, but it turned out that they knew as much or more about these subjects than he did.[17] He reacted by withdrawing from his medical colleagues, openly attacking several of them, and creating an atmosphere of distrust and isolation. He then turned to an old friend, Dr. Josef Breuer, who was to assume great importance in his career.

Through Breuer, he became involved in the classic case of "Anna O," a woman seized by hysteria whom Breuer began treating with hypnosis and the cathartic, or "talking" cure, back in 1880. Six years later, Freud persuaded Breuer that they should jointly resume the work on hysteria and the cathartic cure, which led to their book, *Studies in Hysteria* (1895). In it is formulated the idea that patients with hysteria (a type of mental illness more prevalent at that time) suffer from the repressed memory of traumatic events that they could not handle at the time the events occurred. Freud claimed that these traumatic events were based on sexual abuses passively suffered during childhood. Freud also introduced "free association" as a psychotherapeutic method to overcome the limitations of hypnosis. While he credited Breuer for his discoveries, Freud later criticized him, and Breuer ended their collaboration.

Freud was then on his own. He still had not made his great discovery, and his interests had taken him further away from mechanistic physiology into the indefinable realm of the unconscious. He feared his own tendency toward abstract speculation and sought to curb it.[18] The idea that he should break from the mechanistic viewpoint was unthinkable, given his conservative nature. His dream of fame and his idealized image of the scientist were fundamentally threatened.

In the lonely years 1895–1899, Freud entered a soul-searching self-analysis shared only by his friend Wilhelm Fliess. It was a time fraught with depression, with an alternating sense of great discovery and self-doubt, and with a relentless search for a monumental discovery—a last chance before age would rob him of his destiny.

In 1900, he emerged from this self-tormented period—a neurotic illness as some saw it, a creative illness to others—published his *Interpretation of Dreams*, and proclaimed his earthshaking discovery of the "science of

Psychoanalysis." Since he could not bend the subject of his inquiry to the rigorous demands of science, he bent science to fit the subject. In the sexual instinct, he claimed, lay the irreducible basis of all mental functioning and neurosis. He announced that he had achieved a "true science" of the psyche by discovering the rules and forces that completely determine man's behavior. This work contained the real gems of Freud's genius—his psychotherapeutic discoveries and the notion that the origin of adult neuroses could be traced to experiences in childhood. Ironically, Freud believed his real achievement to be the "scientism" he superimposed on his discoveries.

ADLER PURSUES A DIFFERENT PATH

When Adler began his medical studies at the university, in 1887, he was set on becoming a practicing physician rather than pursuing research. As a result, he was little influenced by the dominant mechanistic approach. He was more inclined to the far older tradition of clinical bedside teaching, which focused on the investigation and treatment of disease by studying real patients. This approach historically marked the beginning of modern medical education and practice.[19] The University of Vienna and its allied hospital, the Wiener Allgemeine Krankenhaus, were together the foremost clinical medical center in the world, each department being directed by an internationally renowned specialist. In contrast to the remoteness of the physiological laboratory, the clinical approach continually brought the physician face to face with people in all their suffering and with their idiosyncratic response to illness and its treatment.

While Adler was a medical student, anti-Semitism reemerged in Europe. At the university, the once liberal German nationalist student groups became increasingly anti-Semitic, racist, and conservative. That minority of the student body interested in social betterment then united under the emerging socialist movement, Adler and his close friend, Carl Furtmüller, among them. An intense intellectual spirit characterized this circle as they debated Marxist and socialist philosophy into the early morning hours in Vienna's cafés.

It was at such meetings that Adler met Raissa Timofeyevna Epstein, an aristocratic young Russian woman. They married in 1897. Her independence, fearlessness, and political activism played a role in shaping his ideas about "masculine protest" and equality between the sexes.

Adler received his medical degree in 1895 and spent the next two years working in the ophthalmology department of the Vienna Poliklinik, a benevolent institution that provided free medical care to the working class and appealed to his humanitarian ideals.

Two years later, he began a general medical practice in a lower-middle-class, mostly Jewish, neighborhood. He soon became a popular physician, and his future success seemed assured. He published his first book, *Health Book for the Tailoring Trade*, in 1898.[20] It exposed the shocking working conditions of the tailoring trade, whose methods helped transmit infectious diseases and therefore posed a serious health hazard to the general public.

Near to Adler's office was the Prater, Vienna's famed amusement park. Adler frequently treated the artists and acrobats who worked there. These people, who earned their living through their extraordinary body strength and skills, revealed in confidence to Adler their attitudes about their physical weaknesses and ills. Such patients stimulated Adler's earliest ideas about physical and mental compensation.

To better understand and help his patients, Adler delved into the study of psychology and psychiatry. His thorough survey of both fields led him to conclude that their progress as sciences was unsatisfactory.

The Clash of Genius

When Freud's *Interpretation of Dreams* was published, it was subjected to caustic attack in the local press, which traditionally ridiculed every new idea in the arts and sciences. Adler disliked hackneyed opinions and was intrigued to learn more about Freud's ideas. Like Freud, he too was trying to unravel the "psychological connection of the various neuroses." Adler reflected, "At that time, nervous disorders . . . were treated simply symptomatically, through cold water cures, etc. . . . All these methods, to which hypnosis also belongs, seemed not to get at the root of the problem, and to be essentially not more than miracle cures."[21]

Adler was then thirty years old, fourteen years younger than Freud. A short, sturdy man, Adler was not handsome, but his engaging expression, ready wit, and empathic manner made him appealing. A sociable person totally lacking in pretense, he loved Vienna's congenial café life and its free interchange of opinion.

Adler realized that Freud's book on dreams was a significant work that could open new paths in psychiatry. He drafted a defense of Freud's position, which he sent off for publication.[22] Freud was pleased to learn of Adler's support. In 1902, Adler recalled, "I was invited to discuss with Freud and some of his pupils the problems of neurosis."[23] Thus began the Wednesday Psychological Society, which gathered weekly at Freud's home. Meeting in a room clouded with cigar smoke and filled with ever-present cups of thick, black coffee, its five members reported on their respective researches in light of the new concepts of Psychoanalysis.

Although Adler was keenly interested in Freud's new approach to psychiatry, he doubted that he and Freud were in fundamental agreement. His own ideas about organ inferiority and its psychical and physical compensations had already begun to occupy him. Freud persuaded him that by joining the group Adler would have his ideas heard also. When he joined, he hoped to influence Freud with his innovative ideas as much as Freud hoped to make Adler a flag bearer for his science of Psychoanalysis.

In Adler, Freud hoped to find a younger protégé who would devote himself, in a selfless manner, to promoting Freud's greatness. (Freud considered himself equal in greatness to Copernicus and Darwin.)[24] But Adler's independence of mind, directness, and skeptical nature made it impossible for him to serve Freud's ambitions. Eventually, this evoked in Freud a festering envy toward Adler. He was the notable first in a succession of men—including Carl Jung, Wilhelm Stekel, and later, Otto Rank and Sandor Ferenczi—who experienced Freud's initial solicitousness, only to be followed by extreme hostility and vituperous attack when they failed properly to appreciate Freud's specialness.

Early in their relationship—which never had the quality of a warm friendship—difficulties arose between Freud and Adler. These were largely bridged by Freud, who found Adler's collaboration essential. So Adler remained in the group, and "while he could not restrain himself from speaking out . . . he never forgot that Freud was the older man . . . who had achieved a historic progress in psychology, and the host."[25]

What Adler admired most in Freud's theory was the idea that insight into the relationship between the elements of a patient's mental life would be essential to any cure. Further, techniques could be found to achieve such insight. Adler tested the techniques Freud had described, such as the interpretation of dreams and early recollections. Their personal styles, however, were so dissimilar that these techniques soon acquired a different character and meaning in Adler's hands. For instance, Freud insisted that the patient be a docile subject, assuming a passive and subordinate position on the couch, while Freud sat behind, listening but not visible. By contrast, Adler was warm and outgoing and treated his patients as his equal. Both sat in easy chairs and engaged in a conversational dialogue guided by Adler to help the patient gain insight about himself, understanding of his problems, and renewed hope.

Adler's originality as a theoretician became obvious when his *Study of Organ Inferiority* was published in 1907.[26] In it, he presented a systematic theory of organ inferiority and the principle of compensation, describing the interaction of the organism with the environment and its capacity to compensate for inherent weaknesses. While mostly applied physiologically, it also recognized psychological compensation, a notion that evolved later into Adler's psychological theory of inferiority feelings. The book received favorable reviews and even Freud's unqualified commendation.

The following year, Adler diverged further from Freud and challenged the primacy of the sexual drive, contending that there was an aggressive drive that was equally important. Shortly thereafter, he subordinated this drive to the general "striving for overcoming" and defined aggression as the pathological form of this striving. Freud initially rejected Adler's concept of an aggressive drive, only to reintroduce it some fifteen years later as the death instinct.[27]

Freud and Adler disagreed on the role of the unconscious and the unity of the neuroses. The source of sexual dysfunction, whether it was based on Freud's biologically based "penis envy" or Adler's socially based "masculine protest," was a major source of contention between them. Adler was steadily moving from a biologically oriented, objective psychology to a socially oriented, subjective psychology.

In the meantime, Carl Gustav Jung had joined the Freud circle, which by 1907 had grown considerably and had achieved international renown. In 1910, Jung became president of the newly formed International Psychoanalytic Society, and Adler became president of the local Vienna Psychoanalytic Society. That same year, Adler and Stekel became co-editors of a new journal for Psychoanalysis, while Freud served as its editor-in-chief. So, it was clear that despite their growing disagreement, Freud still regarded Adler as a valuable figure in the psychoanalytic movement.

Freud's most loyal disciples disliked Adler's growing dissidence, and repeatedly prodded him to make explicit his criticisms of Freud's concepts. Early in 1911, at Freud's invitation, Adler gave three lectures outlining his criticisms of Freud's sexual theory and presented his own theory of the masculine protest.

"I was not prepared for what followed," Wilhelm Stekel recalled. "One Freudian after another got up and denounced, in well-prepared speeches, the new concepts of Adler."[28] Another witness described how the Freudians made a mass attack upon Adler almost unequaled in its ferocity. The onslaught produced, he wrote, "the impression of being a concerted one. Freud had a sheaf of notes before him and with a gloomy mien seemed prepared to annihilate his adversary."[29]

That summer, Adler resigned his editorship and resigned from the Vienna Psychoanalytic Society as well. Other members of the Freudian society who aligned with Adler began to gather informally with him at the Café Central. When the Freudian group reconvened that fall, "Hanns Sachs read the indictment against Adler, and moved that it was incompatible to belong to both [groups]. Carl Furtmüller replied in a brilliant speech, but the motion was carried and [the] six Adlerians rose, left, and went to the Café Central where [they] celebrated with Adler."[30]

Beyond Adler's "excommunication," Freud proscribed the quoting of Adler in any paper published by a Freudian (although Freud himself polemically railed against Adler whenever he chose). Indeed, one can examine the vast literature produced by the Freudians over the decades and rarely find Adler mentioned. Yet, strangely, Adler's concepts often appear in thinly disguised form and in some cases almost verbatim renditions.

So in that fateful year, Freud and Adler went their separate ways. Yet neither ever seemed to have gotten the other out of his mind.

ADLER CREATES HIS OWN SCHOOL

In the brief period between 1911 and 1914, Adler established his own school of psychology. At first, the small group that gathered called themselves Free Psychoanalysts to express their new freedom from the intellectually oppressive atmosphere of Freud's group. But Adler insisted that the group look to the future and not the past, and they eagerly studied Adler's theories and related them to doctrines and discoveries of other fields. Key figures in this early group were Carl Furtmüller, Alexander Neuer, and Erwin Wexberg. Furtmüller had been Adler's closest and most faithful friend since their university days, a fellow member of the

Freud circle who departed with Adler, and an outstanding educator. Neuer, on the other hand, was a man equally brilliant in both psychology and philosophy, while Wexberg was a clinical physician who possessed superb insight and broad experience.

Adler's professional activities changed in their emphasis. Now he devoted his practice almost exclusively to psychiatry, although he was still consulted in matters of general medicine because of his highly regarded expertise. With his wife and four children, he moved into a large apartment at No. 10, Dominikanerbastei, a street near the center of the city that stood on the remnants of Vienna's ancient fortifications. Here he lived and worked until he left Vienna permanently in 1934.

The weekly meetings of Adler's group attracted new members, mostly younger men and women, including physicians, philosophers, and teachers. Often these meetings and discussions were continued late into the night at Adler's favorite café, the Central, then the foremost gathering place of Vienna's avant-garde thinkers. An informal atmosphere prevailed in the group, where freedom of expression contrasted not only with the Freud group but with the formality of most scientific meetings. It greatly enhanced the breadth and scope of their explorations:

> The philosophers took the lead and began to study the problems of methodology, causality and finality, and of ethics. There were students of Spinoza, Kant, the neo-Kantians, Nietzsche, and Bergson in the group. Besides psychoanalysis, other schools of modern academic psychology were discussed. . . . The contributions of great writers to a living psychology were appraised, with Dostoevski in the center, and comparison of the artist's approach and work processes with those of the psychologist brought deeper insight into methodology. The psychological bases of current social phenomena were discussed, [including] the German Youth Movement whose influence was beginning to be felt in Austria.[31]

In 1912, Adler announced his original system of psychology with the publication of *The Neurotic Constitution*.[32] A brilliant work, it synthesized his creative insight with his empirical experience as a physician and psychiatrist. It radically departed from both Freud and the basic trends of academic psychology by rejecting their uncompromising mechanistic stance. His system was in concert with the emerging trends of the twentieth century—the renewed belief in creative and organizing forces in biology and the concept of a relativistic universe. The new biologists agreed that a living organism cannot be equated with a machine. A machine can only wear away, while an organism can grow and repair itself. Machines are set in motion by external forces, whereas a living organism can move under its own impulsion. An organism cannot be understood solely in terms of the limited strictures of cause and effect but must also be regarded in terms of its inner purpose.[33]

In *The Neurotic Constitution* can be found the most basic assumptions of Adler's psychology:[34]

Unity and Indivisibility. Each individual is unique and can only be understood as a totality and a unity—including the unity of body and mind, thereby eliminating the dualism that had plagued psychological thinking since Descartes. The individual is further understood as indivisible: That is, to examine only a piece of behavior instead of perceiving the individual as a totality is to risk missing the individual altogether. The individual's uniqueness implies the idea that all one's drives, emotions, thoughts, and experiences are subordinated to a subjective and self-created life plan, or "life style" as Adler later termed it.

Purposeful Behavior. The unity, the future orientation, and the law of movement of the individual lead to the notion that all human behavior is goal-oriented and purposeful. Man is not pushed by causes; his behavior is not determined by his heredity nor by his environment. Instead, he is pulled toward the goals he creates and chooses to pursue. The basic motivating force is a dynamic striving toward superiority, mastery, perfection. Life is therefore not a state of being but a process of becoming.

Biased Perception. From infancy on, the individual develops from his experiences convictions about life. These convictions, based upon the child's subjective evaluations and conclusions, are necessarily biased and, at least in part, erroneous. The child accepts these conclusions about himself and the world *as if* they were true.[35] The family constellation and sibling birth order provide the framework for the child's *subjective* interpretations about life.

Striving for Superiority. Life begins from a position of smallness, weakness, and dependency, which gives rise to feelings of inferiority. This sense of inferiority is not in itself a detriment—on the contrary, it provides much of the thrust and direction for the striving for superiority or perfection. Everyone feels inferior. But it is the heightened sense of inferiority, often fostered by misdirected upbringing—overprotection, pampering, or neglect—which robs one of the courage to face the challenges of life and which can result in a safeguarding retreat into neurosis.

One way in which some individuals overcompensate for their exaggerated feelings of inferiority is through the "will to power," a term Adler borrowed from Nietzsche. This usage has resulted in frequent misinterpretation over the years. For Nietzsche, the "will to power" stressed the "superman" concept, a power over others that he admired. For Adler, such striving for power *over others*, as opposed to striving for one's own perfection, was a goal on the "useless side of life," a form of neurotic behavior.

Social Nature. Man is a social being first and foremost. The focus of Adler's psychology was not only on the self-created uniqueness of each individual but also on the primacy of his interpersonal relationships, as well as his relationship to the society. In this view, man is not seen as being in conflict with the demands of society. Instead, society is seen as the matrix from which he develops, functions, reveals himself, and chooses among the alternatives available. Neurosis—and all human problems for that matter—are then seen as social problems and can only be understood and resolved within a social context.

Equality Between the Sexes. Adler was often accused, largely due to the Freudian propaganda, of having dethroned love and belittled sexuality. Actually, Adler held that "sexuality plays an outstanding role in the development and manifestation of the personality, but it is not the predominant characteristic." Rather, it is subsumed within the overall life style. The individual's response to the other sex is one of the three basic challenges of life; the others being the challenge of work and the challenge of relating to others and to society. "No human being can bear to be dominated by another," Adler always stressed. He was the first and greatest champion among modern psychologists of women's rights, a fact almost completely unknown to current students of women's liberation. Whereas Freud believed that women are destined by biology to inferiority because they lack a penis, Adler countered that it is woman's status in society—not her sex organs—that cause her to rebel and feel deprived of her rights. "Masculine protest" is the compensating and sometimes neurotic behavior of women in response to a social structure based on the assumption that women are inferior to men. But it also applies to men who doubt their sexual role or who fear not being able to measure up to their image of it. Such fear often increases their claims of superiority over women. For Adler, women and men are of equal value, even though their biological functions differ, and he encouraged women in every form of self-reliance and self-development. Their imposed inferiority "not only prevented humanity from using half its powers, but it seriously impeded the goodwill between men and women."[36]

The year after *The Neurotic Constitution* was published, Adler and his group adopted a new name for their school, Individual Psychology, and in 1914 began to publish a journal, the *Zeitschrift für Individualpsychologie*. They chose the name Individual Psychology to express their independent existence and also to avoid being identified with Psychoanalysis, a term Freud insisted should be reserved exclusively for his theory. However, *psychoanalysis* as a term never remained solely identified with Freud's ideas but came to be used as a generic term for a variety of psychiatric theories and psychotherapeutic practices. This has had a confusing and misleading effect even among professionals and has heightened Freud's stature disproportionately while diminishing the recognition given to Adler for his profound influence on contemporary thinking.

The name Individual Psychology, although chosen with care, has also led to misunderstanding. Often the name leads to the expectation that this is a psychology of the isolated, perhaps exalted individual, whereas in fact, it is a socially based psychology. To avoid such misconceptions, one must realize that the term *individual* implies both unity and indivisibility, contrary to the notion that the psyche can be analyzed into its parts. It further implies that all psychological manifestations can only be understood from the individual's own perspective.

SOCIAL INTEREST

The tragedy of World War I changed Adler. "He was never quite the same," a friend observed. "He was much quieter and stronger; . . . it was as if he had concentrated all his powers into a single purpose."[37]

Adler's wartime experiences as a neurologist in the army, combined with the need to deal with such devastated social conditions, precipitated his development of the concept of "social interest," which became the keystone of his psychological system. Beyond its psychological meaning, social interest linked his system to mankind's social evolution and offered a norm for human behavior.

Social interest, as Adler subsequently elaborated, expresses the innate capacity within all humans for cooperation and social living. There is no such thing as a totally autonomous human being. What we call human is intrinsically social and hinges on the interactions with and connectedness to others. Man's social nature is essential to his survival in an evolutionary sense. Social interest is like language. Both capacities are inherent, but both must be consciously taught and developed, or they wither and die.

By describing social interest as an innate capacity, Adler veered from the conviction of Freud and others that *Homo sapiens* is by nature anti-social. To Freud, civilization meant the repression and inhibition of ego-tistical, aggressive, and sexual drives. It became a negative concept, a set of laws restricting man's lusting appetites and curbing his freedom and individuality. This is the view of the so-called "muscular" social Dar-winists, who, in applying the concept of survival of the fittest to hu-manity, saw instinctual aggression, physical strength, and rugged competition as necessary to human evolution. Adler, on the other hand, believed that social interest—altruistic and cooperative acts for the mu-tual benefit of self and others—was the essential ingredient for mankind's survival.

In Adler's view, social interest is the logical antidote to universal feel-ings of inferiority and insecurity. It evokes a sense of belonging and the notion of an "extended self" bound inextricably with others. Included in it are the notions of empathy, identification, and common sense. The func-tion of social interest is to direct the individual's innate striving for perfec-tion to the socially useful side: "By useful, I mean in the interests of mankind generally. The most sensible estimate of the value of any activity is its helpfulness to all mankind, present and future, a criterion that applies not only to that which subserves the immediate preservation of life, but also to higher activities such as religion, science and art."[38]

With his concept of social interest, Adler added the last major pillar to the theoretical structure of Individual Psychology, and he viewed it as his crowning achievement. By 1918, Adler and his colleagues had articulated a coherent system of psychology so well conceived that it has changed remarkably little over the decades and has stood well the test of time. Commenting on the significance of Adler's contribution, psychiatrist Vik-tor E. Frankl wrote that what he "achieved and accomplished was no less than a Copernican switch. No longer could man be considered as the product, pawn and victim of drives and instincts; on the contrary, drives and instincts form the material that serves man in expression and in action."[39] But as Dreikurs often remarked, Adler was conceptually far ahead of his time, and full appreciation of his genius still awaits dis-covery.

Notes for Chapter 3

1. Dreikurs, "Guiding, Teaching, and Demonstrating," p. 148.
2. Rudolf Dreikurs, "Determinants of Changing Attitudes of Marital Partners Toward Each Other," in *The Marriage Relationship: Psychoanalytic Perspectives,* ed. Salo Rosenbaum and Ian Alger (New York: Basic Books, 1968), p. 102.
3. Alfred Adler, *Social Interest: Challenge to Mankind* (New York: Capricorn Books, 1964), pp. 154–155.
4. Ernest Jones, *The Life and Work of Sigmund Freud,* vol. 1 (New York: Basic Books, 1953), pp. 5, 30.
5. Franz G. Alexander and Sheldon T. Selesnick, *The History of Psychiatry* (New York: New American Library, 1966), p. 239.
6. Henri F. Ellenberger, *The Discovery of the Unconscious: The History and Evolution of Dynamic Psychiatry* (New York: Basic Books, 1970), p. 458.
7. Adler, *Social Interest,* p. 45.
8. Ellenberger, *Discovery of the Unconscious,* p. 463.
9. Jones, *Sigmund Freud,* pp. 21–22.
10. Phyllis Bottome, *Alfred Adler: A Portrait from Life,* 3rd ed. (New York: Vanguard, 1957), p. 27.
11. Adler, *Social Interest,* pp. 32–33.
12. Bottome, *Alfred Adler,* p. 33.
13. The mechanistic physiological school of thought originated with the brilliant Johannes Müller in Berlin and spread to Vienna and elsewhere in Europe through his students, Emil du Bois-Reymond, Ernst Brücke, Hermann Helmholtz, and Carl Ludwig.
14. According to George Rosen, "Freud was casting about for some way to take hold of his life and develop a personal identity, and the physiologists provided him with a social role . . . a pattern of behavior and set of values he could accept and use to satisfy his needs" (George Rosen, "Freud and Medicine in Vienna," in *Freud: The Man, His Work, His Influence,* ed. Jonathan Miller [Boston: Little, Brown, 1972], p. 22).
15. Ellenberger, *Discovery of the Unconscious,* pp. 433–434.
16. Ibid., p. 436.
17. Ibid., p. 440.
18. Fritz Wittels, *Sigmund Freud: His Personality, His Teachings and His School* (London: Allen & Unwin, 1924), p. 20.
19. Gerhard von Swieten introduced clinical bedside teaching at the University of Vienna medical school in the late eighteenth century.
20. Alfred Adler, *Gesundheitsbuch für das Schneidergewerbe* (Berlin: C. Heymanns), 1898.
21. Carl Furtmüller, "Alfred Adler: A Biographical Essay," in *Superiority and Social Interest: A Collection of Later Writings,* by Alfred Adler, ed. Heinz L. Ansbacher and Rowena R. Ansbacher, 2d ed. (Evanston, Ill.: Northwestern University Press, 1970): pp. 336–337.
22. Although mentioned in nearly every historical account, the critical review of Freud's book and Adler's defense of it in the *Neue Freie Presse* have never been found.
23. Furtmüller, "Alfred Adler," p. 337. The members of the original group were Freud, Adler, Wilhelm Stekel, Max Kahane, and Rudolf Reitler.

24. Sigmund Freud, *A General Introduction to Psychoanalysis* (1917), trans. Joan Rivere (Garden City, N.Y.: Garden City Publishers, 1943), p. 252.

25. Furtmüller, "Alfred Adler," p. 339.

26. Alfred Adler, *Studie über Minderwertigkeit von Organen* (Vienna: Urban and Schwarzenberg, 1907). English ed.: *Study of Organ Inferiority and Its Psychical Compensation*, trans. S. E. Jelliffe (New York: Nervous and Mental Disease Publishing Co., 1917).

27. Alfred Adler, *Superiority and Social Interest: A Collection of Later Writings*, ed. Heinz L. Ansbacher and Rowena R. Ansbacher, 2d. ed. (Evanston, Ill.: Northwestern University Press, 1970), pp. 37–39; Alfred Adler, *The Individual Psychology of Alfred Adler: A Systematic Presentation in Selections from His Writings*, ed. Heinz L. Ansbacher and Rowena R. Ansbacher (New York: Harper Torchbooks, 1964), p. 93.

28. Wilhelm Stekel, *Autobiography* (New York: Liveright, 1950), p. 141.

29. Wittels, *Sigmund Freud*, p. 20.

30. *Journal of Individual Psychology* 20 (1964): 124.

31. Furtmüller, "Alfred Adler," p. 355.

32. Alfred Adler, *Über den Nervösen Charakter* (Wiesbaden: Bergmann, 1912). English ed.: *The Neurotic Constitution*, trans. Bernard Glueck and J. E. Lind (New York: Moffat, Yard, 1917). (Long out of print, the English edition has recently been reissued by Books for Libraries Press, Freeport, N.Y.)

33. Lewis Way, *Alfred Adler: An Introduction to His Psychology* (Baltimore: Penguin Books, 1956), p. 35.

34. The formulation of Adler's teleological, holistic, and unified concept of the individual can be traced to several sources, the most important being Rudolf Virchow, Henri Bergson, Immanuel Kant, and Friedrich Nietzsche. Adler's concept of inferiority feelings drew upon Pierre Janet's *sentiment d'incompletitude*.

35. With the notion of "as if," Adler introduced the concept of fictions into his psychology, an idea he adopted from and credited to Hans Vaihinger (1852–1933). He wrote, "It was good fortune which made me acquainted with Vaihinger's ingenius *Philosophy of "As If"* (Berlin, 1911), a work in which I found the thoughts familiar to me from the neuroses presented as valid for scientific thinking in general," in Adler, *Über den Nervösen Charakter*, p. 22. Vaihinger's position, which he called an idealistic positivism, reflects a certain pragmatism. He held that ideas that are incapable of proof (such as God, morals, and so forth) do possess practical value. We cannot establish any absolute truths, but for our own well-being we must live as if God, free will, and moral laws really exist. See Alfred Adler, *Individual Psychology of Alfred Adler*, pp. 76–87.

36. Bottome, *Alfred Adler*, pp. 163–166.

37. Ibid., p. 120.

38. Alfred Adler, *Problem of Neuroses* (New York: Harper Torchbooks, 1964), p. 78.

39. Viktor E. Frankl, "Forerunner of Existential Psychiatry." In "Tributes to Alfred Adler on His 100th Birthday." *Journal of Individual Psychology* 26 (1970): 12.

4

Medical Training
in a Time of Social Ferment

I then and there decided to train my diagnostic skill, but
in such a way that I could communicate to others the reasons for my conclusions.

Rudolf Dreikurs
"Guiding, Teaching, and Demonstrating," 1967

Conditions at the University of Vienna in the years 1918–1923, when
Dreikurs attended medical school, were radically different from the earlier, more glamorous days of Freud and Adler. The war was still in
progress when Dreikurs began his studies, and Vienna and its people
were in a state of desperation. After four long years, Dreikurs recalled,
"We who were in the midst of it almost became reconciled to an unending
state of war, and I became rather sympathetic to the growing rebellion
against the war and the monarchy."[1]

When the war finally ended for Austria in November 1918, it was not
by military defeat but by a bloodless revolution. Overnight, the once
mighty empire of fifty million people that stretched across central Europe
went to pieces as if shattered by an explosion. Austria emerged as a
diminutive republic of six million people, of whom nearly 30 percent lived
in the city of Vienna. Conditions in the city deteriorated even further as
trainloads of demobilized and wounded soldiers poured in. Unemployment and inflation soared, starvation was rampant, and Vienna, once the
flower of Europe, was reduced to a cheap soup kitchen.

These were difficult years for Rudolf and Steffi, filled with deprivation
and unending financial struggle. For a while they lived with her parents
and then moved into a humble flat of their own in some jerry-built bar-
racks left from the war. Steffi's modest income as a bank clerk provided
their basic support, although Rudolf's father probably assisted with

47

money for tuition and books. Adequate food and clothing were particularly scarce in the outrageous black-market conditions, and Rudolf struggled along like other men wearing the threadbare remnants of army uniforms.

After seven hundred years of Hapsburg rule, Austria finally entered the modern era of republican government under trying circumstances. For the brief but hopeful period that lasted from 1918 to 1934, when totalitarianism succeeded with crushing finality, Austria's struggle for self-rule was shaped by three opposing political forces: The prodemocratic labor movement as represented by the Social Democratic Party; the right-wing, authoritarian Christian Socialists; and the growing German Nationalist Party, which sought union (*Anschluss*) with Germany and which would later link with the Christian Socialists. Both Adler's and Dreikurs's sympathies rested with the Social Democrats.

Vienna came under the control of the Social Democrats and rose remarkably from the shambles of war largely due to the dedicated leadership of Mayor Karl Seitz. His administration launched a spectacular program of sweeping reforms in working conditions, health, welfare, and education, in which Adler and his co-workers (including Dreikurs) played an important role. Included were revolutionary programs in health care and preventive medicine that provided new hospitals, prenatal clinics, and free clinics to curb syphilis, tuberculosis, and alcoholism. An excellent adult education system, kindergartens, day-care programs, public baths, parks, and recreational areas were also established, as well as a massive housing program that provided decent apartments for the working class, who had previously lived under the most wretched slum conditions. All this was carried out in the space of a few short years "by men of superior capacity and tireless zeal whose first motivation was a true love of the people."[2] Her skeptical, smug Anglo-Saxon friends called her "Red Vienna," but quickly sent their planners and their health and education experts to find out how it was accomplished.

Dreikurs's medical training coincided with this challenging postwar period, and he soon emerged as an active leader of the students' movement of the Social Democratic Party. His experiences in the youth movement and the war had paved the way to leadership, and he was not now about to take a backseat to life around him. An outspoken champion in behalf of the underprivileged members of society, his manner was argumentative and often abrasive to others. But what he lacked in tact was compensated for by the clarity of his ideas and his dogged willingness to champion his beliefs.

In response to labor's demand for a role in deciding community issues, elected workers' councils were set up in each district of the city. Dreikurs and others agitated for the right of the university students to be represented, and when they won, he was elected chief delegate of the three students given seats on the council.

"I was twenty-two years old at the time and had quite an influential position," Dreikurs reflected. "But it never registered with me what leadership I had. I only became conscious of it many years after I had come to the States, when I met people from those early years and realized to what extent they looked to me as a leader. My interest in the labor movement had perhaps one lasting effect on me: I became an organizer. Recently someone said to me, 'Even in psychiatry you are a politician.' It is true. I am interested in organizing, in movements."

Because both Adler and Dreikurs were significantly involved in this vital period of Vienna's life, it is important to realize that the labor movement that developed there was much broader than it was in the United States. A major part of labor's efforts was devoted to education and cultural enrichment. The *Volksheim* (People's Institute), a popular adult education center sponsored by the labor party where Adler lectured for years, featured eminent scholars and poets who considered it an honor to teach there. While the brand of socialism that developed in Austria drew upon Marxist ideas, it was also clearly anticommunistic and nonautocratic. Speaking of this period, Dreikurs remarked: "The party leadership was always democratic, and there was much participation of rank-and-file membership. When we speak of Austrian socialism, we should not compare it to any kind of dictatorial, revolutionary socialism. It was a truly democratic party, and that is the reason why Adler and many others were in it. When today they speak of Adler as a 'socialist,' it is a mistaken idea. You have to understand why many of us were socialists."[3]

Adler also participated in the Social Democratic Party after the war and was elected vice-chairman to his own local council because of his deep involvement in educational reform. His political career, however, was short-lived, and in later years he assiduously avoided having his psychology identified with any political party or religion and reacted against those who attempted to do so.[4]

It was through Adler's and Dreikurs's mutual involvement in the workers' councils that they first met personally. By then Adler had an international reputation in psychiatry and was considered a leading authority in education as well. Twenty-seven years younger than Adler, Dreikurs was pleased by this chance association and expressed to Adler his interest in psychiatry. Adler responded by inviting the enthusiastic medical student to accompany him while he visited a patient.

"That became an outstanding experience for me," Dreikurs reflected. "Adler minced no words about every patient having the ability to get well, about every criminal being capable of rehabilitation, if only one wins his trust. . . . Anyone can change and there is hope for everybody. This optimistic outlook was so contrary to what I learned in school that I couldn't accept it, nor believe how anyone in his right mind could hold such an 'unrealistic' opinion. . . . [It] was beyond my grasp—at least then."[5]

Dreikurs came away from this encounter disappointed and perhaps somewhat puzzled given Adler's high esteem in the community. Dreikurs was well-read on current philosophical and psychological issues, and in that light, Adler's compressed statement seemed naïve and simplistic. Besides, his two years of medical training were heavily weighted toward ascribing mental disorders to genetic or physiological causes. This perspective generally scoffed at the idea that the patient played any role in the origin or outcome of his illness. His skeptical reaction was reinforced by his knowledge of Freud's psychoanalytic theory of neurosis, which he had studied in his second semester of medical school.[6] Freud's theory of mental illness not only differed greatly from Adler's but was characterized by a sophisticated intellectualism, against which Adler's unadorned statements paled in comparison.

Not long after this encounter with Adler, Dreikurs's political activities ended with a rude awakening: "My studies suffered . . . and I flunked two examinations. I then decided I had to make a choice, either devote myself to study or continue my political activities. I decided to drop these activities, but not my participation in the educational aspect of the labor movement."

Dreikurs's worrisome financial state also influenced his decision. For in that same year, 1921, their son, Eric, was born. It had been a difficult birth for Steffi, requiring a forceps delivery that injured the infant's nerves, temporarily paralyzing both his arms and resulting in a mild though permanent handicap. No longer able to count on Steffi's income, Dreikurs now faced the added responsibility of providing for all three of them.

Though Dreikurs's political efforts got him into academic difficulties, they also paved the way for the new directions in social psychiatry he later pursued. Because of his efforts to organize a socialist medical students' association, for which he served as president, he won the respect and friendship of his brilliant anatomy professor, Dr. Julius Tandler. An ardent proponent of socialized medicine, Tandler had branched out from a strictly academic career to plan and direct the revolutionary public health and welfare programs mentioned earlier. The devastating effects of war convinced him that the "health of the people as a whole is dependent upon the health of each individual as determined both by his constitution and environment. . . . Any rational, all-embracing policy will therefore need to be governed chiefly by the concept of preventive medicine."[7] He felt the time was past for depending upon private charitable institutions to care for the poor and indigent, a haphazard system that never met the needs of the community. He strongly advocated that the city has an obligation to provide for the well-being of all its citizens. This viewpoint displeased his medical colleagues, and he waged an uphill battle to get his programs established and make them work. Dreikurs helped in this campaign, and Tandler appreciated his efforts.

For the clinical phase of the five-year medical curriculum, the training shifted largely to Vienna General Hospital (*Wiener Allgemeine Krankenhaus*), from which, it has been said, more medical wisdom has emanated than from any other single institution in the world. The largest hospital on the continent, it rambled over a forty-acre site that included sixty-one large clinics and twenty-seven branch hospitals, as well as clinics for instruction and observation. Each clinic was under the direction of an outstanding expert in his field. Dreikurs studied there under some of the great names in medicine: Clemens von Pirquet in pediatrics; Nobel Prize winner Julius Wagner-Jauregg in psychiatry; Julius Tandler in anatomy; and Anton Eiselsberg, recipient of the Lister Prize for his work in brain surgery. Other teachers in psychological and psychiatric subjects included E. Stransky, Otto Pötzl, Paul Schilder, Heinrich Friedjung, and Hermann Swoboda.

Of all his professors, Dreikurs later referred to only three as having particularly influenced him. They were Tandler and Pötzl, who encouraged him in the direction of social psychiatry, and Prof. Franz Chvostek, who taught internal medicine but was also a skilled neurologist. Chvostek intrigued him because of his uncanny ability to make a correct diagnosis by merely looking at the patient.

"Nobody knew whether it was based on vision or smell; but his 'intuition' proved to be accurate even in the most complicated cases. I admired his skill, as did all his associates and students. But I regretted that he could not tell us on what he based his diagnosis. I remember that I then and there decided to train my diagnostic skill, but in such a way that I could communicate to others the reasons for my conclusions. Many believe that this sensitivity is 'innate,' a 'talent' and cannot be acquired by training. I know this is not true."[8]

A DISAPPOINTING EXPERIENCE

Having recovered from the war by the early 1920s, Vienna quickly established itself as the "capitol of psychology" owing largely to the revolution Freud and Adler helped to set in motion. It was the mecca of psychology, to which "all felt obliged to make a pilgrimage before considering themselves qualified to speak with any authority."

Though preoccupied with the demanding requirements of medical studies, Dreikurs maintained his long-standing goal—to explore the mysteries of the mind. He used every opportunity to explore and experience diverse psychological and psychiatric issues. Already familiar with the basic ideas of psychoanalysis and somewhat acquainted with Adler's views, he did not embrace either position, although he was aware of the controversy and bitter hostility that raged between the followers of Freud and Adler. Dreikurs was also acquainted with Wilhelm Stekel, another important Viennese figure in psychology in those years:

> During these student days I also attracted the attention of Wilhelm Stekel through the stand I took in a public meeting of faculty representatives with a "mind reader." At that time I was interested in parapsychology and expected to go into the exploration of its phenomena. However, the suicide of a greatly respected psychiatrist who worked in this field, only to find out that he had been duped by the medium with whom he worked, convinced me that I would not be clever enough to deal with frauds. It was then only natural that I became interested in another avenue of exploring the mind, namely, psychotherapy.[9]

As Dreikurs turned his interests toward psychotherapy, the acrimonious debate between the Freudian and Adlerian groups was brought sharply into focus for him. At first glance, as it often appeared to visitors from abroad who perfunctorily surveyed the conflict, the disagreements reflected little more than the petty rivalries between their brilliant but ambitious leaders. Few grasped that Freud and Adler were moving in fundamentally different directions in their views of human nature. Dreikurs found the undertow of opinions and accusations disturbing. How unscientific! He wrote in his diary in 1920: "We have here a Tower of Babel second to none. No man understands the other, nobody knows what he wants; everybody thinks that he is right—and, what is worse—he is right. If only we could finally realize why we are so limited—why every word has a different meaning to everybody."[10]

A peripatetic questioner who accepted nothing without first challenging and scrutinizing it, Dreikurs was determined to sort out the whole controversial situation and sought to attend each group's meetings and seminars. Among his friends in medical school were Otto Fenichel and Wilhelm Reich, both thoroughly committed to the psychoanalytic school. He asked them if he could observe the weekly meetings of the psychoanalytic group. But to be admitted he would first have to undergo psychoanalysis.

"Why I never became a psychoanalyst is very simple. I was excluded from going window shopping with them. They were an exclusive bunch. One had to commit oneself before one could come in. I didn't want to do that. It was against my nature." Besides, Dreikurs found Freud's sexual theories unappealing: "I thought they were far-fetched and unrealistic."

To attend a session of Adler's group was simple. You just went. No one was excluded, and the door to the weekly Monday meetings was characteristically left wide open. At one meeting Dreikurs got into trouble. Adler made a derogatory remark about Freud, implying that Freud was all wrong.

"Being a young student," Dreikurs admitted, "I was very outspoken on everything I found not to be true, and I became indignant."

He stood up, rebuking Adler. "How can you treat Freud so shabbily? A man with such an international reputation has to know what he is doing, and cannot be simply dismissed."

One of Adler's colleagues took Dreikurs aside and upbraided him for his audacious remarks and naïve understanding of these matters.

"Quite naturally, I lost interest in working with Adler. My first encounters with Adler were negative indeed," Dreikurs reflected. "I think it took quite a while after I had joined his group [before] Adler would trust me. Later I myself carried on his fight with Freud and Psychoanalysis."

At that time, Dreikurs was clearly disappointed with both schools of thought. He was awarded his medical degree in January 1923, and as he entered his internship and psychiatric residency, he temporarily abandoned his interest in psychotherapy.

A Time of Soul-Searching

There is evidence that this was a period of intense personal struggle in Dreikurs's life. Few would have guessed his sense of inadequacy and displeasure with himself. He now sported a bushy red beard that matched his fiery temperament. To others, he seemed outspoken, provocative, and forever haranguing about his favorite socialist causes. Adler's daughter, Alexandra, recalled her impressions of Dreikurs from the days when they were fellow residents in psychiatry: "In Vienna, we laughed at him. He wore a beard. He never got a university appointment. He was in an outlying clinic. We sent our most undesirable patients to him. Most objectionable was his interest in social problems and the fact that he verbalized these concerns constantly. That sort of thing just wasn't done at the University of Vienna, so he was an outcast."[11]

True, Dreikurs did spend the majority of these years in a small substation in Döbling and not in the main clinic of the hospital, but he saw it a little differently: "First of all, the positions in the main clinic were all taken by people who had more pull and connections. The outpatient clinic appealed to me because there was much more of a chance to really participate in [its] activities."

Dreikurs's dissatisfaction with himself was revealed in the student notebook and diary he kept from 1915 to 1923. Filled with sporadic entries, mostly scientific and philosophical, it rarely contained anything personal. However, after he had completed the first part of his internship, he poured out his heart—revealing how deeply displeased he was with himself, with his impact on others, and how much he desired to be respected, to feel a sense of belonging.

May 21, 1923

Even though it was quite short, the first period of my activity as a doctor is over. It presented me with a number of insights, which, even though they are not in scientific or medical areas, are still valuable. They were failure and lack of awareness of deficiencies of my personality. I have abused sympathetic persons, made enemies, and presented myself impossibly in society. I don't know whether a person at this age—I am twenty-six years old—can still change, especially when he has as little energy as I. Yet despite these doubts I will use all insights in order to learn. . . .

The latter part of my studies I spent without human companionship except that of my wife. And I think I can credit her with the fact
that I am able to judge—as I am doing right now—my experiences
with colleagues. . . . I arrived at [Professor] Kovacz's division under
the best possible circumstances. The Professor turned out to be my
uncle's friend which raised my status as a young inexperienced doctor.

The second most important personality of the organization, a casual friend . . . who seriously intended to help me in any possible way
(i.e., through introductions to his friends, working for the student
organization), did as promised until I spoiled our relationship . . .
with my conduct. In the beginning, my colleagues were very friendly
and nice toward me because I looked quite dignified and was
thought of as an intelligent person. But because of my petty quarrels,
I succeeded in spoiling everything for myself. So much so, that today,
after little more than two months, most of the people with whom I
worked closely are glad I have left the division. Why do I do this to
myself?

Then I talk terribly much, I can't bear not to talk. Every time it's
nonsense—I spoil all my relationships. But I *have* to talk, to question
everything instead of keeping my mouth shut.

I had hoped to give a better impression of myself in questions of
organization, since I had worked in this area and believed myself to
be experienced. But even there I could not control myself; I couldn't
keep my mouth shut because I had the impression that others didn't
see what seemed to me to be the most essential point. I had the
impression that I missed every opportunity to make them understand
me. This was worsened by my constant repetitions, my loud voice. . . .
I felt I was hurting the cause I championed more than if I had kept
quiet right from the beginning. But constantly I say to myself, "You
have to help enlighten also." But I wind up sitting down, ashamed,
because it would have been better had nobody taken notice of me in
the first place. . . . So, here again, I showed myself as a person to be
avoided.

I quarrelled with colleagues who tended to be conservative regarding socialism and other modern ideas about the duties of doctors, etc.
I argued so ineffectively that these colleagues became convinced of
the opposite of what I was trying to tell them, and probably say of
me: "So *this* is what the socialists, the revolutionaries look like!"

Right in the beginning I had a row with a nurse. The only reason it didn't turn out badly for *me* was because I was mean and merciless: I reported her, and the doctor had no choice but to discipline her. But I wasn't at all satisfied with my behavior. It didn't help either that my unsatisfied sexuality was practically staring out of my eyes. Because of this, the nurse couldn't excuse my behavior, whereas otherwise she might have, just on the grounds of my being a young, inexperienced, and completely incapable doctor. . . . Tomorrow, I will be transferred to a different section, also under favorable conditions. I wonder what I have learned and how I will fare.[12]

His worry that he would not be able to learn from his soul-searching proved untrue. While some of his "undesirable" traits persisted throughout his life, he did learn to moderate his attacking style with humor and circumspection—except when he considered it absolutely vital. In such instances, he could challenge, provoke, and fight with a tenacity that made his friends cringe. But it was this pugnacious persistence that enabled him to continue fighting for causes he believed in long after others had withdrawn in defeat. In that sense, these qualities were also great assets, sustaining him through the years of opposition that lay ahead.

People were rarely neutral about Dreikurs. They either liked or disliked him. Many found themselves drawn to his ideas if not the man. But others saw beyond these qualities to the real man, who cared deeply and passionately about the well-being of his friends, about people in general, and, perhaps, even his enemies. Of those who knew him as a friend—and there were many all around the world—few knew a truer friend than he. He relished a "good" fight, but he was not one to hold a grudge or to be vengeful. He genuinely respected the right of others to hold different opinions—but he felt that one should at least have the benefit of his point of view, and he saw to it that you received it! He believed that holding opinions was never enough—one must actively promote them.

For example, Dreikurs's early work in social psychiatry involved him in programs to prevent alcohol abuse. A heated issue arose over whether or not hard liquor should be allowed on the premises of a recreation center built for the benefit of the workers in his home district. Dreikurs contended that certain political and economic factions were exploiting the workers by pushing their use of alcohol. A community decision had to be reached, and as the leader of the antialcohol group, he presented a resolution that the center be kept free of alcoholic beverages. When it came time to speak in behalf of the resolution, Dreikurs's friends warned: "You know how you are—always provocative, always too outspoken. You have to be diplomatic. If you speak up, they will probably go after you, and we will have no chance." They suggested that a certain local politician speak in their behalf instead. "He is the right man to represent our cause. He is dignified. Everyone will listen to him."

"I consented," Dreikurs recalled. "I wouldn't say one word. There I sat on pins and needles. The weak argument he made! When attacked, what a weak defense! I don't think I could have made it worse. Of course it was defeated! I decided then and there: I may sometimes provoke, but this polite appeasing when the chips are down . . . doesn't accomplish anything. I don't think I have ever let anyone persuade me to be replaced by a more polite or polished representative of my ideas since."

In this period, Dreikurs also faced the first direct challenge to his professional integrity. In characteristic fashion, he picked up the gauntlet and challenged the opposition:

When he was a resident physician at the university clinic, he recalled:

> I suddenly realized that people were rather distrusting of me, that they were holding back. I tried to figure it out, and finally, one of my colleagues told me. It seems there was a young fellow behind me, the grandson of a professor of psychiatry, and I was in his way. So he told everybody that I never took my examinations in medical school and that I had bought my degree by negotiating with the dean. I was furious, as you can imagine. So I took the matter to court, and he was forced by the judge to write a statement apologizing for the unfounded and damaging rumor. He had to return this statement with the signatures of all the professors to the judge. This did not prevent him from later becoming a professor of psychiatry, one of the leading men in Germany—a Nazi.

This bizarre incident hinted at the undercurrent of anti-Semitism that was growing within the population, seeping into the formerly tolerant professional and upper-class circles.

Because of his secular outlook, Dreikurs probably did not ascribe the incident to anti-Semitism at the time. He reflected an antireligious attitude that was common among Vienna's intellectual and cultured Jews. Although his mother was religiously observant and a Zionist, his father disdained religion and mocked her religious sentiments. Most of Drei-

kurs's friends identified with the progressive political and social movement, and few found much value in the narrow outlook and rigid
strictures of organized religion. Assimilationist and cosmopolitan, they
claimed a more universalist outlook that went beyond the bounds of
traditional religious practice. Dreikurs never denied his Jewish origins,
but like many of his contemporaries, he was neither well-versed nor interested in Judaic traditions.[13]

The "unsatisfied sexuality" mentioned in his agonizing diary entry
hints at another aspect of his life that was troubling him. From subsequent developments it is known that there were serious difficulties in his
marriage, which had followed a youthful, passionate romance, exaggerated by the uncertainties of war.

Steffi was shrewd, ambitious, and calculating. Some thought she was
the driving force behind Dreikurs in those struggling years, that without
her he might not have finished his medical training. But in her rigid and
perfectionistic way, she tried to mold him to her own idea of what a
physician should be. She handled the family finances and directed the
household and his early practice with domineering efficiency. This ran
counter to Dreikurs's own style and roused his aversion to being dominated.

In contrast to Steffi's reclusiveness, Dreikurs was outgoing—always
attending meetings, involved in politics and music, and genuinely interested in other people. Though not considered especially handsome, he
had a softness and a sensuality that conveyed his appreciative attitude
toward women. Women sensed these qualities, were drawn to him, and
valued his friendship. Naturally, he was bolstered by their reciprocated
interest and did not discourage it.

But for Steffi, who tended to distrust the motives of others, such open
friendliness on his part raised her suspicions. She became obsessively
jealous of his activities and interests. Her suspiciousness was disturbing
and created a rift between them. At the time of the diary entry, these
problems had probably begun to affect their marriage seriously.

Notes for Chapter 4

1. The direct quotations of Rudolf Dreikurs, unless otherwise noted, are from the
Dreikurs-Mackaness interview.

2. Charles A. Gulick, *Austria from Habsburg to Hitler*, vol. 1. (Berkeley, Calif.:
University of California Press, 1948), p. ix.

3. Dreikurs's assessment is supported by Charles A. Gulick in his *Austria from Habsburg to Hitler*, where he wrote:

Austrian Social Democratic *theory* embodied a political, economic, and social philosophy well to the left of that preferred . . . by most Anglo-Saxons. . . . The *practice* was "revisionist" and social reformist. Its accomplishments in school reform, social welfare, and housing were recognized and claimed throughout the world. But the most important consideration, which should be kept in mind at all times, is the fact that particularly in the last years of the republic there were only two practical choices for the Austrian who took his citizenship seriously: some form of Fascism or this leftist type of democracy [pp. 11–12].

4. Furtmüller, "Alfred Adler," p. 372.

5. Dreikurs, "Guiding, Teaching, and Demonstrating," p. 148; idem, "Rudolf Dreikurs 1897–1972," in *Psychotherapie in Selbstdarstellungen*, ed. Ludwig J. Pongratz (Bern, Switz.: Hans Huber, 1973), p. 109.

6. Dreikurs's University of Vienna course record book (*Meldungsbuch*), Dreikurs Papers (Manuscript Division, Library of Congress), shows that in the fall of 1918, he took a course, "The Psychoanalytic Theory of Neurosis," which lists Freud as the professor. However, Dreikurs told his family and friends that he never met Freud. So, it would appear that someone else substituted for Freud.

7. Alfred Goetzl and Ralph Arthur Reynolds, *Julius Tandler: A Biography* (San Francisco, privately published, 1944), p. 23.

8. Dreikurs, "Guiding, Teaching, and Demonstrating," p. 155.

9. Ibid., pp. 148–149.

10. Rudolf Dreikurs, student notebooks, October 13, 1920, Dreikurs Papers.

11. Dr. Alexandra Adler, personal communication, 1973.

12. Dreikurs Papers.

13. In the Dreikurs-Mackaness interview, Dreikurs explained his resignation from the Jewish Cultural Community of Vienna in 1922:

When our children were born, I did not want them to get a religious education. But religious education was obligatory in Vienna, because Austria was a Catholic country. You had to send the children. So the only thing to do was to declare openly my "becoming without faith." You had to go to the municipal [Jewish community] agency and make a statement that you, your family and children, no longer belonged to any church; this was then published in the local journals and prevented [obligatory religious education] from happening. The interesting part was that they should take some form of religious education, and they were brought up in my own spirit. When Austrofascism came along, the Catholic control began again. My girl was in grammar school and it didn't affect her too much, but my boy was in high school, and if he didn't get a mark in religion, he would fail. I protested: "If you really force him to take religion, then you will have to instruct him each year in another one, and the first one, the Jewish religion." That stopped them pretty cold because they didn't have any kind of service for that. But it was only the last year before we left before it came to this showdown.

5

Adler's Child Guidance Clinics

> The honest psychologist cannot shut his eyes against the
> fact that conditions exist which prevent the entering of the
> child into the community, prevent his feeling at home, and
> let him grow up as if in enemy country. He must there-
> fore talk and work against all . . . disturbances of the
> spreading of social interest in the family, the school, and
> the social life.
>
> Alfred Adler
> *Social Interest*

In the years following World War I, the school of Individual Psychology
had grown to international proportions,[1] stimulated mostly by Adler's
work in education and the child guidance centers he developed in Vienna.
Adler's outstanding contributions in these fields continually drew Dreikurs's admiration, even if he was at that time dubious about some aspects
of Adler's work. Dreikurs's abiding interest in education never diminished as his career in medicine and psychiatry progressed. Indeed, it
began to weave a basic thread for his entire lifework. His early efforts in
social psychiatry and the mental health movement would lead him to the
conclusion that the "prevention of mental disorder must begin with the
child."[2] Adler's work in child guidance coincided with the direction in
which Dreikurs was heading.

The child guidance clinics that Adler developed were called *Erzie-
hungberatungstellen,* which translates as "advice centers for bringing up
children." Their significance, Dreikurs often emphasized, was that they
were less concerned with treating disturbed children than with providing
concrete guidance for parents in their difficult task of properly raising
children. As important, Adler's focus went beyond the parents to the
teachers, who he realized were in a strategic position for reaching those
children who might need the most help but whose parents might be the
least likely to seek it. Drawing upon years of clinical experience, Adler
creatively applied his findings to developing a counseling model that

pioneered the way in group methods and family therapy. This model is especially well suited to the needs of a democratic society and remains far in advance of today's groping efforts in this direction. Its long existence and proven success seems paradoxical in view of its lack of recognition by many contemporary practitioners. This dilemma prompted Dreikurs to wage a lonely campaign, against stiff opposition, to see this guidance model revived on American soil.

Both Adler's and Dreikurs's sustained interest in education can be traced to their own unhappy experiences in Austria's old "obedience" schools, which mirrored the autocratic government's ideal: "obedient children to be made into obedient adults." Adler reflected:

> When I became a physician, I realized what this meant in terms of human life, what the influence of such a warped, repressed childhood was on intelligence, courage, self-confidence, independence. It seemed to me that only the physician's skill and outlook would transform these school-prisons into a scheme of real education. In 1898, I wrote my first article developing my idea of the relationship between medicine in the larger sense and the school. . . . I had learned that it is not true that a child's intelligence is constant throughout life. Characteristics of both child and adult can be modified.[3]

Adler also discovered that most of the mistaken ideas of children that later lead to behavior problems originate in the home. But it is almost impossible to see these faults until the child enters the more challenging environment of school.

Adler attempted his first child guidance clinic sometime before World War I. But it attracted little attention: "Once in a while teachers came to me, or children with teachers, or even an occasional parent. But it was only a small beginning and a very unsatisfactory one. . . . Out of the discouraging futility of my very first clinic was born the plan to teach the teachers, to give them an understanding of character through psychology."[4]

Conditions in Vienna were ripe for Adler's ideas on child guidance in the problem-ridden years following the war. The city was beset with large numbers of wayward, malnourished, and rootless children. The enlightened social welfare and public health programs instituted by Julius Tandler did much to restore these innocent victims of war to health. But they were not enough. Education was recognized as the key to shaping youth to the demands and responsibilities of a society in transition from autocracy to democracy. Under the inspired direction of Otto Glöckel, minister of education, an unprecedented program of educational reform was begun.[5]

The school reform involved radically changing the organization, methods, curricula, and goals of the schools, but it was neither conceived nor carried out in haste. Such a massive reform also required a major reorientation of the teachers and a conscious effort to win the parents to a new educational philosophy applicable in the home.

Adler's efforts were moving in a similar direction. With the new emphasis on "social interest," he began to devote the major part of his energies to educating the public, especially parents and teachers, to a better understanding of human nature. His lectures at the *Volksheim*, the institute for adult education, honed his captivating style, cultivated his insight, and drew large and enthusiastic audiences.

From 1919 to 1922, Adler conducted seminars devoted successively to the young child, the school-age child, and the adolescent. These influenced a group of young educators, who learned a concrete applicability that had been totally lacking in their academic training. Among them were Ferdinand Birnbaum, Oskar Spiel, Regine Seidler, Alice Friedman, and Ida Löwy, who later helped to develop the educational component of Individual Psychology.

Adler's first successful child guidance clinic evolved from these seminars in 1920. Where his earlier, prewar effort had failed, now, in the exciting atmosphere of widespread reform, his clinic filled with teachers who were seeking ways to help the many difficult children they felt incapable of handling. Their problems included "backwardness" (underachievement), disruptive acts, and delinquent behavior.

Otto Glöckel, the head of the Vienna schools, was impressed by Adler's efforts on behalf of the teachers and invited him to direct more than two-thirds of the state child guidance clinics, all of which were attached to the schools. The clinics directed by Adler and his colleagues were conducted on a voluntary basis.

Adler's clinics were not the first ever established. Pioneering efforts had already begun in the United States, Germany, and Switzerland, and Adler was familiar with them.[6] However, Adler's distinctive theoretical and practical approach, and the urgency of conditions in Vienna, gave his clinics a unique character that distinguished them from those established elsewhere. Their special character derived from their public format, which evolved, as discoveries often do, serendipitously.

Adler's basic orientation to child guidance differed from that of others in that he was primarily concerned not only with helping the child but also with conveying his knowledge and skills to others. In contrast, the typical model that evolved in the United States became almost exclusively concerned with helping the individual child in the seclusion of the private consulting office. Right from the beginning, Adler's was a teaching model designed to reach a great many teachers and schools as rapidly as possible.

To accomplish this goal, he decided to demonstrate his methods with actual cases. Thus began his unorthodox and daring practice of counseling the child in the presence of a limited audience of students. A teacher would bring in the problem child accompanied by the consenting parent. The session would begin with an oral or written report by the teacher, from which Adler would begin to sketch the character or life style of the child, his problems, and the family situation. Approaching each case with a view toward grasping the child holistically, he would look for a consistent, unified pattern of behavior and make a guess about the purpose of the child's misbehavior. Adler would next interview the parent, then the child. Even before the child entered the room, Adler often guessed how he thought the youngster would act. Because mind and body are a unified expression of personality in Adler's psychology, "body language" (although he did not use the term) provided valuable clues for discovering an individual's approach to life.

When the child did appear, many in the audience were struck with Adler's uncanny knack for accurately fathoming the child's character from only the brief report and interview with the teacher and parents. The child was then faced with his own particular misinterpretation of events and his mistaken goals. This was never done in an attacking, fault-finding, or moralistic manner. Instead, in a hypothetical, problem-solving fashion, Adler would explore with the youngster his situation and his mistaken purposes. Most important, he discussed with the child useful, alternative behaviors. After interviewing the child, Adler discussed the case comprehensively with his students, emphasizing its implications and its applicability to other cases.

Adler's opponents, especially the Freudians, decried his violation of the sanctity of counseling in private. However, Adler had discovered unexpected benefits from counseling before a group: "I found that treating the child as part of his group was often very effective. It made the child realize that 'no man liveth unto himself alone,' and that the mistakes of every individual affect many lives and are of public concern. The boys and girls could be brought to see themselves as social beings, not as isolated units."[7]

Concern that the child might be embarrassed appearing before a group of adults proved groundless. The child found that he was treated respectfully and quickly sensed that he was among friends where he might at last be understood. Any self-consciousness about the audience was quickly lost as he became absorbed in self-knowledge. "I have never known a child who could not understand his difficulties when they were set before him," Adler asserted. "If I find a child who fails to follow me as I trace the roots of his mistakes, I can always be sure I have blundered either in interpreting his situation or in describing it to him. Every normal child is capable of fathoming the springs of his own action and reaching a true understanding of his own life."[8] Adler's deft skill at eliciting self-awareness in youngsters is illustrated in the following dialogue with Willie.

As the blond boy approached the stage where Adler sat, his expression was resentful, and he clenched and unclenched his fists along the seams of his knickers.

"Ah," the doctor said as he quickly read through the teacher's report, "he throws erasers at the teacher. The principal sends him home many times, but he still throws." Looking at Willie, he queried, "You do this when the teacher's back is turned?" The boy looked down at the stage floor.

"You will please answer," the doctor said gently. There was no reply.

"Are you afraid of me?"

The boy looked up at once. The word *afraid* was a challenge to him.

"How old are you?" Adler continued.

The boy began swinging his foot in a circle. "Ten," he replied.

"Ten?" Adler repeated, backing away. "You are little for ten, are you not?" Willie's little blue eyes pinned the doctor with venom.

"Look at me," Adler said. "I am little at fifty. We who are little must prove we are big. We throw erasers at teachers. Is that not so, Willie?"

Willie's eyes remained fixed on the floor. There was a slight shrug.

"Come, Willie, look at me. What am I doing?" Adler slowly raised himself on his toes and let himself down. He did it again. "You know what I am doing?" The boy looked up. "Willie, I am making myself bigger than I am."

The boy almost smiled, then stifled it like a yawn in church.

"Do you participate in sports, Willie?" The youngster began to show interest. "Of course you do. Bet I can tell you which is your favorite." The little boy's body sagged in relaxation.

"You play rugby." Willie's eyes opened wide. "You play rugby because it is a rough sport. You must always prove you are big. I can guess what position you play," Adler continued. "You would be the goaltender, no?"

Willie nodded slowly. "And why are you the goaltender? I will tell you. How else can you prove how big you are than by preventing a goal?" The boy was popeyed. Adler slowly raised himself on his toes and lowered himself again. "I must be bigger than I am," Adler repeated. "I must prove it to everybody and myself. I must play better than the big boys. I must fight better than the big boys and I must defy authority—like throwing erasers at my teacher."

Adler then called Willie's teacher onstage and whispered something to her. She nodded and left, taking Willie with her.

Almost a year later, Adler's assistant wrote a postscript to the case. "Willie returned to class. Behavior excellent. One remission. Teacher said it occurred after first three weeks. She was at blackboard. Eraser hit blackboard next to her head. She said nothing, walked over to the aisle where Willie sat, stood before him, raised herself on her toes twice, and resumed classwork. No problems since."[9]

The audience did not remain passive observers. Adler often turned to them asking whether anyone had experienced similar difficulties to those of the child before them. The admission of childhood difficulties by the now successful adults was not only encouraging to the child but helped the adults understand the purposes of children's behavior.

Adler's initial school-based clinic was conducted in a district that included sixty-seven schools and served 19,780 children.[10] Both teachers and administrators attended the fortnightly sessions, which lasted several hours, during which two or three children would be counseled. Each case was handled comprehensively.

What was the reaction among the classroom teachers, who had traditionally felt their only obligation was to teach curricular subjects and maintain discipline?

> [At first,] many teachers actively resented my offer to show them a new and better way to go about their work. Even those who were mildly interested often complained that they had so much to do, with thirty or forty pupils under their care, that they could not give individual attention to each child. Little by little they began to realize that what I taught them, far from being an added burden, greatly lightened their load. . . . I talked about school matters with them and tried to point out that the behavior difficulties that made their work

so hard . . . were seldom the fault of the school or of inheritance but mistakes made in building up the style of life. Then I tried to make clear to them, that for this very reason, the school was the only place where these children, freed for a little time from these home influences, could be studied and helped. In one school, and then in another, teachers began to put into practice what I had taught them, and the results excited the interest of other teachers.[11]

As the teachers put Adler's new ideas into practice, they began to sense an improved atmosphere in the classroom and even with problems in their own families. "The effect of our work was so striking," Adler reported, "that the teachers went to the Board of Education without my knowledge and asked for my appointment [to] the Pedagogical Institute of Vienna, in which the teachers . . . are trained."[12]

He began lecturing at the institute in 1924, and the immense popularity of his ideas is shown by the fact that more than six hundred teachers, comprising a great part of the public school staff, elected to attend his course in its first three years. His faith in and dedication to the teachers was total: "He never once missed, through all the years that followed until he went to live in America, giving this fortnightly lecture to teachers."[13] These lectures formed the basis of his book *The Education of Children* (1930).

Adler's dream was to generate a true community of parents and teachers who would work together to foster courage and social responsibility in youth. And before long the teachers' enthusiasm did infect the parents, especially through the parents' associations. As a result, a number of child guidance centers were opened to the general community for parents and other interested parties.

As the demand for the child guidance centers grew, Adler found it essential to train others to continue his work. Dreikurs, who had attended the Adlerian clinics since the early 1920s, was among a core group of physicians, educators, and social workers who trained to work together as "medico-pedagogic" teams in the new centers. By 1927, there were approximately thirty such centers in Vienna. In addition, a number were opened in Germany and in Holland.[14] No record remains of Dreikurs's personal experiences with Adler at this time—other than a summary remark to the effect that Dreikurs began conducting such a child guidance center as early as 1923.[15] by 1926, he was listed as a codirector of a child guidance center.[16]

The guidance model Adler created made excellent sense to Dreikurs. He saw it as the logical counterpart to his own pioneering efforts in the fields of social psychiatry and mental health. While others were dubious about the public sessions, he immediately recognized the unique advantage they offered. He had only to remember the youth movement to recall how an "open" policy had salvaged his discussion group when it was threatened by the suspicious fears of the parents and the school authorities.

Whenever the question of "values" comes up, as it inevitably must when the discussion is centered on education, social relations, politics, or sex, parents are naturally going to be fearful of the possible influence of others in what they regard as their privileged sphere of responsibility. With open groups, all can observe, participate, and judge for themselves whether it is contrary to their own values or not. Many a teacher and parent, hearing of the work of the centers, came to challenge and confront these new ideas on discipline and education. Much to their own surprise, they often stayed and became actively involved.

Dreikurs's exposure to Adler's ideas provided him with revealing insights about himself, his upbringing, and his role as a parent. Like other intelligent and well-meaning parents, he had fallen into the trap of setting discouragingly high standards for his son and resorting to harsh discipline when he failed to live up to those expectations. In spite of Dreikurs's resentment toward his own father for beating and humiliating him as a child, he was shocked to find he had succumbed to the same mistakes in dealing with his own son. After exposure to Adler's discoveries in child development, he realized how discouraging such treatment is to a child and how contrary it was to his own humanistic philosophy. With this new understanding, his harshness and autocratic behavior as a parent ceased.

THE ADLERIAN EXPERIMENTAL SCHOOL

Adler yearned to see a school established where his psychological and educational principles could be comprehensively applied. That dream became reality in 1931 with the founding of the Individual Psychological Experimental School—a secondary school for boys aged ten to fourteen. Located in an impoverished district, the school was directed by two of Adler's most skilled educational co-workers, Drs. Ferdinand Birnbaum and Oskar Spiel.

"The great importance of Adler," Birnbaum believed, was "that he showed the road to outward political democracy as well as to inner personal democracy. . . . His road is that of psychology, a road of more or less self-discovery."[17]

The essential challenge Birnbaum and Spiel successfully met was that of translating techniques for counseling one child in the clinic to methods of guiding many children in a group. By 1924 they had worked out a complete theoretical and practical model for classroom use, a distinguishing feature of which was the system of "class discussions." In the years 1925–1930, this approach was implemented by many teachers, whose classrooms were frequently visited by guests from abroad.

When the experimental school was opened,[18] it was under the most difficult conditions. Vienna's school authorities made clear that it could not be a specially favored educational experiment and that there could be no deviation from curriculum standards set for all the public schools. By then, the Great Depression had largely destroyed economic stability, and unemployment was widespread, which directly affected the physical facilities of the school and the students who attended. The children came from one of the worst slum neighborhoods in the city, were generally underfed and inadequately clothed, and were in no way specially selected for the program. The school building was as bad as any slum school in the States. There was no yard or recreational area, and the children were confined to their classroom for the entire day. Because of a fuel shortage that beset Vienna, the building remained unheated throughout the long winter months. Consequently, the teachers labored under the most miserable, failure-prone circumstances—conditions that would have given ample excuse for failing to teach these children. Yet the school was an acknowledged success.

"As to the results we had with these children," Birnbaum wrote, "we insist that they can certainly be obtained in other schools. Nobody must be given the opportunity to say, 'Yes, if we had these desirable conditions, we, too, could apply your fundamental ideas.' "[19]

Birnbaum and Spiel had demonstrated that the principles of Individual Psychology could affect a whole school by improving the teaching methods and educating children to solve their own problems. Through collective class discussions and counsels, they stimulated individual endeavors toward self-understanding and improvement. The school continued its valuable work, which was the subject of numerous reports, until February 12, 1934, the day the Austrian fascists took over and closed it down.

Dreikurs closely followed the work of Birnbaum and Spiel in those years and became thoroughly grounded in the educational problems they encountered and methodological solutions they devised. Their work attracted his attention because of his long-standing interest in education and because he recognized the tremendous value of group methods and their potential role in promoting mental health. Later, in the United States, he drew upon the outstanding educational work of Birnbaum and Spiel as he himself began to "teach the teachers."

Notes for Chapter 5

1. Heinz L. Ansbacher, "Alfred Adler and G. Stanley Hall: Correspondence and General Relationship." *Journal of the History of the Behavioral Sciences* 7 (1971): 337–352.

2. Rudolf Dreikurs, "Early Experiments in Social Psychiatry," *International Journal of Social Psychiatry* 7 (1961): 144.

3. Alfred Adler, "A Doctor Remakes Education," *Survey Graphic* 58 (1927): 490–491.

4. Ibid.

5. Ernst Papanek, *The Austrian School Reform* (New York: Frederick Fell, 1962). See also: Charles A. Gulick, *Austria from Habsburg to Hitler.* See also: Furtmüller, "Alfred Adler," pp. 375–378.

6. Furtmüller, "Alfred Adler," 380n.

7. Adler, "A Doctor Remakes Education," p. 491.

8. Ibid., p. 493.

9. Adapted from, "The Little Man and the Little Boy," *Alfred Adler Institute Student Association Newsletter* 2, no. 1 (1976): 6.

10. Regine Seidler, "School Guidance Clinics in Vienna," *International Journal of Individual Psychology* 2 (1936): 76.

11. Adler, "A Doctor Remakes Education," p. 493.

12. Ibid.

13. Bottome, *Alfred Adler*, p. 314.

14. The first child guidance center established on Adler's model outside Vienna was opened in Munich in 1922 under Dr. Leonhard Seif. Others were established in Berlin, Dresden, Chemitz, Linz, Düsseldorf, Heidelberg, Karlsruhe, Cologne, Magdeburg, and Stuttgart. All these centers were halted in 1933 when Hitler came to power.

15. Rudolf Dreikurs, "Group Psychotherapy: General Review," *Proceedings of the 1st International Congress of Psychiatry*, Paris 1950. Part 5. *Actualities Scientifiques et Industrielles*, no. 1172. (Paris: Hermann & Cie, 1952), p. 228.

16. *Internationale Zeitschrift für Individualpsychologie* 4 (1926): 169.

17. Ferdinand Birnbaum, "The Importance of Alfred Adler for the Present," *Individual Psychology Bulletin* 6 (1948): 174.

18. For a detailed account of the Adlerian experimental school, see Oscar Spiel, *Discipline Without Punishment* (London: Faber & Faber, 1962).

19. Ferdinand Birnbaum, "Applying Individual Psychology in School," *International Journal of Individual Psychology* 1 (1935): 118.

6

Pioneering Social Psychiatry

Therapy . . . serves mainly the interest of the individual;
only prevention has social significance.

Rudolf Dreikurs
"Early Experiments in Social Psychiatry"

Disillusioned with his initial explorations into psychotherapy, Dreikurs
began to devote his attention to the newly emerging field of social psychiatry. Between 1923 and 1928, Dreikurs first completed his year of internship at Vienna General Hospital and then undertook his residency in
psychiatry and neurology at the University Psychiatry Clinic under the
direction of Professors Wagner-Jauregg and Emil Mettauschek. Mettauschek was favorably disposed to the new programs in social welfare and
preventive medicine instituted in Vienna by Julius Tandler. He recognized
the need to extend these services to mental patients. Knowing Dreikurs's
interests, Mettauschek asked him to develop social welfare programs that
would enable mental patients to leave the hospital as soon as possible.
The need for such programs had become acute following the war when
the number of mental patients requiring hospitalization nearly tripled.

Dreikurs began by enlisting charitable private agencies that would provide money, clothing, and financial support for needy cases, but was not
successful. Trying, through these same agencies, to find jobs for discharged patients, whose very illness had stemmed from the distress of unemployment, through the help of private agencies likewise met with little
success. Finally, the federal Department of Social Welfare offered to refer
patients for jobs and to retrain them if necessary. This proved to be decisive in resolving several critical cases. It became increasingly evident to
Dreikurs that social conditions such as bad housing and unemployment
influenced the development of mental disorders, and in some cases posed
insurmountable difficulties for already deeply discouraged individuals.

Finding charitable agencies ill-prepared and inadequate to provide
these services, Dreikurs proposed the establishment of a welfare and

counseling center sponsored by the municipality. Through these efforts, Dreikurs initiated psychiatric social work in Vienna and throughout Austria. In so doing, he extensively researched similar efforts outside of Austria and reported his findings in his first published paper, "Social Work in Psychiatry" (1925).[1] He soon realized that social measures were needed for alcoholics, psychopaths, and epileptics, and in 1926, he published four additional papers that spelled out the problems and proposed solutions.

Dreikurs's work with psychiatric social welfare logically led him to a deeper understanding of the connection between social conditions and psychic abnormality:

> The consequences of a mental illness depended on the social milieu of the patient. One of the essential characteristics of psychopathy is the diminished ability to adapt to given conditions and the low resistance to unfavorable influences. . . . In this way, concern with extra-mural care led to Social Psychiatry. Its task was not only to determine the influence of social conditions upon the development of a mental disease and the course it took, but also to examine the social significance the disease posed. This was particularly true for psychopathic disturbances which constituted primarily social malfunctioning.[2]

The advent of social psychiatry has been hailed as one of the most enlightened developments of the treatment of the mentally ill. It heralded the attempt to understand the patient not just in terms of his intrapsychic dynamics but also as a member of the community.[3] Indeed, the origins of social psychiatry—which includes family and group therapy as well as community psychiatric approaches—can be traced to developments in Vienna in the 1920s, where Adler and his co-workers were key innovators.

Dreikurs's initial efforts regarding the welfare needs of mental patients now led to a fundamental conclusion. Since social psychiatry focused on the social connections of mental disorders, it led directly to the need for prophylaxis. "The therapy of a manifest disorder serves mainly the interest of the individual. Only prevention has social significance," Dreikurs wrote in 1928.[4]

Prevention of mental disorders was first systematically addressed on a major scale in the United States with the founding of the mental hygiene movement. Inspired by Clifford Beers's *A Mind That Found Itself*, it grew rapidly owing to the vital support of Adolf Meyer, a major figure in

American psychiatry. But it did not have much impact in Europe initially and was only introduced into Austria in 1927, in great measure due to the efforts of Dreikurs. He wrote several articles demonstrating the need for and proposing the creation of an Austrian Committee for Mental Hygiene. When it was created, he became its first secretary. In 1929, he published the first report about Vienna's developments in mental hygiene and described all the prophylactic efforts then functioning. What especially impressed him was that this work did not reflect the thinking of isolated psychiatrists or the efforts of a few private agencies, but rather it constituted a movement, an integration of well-defined problems and tasks directed toward a definite goal. Only in this way could the results have a real impact.[5]

As part of Dreikurs's ambitious and innovative efforts on behalf of mental hygiene and community psychiatry, he founded and conducted several clinics and dispensaries for psychopaths as well as alcoholics. These were developed in connection with various private agencies and municipal authorities and with the support of the adult education programs of the Social Democratic Party. Working with the Ethical Society, Dreikurs helped create, and served as a psychiatrist at, the *Lebensmudenstelle*, a suicide prevention center. Staffed by forty volunteer counselors and social workers, the center operated day and night to assist anyone who felt the need for help. More than fifteen hundred people came in the first year of operation. Although suicide prevention efforts had been started early in the century by General Booth of the Salvation Army, the programs undertaken in Vienna, in which Dreikurs played an important role, constituted the first systematic and organized fight against suicide.[6]

By the time Dreikurs had completed his residency in 1928, he had already demonstrated a genuine concern for the mental well-being of his fellow citizens and a definite knack for getting things moving in the community. He was willing to spend the time and energy needed to carry out the organizational aspects of these many programs. He had revealed himself to be a good writer, knowledgeable in his subject matter and the precedent work of others. His early writings reveal his outstanding skill as a clarifier. Keenly observant, he analyzed and ordered what he saw, unveiling facets of psychological processes and problems that others had perhaps sensed but never conceptualized.

THE LINK WITH ADLER

Dreikurs's admiration for Adler's work grew during the 1920s. What had seemed a simplistic statement to the young medical student back in 1920, when Adler declared that "anyone can change, and there is hope for everybody," had by now taken on a deeper and infinitely more challenging meaning. With the experience he had gained in the neuropsychiatric clinic, in social psychiatry and mental hygiene, and in the child guidance clinics, he now realized that to assume other than that "anyone can change" was to undermine the whole basis of education and psychotherapy. It asked the fundamental question—whether man chooses his fate and is therefore responsible for his actions, or whether he is the victim of instinctual drives and environmental determinants.

Dreikurs had still not formally identified himself with the Adlerian group, even though he had been involved with their child guidance clinics since 1923. Something was missing that prevented him from grasping the totality of Adler's system—from recognizing that it embraced the whole spectrum of human functioning in a coherent and unified way.

It was by happy coincidence for Dreikurs that he got to work with Alexander Neuer during his residency training. Neuer was the brilliant theoretician who had been associated with Adler since the days of the Freud circle. Together, Adler and Neuer hammered out the revolutionary view that human behavior was not caused in a mechanistic fashion but that it was teleological and purposeful. They directly challenged the mechanistic interpretations of psychological functioning that dominated scientific thought.

Besides being a philosopher, Neuer was a physician, but apparently he undertook his formal residency training in psychiatry later in life. So it happened that Neuer and Dreikurs worked together in Mettauschek's department. They debated psychological concepts in depth as well as the philosophical issues of modern science. These discussions with Neuer proved crucial: "It was [Neuer's] influence," Dreikurs recalled, "which made me become increasingly interested in Adler's psychology. He pointed out that my ideas agreed with Adler well. . . . He encouraged me to take a seminar with the Adlerians, and what I heard there made so much sense to me that I joined their association."[7]

But Dreikurs was still reluctant to identify himself completely as an Adlerian. That came about shortly thereafter, when Dreikurs opened his own private practice in 1927, and was confronted with a particularly perplexing case. "Turning to the literature," Dreikurs recalled, "especially the writings of Freud, Stekel and Adler, I found, to my great surprise, that Adler not only understood the problems of this patient, but had demonstrated how he was to be treated. A full understanding of his methods can come only when you apply them in practice. For me, this was an experience I had over and over again."[8]

In a flash of discovery, the real impact of Adler's psychology as a psychology of "use," and not "possession," finally came through. Adler's ideas took on a whole new meaning. Now Dreikurs grasped the deeper implications of holistic and purposive thinking. With that, he realized how incompatible his traditional training was with his new way of looking at behavior. He explained: "The theory which Adler has fashioned can be understood when it serves as a basis for actual operations. The concept of man as holistic can be comprehended only when we know the techniques for experiencing man as a 'whole.' To speak of man as self-determined in all he does and his behavior as goal-directed is not very convincing until it can be demonstrated in the concrete instance. Adler's ideas go against all the commonly recognized conceptions. . . . It takes courage to go against the myths we have learned in school . . . to dismiss what the social and behavioral scientists have put before us."[9]

Dreikurs soon encountered the difficulties involved in going against the accepted practice of the day and the need for courage sufficient to surmount them. An incident occurred not long after he had entered private practice that left a deep impression:

> One of my patients suffered from senile depression and was in a sanitarium outside of Vienna. At that time there was, of course, neither chemotherapy nor shock therapy, and this patient was in a horrible state of disintegration. I proposed moving him from the sanitarium to a pleasant rustic setting where he could be cared for by a male nurse. His family, however, would not hear of it. So I proposed that we call in Adler as a consultant.
>
> He came to the sanitarium and began to interview the patient. All the psychiatrists, the residents and nurses stood around in a circle while Adler began to interview the patient. It was an unforgettable scene which developed. He asked him a question about himself and the patient began to respond in the characteristically slow way of a depressed person. But Adler did not wait until the patient finished

the sentence—and threw another question at him. Again, the patient began to answer slowly; again Adler did not wait and fired off another question.

At this point, I felt distinct embarrassment. After all, Adler was my teacher, I felt identified with him—and here he was, apparently ignoring the basic rudiments of a psychiatric interview. Doesn't he know that a depressed person speaks slowly? Why doesn't he wait for his answers if he wants to talk with him? What kind of impression would he make on the other professionals standing around? Frankly, I began to feel ashamed of him. When suddenly—to everyone's surprise—the patient began to speak rapidly in order to say what he wanted to express. That was Adler's genius! He simply did not play along with the myths that we all had about patients, such as the notion that deeply depressed people can only speak very slowly. He understood that such patients speak slowly because they do not want to contribute, yet they are capable of contributing whenever they want to do so. Knowing they could, he refused to be party to a well-accepted practice and theory of abnormal behavior which he knew was fallacious.

This kind of optimism, this trust in people, even those who were very disabled, is a characteristic of Adler and all his students. . . . We do not know whether a given patient will change, but we are convinced that, should he want to, he can change.[10]

Now, as he looked back, Dreikurs could chuckle at that memorable incident when he attacked Adler for his criticism of Freud and was forthrightly put down for his naïve understanding of the issues involved. As it turned out, Adler, and Dreikurs too, never failed to credit Freud for having launched a revolution in psychiatry—a new way to explore the psychological dynamics of behavior. What they strenuously objected to was Freud's reductionist generalizing across the board, from his neurotic patients—with their fantasies, fears, and phobias—to the proposition that *all* behavior originates in a narcissistic, sexual impulse for pleasure and in a desire to return to a state of rest (the death instinct).

Equally objectionable was Freud's conclusion that the individual's instinctual needs are in opposition to the needs of society, requiring one to sacrifice his own self-interests to society. For Adlerians, man is human only in a social context, his whole life an ongoing process of "becoming" that is inexorably tied up with his social relations to others. For Freud, freedom was an illusion. Art, music, and other magnificent creations of man were nothing but the sublimation of sexual impulses, nothing but rationalization. This was an absurdity to Adler, although one he felt carried grave implications because it made every accomplishment, great and small, suspect of being nothing more than well-managed sexual frustration! The most damaging consequence was that by attributing all behavior to irrational and unconscious impulses the individual could not be held responsible for his acts. They were out of his control. Man now had an excuse for all his misdeeds and transgressions against others—"he couldn't help it." The notion that our acts are beyond our control, that we play no decisive part in how things turn out, was the logical implication. It would play havoc with our social philosophies and programs as they are juxtaposed with the increasing democratic and self-determining trends of this century.

Dreikurs declared himself an Adlerian. Adler's fight now became his fight.

Notes for Chapter 6

1. Rudolf Dreikurs, "Die soziale Fursorge in die Psychiatrie," *Jahrbuch für Psychiatrie und Neurologie* 44 (1925): pp. 247–266.
2. Dreikurs, "Early Experiments in Social Psychiatry," p. 143.
3. Alexander and Selesnick, *History of Psychiatry*. (New York: New American Library, 1966), p. 415.
4. Rudolf Dreikurs, "Die Entwicklung der psychischen Hygiene in Wien, unter besonderer Berücksichtigung der Alkoholiker und Psychopathen- (Selbstmörder-) Fürsorge," *Allg. Z. Psychiat.* 88 (1928): 471.
5. Dreikurs, "Early Experiments in Social Psychiatry," p. 143.
6. Ibid., p. 145–146.
7. Dreikurs, "Guiding, Teaching, and Demonstrating," p. 149; Rudolf Dreikurs, 1897–1972," in *Psychotherapie in Selbstdarstellungen*, p. 113.
8. Dreikurs, "Rudolf Dreikurs, 1897–1972," p. 113–114.
9. Ibid., p. 114.
10. Ibid., p. 110–111.

7

Innovations in Group Psychotherapy

> Group psychotherapy is more than a therapeutic method;
> wherever it is practiced it affects human relationships and
> the social climate. . . . It establishes a truly democratic
> atmosphere as it cannot exist save in a democratic setting.
>
> Rudolf Dreikurs
> "The Contribution of Group Psychotherapy to Psychiatry."

Dreikurs's involvement with the Adlerian child guidance clinics and their group setting paved the way for his pioneering work in group psychotherapy. Adlerian group approaches evolved from the demonstration clinics. What was originally a teaching model became a standard therapeutic practice. However the singularity of this innovation was not acknowledged or given a special name.

"This apparent 'negligence,'" Dreikurs pointed out,

> can be understood only in connection with the psychological atmosphere of the time. The Adlerian psychologists who developed the group approaches always considered man as a social being and as socially motivated, in contrast to the psychoanalytic and other approaches. We observed the difficult child together with his parents and siblings, we always treated the whole family, not the isolated patient, even in so-called "individual" psychotherapy and counseling. . . . When we started group counseling, we were utterly unaware that we had entered a new phase of psychiatric exploration and therapy. . . . Consequently, "Collective Therapy," as it was called at that time, was merely a by-product of our general therapeutic orientation. When I published the first report on group psychotherapy, it was

done only as part of a general report about mental health developments in Vienna.[1]

Dreikurs's innovations in group psychotherapy can also be traced to his efforts in social psychiatry, especially his involvement with alcoholics. At that time only two agencies were concerned with alcoholics, the mental hospitals and the police department. Dissatisfied with his efforts to rehabilitate individual alcoholics Dr. Julius Metzl, a police physician, began to experiment with counseling alcoholics in a group in 1925. His approach, in which former alcoholics took an active part in helping new recruits, was carefully developed, and it proved effective. Intrigued by Metzl's work, Dreikurs joined in his experiments that same year, and then instituted a similar consultation center in his home district of Döbling. This early effort at group therapy comprised two elements: a regular discussion group with the patients and their wives, and the mutual self-help that the patients gave one another. He was especially impressed with the self-help aspect and predicted that it might be of extreme importance.[2] Later, in the United States, the successful work of Alcoholics Anonymous hinged on this self-help approach.

The centers, in addition to their counseling work, engaged the volunteers, mostly ex-alcoholics, in trying to counteract the growing problem of alcohol abuse, particularly among the working class. By so doing, Dreikurs helped to bring the prevention and treatment of alcoholism under the umbrella of mental health prophylaxis.

Metzl published the results of his experimental "collective counseling" of alcoholics in an obscure journal in 1927. A year later, Dreikurs published a historically important paper, "The Development of Mental Hygiene in Vienna."[3] In it he outlined a comprehensive plan for the prevention of mental disease in Vienna and cited Metzl's methods of working with alcoholics. More importantly, he described in detail, probably for the first time anywhere, the dynamic differences between individual and group therapy. This paper appeared in a well-known European journal of psychiatry, but as Dreikurs pointed out, he did not identify the significance of these early experiences as the beginning of an important new trend in psychiatric practice until years later.[4]

In 1928, Dreikurs introduced group psychotherapy into his private practice, becoming probably the first psychiatrist ever to do so. It happened quite by accident. Dreikurs had developed a busy practice by then, although it was not a lucrative one: "My fees were relatively small. I couldn't ask for much money—people were very poor."[5] Once, due to an overcrowded schedule, he suggested that three of his patients come for a joint interview. The two men and one woman were all at a stage in their therapy where Dreikurs wanted to give them some theoretical insights. He also felt that in this way he could save considerable time.

When the session ended, all three agreed that they had benefited more from the group discussion than from individual interviews and proposed to Dreikurs that they continue to work together. In the case of one of the men, the session proved very productive, for he overcame the resistance he had shown in individual sessions. What started out as a time-saving and economically advantageous experiment turned out to be a more effective way of reaching people. Thereafter, Dreikurs used group therapy as an adjunct to individual therapy throughout all his years of practice both in Vienna and in Chicago.

Dreikurs described his early work regarding group psychotherapy before the Individual Psychology Physicians' Seminar in 1930. The minutes of that meeting, including a summary of remarks, were preserved and reveal some of the earliest thinking on the practice of group psychotherapy:

> Dreikurs started by discussing case histories and incidents so that no one, except the patient himself, knew that they concerned him. This offered an opportunity to bring up individual cases for discussion. All expressed their opinions, until one or the other was ready to report about himself. Even the most reluctant patients were drawn into such a group; in this way one could convey to them points they otherwise would never have permitted anybody to present to them. The impersonal attitude of the other patients had a disciplinary effect. The goal-directedness of all actions could be clearly established, so that each was able to gain insight. . . .
>
> Dreikurs had first assumed he would have to be satisfied with [discussing] special questions which the patients had in common. But on one occasion a patient requested that they should discuss everything together. . . . Soon everything was discussed, after some hesitation, even sexual problems. It was obvious that each patient could understand what pertained to another patient more than what concerned himself. Occasionally some patients became irritated because they could not evade the issues so easily. They recognized their annoyance as an expression of their resistance to change. One of the

most important aspects seemed to be that in collective therapy the physician is not the center of activity. It is different when one patient recognizes the maneuvers of another than when the physician discloses them. In the former case, there is no fight for prestige. . . .

The following aspects of collective therapy seem to be important: (1) It destroys the illusion of the uniqueness of personal problems and deficiencies. It is quite an experience when a patient recognizes that others suffer from the same symptoms; what he considered as his difference from others now becomes the link to others. (2) Collective therapy indicates the only way in which psychotherapy can be introduced when large numbers of patients are involved.[6]

While Dreikurs was one among several pioneers in the use of group psychotherapy, a term coined by Jacob L. Moreno in 1932,[7] his early work stands out for several reasons. He was probably the first psychiatrist to move group therapy from a clinic or institutional setting to the sphere of regular private practice. Second, others who developed group methods generally restricted them to very specialized areas, for example, J. H. Pratt's work with tubercular patients, W. R. P. Emerson's work with undernourished children, and E. W. Lazell's work with dementia praecox patients.[8] Their techniques often relied upon lectures and inspirational appeals in a group setting that did not, except indirectly, deal with anyone's specific problems and personality. Dreikurs was perhaps the first to employ group therapy for providing insight into each participant's style of life: "The characteristics and life style of the patient are shown with emphatic clarity in the course of *collective therapy*," he wrote in 1932.[9] Years later at the First International Congress of Psychiatry in Paris in 1950, he pointed out:

All the elements of our Adlerian approach with individual patients can be found in our G.T. [group therapy]. Sometimes the individual life style of one member is re-examined, as we do repeatedly in individual therapy. Often concrete situations are evaluated and analyzed, sometimes dreams interpreted, general psychological principles explored and mistaken values examined and evaluated. The main difference between [individual and group therapy] is the active participation of all members of the group in the discussion. The therapist explains and interprets less, but rather leads the others in a process of thinking the problem through together.[10]

In the years before the era of Austrian facism, from 1927 to 1934, Dreikurs used group therapy in his work with alcoholics, in his counseling centers for parents and children, and at the Vienna Poliklinik under Dr. Hans Hoff. The advent of the totalitarian regime in Austria brought an abrupt halt to all forms of group approaches in public and institutional settings, thereby interrupting a historically important advance in psychiatry. Thereafter, the development of group psychotherapy shifted to the United States, where Dreikurs continued to play an important role after his arrival in 1937. When he returned to Europe in 1950 for the Paris Congress, he was chagrined to find that group psychotherapy, then flourishing in America, was nonexistent in Vienna and otherwise lagging in other parts of Europe.

"It then became clear," he reflected, "that group psychotherapy is essentially a democratic procedure, and its use reflects the political climate of a nation. It cannot flourish except in a free atmosphere; it needs a unique social climate, and in turn, creates it."[11] In time, he identified this fertile period that saw the advent of Adler's social psychology and therapeutic methods and the emergence of group approaches in Europe and America as the start of a "third psychiatric revolution," marking a fundamental change in our concept of man.[12]

Notes for Chapter 7

1. Rudolf Dreikurs. "Early Experiments with Group Psychotherapy," *American Journal of Psychotherapy* 13 (1959): 884.

2. Dreikurs, "Group Psychotherapy: A General Review," pp. 223–237.

3. Dreikurs, "Die Entwicklung der Psychische Hygiene in Wien," pp. 469–489.

4. Dreikurs, "Early Experiments with Group Psychotherapy," pp. 882–883.

5. Mackaness, *Biographical Study*, pp. 91–92.

6. Dreikurs, "Early Experiments with Group Psychotherapy," pp. 887–889.

7. Jacob L. Moreno and E. S. Whitin. *Application of the Group Method to Classification* (New York: National Committee on Prison and Prison Labor, 1932). Commenting on Moreno's activities with groups in Vienna, Dreikurs said: "His work in Vienna had nothing to do with group psychotherapy as we understand it today, namely, with the use of the group method for treating and counseling. The books and papers which he published under the name of Levy are mostly philosophical and poetical. The Improvised Theater, as well as his impromptu experiments, can be regarded as forerunners of psychodrama, which later in America became a method used for the treatment of patients and of which he is undoubtedly the founder" (Dreikurs-Mackaness interview).

8. Dreikurs, "Group Psychotherapy: A General Review," pp. 226–227.

9. Rudolf Dreikurs, "Einige wirksame Faktoren in der Psychotherapie," *Internationale Zeitschrift für Individualpsychologie* 10 (1932): 175.

10. Dreikurs, "Group Psychotherapy: A General Review," p. 230.

11. Rudolf Dreikurs, "The Cultural Implications of Group Psychotherapy," *Zeit. Diagnos. Psychol. Persönalichkeitsforsch.* 5 (1957): 186–197.

12. Rudolf Dreikurs, "Group Psychotherapy and the Third Revolution in Psychiatry," *International Journal of Social Psychiatry* 1 (1955): 23–32.

8

Departure from Europe

Fear is the sin of free men.
Rudolf Dreikurs
"Educational Implications of the Four Freedoms"

Dreikurs opened his private practice in psychiatry in 1927. He was a dedicated social psychiatrist with no intention of establishing a practice that catered exclusively to the neurotic ills of the upper class. Instead of choosing the elegant "doctors' row" of inner Vienna for his office, he took a double apartment in his old neighborhood of Döbling, using one apartment for his office and one for his residence. In so doing, he was among the first to provide the specialized services of psychiatry and neurology in a lower-middle-class neighborhood.

It was a modest beginning but not free of financial difficulty. Most of Dreikurs's patients were struggling young intellectuals associated with the Social Democratic and labor movements, and few were able to pay adequately for his services. Still, there was time for his favorite pastimes of collecting stamps and playing chamber music, time to sit down for the big family meal at midday, time to attend concerts, and time to take his beloved Sunday excursions in the Vienna woods. Apart from his private practice, he was deeply involved in community work with alcoholics, potential suicides, the child guidance clinics, and increasingly with the professional activities of the Adlerian Society.

Just as he was getting settled in his career, he was faced with a devastating tragedy in his family. Steffi became mentally ill. While she was pregnant with their second child, the distrust in her personality, which had intensified over the years, reached a critical stage. Rudolf loved Steffi and understood that the origin of her condition could be traced to events in her life that had occurred long before they met. But now, as her husband and the prime target of her suspicions, he knew that he alone could not help her.

Of course he sought the best psychiatric help. (Unfortunately, Adler could not be engaged because at that time he was spending most of each year in the United States and therefore could not take on new patients who required intensive and long-range therapy.) Within months after the birth of their daughter, Eva, Steffi's paranoia reached such a destructive stage, in terms of herself and others around her, that hospitalization was the only recourse. Her illness was a type most difficult to treat because the hostility and distrust extended to everyone, including the therapist. At that time, no psychotropic drugs or other techniques were available to help her reach a stage of trust with which she could understand what was happening and possibly return to a normal life. Steffi never recovered and was confined to hospitals for her remaining years.

Beginning with this troubled period, Dreikurs was left as the sole parent. When Eva was nearly two years old, Josie Pollack (no relation to Mimi), Dreikurs's cousin, came to live with them and to take care of the children. A cheerful and sturdy young woman with a loving disposition, Josie remained with the family until they resettled in the United States in 1938.

The qualities that stood out about Dreikurs in those Vienna years, Josie recalled,[1] were his boundless energy and total dedication to his work. He was forever going to meetings, gave much professional help for little or no remuneration, and spent long hours writing his numerous early papers and books. He was good-natured and friendly and an excellent parent, she remarked. Often, he took her along to the Monday night meetings of the Adlerian group, and as the months lapsed into years following Steffi's hospitalization, he could be found accompanied by women friends who found him attractive, intellectually stimulating, serious, and yet fun loving. Probably most memorable from those years were the Sunday evening chamber music concerts that Dreikurs organized in his home. On such nights all of the rooms of the apartment and adjacent office were opened and filled with invited friends who came to hear the amateur musicians perform.

ADLER AND DREIKURS

Dreikurs's formal link with Adler in 1927 came at a time when the pattern of Adler's life and the subsequent direction of Individual Psychology were undergoing far-reaching changes.

Adler, in his late fifties and as robust and energetic as ever, was by now an internationally established figure in psychological and educational circles. The *Zeitschrift* and the International Society of Individual Psychology were flourishing. Local societies had developed in Holland, Czechoslovakia, Hungary, England, the United States, and in all the major cities of Germany. International congresses were held in Berlin, Düsseldorf, and Vienna, although it had been only a short time since the first one in Munich in 1922. These hastened the spread of Adler's ideas throughout the world. Several Americans came to Vienna to learn firsthand of Adler's work, including psychologists Prescott Lecky and Rollo May, and Carleton Washburne, an educator who later played an important part in Dreikurs's work in Chicago.

The lonely stand Adler had taken against the mechanistic approach that dominated academic psychology and psychiatry drew considerable support with the development of Gestalt and phenomenological psychology. Both focused on the subjective and holistic aspects of human behavior. Adler's approach was further supported by the development of the concept of "holism" by Jan C. Smuts, who coined the term in 1926.[2]

Yet, the major thrust of Adler's efforts lay in directions other than that of refining and systematizing his theoretical concepts. He chose instead to devote his considerable energies to disseminating the knowledge he had acquired: "The study of human nature cannot be pursued with the sole purpose of developing occasional experts. Only the understanding of human nature by every human being can be its proper goal."[3] This decision had far-reaching ramifications and led to much misunderstanding and difficulty for Adler.

"I believe Adler would have done better sticking to science and working through scientists," his friend Furtmüller remarked. "He believed in making his science universal and imparting it directly to his fellowmen. Who can say which of us is right? Time alone can tell."[4]

It seems as if Adler had decided that his conceptual system was, for the most part, complete, and therefore he was less willing to engage in hairsplitting debates or elaborate on the fine points of definition. He had little patience for those who wanted to play with his ideas rather than live them. Moreover, he refused to turn away anyone who sincerely sought to learn, and several of his more brilliant colleagues were distressed to have to share him with the number of ex-patients and hangers-on who perpetually surrounded him.

Some felt it was wrong and dangerous to entrust the people with psychological knowledge. Adler thought it more dangerous to keep this knowledge in the hands of an elite few. For these reasons, he tended to lose the support of many powerful men in his profession and in academic circles. They were offended, which explains much of the prejudice toward him in succeeding years—a prejudice that was expressed by undervaluing his work and dismissing it without studying it.[5] Similar experiences were to confront Dreikurs.

Because of his goal, Adler concentrated on presenting his ideas in an uncomplicated fashion. All of Adler's later books, *Understanding Human Nature*, *The Science of Living*, *What Life Should Mean to You*, *The Education of Children*, and especially his last work, *Social Interest: Challenge of Mankind*, were compiled from his extensive lectures around the world and reflect his determination to communicate simply his psychological insights. He refrained from coining special terms that only the professionally initiated could understand, although his use of language was precise. To the accusation that he was simplistic, Adler's famous reply was: "I have taken forty years to make my psychology simple. I might make it still more simple by saying 'all neurosis is vanity' but that also might not be understood."[6]

Because Adler was away from Vienna for so much of these later years, the opportunities for Dreikurs to work closely with him were far more limited than had been the case with Adler's earlier colleagues. Dreikurs was considerably younger and more properly fit in with the second generation of Adlerians, all trained by Adler and deeply involved in the functioning of the child guidance centers, various clinics, and the activities of the Society of Individual Psychology.

It would appear that Adler saw in Dreikurs a man of unusual potential. He had known this vigorous young man for nearly a decade and had witnessed Dreikurs's courageous support of social causes that drew the snickering criticism of more conventional colleagues. Adler sensed that this man was not afraid to go against the mainstream, as he himself had done, even at the risk of personal prestige and financial success. And he knew that Dreikurs truly shared his goals and depth of commitment. He must also have known Dreikurs's shortcomings—especially his provocativeness, which was alien to his own temperament—but he did not view them as an insurmountable obstacle.

While little documentary evidence of their relationship remains, Adler's growing regard for Dreikurs can be glimpsed in a letter he sent from New York in 1929:

The Windermere
New York City
22 November 1929

Dear Dreikurs,

Your letter brought me great joy. I observe with great satisfaction how you and others progress and that you will soon arrive at the right place. If you should succeed in getting more doctors for our work, then we'll be over the hump. Please try to collect interesting educational material for the future.

Here everything is developing beautifully. I am overburdened with lectures and in the clinic up to May "because of the excellent results," and I have hardly any free time. Therefore, don't be too cross if I don't write very much. . . .

Of political conditions in Vienna I don't know very much, and of the little I do know, only sad things. But I didn't expect anything else. There were just too many dumbheads playing around—they are the ruin of everything.

Don't forget the out-patient clinic and the counseling centers. Under no circumstances must we give up what we have won thus far.

Greetings to all our friends and tell them that I have not forgotten them. But they should not think that I am omnipotent and that I could fulfill God-knows-what wishes.

Best regards,
Your
Adler[7]

Dreikurs delivered his first paper before the Vienna Society of Individual Psychology in February 1930 as part of a *Festschrift* held in honor of Adler's sixtieth birthday. He spoke on the topic "self-knowledge" (his talk was subsequently published in both English and German[8] and has a refreshing relevance to this day).

Dreikurs recognized the value of self-knowledge but cautioned us not to be misled by our own self-deceptions. The desire to " 'know thyself' often furnishes a convenient *pretext* for behavior that is anything but productive of socially useful results."[9] Or it winds up as "fruitless *self-reflection*, which usually has as its chief result merely the useless acknowledgment . . . that the road to hell is paved with good intentions."[10]

Change in behavior, he continued, is the only reliable clue to real self-insight. It is not what one *says* or *feels* but what one *does*; or, to use Martin Luther's aphorism, "Do not look at a man's mouth but at his fists." Self-deception often results because we base our opinions about ourselves on our "thoughts, desires, and emotions [and] fail to give sufficient . . . consideration [to] our *actions*—to what we *do*."[11]

"Genuine insight," he asserted, "is that insight which reveals to the individual his particular conception of the world, his particular goal and his methods for achieving that goal—in other words, his own particular life style."[12] For that, our observations must turn to "what we *do* in relation to the world and people about us . . . the specific manner in which we individually *relate ourselves to the outside world*." He concluded that the persons most capable of acquiring real self-knowledge are those who have the "courage to be imperfect"—to risk making mistakes, to risk the uncertainty of living and doing, thereby overcoming their own safeguarding tendencies toward self-deception.

In Dreikurs's earliest presentation as an Individual Psychologist, he used the phrase "the courage to be imperfect," which came to be a leitmotiv in his subsequent work. While he properly credited Sofie Lazarsfeld, the late Adlerian psychotherapist, who coined the phrase, it was he who developed it into a theme he taught others.

Dreikurs published his first book in 1931. Entitled *Psychic Impotence*,[13] it was an original attempt to compare and contrast the concepts of Freudian and Adlerian psychology. He used an actual case study from a psychoanalyst and then reinterpreted it from an Adlerian standpoint. When the Nazis seized control, this book, along with thousands of others, was confiscated and destroyed. Dreikurs managed to salvage one copy, but it has never been republished. The next year he published a second book, *The Nervous Symptom*,[14] which also has never been translated or reissued.

The longer he worked with Adler, the more impressed Dreikurs was with his mentor's diagnostic and therapeutic skills: "I have never seen anyone since," he stated, "who could recite by memory fully and lucidly a person's life history as Adler did. Equally unique was his remarkable ability to find a characteristic phrase to describe a person's life style, like 'a beggar holding out his hands,' 'a dethroned king,' or 'a man who carries the burden of the whole world on his shoulders.' "[15]

Historian Henri Ellenberger agreed and recently wrote:

> Those who have known Adler agree that he possessed the gift of *Menschenkenntnis* (intuitive practical understanding of man) to a

supreme degree. . . . In the presence of a new patient, about whom he knew nothing, he would look at him for a moment, ask a few questions, and then get a complete picture of the subject's difficulties, clinical disturbances, and life problems. . . . He came to be able to almost instantaneously guess any person's position in the sibling constellation. Adler was also reputed for his gift of rapidly establishing contact with any person, including rebellious children, psychotics and criminals. He felt a genuine interest for all human beings and compassion for their sufferings, but like [Pierre] Janet he would immediately detect the part of play-acting and mendacity.[16]

Many of Adler's associates felt that his unique skill reflected an inborn talent that arises in only the rarest of persons, cannot be matched, and is only poorly imitated. Adler disagreed, but he never devoted much time to analyzing what he did in the therapeutic process except in a rather general way. Dreikurs was intrigued with Adler's remarkable diagnostic skills, much as he had earlier been by Professor Chvostek's, and dedicated himself to determining what were the components and logical steps in Adler's therapeutic processes. Why did Adler ask the questions he did, in the way he did, or at the time he did? What clues was he listening and looking for? In pursuing this, he not only developed his own diagnostic and therapeutic skills to a superb degree but succeeded remarkably in teaching them to others, many of whom initially would not have believed it possible.

Dreikurs began to demonstrate his insights and explanations of the therapeutic process in a paper delivered in 1931 before the Adlerian Physicians' Seminar.[17] It revealed his skill as a "clarifier," as he examined issues that are central to understanding what takes place in therapy. He described several special techniques that can help overcome stalemates and resistance; for instance, the use of surprise, irony, "collective therapy," and "antisuggestion" (a technique Adler innovated that was later termed "paradoxical intentions" by Viktor Frankl). His insights into the pitfalls encountered in therapy are as pertinent today as they were then.

Dreikurs's activities and contributions as an Adlerian therapist and educator soon reached impressive proportions and belied his own mistaken self-image as lazy. But then, this mistaken self-perception probably provided impetus for his ambitions. Beyond his private practice and clinical work, Dreikurs frequently lectured before the Vienna Society of Individual Psychology (IP). He served as president of the IP Physicians' Seminar. He conducted a course entitled "Practical Problems of Individual Psychology" in his home every Saturday afternoon, which was designed to help parents and teachers handle everyday problems. He also taught a course for physicians, "Individual Psychological Therapy," weekly in his home and, in addition, gave a lecture course on the "Fundamentals of Individual Psychology for Physicians" at the Vienna Academy of Psychological Medicine. Furthermore, he conducted two child guidance clinics each week as well as continuing to write.[18]

Dr. Edward Schneider, an early colleague, recalled the establishment of the child guidance clinic in Heiligenstadt (a section of Vienna):

> for which, in the main, Dr. Dreikurs was responsible. I can never forget his skillful organization, selection, and supervision of the staff members and his leadership there. He pioneered in consulting and advising not only the child but his surrounding siblings, parents, and even teachers. The institute enjoyed great success locally and attracted many foreign students of psychology [already] in Vienna. To achieve his aim, he worked harder than any of us; hours did not count, only performance. His patience was proverbial. He never seemed tired . . . and he always had an encouraging word for the staff and patients.[19]

THE HANDWRITING ON THE WALL

It must be about twenty years since I tried to foretell the future of Individual Psychology. . . . It will have a permanent influence on the thought, poetry and dreams of humanity. It will attract many enlightened disciples, and many more who will hardly know the names of its pioneers. It will be understood by some, but the numbers who misunderstand it will be greater. It will have many adherents, and still more enemies. Because of its simplicity many will think it too easy, whereas those who know it will recognize how difficult it is. It will bring its followers neither wealth nor position, but they will have the satisfaction of learning from their opponents' mistakes. It will draw a dividing line between those who use their knowledge for the purpose of establishing an ideal community, and those who do not. It will give its followers such keenness of vision that no corner of the human soul will be hidden from them and it will ensure that this hard-earned capacity shall be placed in the service of humanity.

Adler wrote this in his foreword to Dreikurs's *Introduction to Individual Psychology* (1933).[20] In this brief but penetrating book, Dreikurs presented the fundamental postulates of Adler's psychology recast in his own succinct and lucid way. In introducing Dreikurs, Adler wrote, "The author of this book is well fitted to speak in the name of Individual Psychology. His life, his work, his first book on *Psychic Impotence* . . . are all evidence of a mode of thought which is characterized by acceptance of Individual Psychology, enthusiasm for co-operation and specialized knowledge. It may well . . . disclose to many darkened minds the secrets after which they are groping."[21]

The book derived from Dreikurs's lecture course for the Vienna Academic Society for Medical Psychology in 1932/1933. Translated into English, Czech, Dutch, Greek, French, and Italian, it has proven to be a clear explication of Adler's concepts, a work that reveals Adler's meaning to many, which is exemplified in the following rather typical account by a contemporary Adlerian: "I found Adler's *The Neurotic Constitution* and *The Practice and Theory of Individual Psychology* most difficult reading; in fact, I doubt if I understood much. Reading Dreikurs' *Fundamentals*, however, suddenly made things more clear, like a flash of lightning illuminating the darkness, a sudden insight into what it is all about."[22] (When Dreikurs published his first American edition in 1950, he retitled it *Fundamentals of Adlerian Psychology*.)[23]

An interesting aspect of the book is Dreikurs's insight concerning the opposition that Adlerian psychology most frequently encounters, one that springs from the human tendency to evade the issue of self-determination:

> Anyone who has grasped the simple truths upon which Adler's psychology has been built up soon realizes why people underrate it and why acceptance of it involves certain difficulties. It provides a set of very simple tools for investigating complex character formations. Simplicity characterizes the fundamental laws of social interest, its counterpart the inferiority feeling (which is the source of all striving for significance), the unity of the personality and the individual life style. Whoever refuses to allow himself to be convinced that such laws govern all the activities of the mind forgets that fundamental laws have always proved to be simple in essence though applicable to complex modes of life. One has only to think of Newton's law of gravitation, which enabled so many varieties of motion of inanimate

matter to be deduced from the same fundamental formula. It is not surprising, therefore, that it should be possible to apply the fundamental laws discovered by Alfred Adler to *all* psychological manifestations. How little justification there is in the accusation that these laws fail to take [heredity] and the part played by the instincts into account. . . .

It is evident that the teachings of Adler are intelligible to all, and many people even agree with them so long as no personal problem appears to be attacked. The findings of Adler win their assent when they refer to other people, but they try to feel skeptical and raise objections as soon as their own behavior comes under observation. They object that our laws cannot explain everything. Yet it is significant that each one takes exception to something different while readily assenting to statements which another person has difficulty in accepting. Whoever has deeply explored human nature will have no difficulty in understanding this. Everyone refuses to understand what does not agree with his own bias and involves the recognition of his own responsibility. This explains why people are constantly emphasizing the special importance of [heredity] and the instincts. They represent the greatest limitation of individual responsibility.[24]

The hint of pessimism in Adler's foreword, so contrary to his optimistic stance, suggests his sense of impending social and political disaster. It was 1933—the year Hitler took control in Germany. In March of that year the Austrian Parliament was dissolved by Chancellor Dollfuss, and all political parties with the exception of the Fatherland Front were forbidden. The haunting prediction of the Austrian poet Franz Grillparzer: "The path of departure from humanity is via nationality to bestiality," was launched on its fateful course. Adler and Dreikurs were keenly aware of the deteriorating political conditions.

Adler had spent most of the previous seven years in America and had by that time transplanted his hopes there. There, he believed, "lay the hope of humanity at large: there liberty could be preserved and a reasonable freedom practiced. Man could become a 'whole human being' in America better than anywhere else."[25]

The decisive blow to democracy and freedom in Austria came in 1934 following the "Vienna Massacre," when Dollfuss turned the army against the striking workers, killing and wounding hundreds of citizens. Dollfuss found himself caught in an iron-clawed vise. On the one side, Hitler and

Mussolini each demanded that he destroy the socialist and communist movements in Austria. On the other side, he sincerely wanted to maintain Austria's independence and sovereignty, but as a dictatorship. Figuring that if he appeased the former demands, he could salvage Austria as a nation, he turned against the Social Democratic Party and the workers. In so doing, he made a fatal mistake, for they were the only significant group that could have waged a genuine and sustained fight to preserve Austria. In the end, all lost: Austria's courageous experiment in democracy; the Social Democrats, whose leaders were arrested and many executed; Dollfuss, who later that year was assassinated by Nazi fanatics; the Jews of Austria, who found themselves to be increasingly detested "aliens" in a culture they, as much as anyone, had helped to shape; and Austria itself, which ceased to exist as a nation four years later with Hitler's *Anschluss*.

One of the first acts of the Austro-fascist regime after the takeover was to end the school reform and to close down the child guidance clinics and the Adlerian experimental school. Dreikurs recalled:

> I went to the school and found the door to the child guidance center locked. I was told by the janitor, "There is no more center—go down to the Board of Education." They told me, "We don't need these new-fangled ideas. Our teachers know what to do. There is no problem with a child that cannot be cured by a rod."
>
> So that was the end. I saw the danger signal. I saw Hitler coming, and it was getting worse. There was no freedom anymore. I had to restrict my activities to my own private groups because of the tremendous fascist pressure. Austrian fascism wasn't as violent as Hitler's, it wasn't as anti-Semitic, but it was bad enough. Much too bad for me. I had no interest in staying, and I prepared myself to leave.[26]

Another foreboding incident took place when Dreikurs traveled to Krakow to deliver a paper for the International Congress of Moral Education in 1934:

> I met a psychiatrist there from Germany who had been one of the most modern pioneers in the field, very advanced. He expressed his Hitlerism—about the superiority of the German race, and about the Jews.
>
> "How could you, a man with your knowledge, fall for that?" I asked.

"Fall for that," he replied, "Hitler opened my eyes!"

He became convinced that it was so. I realized the tremendous, almost hypnotic power which can overcome even the brightest of minds. It seems impossible to visualize how this scientist, with such grand ideas, could become a victim. But you see, nobody could attend a meeting of the Nazis and express opposition. If you dared to make any interruption, you were beaten down and were lucky if you left the room alive. So the people who were exposed to this harassment never could mount any opposition.[27]

That same summer was Adler's last in Vienna. The city was no longer alive for him. "I want very much to get away from it. Our duty is always toward the living," he remarked to a friend.[28] It was not as easy for Dreikurs to leave as it was for Adler. He had neither the international reputation nor the connections to secure a position overseas, and he knew he would need to raise money to finance a move for himself and his family.

It took three long years before he was able to leave Vienna. Those were heartbreaking years for him and his Adlerian co-workers as they watched their activities in the community being increasingly restricted and were powerless to do anything about it. The Vienna Society of Individual Psychology continued to meet, and Dreikurs became a key leader of the group, but there was a decline in all their activities. This is reflected in the size of the *Internationale Zeitschrift*, which grew smaller and smaller and ceased altogether with Adler's death in 1937.

In the last year of freedom in Austria, Dreikurs published five short papers in professional journals, but no others after that, with the exception of a brief tribute to Adler upon his death.[29] However, it is clear that he continued to gather research material in several key areas—child rearing, education, sexuality, and marriage—which served as a basis for his later books. There is even indication that he published a book in 1935 in Vienna that has never appeared in any of his bibliographies and that was perhaps destroyed in the cultural upheavals of the times. He referred to this book only once, in a résumé of his career drafted around 1940–1941: "I undertook the task of uniting the different groups interested in modern education and child guidance. With the help of one of the most important women's organizations, we accomplished this task, publishing in 1935 the 'Advice for Bringing Up Children.' It included for the first and, I think, the only time in history, the united views of the most antagonistic and scientific groups and schools."[30]

Soon thereafter, Dreikurs managed to get a manuscript that was the forerunner of the *Challenge of Parenthood* to Holland, where it was translated by Peter Ronge, an Adlerian leader there, and published in 1936 in Dutch as *How Do I Raise My Child? Education Without Coercion*.[31] The publisher was Erven J. Bijleveld, and his son, J. B. Bommelje, recently remarked: "When the book was published in 1936, it immediately became a best seller, and until the war broke out, all of Holland seemed to be raising their children using Dreikurs's methods. Then, after the war, many young psychologists literally stole his ideas, gave him no credit, and sold them as their own. His theories remained very popular for many years to come, and now it has all sort of merged into a general philosophy of raising children."[32]

Once Dreikurs made the decision to leave Vienna, a crucial matter had to be resolved in his personal life. His wife's mental condition had never shown the slightest improvement after years of hospitalization. No longer able to recognize members of her own family, she was tragically lost to them and the world.

Dreikurs longed to have a meaningful relationship with a woman who would be his companion, wife, and a mother to his children. While he cared deeply about Steffi, he was not a sentimentalist and knew that there was no hope for the two of them. He also knew that her own family would see to it that everything possible was done for her. So in July 1934, he and Steffi were perfunctorily divorced, moving him one step closer toward a new life.

Living in the city became increasingly oppressive as political events continued to deteriorate. Dreikurs needed to get away, to find peace and reprieve from the ominous shadow cast over individual freedom. He decided to open a summer camp for troubled children in the lovely Austrian Alps, where he could work with children, be in the country, and possibly earn additional income.

He went to see Elly Rotwein, a member of the Adlerian group who had operated a successful summer camp. Spunky and independent, Elly was an ardent socialist and an Adlerian and had known Dreikurs for years. There was a certain competitiveness between them even then, a sort of brother-sister teasing, but underneath lay an abiding respect for the integrity of the other's work. Later, in Chicago, she would work with Dreikurs in the struggle to see Adler's ideas reestablished in America. From her he got some basic advice for setting up his camp, the *Kinderheim*.

The inauspicious camp that first year of 1935 was little more than a primitive cottage in the mountains, but sufficient for the six or eight children who attended. The following summer there were twenty children, and a bigger country property was rented. By the third and last summer, this time in Seebenstein, forty or fifty children attended, with a hired staff under Dreikurs's direction.

He was very different at the camp, Josie recalled. Carefree, relaxed, and removed from the harassment of city life, he thoroughly enjoyed living and working with the children. Many were problem children, and in "Uncle Rudi's" camp they found a new respect for themselves and the encouragement they sorely lacked in their home life. He was their good friend, with whom they could discuss anything without fear or humiliation. At night he made wonderful campfires, at which he sang and played guitar. He organized and participated in every aspect of camp life and thoroughly enjoyed it. He had staff conferences where he taught the psychological principles for working with children, and he also conducted group discussions with the children. The children learned a great deal, and so did he.

Dreikurs later reminisced:

> One important event concerned a little boy, Peter, who stayed with us. His mother put him in our home because she was a widow and had no place for him. He was a particularly bright boy, about three or four years old, but not one of the regular children, since he was far below the age level. Once when I was sitting in the garden with a bunch of boys, I was talking to them psychologically—why they do certain things—in the way we have our group discussions. At one point, something rather difficult came up, and none of the boys knew the answer. All the while, little Peter, who was running around completely unnoticed by us, came up with the answer. From then on, I knew you could talk psychologically with young children. As soon as they understand the meaning of your words, so too they can understand psychological meaning. The pity is that people say that children can't understand psychology until they can think abstractly—what these people consider "psychology" is something unnatural that children don't grasp. But when you speak to children, if your psychology is a real psychological interpretation of what is going on in their minds, then they understand perfectly well what is going on.[33]

It was early in 1937 before Dreikurs's plans to leave Vienna began to finalize. One opportunity opened through Wilhelm Stekel, who had just returned from a trip to Brazil. Stekel said that he had gone to Brazil at the invitation of Dr. Antonio da Silva Mello, a well-known Brazilian physician who had studied in Germany and was trying to introduce modern psychodynamics into Brazil. Stekel suggested that Dreikurs contact da Silva Mello. Dreikurs did so and received an invitation to lecture at Brazil's Academy of Medicine. But he was also considering going to the United States.

"Adler wanted me to go there," he recalled. "That's where the future was anyway. The group in Chicago, who published the journal, negotiated with me to come. It wasn't clear whether I would go there or to Brazil."[34]

Then came the shocking news. It was May 28, 1937. In Aberdeen, Scotland, Alfred Adler collapsed and died in the street on the way to giving a lecture. The news stunned his friends and colleagues in Vienna. Another bright light for humanity was extinguished in a world of growing darkness. Sad as Adler's death was, it was made more tragic by circumstances in his beloved Vienna. When memorial services were held, no public honor was shown to him. The city authorities, who were invited to attend, sent a letter curtly refusing. All the known psychiatrists, no matter to what school they belonged, were invited to attend so that science might hold the torch of tolerance higher than any personal enmity. The Freudians accepted the invitation but forgot to come. An obituary sent to the *Neue Freie Presse* was not printed, the editor replying "that it was not a suitable moment to bring out an article on Alfred Adler." Phyllis Bottome, Adler's biographer, lamented, "Thinkers belong to Time, but the Viennese contemporaries of Adler felt they belonged to Hitler."[35]

Dreikurs was sick at heart, and the urge to leave was redoubled. Then came an invitation, this time from Williams College in Berkeley, California, where Adler had been scheduled to give a summer course. Because of Adler's sudden death, Dreikurs was invited to substitute. He was elated with the invitation, and he began to study English in earnest. But suddenly the correspondence collapsed, and nothing further came of it. Ten years elapsed before he learned that the woman who had invited him had also died. So, until the last two or three weeks before his departure, he was not certain whether he would go to Brazil or to the United States:

> Before I left, everyone was after me—I am irresponsible, I leave my children, my parents, my practice. . . . Even my Adlerian friends; everyone was against me. There were some who left before me, but

nobody realized the danger of Hitler at that time. I had to fight them to go, and it proved to be right. It saved my life.

Fortunately, I got my papers and my passage on the boat. . . . My mother and aunt said good-bye. My father was still angry: If I had only been more of a success in Vienna, I wouldn't have to leave just now.

They had a good-bye party for me at the camp, and the children cried that I was going so far away. I took a bus to Venice, and when it passed some miles from the camp, the children, including my son, came on their bicycles to meet me at the crossing, and there again say good-bye. I didn't see my children until eleven months later.[36]

Notes for Chapter 8

1. Josie Pollack, personal communication, May 1974.
2. Jan C. Smuts, *Holism and Evolution* (New York: Viking Press, 1961).
3. Alfred Adler, *Understanding Human Nature* (New York: Fawcett, 1954), p. 15.
4. Bottome, *Alfred Adler*, p. 51.
5. Way, *Alfred Adler*, pp. 42–44.
6. Bottome, *Alfred Adler*, p. 13.
7. Dreikurs Papers.
8. Rudolf Dreikurs, "On Knowing Oneself," *International Journal of Individual Psychology* 3 (1937): 13–23.
9. Ibid., p. 13.
10. Ibid.
11. Ibid., p. 18.
12. Ibid., p. 22.
13. Rudolf Dreikurs, *Seelische Impotenz* (Leipzig: Hirzel), 1931.
14. Rudolf Dreikurs, *Das Nervöse Symptom* (Vienna: Perles, 1932).
15. Rudolf Dreikurs, "Recollections of Alfred Adler," Dreikurs Papers.
16. Ellenberger, *Discovery of the Unconscious*, p. 594.
17. Rudolf Dreikurs, "Certain Factors Effective in Psychotherapy," *International Journal of Individual Psychology* 2 (1936): 39–54.
18. *Mitteilungsblatt für Individualpsychologie Veranstaltung*, vol. 1, 1932.
19. Dr. Edward Schneider to Dr. [Raymond J.] Corsini, [June] 1967, Dreikurs Papers.
20. Rudolf Dreikurs, *Einführung in die Individualpsychologie* (Leipzig: Hirzel, 1933). Quoted from the American edition, *Fundamentals of Adlerian Psychology* (New York: Greenberg, 1950), p. vii.
21. Ibid.
22. Dr. Abraham Waxman to Dr. Raymond J. Corsini, May 25, 1967. Dreikurs Papers.
23. Rudolf Dreikurs, *Fundamentals of Adlerian Psychology* (New York: Greenberg, 1950).
24. Ibid., pp. 109–110.

25. Bottome, *Alfred Adler*, p. 220.

26. Dreikurs-Mackaness interview.

27. Ibid.

28. Bottome, *Alfred Adler*, p. 225.

29. Rudolf Dreikurs, "In Memoriam—Alfred Adler." *Psychotherapeutische Praxis* 3 (1937): 208–209.

30. Rudolf Dreikurs, personal data, Dreikurs Papers.

31. Rudolf Dreikurs, *Hoe voed ik mijn kind op? Techniek van een opvoeding zonder dwang* (Utrecht: Bijleveld, 1936).

32. J. B. Bommejle, personal communication to Sadie Garland Dreikurs, August 1974.

33. Dreikurs-Mackaness interview.

34. Ibid.

35. Bottome, *Alfred Adler*, pp. 267–268.

36. Dreikurs-Mackaness interview.

PART II

CHICAGO:
TRAINING GROUND
IN ADVERSITY
1937-1957

9

Brazilian Interlude

I have fallen into the world, and will now have to swim.
Rudolf Dreikurs
"Report," November 24, 1960

Dreikurs departed Genoa for the twelve-day Atlantic crossing to Brazil on August 19, 1937. During the voyage, he felt as if suspended between two worlds. He didn't belong to Europe anymore and, with each day, Vienna became more dreamlike.

"Since I left on my own, before the Nazis drove me out," Dreikurs remarked, "I never felt myself to be a refugee. On the contrary, leaving the modest opportunities that a small country like Austria had to offer was a happy thought. For me, the whole world opened up—I could go anywhere I wanted. There was no resignation, no loss, only the tremendous excitement of adventure. For me, life was always an adventure."[1]

The ship encountered rough seas, causing much seasickness among the passengers. In his letters home Dreikurs noted that he was spared, a fact that he attributed to his knowledge of the psychological power of "antisuggestion." The principle behind this technique is that a neurotic symptom can be stopped, at least temporarily, by suggesting that the patient try to produce the very symptom of which he complains. Contrary as it might seem, Dreikurs contended, neurotic symptoms are actually maintained by fighting against them.

Dreikurs first learned that this paradoxical effect, which was already practiced by Adlerian therapists, could be useful in other contexts. He had read about a North Sea fishing company that used "antisuggestion" to combat seasickness among the private passengers they routinely carried on their voyages. As an experiment, the company promised that any passenger who became seasick would receive a beautifully carved silver spoon. Much to their surprise, thereafter nobody got sick. Intrigued, Dreikurs tried it with the children at the camp. They often took bus trips, and there were always several children who got motion sickness. So he promised the first one who got sick a schilling, and much to his relief, not one of the children claimed the reward.

Years later, Dreikurs told about an Israeli woman who often traveled by ship between Israel and America to raise funds. One time, she mentioned to him how leery she was about her upcoming voyage because she always suffered from seasickness.

"Oh?" said Dreikurs with a twinkle in his eye. "I can stop you from that."

"Impossible," she replied. "I've tried all the drugs and nothing helps."

"But," he interjected, "you are here on a mission to raise funds for Israel. Anytime you get seasick, I will give you one hundred dollars for the fund."

She laughed, thinking she had a crisp hundred-dollar bill practically in the palm of her hand. Dreikurs's mischievous smile did not dampen her certainty in the least.

"Well, she wrote back that shortly after the ship left New York, they ran into rough seas, and most everyone got sick—but she could not. You see, you can only get seasick when you fight against it. Most people don't know that."

Dreikurs arrived in Brazil and was greeted by Dr. Antonio da Silva Mello, the Brazilian physician who sponsored his trip. Da Silva Mello came from one of Brazil's noble families, but his regal image was not reflected in his thinking. Dreikurs felt an immediate rapport with this hardworking physician who tirelessly dedicated himself to improving the health and well-being of his fellow Brazilians.

Trained in Europe, da Silva Mello was not a psychiatrist, but a professor of internal medicine at the University of Rio de Janeiro and had gained distinction through his scientific research, his writings, and his considerable efforts to strengthen the training of Brazil's doctors. From years of practice, he concluded that medicine focused too much on the physical aspects of illness to the neglect of the mental components. He began, therefore, to turn his interests to psychology and particularly psychosomatic medicine.

Brazil at the time was just beginning to address itself to modern issues of psychology and education.[2] In the mid-1930s, da Silva Mello returned to Europe, where he worked with Stekel in Vienna for several months. While Stekel took a theoretical stand somewhere between Freud and Adler, his therapeutic methods emphasized brevity and were closer to Adler's. This appealed to da Silva Mello, who knew that a broad and practical approach was essential if any real progress was to be made on Brazil's extensive problems. When Stekel told him about Dreikurs and his work, da Silva Mello arranged for his invitation to lecture at the Academy of Medicine.

Dreikurs was amazed at the program of activities da Silva Mello had arranged for him. There were lectures and courses for physicians, for psychologists, and for educators at Rio's most important institutions. There were opportunities to treat patients and consult with other physicians and to meet the highest-ranking people in government and science. Two young physicians were assigned to work with him as assistants. In short, he was treated like a dignitary, which, though flattering, was also tremendously challenging. He plunged into the work with his typical enthusiasm and made such an impact that his activities were recorded almost daily in the local papers. Interviews were published and he became something of a celebrity.

It was difficult to engage in complex professional activities such as teaching and discussion in a foreign land surrounded by strange languages and customs. Dreikurs worried about his language skills. Since his youth, he was convinced that he had no talent for languages. Before he arrived in Brazil, he began boning up on his rudimentary French, the official language used in Brazilian professional circles. As for the native language, Portuguese, he felt incapable of even attempting it.

One of his primary obligations in Brazil was to give a lecture before the Academy of Medicine. When da Silva Mello recognized Dreikurs's poor grasp of French, he exclaimed, "For heaven's sake, you can't give a lecture in French. You simply don't know it well enough!"

"You see," Dreikurs reflected later, "though I never knew much of the language, I always had the ability to communicate—that was my strength. Even then I knew that much. Well, I gave the lecture, but whether anyone understood it or not I don't know, and neither of us worried too much about it."

Shortly thereafter, Dreikurs received an invitation to lecture before the Academy of Letters, Brazil's most prestigious institution. There da Silva Mello drew the line: "No. I let you give your talk before the Academy of Medicine, first of all, because it was the basis of your visa, and secondly, it didn't make much difference. But the Academy of Letters is the most scholarly body in Brazil, where all the famous French professors come. And you, with your French—it's just ridiculous. I can't let you expose yourself like that. It would be pathetic."

So Dreikurs declined the invitation, and the matter was dropped. Over the next busy weeks as he lectured, consulted, and saw patients, he was unconscious of his growing facility with the language.

Eventually another invitation to lecture before the Academy of Letters came. This time, his friend said, "All right, you want to lecture, go ahead."

Dreikurs gave the lecture, but afterward was deeply disappointed in himself. When he saw his friend thereafter, he said:

"I don't know what happened to me. I don't ever remember giving such a poor speech. I couldn't get a word out."

Da Silva Mello laughed: "Don't you know why?"

"I haven't the slightest idea," Dreikurs replied, obviously perplexed.

"Because, when you came on the stage and started to speak, you apologized for using such poor French where all the famous French scientists have spoken. You were embarrassed and couldn't speak."

What happened was that over those hectic weeks Dreikurs had mastered French but did not realize it. His friend felt he could now accept the invitation to speak before the academy. But Dreikurs still believed he was incapable of mastering the language. When he stood to speak, the old message was still playing in his head, and he suddenly couldn't find the words:

> It hit me like lightning! I was a fool to assume I couldn't learn other languages. Just as suddenly, it came to me that I can go anywhere in the world and learn any language. That was the beginning of a new awakening about myself, the first breakdown of my assumed deficiencies.
>
> Without this experience in Brazil, I don't think my development in America would have been the same. When I went there, I didn't know English either, but I didn't worry about it. In time I developed a command of the language in speaking and writing, equal to the best Americans.[3]

A Taste of Opposition

Toward the end of Dreikurs's stay in Brazil, he was invited by the governor of the state of São Paulo to spend a week teaching the psychologists and educators at the University of São Paulo.

At São Paulo's Educational Institute, Dreikurs taught and demonstrated his counseling techniques with families. Because he was working with the general population, Portuguese was used, and Dreikurs had to rely upon an interpreter. This slowed his style somewhat, but even so the rapidity with which he handled each case was shocking to the professional audience.

A professor of educational psychology who was very knowledgeable in her field and who claimed to have studied with Adler in New York challenged him. He recalled:

"The first day, everything went fine and they were quite impressed with my ability to find things out and to understand the total situation. The second day, I recognized some restlessness which I couldn't quite account for, but on the third day, a storm broke loose. It seems that one of the assistants at the institute was a woman psychologist from Germany. She let me have it, and she didn't mince any words about it like Germans rarely do."

"What you are doing," she accused, "is just plain quackery! When we get a child, it takes us two months to find out what is wrong with him, and even then we are not sure. Yet you, in half an hour or an hour, dare to think you know what the situation is all about and to make recommendations. That's just impossible!"

Tension filled the room, and Dreikurs knew he was in a tough situation. Fortunately, da Silva Mello, a man highly esteemed by the others, rose and responded, "Instead of telling Dr. Dreikurs it can't be done, you'd be better off learning from him how it is done."

Da Silva Mello argued heatedly with her. Realizing they were getting nowhere, they agreed to test Dreikurs's ideas. They challenged him— would he agree to examine a boy whom the institute had already carefully studied and whose case was fully documented and make his own independent interpretation about him?

"Of course, and why not," Dreikurs reacted. "What I do is a systematic technique, not black magic."

The next day at the Criminological Institute, Dreikurs met his test case, a juvenile delinquent about seventeen years of age who had been charged with a holdup. Dreikurs sat with the youth and began asking the typical questions concerning family constellation and early recollections in order to determine his life style. He recalled:

> But this time, I was a little more cautious. I took a whole hour getting the facts down. I don't remember the details of his life style,

but the main idea was that he couldn't say no. He had to please everybody, and he couldn't let you down. So when his friends decided to break into a building and asked him to be a lookout for the police, he did so and got caught.

Then I was asked the crucial question: Would I be willing to let him go out and take my keys with him and trust him to come back on his own?

Completely, I replied, because if you tell him to be back, he can't let you down.

That was exactly what it took the institute months of testing to determine—that the boy was trustworthy.

"I just talked to him," Dreikurs went on, "and without any psychological tests, no TAT, no projective test, nothing of that sort, came to the same conclusion they had. From then on, the opposition was gone."

Buoyed by his successes and the solid support of da Silva Mello and others, Dreikurs grew more outspoken concerning his observations of professional activities in Brazil. At a lecture before the São Paulo Society of Medicine, his remarks drew sharp criticism from Dr. Antonio Pacheco e Silva, one of Brazil's upcoming leaders in psychiatry and director of the School of Sociology and Politics. During the debate, which was reported in the newspapers,[4] Pacheco e Silva asked Dreikurs whether psychiatrists were not also psychologists?

"But of course," Dreikurs countered, "only generally they are poor psychologists."

This remark hardly soothed Pacheco e Silva, but Dreikurs's aim was not to smooth over differences but to foster genuine debate within professional circles. Indeed it did, because after the lecture a heated discussion started between Pacheco e Silva and those who took Dreikurs's position, a debate that Dreikurs knew would continue even after he left.

Dreikurs returned to Rio to find his renown spreading and his trip a great success. In the course of a brief nine weeks, he had had a considerable impact on the emerging psychological profession in Brazil. His courses attracted several enthusiastic students, including some who were determined to carry on the theories and practical techniques he had taught them.

He felt that his greatest accomplishment in Brazil was the establishment of an Individual Psychology Association, the first in Latin America. Its creation reflected not only the viability of his ideas but his great skill in mobilizing others. The association's dedicated leaders included Dr.

Januario de Bittencourt, professor of education in Rio, Dr. Luiz Viana, and Dr. Manoel B. Lourenco Filho, an outstanding Brazilian in the field of educational psychology and director of the Institute of Pedagogic Studies in Rio.[5]

What Dreikurs cherished most about his trip was his relationship with da Silva Mello, which rapidly developed into a deep and enduring friendship. Da Silva Mello admired Dreikurs greatly and took every opportunity to sponsor his work. Nearly twenty years later, da Silva Mello wrote:

> In Adler's doctrine a new and fertile view was uncovered, which when followed up yielded abundant material of incalculable value. ... [His] discoveries ... gave us a better understanding of our lives, our behavior in relation to ourselves and others, in the school, in the professions, in our family, and in society, with regard to our affective and amorous life, our tendencies and aversions, our capacities and shortcomings, our successes and failures. And all this was so unexpected, had so many practical consequences, so obviously close to the truth, and so easy to check by its constant repetition that, without any further proof being adduced, it appeared to demonstrate the insufficiencies of Freud's theories.[6]

For da Silva Mello, the depth and practicability of Adler's ideas came to life through Dreikurs. His demonstrations with clients were decisive. In a matter of minutes, he brilliantly stripped all but the core issues for the individual or family before him and vividly demonstrated the universal applicability of Adler's ideas to men, women, and children from all walks of life. If it smacked of showmanship, it was largely because he revealed that behind the seeming mundanities of life was an unfolding drama of conflicts, high purpose, resolution, and, most of all, hope that gave each individual a new sense of his own dignity and worth. It was indelibly convincing. In 1970, many years after Dreikurs's visits to Brazil in 1937 and again in 1946, da Silva Mello recalled: "The time spent with Dreikurs was for me extremely rich, because Adler himself in his own writings seems to be not very precise nor convincing, perhaps incapable of expounding his own doctrine to the point of making it sufficiently comprehensible and apt to produce the fruits it can so easily produce."[7]

Professionally and personally, Dreikurs made such an impact that the Brazilians did their best to tempt him to stay. He considered the matter but decided to go on to the States as planned.

"When I came back to Brazil in 1946," he reflected, "I realized the wisdom of my decision. True, I had tremendous difficulty starting in America. I came from Brazil with all the honors, with money, as a big shot. In America, I started as the lowest, a nobody—an Adlerian just didn't count at all. But, when I came back in 1946, I was a full professor and had established myself, and I realized that I had gotten much further than I ever would have in Brazil."

On November 5, 1937, he boarded the S.S. *Western World*, an American ship, and embarked on the last leg of his journey to the United States. Once onboard, but before the ship was out of Rio's harbor, Dreikurs sensed a totally new atmosphere and flavor. He imbibed it, listened intently to the English, the meaning of which mostly escaped him, and sought to fathom the new faces and mannerisms of the Americans. But it was also a time for reflection. He wrote:

> I first thought about it on the ship just about the time when the lights of Rio moved slowly backward and fused into a single sea of light. Strangely, I experienced a certain uneasiness. I was not satisfied with myself—I thought about this and that, things I should have done in a different way. This is something I experienced several times in Rio: I really thought I would have to be perfect. I am still much too vain, I still have too many doubts in myself. Thus I take small mistakes much too tragically, just as on the other hand, I am much too over-joyed about small successes. . . .
>
> Perhaps I could have done this or that better, but in general I believe I can be satisfied. . . . I have seen much, experienced many beautiful things, but I have also learned much. . . . Not only have I familiarized that part of the world with the teachings of Alfred Adler, but I have managed to win enthusiastic disciples as well. Thus, I have accomplished what really was to be accomplished.[8]

Notes for Chapter 9

1. This and other direct quotations from Dreikurs are from the Dreikurs-Mackaness interview.

2. Manoel B. Lourenco Filho, "Present State of Psychology in Brazil," *Inter-American Psychologist*, monograph 1 (1955): 20–26; Carlos A. Leon, "Psychiatry in Latin America," *British Journal of Psychiatry* 121 (1972): 121–136.

3. Actually, Dreikurs always retained a heavy Viennese accent, which lent a decidedly authoritative charisma to his whole demeanor. His conversation and even his

speeches, which he rarely read from prepared texts, were flavored throughout by a rich peppering of Teutonic structures and phrasing.

4. *Folha da Manha* (São Paulo), October 23, 1937.

5. *Individual Psychology Bulletin* 2 (1942): 60; and *Individual Psychology Bulletin* 5 (1946): 91–93.

6. Antonio da Silva Mello, *Man: His Life, His Education, His Happiness* (New York: Philosophical Library, 1956), p. 41.

7. Antonio da Silva Mello, *Psicologia de Fatos Cotidianos* (Rio de Janeiro: Civilizacao Brasileira, 1970), p. 222.

8. Rudolf Dreikurs, [Travel] Report no. 20, "On Board Ship," November 5, 1937. Dreikurs Papers.

10

The Strange Fate
of Adler in America

Most observations and ideas of Alfred Adler have subtly
and quietly permeated modern psychological thinking to
such a degree that the proper question is not whether one
is an Adlerian but how much of an Adlerian one is.

Joseph Wilder
Essays in Individual Psychology

As the S.S. *Western World* steamed northward to America, Dreikurs laz-
ily basked under the hot equatorial sun, passing the time reading American newspapers and a detective story in order to bone up on his English.
Even onboard the ship—a tiny outpost of America—he sensed an air of
freedom he had not known in years.

He was forty years of age. Although he had considerable and acknowledged talents, he had known only difficulty and financial struggle in his
entire adult life, due to the economic and political hard times that had
plagued Vienna.

His optimism was buoyed by his triumphant tour of Brazil. However,
his worries began to mount as he sensed the worsening conditions in
Europe and the growing threat to Austria. He realized the potential danger to his children and family back in Vienna. Yet here he was venturing
thousands of miles away, helpless to give assistance should they need it.
All he could do was to monitor events and, hopefully, sound the warning
bell in time.

Dreikurs never considered himself a refugee forced to flee his homeland, but the fact is that had he delayed his departure a mere seven
months, he might have lost the chance to leave altogether. Unknown to
him, he was part of a small, yet most remarkable wave of immigration to
America. The "illustrious immigrants," Laura Fermi aptly called them—

the cream of Europe's scientists and intellectuals who managed to escape the Hitler madness and make their way to America. Included were such outstanding physicists as Albert Einstein, Enrico Fermi, and Leo Szilard and a host of brilliant figures whose talents ranged from the theoretical sciences to philosophy, medicine, literature, music, and the performing arts—John von Neumann, the mathematician; the philosopher Rudolf Carnap; architects Walther Gropius and Ludwig Miës van der Rohe; composers Béla Bartók, Arnold Schoenberg, and Alban Berg, to mention but a few. These men and women who slowly filtered into our universities and communities played a vital role in transforming the United States into the world's leader in science and the arts in the aftermath of World War II.

Psychiatry and psychology, two differing yet overlapping disciplines were also affected by the transplantation of Europe's leading minds. Before the war, Europe was regarded as the most important center of modern psychiatry and experimental psychology, to which aspiring psychologists and psychiatrists made obligatory pilgrimages to gain expertise and prestige. Freud and Adler in Vienna, and Jung in Switzerland, were the unquestioned giants of psychiatry, and to this day nearly every psychology textbook opens by paying tribute to all three. Yet, Adler's contributions are treated with remarkable ignorance. Beyond crediting him with discovering the "inferiority complex" and "will to power," they say almost nothing of his brilliant concept of the "life style," his revolutionary teleoanalytic approach, his contributions in child guidance, or his momentous concept of social interest. Instead, these books generally give the impression that Freud singlehandedly revolutionized our ideas of human nature. Adler's original contributions were swallowed up in the overwhelming intrigue with Freudian dogma.

Adler and Individual Psychology were victims of the cultural upheaval in Europe in the 1930s. The disembowelment of Europe's intellectual centers and their fitful shift to America was not an orderly process. Civilization experienced a rupture in its spirit and institutions. Much that went before was cut off and set adrift in history and soon forgotten in the disillusionment and chaos of the time. The relative positions of Freud and Adler were dramatically altered by these events, especially in the United States, which became the creative center of modern psychology and psychiatry. (Situated in neutral Switzerland, Jung and his school were not disrupted and therefore were not so affected as were Freud and Adler.) As he approached the States, Dreikurs could not possibly have known the puzzling fate of Adler's psychology in America, but its impact would energize and color his life in the years ahead.

ADLER'S INFLUENCE IN AMERICA

Gauging from the history books, one would think that Adler had little exposure in this country and that his influence was negligible. Nothing could be more erroneous! Of the great triumvirate who revolutionized psychology in this century, Adler's ideas were philosophically the most compatible with the basic American outlook. His underlying concept of man as a purposeful, self-determining being fit well with the predominant American spirit of optimism, pragmatism, and the basic belief in man's ability to shape his own destiny. The paradox of the apparent neglect of Adler's ideas while they were concurrently so compatible with the American spirit is only resolved when we understand the intellectual forces that flowed in America in those decades.

This discrepancy suggests the possibility of inadequate exposure, for the greatest discoveries are useless artifacts if there is no opportunity for them to be heard, absorbed, and tested against the reality of experience. Right away, a curious fact emerges; of the three great pioneers, only Adler had a prolonged, direct contact with the American people and their institutions. Adler spent the major portion of his last ten years in the United States, eventually making his permanent home here. His exposure was not isolated or limited to a few colleagues in some remote academic niche. With boundless energy, he crisscrossed the continent, lecturing and teaching wherever he went and attracting the interest of physicians, psychologists, social workers, criminologists, mental health workers, and educators. Even before Adler set foot in America, his brilliant discoveries had begun to take root.

When the "earthshaking" discoveries of Psychoanalysis were proclaimed by Freud at the turn of the century, psychology and psychiatry were newly emerging disciplines still casting about for a definitive role in America. In psychology—newly elevated to the status of a "science"—the pioneering leaders in America modeled their university departments after the experimental research approach that originated with Wilhelm Wundt in Germany. The Wundtian tradition, which focused on observing and measuring the sensate aspects of consciousness, was enthusiastically adopted here. However, before long it was overwhelmed by Watson's behaviorism, which, in its worship of pure mechanistic causality, outdid even the Germanic tradition. It removed human consciousness altogether from the proper study of psychology. In the end, a rigorous empirical research model became the entrenched and dominant force in American academic psychology. In its quest for professionalism and scientific respectability it emulated the scientific method. Academic psychology became increasingly remote from the real problems of human affairs and produced little that gave any insight into understanding human behavior. The dictum of America's first and greatest philosopher-psychologist, William James, that "only a science which is directly related to [enhancing] life is really a science," was forgotten along the way.

At the same time, psychiatry too was groping for new directions as a profession and stirring to break out of its confining cocoon. Psychiatry had arisen as a special branch of medicine nearly one hundred years earlier when Philippe Pinel symbolically unshackled the insane and declared that they were sick people who deserved the same compassionate care given those suffering physical symptoms. From that humanitarian act evolved the tradition that the treatment of the insane was the proper jurisdiction of medicine, represented by the psychiatrist. For most of the nineteenth century, psychiatry was practiced within the confines of asylums, and the patients were mostly psychotics whose bizarre or threatening behavior made them outcasts from their families or communities. But there was little treatment, little hope of a cure, and too often the inmates were treated no better than criminals. Insanity was regarded as another medical pathology; its cause was attributed to genetic defects, organic malfunctioning, or physical imbalances in the body. Little attention was paid to personal experiences, feelings, or social circumstances as precipitating factors, let alone the source of illness. Toward the end of the nineteenth century, Emil Kraepelin of Berlin brought considerable order to the chaotic riddle of mental illness with his classification of the various illnesses and their symptoms. While this did little to improve treatment, it served to keep mental illness under medical wraps by cloaking behavioral disorders in Greco-Latin cant. While profound advances in general medicine brought the profession unprecedented prestige and stature in society's eyes, the specialty of psychiatry was left behind, within the walls of the asylum along with its hopeless inmates.

But there was a fresh breeze stirring that would alter the status of psychiatry in America, and it arose from two directions. First was the change in the conception of mental illness that has symbolically come to be known as the Freudian revolution. Its point of departure was the exploration of the psychological elements that caused mental disturbance and was a direct challenge to the older approach. Freud's psychogenic approach centered on the neuroses and not on the more intransigent psychoses. Until then, the neuroses were poorly understood, and while they caused real suffering in the patient, they rarely resulted in confinement in insane asylums. The Freudian revolution opened new areas of investigation and treatment. Because neurosis is the major type of psychiatric disorder in which the patient feels ill and voluntarily seeks help, psychiatrists began to shift their interest to it. In so doing, they left the confines of the mental institutions, entered private practice, and took their place alongside their already prestigious and influential medical brethren.[1]

The other factor that affected the status of psychiatry in America was the emergence of the mental hygiene movement, a humanitarian effort that linked laymen and specialists in a genuine desire to improve the shameful conditions in mental hospitals and to promote sound mental hygiene principles. The psychiatrists emerged as the authoritative experts in this area and soon advanced to the forefront of the movement. In the process, they formed close ties with the social and political policy-making bodies.

Freud's startling discoveries had little impact on this side of the Atlantic before his brief and only visit to America in 1909, at the invitation of G. Stanley Hall, then the "dean" of American psychology. The occasion was the great conference at Clark University, which brought together America's most influential figures in psychology and the social sciences. Dismayed by the lack of appreciation for his discoveries in Europe, Freud regarded the invitation to America as exceeding his fondest dreams,[2] and he playfully referred to Hall as a "king maker." In fact, Hall was an outstanding figure: the founder and first president of the American Psychological Association and the founder and editor of the first American journal of psychology. While Freud saw his visit as a great opportunity for recognition, he harbored no fondness for the United States. Cynical and aristocratic in outlook, he expressed a deep dislike for its democratic ideals and referred to America as a gigantic mistake. En route to the United States, he remarked to a companion, "We are bringing them the plague,"[3] which suggests a pessimistic disdain for his own theories. Assessing the impact of his lectures at Clark University, he curiously remarked that "Psychoanalysis was no longer a product of delusion; it had become a valuable part of reality."[4]

Adler's and Freud's polar positions on human nature were reflected in their attitudes toward America. One thing they had in common was that both were introduced to America through Hall's energetic efforts. Hall was open to new ideas and was interested in childhood education as well as psychology. Through his role as organizer, editor, and professor, he facilitated an easy exchange of ideas among his students and colleagues. While impressed with Freud's psychogenic approach to mental illness, he expressed grave reservations about its exclusive basis in infantile sexuality and soon discovered that Adler's ideas were much closer to his own experience and thinking.[5] By 1914, Hall introduced Adler's theories of compensation and inferiority feelings and described them as more fundamental to understanding behavior than Freud's.[6] Hall corresponded with Adler and hoped to bring him to this country to lecture, but World War I intervened, and the visit was delayed some thirteen years. However, Adler's ideas attracted sufficient attention to warrant American editions of his early works on organ inferiority and the neurotic character, both of which appeared in 1917.[7] The publication of these works was largely due to Bernard Glueck, Smith Ely Jelliffe, and William Alanson White—all of whom, ironically enough, were influential pioneers in promoting and establishing psychoanalysis in American medicine.[8]

That members of Freud's first-string team in America should introduce Adler's works some six years after Freud's and Adler's irrevocable break seems strange indeed. However, awareness of the schisms in Vienna was slow in reaching America, and few here had any direct, emotional stake in it—at least not at first. Besides, "American physicians gloried in their eclecticism,"[9] and were critical of the formation of "schools." They looked upon psychoanalysis as essentially a new methodology that was merely enlarged and improved by Adler and Jung. Few besides Adler and Freud themselves were aware of how incompatible their views were. Freud wrote to Hall, "It cannot possibly escape you that a complete rejection of psychoanalysis is an essential part of Adler's teaching."[10]

By 1916, Freud's ideas had penetrated American medicine, largely due to a few highly influential doctors who promoted psychoanalysis, including James J. Putnam and Morton Prince in Boston, A. A. Brill and Smith Ely Jelliffe in New York, Adolf Meyer in Baltimore, and William Alanson White, the powerful superintendent of the government-run Saint Elizabeth's Hospital in Washington, D.C. Men like Prince, Meyer, and White, all brilliant thinkers in their own right, never strictly adhered to orthodox Freudian theory and methods. The nature of the psychoanalysis which evolved through their eclectic outlook was a diluted and piecemeal mixture of favorite themes and concepts. If it appeared as a unified movement to those outside and to the less discerning adherents within, it was because Freud had also created a highly specialized language for his conceptualizations, including words and phrases such as *libido, id, super-ego, the Censor, Oedipus complex, anal and oral eroticism, castration complex, transference, reaction formation, cathexis,* and the like. As psychoanalysis became the mainstream in psychiatry, one could jump aboard the bandwagon by simply employing this special language, even if it was used in a way that was different from Freud's meaning. To be part of the mainstream was considered vital to most practicing psychiatrists. Its leaders were the power brokers who held the key to hospital appointments, professorships, and publishing opportunities—in sum—to recognition and success.

Adler's contributions were initially regarded as an important part of the psychoanalytic corpus. This changed at about the time Adler's American editions appeared. Freud never forgave Adler's dissidence, and in the years that followed he wielded his eloquent pen to encourage his loyal followers to deny or discredit Adler's discoveries—to keep Adler forever in the shadow of his own greatness. Freud knew the power of legend, and when he wrote his history of the psychoanalytic movement, which was reprinted in the United States,[11] in 1916, he presented his own prejudiced version of the split with Adler, scurrilously attacked him, and judged his ideas as "radically false." In this way, he got his account of these events into the history books long before it seemed important to anyone else.[12] This affected Adler's image in America both immediately and in the long run.

Unlike Freud, Adler had no strong following in America, and there was no one to respond to Freud's attack. Nobody had worked or studied with Adler, whose own school had only been formalized in 1914, the same year war broke out, disrupting activities and communication. Freud's most orthodox followers in the United States mimicked practically word for word Freud's arguments against Adler and implied that he was a dangerous heretic. For instance, Dr. James J. Putnam, a venerable Boston Brahmin and champion of Freud, wrote: "A great longing has been felt by many conscientious students of human nature to find some way of escape from accepting Freud's conclusions. . . . To such persons Adler's mode of explanation is only too attractive. In plain terms, it offers a weapon with which Freud may be conveniently struck down by those . . . so minded."[13] The "hot" battle in Vienna was transplanted to America as a cold shoulder.

The impact of Freud's curse on Adler was notable, and when Adler's *Study of Organ Inferiority* and *The Neurotic Constitution* appeared the following year, the reviews in the psychiatric literature were few and terse, with one notable exception. Bernard Glueck, the psychoanalyst who had translated *The Neurotic Constitution* and who therefore knew its contents better than anyone, wrote a long, enthusiastic review in which he said:

> In this book on the neurotic character Adler . . . has perhaps given us thus far the most complete and technically most perfect description of the neurotic constitution. As we peruse this book we are struck again and again with the most thorough and incisive manner in which he proceeded in his search after the truth. His investigation into the forces which are operative in giving the life-spark and sustenance for the creation and moulding of the neurotic character carry him to the very beginnings of life and perforce create the profoundest admiration, whether or no we accept his views. In following him upon his journey of exploration, new vistas are constantly revealed to us and in the end, the neurotic stands before us like an open book. . . . The chief distinction of Adler's mode of approach . . . is his endeavor to discern the whys and wherefores, the object of the neurotic symptoms, aside from having given us a much more dependable etiological basis than has heretofore been furnished for the neurotic condition.[14]

But the die was essentially cast for Adler's place within American psychiatry. A select few ideas—organ inferiority and its psychic compensations, and "the will to power"—became incorporated into psychiatric theory, but Adler's name was disregarded and soon forgotten. To mention Adler or openly advocate his ideas was a risky stance against the mainstream of the profession. It hardly seemed warranted in view of the extreme value placed upon eclecticism. Few understood that Adler offered a radically different way of looking at behavior or treating mental problems. Thus, for many professionals, Adler's ideas became frozen at an early, incomplete stage of development. Consequently, his later thoughts were largely ignored in psychiatry.

The decade between the American publication of his books and his first visit to America witnessed a major shift in the direction of Individual Psychology. The concept of social interest was the point of departure, firmly linking the individual and society in a mutually dependent community and providing a workable guideline for distinguishing normal (useful) and abnormal (useless) functioning. From it evolved Adler's bold leap from a medical-psychiatric model of curing mental illness to a broad, socially based, educational model of prevention. The schools and free child guidance clinics of Vienna were the testing grounds, offering dramatic proof of what could be done when psychologists, teachers, and parents united in a common effort to reach the troubled children of the city. Individual Psychology achieved international fame, and in Europe, Adler's repute even outstripped Freud's.

By the time of Adler's first visit to the United States, he had acquired a number of dedicated American friends who had studied with him in Austria. His ideas were highly regarded by progressive educators and within the mental hygiene movement. The extent of Adler's impact on modern thinking about behavior was widely appreciated. For instance, acknowledgment of Adler's arrival by the *New York Times*, reported in its usual restrained manner, inspired this rejoinder in the *New Republic* (January 5, 1927):

Doctor Adler Incognito

New York's greatest newspaper (not the *Daily News*) missed a trick the other day when it recorded, under the quiet headline "Brings New Psychology, An Even More Modest Arrival": "Among the passengers (of the fogbound *Bergenland*) was Dr. Alfred Adler, a Viennese psychologist, who at one time worked with Freud and Jung, and parted from them . . . years ago. He said he was the exponent of individual psychology, based on studies of so-called inferiority and insecurity feelings gained early in childhood or caused by an inferior constitution." Doctor Adler is not merely *a* psychologist, he is almost *the* psychologist. Indeed, he is *the* Dr. Alfred Adler, from whom Freud and Jung learned as much as he learned from them. Further still, he is the originator of the theory and phrase "inferiority complex," and as such, deserving of flaming headlines, a long interview, a column, a column and a half. But all that the father of the most famous of complexes received was a paltry stick of small type which might well have given him a taste of his own discovery.

In the event-packed period from January to mid-April 1927, Adler crisscrossed the nation delivering more than three hundred lectures in his heavily accented but lucid English. That averaged out to more than three lectures a day including Sundays! Highlights of his itinerary were lectures at the New School for Social Research, the Child Study Association, the Mental Hygiene Society, and the Neurological Section of the Academy of Medicine—all in New York City. In Boston he lectured at Harvard, was warmly greeted by Dr. Morton Prince, and was the guest of Dr. William Healy, who founded the Judge Baker Child Guidance Clinic, which became the standard model for such clinics in America.

In Chicago, Adler lectured before the Child Study Association to an enthusiastic, overflow audience of physicians, teachers, and social workers. He interpreted cases before the physicians and staff members at the Institute for Juvenile Research and lectured at the University of Chicago.[15]

In the succeeding nine years, he lectured at some of America's leading universities—Harvard, Yale, Columbia, Chicago, Stanford, and the New School for Social Research. From 1929 to 1931, Adler was a visiting lecturer at Columbia University, where he gave courses at the College of Physicians and Surgeons, the Institute of Arts and Sciences, and to graduate students in psychology. Adler's public lectures at Columbia University's McMillan Theatre in 1930 (subsequently published as *What Life Should Mean to You*) broke all previous attendance records there, according to university authorities.

During the last five years of his life, Adler was visiting professor of medical psychology at Long Island Medical College (now the Downstate Medical Center, State University of New York), and after 1934, he made the United States his permanent home. Adler's ideas became widely disseminated not only through his lectures and courses but also through the popularity of his books.[16] Popular and professional magazines featured articles about his psychology. By the mid-1930s, professional societies of Individual Psychology existed in New York, Chicago, and Milwaukee, and in 1934, the *International Journal of Individual Psychology* was launched in Chicago with Adler as editor-in-chief.

Adler's unique child guidance model also had considerable exposure. Apart from his demonstration clinics conducted all over the country, at least three clinics functioned for a number of years, under the direction of Drs. Walter Beran Wolfe, Max Strauss, and Samuel Plahner.[17]

The mindlessly repeated notion that Adler's ideas had a negligible influence in America can be put to rest. Adler's basic concepts of inferiority feelings, compensating behavior, and the ceaseless striving for superiority —mastery, a place in the sun—were absorbed and incorporated into the American consciousness. They became part of the commonsensical, almost intuitive way we generally anticipate, perceive, and interpret human behavior. American psychiatrist Merrill Moore wrote: "We can scarcely detach Adler from the world as we know it today or imagine what modern thought would be like if he had never lived; for so much of our present day thinking rests upon his creation. When we read what he says, we may sometimes think, "Everybody knows that." Only when we stop and look back do we realize that everybody knows it because Adler taught it to everybody."[18]

To correct another misconception, the commonsense quality of Adlerian concepts is not a defect, not a sign of simplistic superficiality as the Freudians have always charged. "Common sense, or consensual validation (Harry Stack Sullivan's term), refers to the communality of thinking that enables men to understand each other, to come to an agreement, and to share opinions and convictions."[19] Thus, common sense is basic to the orderly functioning of any community. Perhaps common sense is better appreciated when we look at it in relationship to the concepts *to know, to comprehend*, and *to understand*. To know something is to be aware of something as a fact or truth; to comprehend is to know something thoroughly and to perceive its relationship to other ideas and facts; but to understand is to be fully aware not only of the meaning of something but also of its implications. Only when we realize the implications of what we know do we feel a solid basis for practical *action*. The common sense of Adlerian concepts lies in their making daily behavior understandable. Individual Psychology, in effect, provides a special orderliness, a subtle insight into the underlying functioning and relationships of what was always before our eyes but somehow escaped our understanding.

One definition of genius is the capacity to create a new obviousness,[20] and that is precisely what Adler did. This is why many people, when they encounter his ideas for the first time, find them so exciting. They illuminate at once the experience of reality and generate the typical "But of course! Why didn't I think of that myself?" kind of response. It was that kind of reaction, that awareness of a new obviousness that enabled Adler's ideas to penetrate effortlessly into our general thought patterns.

Ironically, it was the very ease with which Adler's ideas filtered into modern thought that kept their creator from being credited for his discoveries in the social turmoil of the 1930s. As Adler's ideas became popular, others freely borrowed his themes and turned them to their own purposes. This resulted in a spate of books that distorted and misconstrued his thinking. The "inferiority complex" and the notion of "the will to power" were especially plucked from Adler's psychological system and became the basis of numerous "success" manuals and do-it-yourself psychology books that flooded the market.

Freud's and Jung's ideas were subjected to a similar ransacking and likewise suffered distortion at the hands of conceptually weak but verbally nimble popularizers. Grace Adams, a noted critic of the time, wrote in dismay: "As article followed article, and book followed book, and theory superceded theory, the essential nature of man, instead of becoming increasingly clear, seemed more obtuse and difficult to understand—until at last it was all but obscured by a mass of conflicting, unintelligible verbiage."[21]

THE CULT OF FREUDIANISM

While Adler's ideas penetrated everyday consciousness, it was Freud's seductive ideas about our lurking unconscious, our instinctual sexuality, our lost freedom in a repressive society that captivated the intelligentsia, and the opinion makers. The intellectuals found in Freudianism a new weapon for maintaining their exalted position and enthusiastically applied psychoanalytic ideas to all human endeavors—the arts, religion, anthropology, education, history, and politics. The novelists and dramatists soon learned that facility with Freudian ideas and a glibness with its jargon were far more profitable than clear prose or real insight into character. The result was that any aspect of life, any conscious act, gesture, or creation, was subject to the scrutiny of the Freudian lens for "its hidden, repressed sexual meaning," thereby casting doubt upon and demeaning our beliefs and actions. The fact is that psychoanalysis, while clamoring for libido liberation in the name of individual freedom, was actually chaining man to his instincts, thereby denying his free choice, his self-determination, and his responsibility.

The intellectual appeal of Freudianism boosted the status of psychiatry immensely. The sophisticated, the prominent, and the well-heeled who could afford it, flocked to the couch to reveal all, and spent years learning about their infantile fixations, inhibitions, and repressions. The psychoanalytic model of childrearing, which promoted pampering, the avoidance of frustration, and permissiveness, influenced the schools, guidance clinics, and parenting. The psychoanalyst became a super-authority in every aspect of modern life and human conduct.

Psychoanalysis, already the mainstream within psychiatry, now assumed a virtual hegemony over the entire profession. That hegemony moved out of the confines of psychiatry to dominate the direction of the mental health movement, social work, child guidance clinics, and general education. As psychoanalysts became preeminent, they grew less tolerant of opposing points of view. Psychoanalysis was loudly acclaimed as a scientifically proven body of theory and practice, and those who actively challenged or opposed it within the professions were discredited as the simple unwashed—that is, the unanalyzed and therefore unknowing and superficial. Even eclecticism became ensnared in the defense of psychoanalysis. Since psychoanalysis was regarded as an established truth, it therefore became "uneclectic" and dogmatic *not* to acknowledge its basic truths. In other words, if these truths were acknowledged and the catechism of Freudian phrases was repeated, one could acquire the luster of revered "objectivity."

But there were those—Adler perhaps the wisest among them—who saw through the pseudoscience of psychoanalysis and whose integrity would not allow them to lend support to a burgeoning professional edifice built upon a dubious foundation. But Adler was no match for the advancing army of Freudianism. His views were incompatible with the professional power structures, and he was unable to counter their influence effectively.

The final blow to Adlerian psychology in Europe and America occurred after 1937. While Adler's and Freud's schools were equally condemned and destroyed by the Nazis in Europe, the consequences for each were quite different. The great esteem psychoanalysis had acquired and its links to influential circles assured the success of the refugee psychoanalysts in the United States. Analysts, who in Vienna or Berlin had been relatively undistinguished, found a reverent audience. "Patients were eager to be treated by Europeans," Laura Fermi remarked, "because the famous among them cast a bright aura on the others."[22] These Freudian émigrés rapidly acquired important hospital positions and rose to powerful leadership roles in psychiatry and in the community.

Adler's European co-workers were not so fortunate. Adler's sudden death in May 1937 was a devastating blow that demoralized his followers. In America, they were left leaderless and incapable of providing much assistance for the plight of their European colleagues. Many European Adlerians perished later in the Holocaust. Those who made their way to America faced a desperate struggle to become reestablished in a new country, where their Adlerian training and experience became a liability rather than an asset.

A RUDE AWAKENING

As the S.S. *Western World* drew close to New York, Dreikurs's hopes and expectations ran high. He had no inkling of Adler's diminishing esteem in American professional circles or of the hardships and difficulties that awaited him.

His stay in New York was brief and jammed with activities. He visited his several relatives and spent hours walking the streets of New York, enthusiastically absorbing all the sights. He contacted the local Adlerian group in New York, which was expecting him, and paid his respects to Adler's widow, Raissa, whose courageous expression could not conceal her tragic loss.

A reception was arranged on Dreikurs's behalf at the home of Dr. Frederick Dey, a psychiatrist and president of the New York Society of Individual Psychology. Adlerian psychology was then at a low ebb, and the New York group, numbering less than thirty, served as an advisory center for new arrivals from Europe.

Dreikurs never forgot the advice he recieved that night. He was firmly warned not to declare himself an Adlerian. To do so was to risk future hospital appointments and professional viability. Shock and anger welled within him: "I was pretty furious. What kind of cowards are they? I couldn't imagine that in the land of democracy you would be ashamed to declare your own professional orientation."[23]

Notes for Chapter 10

1. Dreikurs, "Group Psychotherapy and the Third Revolution," pp. 26–27.

2. Sigmund Freud, "Autobiography." In: *The Standard Edition of the Complete Psychological Works of Sigmund Freud* (London: Hogarth Press, 1953), vol. 22, pp. 7–74.

3. Stuart Hampshire, "Review of *Freud*, by O. Mannoni," *New York Times Book Review*, January 31, 1971, p. 8.

4. Sigmund Freud, "An Autobiographical Study," in *Problems of Lay-analysis* (New York: Brentano, 1927).

5. Ansbacher, "Alfred Adler and G. Stanley Hall," pp. 337–352.

6. G. Stanley Hall, "A Synthetic Genetic Study of Fear," *American Journal of Psychology* 25 (1914): 149–200.

7. Adler, *Study of Organ Inferiority* and *The Neurotic Constitution*.

8. John C. Burnham, *Psychoanalysis and American Medicine: 1894–1918* (New York: International Universities Press, 1967).

9. Ibid., p. 184.

10. Ansbacher, "Alfred Adler and G. Stanley Hall," p. 348.

11. Sigmund Freud, "History of the Psychoanalytic Movement," *Psychoanalytic Review* 3; 1916: 406–454.

12. Paul Roazen, "The Legend of Freud," *Virginia Quarterly Review* 47 (1971): 33–45.

13. James J. Putnam, "The Work of Alfred Adler Considered with Especial Reference to That of Freud," *Psychoanalytic Review* 3 (1916): 121–140.

14. Bernard Glueck, "Adler's Conception of the Neurotic Constitution," *Psychoanalytic Review* 4 (1917): 218, 225.

15. *Internationale Zeitschrift für Individualpsychologie* 5 (1927): 225–227, v–viii.

16. Alfred Adler, *Understanding Human Nature* (1927) (New York: Fawcett, 1954); *The Education of Children* (1930) (Chicago: Gateway Editions, 1970); *What Life Should Mean to You* (1931) (New York: Capricorn Books, 1958).

17. John Haynes Holmes, "The Clinic at the Community Church," *Christian Register*, November 1933; Aysa L. Kaydis and Sofie Lazarsfeld, "The Group as a Psychotherapeutic Factor in Counseling Work," *Nervous Child* 4 (1944/1945): 228–235; *Internationale Zeitschrift für Individualpsychologie* 12 (1943): 63.

18. Merrill Moore, "Alfred Adler—Creative Personality," *American Journal of Individual Psychology* 11 (1954): 3.

19. Helene Papanek, "Adler's Psychology and Group Psychotherapy," *American Journal of Psychiatry* 127 (1970): 785.

20. Bernard Grasset, *Remarques Sur l'Action* (Paris: Gallimard, 1928).

21. Grace Adams, "The Rise and Fall of Psychology," *Modern Psychologist* 3 (1934): 115.

22. Laura Fermi, *Illustrious Immigrants: The Intellectual Migration From Europe, 1930–1941* (Chicago: University of Chicago Press, 1971), p. 173.

23. Dreikurs-Mackaness interview.

11

A Warning Not Heeded

No advance is ever made without the consciousness of a
hindrance. It is the thing which appears to be a deterrent
which acts as the incentive.

Alfred Adler
Problems of Neurosis

Now immersed in a totally English-speaking milieu, Dreikurs felt at times
left out and overwhelmed. By listening intently, he managed to understand much, but long conversations left him trailing. He was not discouraged by his language difficulties—his experience in Brazil had taught him
not to be—and he was determined to master English quickly. In those
first days in New York, he spoke English as much as possible, and when
he met with the Adlerian group, most of whom spoke fluent German, he
addressed them in English—clumsily, haltingly, with many errors—but in
English! By the time he boarded the train for Chicago, his English had
improved remarkably in four short days.

What occupied him that long night on the train was the strange warning not to declare himself an Adlerian. Maybe things were bad in New
York, he concluded, but in Chicago everything must be better. After all, it
was Chicago where a strong society had formed, where the *International
Journal of Individual Psychology* was being published, and where Adler
had suggested that he establish himself. Letters from Edyth Menser, the
secretary of the Chicago society, gave every indication that he would be
warmly received and that his skills were needed and wanted. Besides, he
was not totally unknown in America. Adler had spoken of him as a
talented and dedicated colleague, and his reputation as an excellent clini-
cian and theoretician was known throughout Adlerian circles in both
Europe and America. Though he had never written anything in English,
six of his early and important papers had been translated and published
in the American journal between 1935 and 1937.[1]

The gap between his expectations and the bleak reality of his professional prospects hit him shortly after he arrived in Chicago on November 21, 1937. He wrote to his family in Vienna:

> These first few days in Chicago were probably the most difficult ones I have experienced so far. For the first time, the thought occurred to me whether it would not have been better to stay in Vienna. . . .
>
> First, there was the question of my activity here. I was accepted by the people of our group with great warmth and friendliness. It was a beautiful feeling to get into a strange country and immediately to have friends. But there was no preliminary work done on my behalf. I found no work either in the group or outside of it. At the moment, there are no positions at the University, and there is the strong psychoanalytic opposition from the doctors and psychiatrists.[2]

Coming from Brazil, where he was treated as a renowned expert and an honored guest, he found the conditions in Chicago shocking. The Adlerian Society, which he counted on as an initial link to Chicago's professional community, turned out to be a small, ineffectual group numbering about twenty members. The *International Journal*, which was the most important contribution of the Chicago group, ceased publication just when Dreikurs arrived.[3]

His disappointment with the state of the local society deepened when he met his old friend Dr. Erwin O. Krausz,[4] a talented Viennese coworker who had come to Chicago some time earlier. From Krausz, he heard a bitter story of the pettiness and intrigue that had led to Krausz's ouster from the local group. The Chicago group, he further learned, was comprised mostly of teachers and volunteer women, a dedicated enough group but completely under the sway of its president, Dr. Nita Mieth Arnold,[5] a German-immigrant psychiatrist, and the only physician among them. While Arnold was a skilled therapist, she was ambitious and competitive and had little tolerance for anyone who threatened her leadership. Dreikurs sensed that he too would have difficulties with this clique of women, and indeed, for the next few years, until Arnold left Chicago, they posed numerous and sometimes painful obstacles for him. But Dreikurs, they soon found out, was not a quitter. No matter how much they opposed his bold ideas, he was determined to stay and to shape the group to his own vision.

His most pressing concern was to find work. No ordinary or routine kind of work would do, because he was not an ordinary man. His vision

of himself, his fundamental conviction and belief in what he could accomplish, was steadfast. He set his goal and aimed for nothing less than
an important role, that is, a professorship, or some position from which he
could launch his bold ideas, teach others, and have an impact far beyond
the aspirations of most. But the urgency of finding work was also a matter
of economic necessity. The money he brought with him had dwindled,
and his funds could not sustain him for long. Added to that was his
growing concern that money would be necessary to get his children out of
Europe.

In his letter of November 24 he described the circumstances:

> In order to practice medicine, I first need a license which I can only
> get after a year's work and an examination. But where should I work
> until then, that is the question. One doctor whom I talked to and
> whose connections I counted on proposed a year of graduate work at
> one of the local universities. This, of course, did not agree with me at
> all. After all, I have a name and a certain scientific reputation which
> I am not going to squander very easily.
>
> The first reports from people I met was that I would either have to
> accept a subordinate position doing office work or laboratory investi-
> gations, or find work as an intern in a hospital. I was assured that it
> would be quite difficult to get an internship because so many young
> American doctors wait in vain for that one year of practical work. So
> this was my first surprise here.[6]

But, as matters improved, his basic optimism resurfaced:

> Then at the right moment came the change, through a curious coin-
> cidence which so often has played a role in my life. I visited a
> professor of psychiatry here, Professor [Abraham] Low,[7] a former
> Austrian himself, who encouraged me tremendously. He gave me a
> recommendation to the local Jewish Hospital [Michael Reese], one
> of the largest and most influential hospitals in the city. I knew, how-
> ever, that neither he nor the man to whom he directed me [Dr. Jacob
> Kasanin],[8] could really help me. I was very sad and down. The next
> morning in bed, I was thinking whether I actually had my medical
> degree with me. I jumped out of bed . . . but as I went through my
> documents, I found something I never thought would be of any
> importance at all. It was a letter from Saphir to his brother [Otto

Saphir][9] here in Chicago. I knew the man . . . and now I found out that he is a professor at the same hospital where I could possibly get work and a corresponding position if I had the necessary backing. I called him at once. . . . He spoke immediately to the man to whom I was referred. This, of course, provided me with an entirely different entrée when I appeared there. Thus, I found the letter at the decisive moment. One day later and it might have been too late. Isn't that funny?

This Professor [Kasanin] took me with him to a lecture, and this was my first important experience in this city. In this large public hospital were a number of doctors and social workers who discussed in detail the case of a patient. . . . They discussed it purely psychoanalytically, but nevertheless, it was psychology. And this, of course, is where I am at home! All of the professors participated in the purely psychological debate. Then it became clear to me: This is where I have to get in, one way or another. I do belong in these circles and here is where I have something to give. If during the last couple of days I often asked myself the question, "Do these people here really wait for me, as my friends would lead me to believe?" Then here I found the confirmation. Adler is dead and hardly anybody is here who can really forcefully represent his theories. Our group has really fine results, but what is missing is the doctors, and especially.————[10] [Dreikurs!].

Three days later, Dreikurs was offered an internship. In accepting the appointment, he entered, as he put it, the psychoanalytic "lion's den": Warned not to propagandize his Adlerian views, he probably tried to comply, in all sincerity. But, being a man of integrity, he could not compromise the principles in which he believed, nor did he lose sight of his primary obligation—the well-being of the patient. Therefore, he probably did not equate propagandizing with forthrightly criticizing what he regarded as conceptually and therapeutically wrong. He could not be the "good and quiet" Adlerian that Kasanin insisted upon for Dreikurs's own sake.

"Kasanin himself told me, 'If you are an Adlerian, don't say you are opposed to Freud. You will be professionally killed if you do. If you say you take something from Freud and something from Adler, you may be able to get by with it. But don't make any criticisms of Freud, because you will have no chance.' "[11]

Dreikurs's letters home poignantly revealed his impressions of American psychiatry and the opposition he quickly provoked:

December 6, 1937

It was indeed a special stroke of luck that I found this position. . . . Of course, things are not that simple. From the very first my chief had a fight with me. He told me things not even old Mettauschek would have dared to tell me. . . .

You have to understand my position here. I went directly into the lion's den. All staff members here are psychoanalysts and up to this time, no Individual Psychologist has succeeded in getting into this hospital. Even Adler was prevented from giving a lecture here.[12] . . . That I was accepted in this hospital, especially on the staff—that I owe to Saphir, and the fact that the people here wanted to defend themselves against the accusation that they were exclusively and one-sidedly psychoanalytic which the Board of Directors did not like. So I was accepted in order for them to show their neutrality, but on the other hand, this is what makes life difficult for me. But I am sure I can last it out and it is quite interesting.[13]

Dreikurs later described this clash with Kasanin: "It must have been on the second or third day that an incident occurred, and Kasanin immediately tried to put me in my place. You see, he first told me that I should not do anything, just observe what they were doing and get a feeling for the place. So, I had nothing to do, and there wasn't much to see. On the second day, he invited me to sit in on a case conference with a social agency. They discussed the case of a boy, an ambulatory patient. The doctor who was treating him had gotten nowhere and felt he didn't want to waste any more of his time with him. So they argued back and forth about what to do with the boy. He was obviously disturbed, but nobody had any plan, and there was no one to whom he could be referred.

"At this point I said, 'By the way, I have nothing to do. I would be glad to work with the boy.' Oh, they were quite surprised. One social worker asked me about my background, whether I had ever worked with children. I told her, yes, that I had quite a lot of experience with children. So it was decided that I would work with him. At least I had something to do.

"The next morning when I got to the hospital, Dr. Kasanin called me into his office first thing and gave me hell. 'Tell me, Dr. Dreikurs,' he exclaimed, 'don't the people in Europe know how to behave? Aren't they gentlemen? Do we have to teach you how to be a gentleman?' "

"What did I do?" Dreikurs queried innocently.

"Remember the case conference? Number one, who asked for your opinion?"

"Don't I have a right to speak up?" Dreikurs shot back.

Kasanin fumed, "Nobody asked you. Do you realize what you did? If you took on the boy—and let us assume you succeeded with him—where would it leave this man who couldn't get anywhere with him? You keep your mouth shut until you are asked for your opinion."

"It was quite a shock to me," Dreikurs recalled. "I was almost willing to resign because, after all, I would not have expected that kind of treatment from anyone.[14]

"The greatest difficulty at the beginning was to listen to the hour-long reports of case histories by the social workers," he reflected. "Once, after I began to understand one social worker's hour-long presentation of her findings, I piped up and asked, 'Tell me, after all you found out, what do you think of the case? What did you get from all this information?' I was very rudely rebuffed by the psychiatrist in charge of the conference, who told me, 'The social worker is not supposed to make any interpretations. She is only to prepare the data.' Actually my question was how do you know what data to prepare if you don't know the significance of the data?"[15]

A few days later, Dreikurs wrote:

> Slowly I realize how interesting America really is, and how important it has been for me to come here. . . .
>
> However, for the time being, I am willfully being kept in the background here at the hospital. . . . But, nevertheless, everybody is interested in my work. My chief has already found a real psychoanalytic explanation for it. He says, 'To the extent to which you describe things, you are entirely right and everything fits very nicely, but the essential issue is still much deeper.' When I told him I would be only too happy to learn from him the deeper sources in concrete cases, he said this could only be found through regular psychoanalytic treatment, and this treatment is not being done in the hospital! Therefore, I cannot find out what the real issue is about! Nevertheless, they let me treat patients now, and they are glad when

I can find out what the problem is because they do not treat people effectively or correctly themselves.[16]

An important contact Dreikurs made in these earliest days in Chicago was with psychoanalyst Dr. Franz Alexander,[17] who headed the famed Institute for Psychoanalysis in Chicago and spearheaded the shift to a more ego-based form of psychoanalysis. In his letter of December 13, Dreikurs mentioned that he was meeting daily for lunch with the "Chief of the Psychoanalysts." On the following day, he wrote: "Today I went to lunch with Dr. Alexander who is the 'big man' here. My God, the money that these people have assembled to create a gigantic psychoanalytic institute, equipped in the best, most modern fashion! Bernfeld[18] is now traveling in California making studies there, all at the Institute's expense."[19]

Apart from professional matters, Dreikurs wrote of his impressions of Chicago and American customs and way of life. They provide a fascinating vignette of the times as seen through a foreigner's eyes.

Of American manners he humorously wrote:

> People here, on the whole, are very correct. So much friendliness and politeness cannot be imagined by Viennese. Everything is done correctly, exactly determined. . . . All tell you how happy they are to get to know you, and even so, they don't know you, and nobody will believe the other. The men shake hands and no woman will do the same. . . . Acquaintances are greeted generally only with "Hello." "Please" and "thank you" are said very often, everyone excuses himself as often as he can, and he always finds it "all right," if someone else excuses himself. . . . During dinner one continually has to interchange forks and knives, and during the activity, one keeps the instrument in the right hand, etc. Thank goodness, there are enough Europeans around here to bring a little disorder into these strange customs. Only the Americans get very mad about it. They ask everybody how he likes it here, and are terribly hurt if you have something adverse to say[20]

In the political and social realms, Dreikurs's initial impressions were interesting. Less than a month after he arrived, he wrote:

December 19th, 1937

Last night I had quite an experience. I went to a theatrical produc-
tion by a radical leftist group. First they played a piece describing
life in a work camp. . . . The second was an anti-war piece. The
impression that these plays had upon me was very strong. First, they
reminded me of the numerous pieces "No More War" which we had
participated in ten years ago. But to what effect? . . . Now I see with
amazement how passive and how inactive we were in our thinking
and in our political activities. It is unpardonable! It seems as if our
whole people had fallen into an inactive dream, waiting for the inevitable to come over us.

But here people are still thinking and still have courage. Moreover,
the people are permitted to take courage. . . .

Perhaps this is America's great chance, that here the people are
educated in a way that the respect for personal freedom, and thus,
love for freedom, was never broken, not even through military service and war. Not even the police here appear as forceful authorities.
On the other hand, the criminals profit from this attitude. The
amount of shooting that goes on is unimaginable for Europeans. But
nobody takes any notice of it. . . . Whether there is a connection
somehow between the personal freedom of the individual and the
liberty which the criminal takes for himself because he has never
learned to fit himself to an orderly way of life—perhaps these are
only two different aspects of the same process. (If I should stay here,
I intend to concern myself more with the psychological aspects of the
criminal.)[21]

A YEAR OF DESPERATION AND REUNION

With the dawn of the new year, 1938, Dreikurs had just begun to settle
into his new life. His original plan was that his children would join him in
1939, when Eric would have completed his *gymnasium* education. By
then, he expected he would be satisfactorily established. But plans
changed abruptly as political events in Austria signaled impending disaster.

The ominous signs leading to Nazi Germany's annexation of Austria,
the *Anschluss*, occurred in rapid-fire succession after February 12, 1938,
the day Hitler delivered his ultimatum to Kurt von Schussnigg, Austria's

dictator-chancellor, at a secret meeting at Berchtesgaden. At the last moment, Schussnigg mounted a defiant gesture against Hitler. He called for a plebiscite, the first election in four years, in which the Austrians would decide whether to join with Germany or maintain their independent nationhood.

Sensing the escalating danger, Dreikurs shot off several letters to Josie and his parents: "You are sitting on a powder keg which will explode any minute, and you don't even know it!" Josie didn't believe that anything that bad could happen, but she heeded his instructions to secure passports and to prepare to depart Austria as soon as possible. In contrast, his warning provoked a bitter response from his proud, bullheaded father, who resented any advice from his son and who could not imagine that his privileged status in Vienna could be threatened. Sigmund Dreikurs did not understand what was going on. He saw his son's departure from Europe as a betrayal of his family and his native Austria.

Time was running out. Hitler accurately sensed that the Western powers would not interfere and launched his "rape of Austria." On March 12, his army marched into Austria without so much as a drop of blood shed in her defense. Austria ceased to exist and became a part of the Third Reich. When Hitler entered Vienna on March 14, proclamations had already gone out denying all Jews any citizenship rights and barring them from practicing their professions. In the days following the *Anschluss*, a wave of barbaric and inhuman acts were unleashed against Vienna's Jews by the Austrians themselves that outdid even the Germans for sheer brutality up to that time. By April more than thirty-four thousand enemies of the Nazis were arrested, and Dr. Goebbels, Hitler's minister of propaganda, boastfully declared that Germany-Austria would be *Judenfrei* (free of Jews) by 1942.[22]

Dreikurs was stunned by the lightning speed and ferocity with which all this took place. He feared for his children, his family, his many dear friends and colleagues in Vienna. There was no more mail from Vienna— only a dreadful silence broken by grim news stories on the radio and in the papers. Gripped with a desperate sense of helplessness, Dreikurs agonized with each passing day as he anxiously awaited word of his children.

Unknown to him, Josie was doing her utmost to make the necessary arrangements to leave, but it was no simple matter. The preparatory stages for emigration had become highly systematized in the notorious Central Office for Jewish Emigration, which was administered by the Austrian Nazi, Adolf Eichmann.[23] The applicant for a passport had successively to pass before a series of desks representing the Jewish community, the police, the economic and financial authorities, and the Gestapo. Any flaw in the record, any tax or levy unpaid anywhere along the line, immediately expelled the applicant from the torturously long process, with no recourse but to start the procedure all over again.

After weeks filled with many humiliating experiences, Josie finally secured the precious passports. Their visas were authorized only as far as Sweden, since it was too dangerous to specify the United States as their destination.

It was sometime late in April. "Immediately," Josie recalled, "I grabbed the children and ran. I just left everything—the apartment, the maid—so they would not know we had left." It was a long and harrowing journey across Germany en route to Sweden.

After unbearable weeks of silence, what immense relief Dreikurs felt when the cable announcing his children's arrival in Sweden came, early in May. But it would take another two and one-half months before all three would be united in Chicago. First there were delays in getting their visas for the United States. Far more challenging, however, was the desperate need for funds. Money became a paramount issue. Dreikurs's paltry salary as an intern barely met his personal expenses. Now he needed money to support his children in Sweden and to pay their transatlantic fares to bring them to Chicago. Beyond that, he had to support them here. There were few options open to him for getting more money. It was the depression, and it was difficult to borrow much money from his new American friends, and the few patients he saw outside his hospital duties could not afford to pay him much at all:

> My last penny was gone when the children arrived in New York. A friend of mine who had to be in New York on business picked them up, but I had no money. I really didn't know what to do. Then, in one of those strange coincidences, I got the money needed. I was seeing a patient in the hospital for free. On this very day, his father came by and offered me a hundred dollars as compensation for my work with his son. So, I had the money to get my children to Chicago at least. But, I realized I had to make more money, and I arranged to teach a class for the Adlerian group. But the woman who ran the society called a meeting of the board. They decided that my English wasn't good enough, and so, I had to give back all the money which I had collected and to stop the class. It was all the way around a rather difficult and humiliating experience for me.[24]

Dreikurs's reunion with his children nearly a year after he left them in Vienna was an emotionally charged occasion. It restored his characteristic *joie de vivre*. He felt whole once again, ready to face all challenges.

Indeed, there were plenty of difficulties. Living in a cheap boarding-house in a poor neighborhood near the hospital, he could neither keep the children with him nor could he afford an apartment for all three. He had little recourse but to arrange for Eva to live with friends for the time being, while Eric stayed with him at the boardinghouse. This was hard on Dreikurs, but far harder for Eva, who had just come through a trying ordeal and now faced adjustment to a new culture and language. Late in 1938, Dreikurs was finally able to reestablish his family in their own home, an apartment on Chicago's North Side. By that time, Dreikurs's sister, Bertha, had arrived in Chicago and was living with them, and managing the household. Josie arrived somewhat later, took her own apartment nearby, and remained very close to the family. Life, once again, settled into a normal family routine.

So far, we have glimpsed Dreikurs's early experiences in America both personally and professionally, as seen largely through his own eyes. What of this impact on others? How did they see him?

"I met Dreikurs practically his first day," recalled Bronia Grunwald,[25] one of his earliest American friends and later a dedicated co-worker in the field of education. "I was young—he was young—but in my eyes, he looked like a middle-aged man, probably because of his bald head, the moustache, his old-fashioned glasses, and conservative attire." Bronia, a free-spirited, independent, vivacious young woman was about twenty years old, half Dreikurs's age:

> Of course, as I got to know him, he no longer seemed so old. There was a great zest about him, about everything he did. He walked with a very brisk, determined step and always had an erect bearing that lent an air of great confidence and certainty. But he had a boyish quality too, that was matched by his baby-smooth skin, his rosy cheeks, and his sparkling eyes.
>
> Dreikurs had an amazing belief in himself. He spoke English from his very first days in America, and he used Germanic sentence struc-tures up to his very last. In his early lectures, he'd put the accent on the wrong syllable, the beginning of the sentence at the end, and the end in the middle. Somehow people understood him, and his English improved, but he never perfected it. He concentrated all his energy on the content and on reaching his audience. Years later, when we

wrote *Maintaining Sanity in the Classroom* together, I had a lot of trouble in this regard. As I read certain passages, I'd wince in pain over their construction. "We can't do it this way," I would tell him. He argued with me: "Well, who has written books, you or I? I've written many books, and look how popular they are." He would insist that the passages remain as written, and they did.

Dreikurs also believed in his work. He immediately gathered around him people with whom he could discuss ideas, although such gatherings usually wound up with him lecturing and doing most of the talking. I, too, became interested and involved in the activities of the Adlerian group.

Some months after we had been working together, Dreikurs said to me, "Why do you want to study acting? I think you should give up dramatics and concentrate on education—because I need you." Actually, I was taking some education courses at the time, but I was mostly interested in dramatics, in becoming an actress. "What do you mean, you need me?" I responded. "Well," he said, "we need somebody who can break into the schools and begin to illustrate Adlerian techniques in education. You seem to have a good understanding of our ideas. I need you, and you should get your degree in teaching as quickly as you can." In fact, that is exactly what I did.

After I made the switch, he asked me to report what I did in the classroom, and he guided me. He told me what he thought I did wrong, what I misunderstood, and he encouraged me to try this or that approach. When I was successful, he would always say, "You must write it up immediately." When next he would see me, he would query, "Did you write it up?" I'd say, "No, I didn't." He would get very annoyed with me: "What do you mean, you didn't? This is important because we—you—will need it when we train other teachers later on. You've got to go home and write it up."

While Dreikurs could be the gentlest and most understanding human being when working with children or his patients, he was a tough and scrappy fighter in the professional arena. Intolerant of ineptitude and shoddy or dogmatic thinking among his colleagues, he lashed out and let them know it in no uncertain terms. He confided to Bronia all the indignities and shabby treatment he received at Michael Reese Hospital. It fired his anger, and he felt he had to fight back. Bronia was among the first of many friends over the years who challenged his pugnacious style. "You know, Dreikurs," they would typically say, "perhaps if you didn't fight so much, you could probably get where you want much faster, and then you could use your own techniques." Always, Dreikurs strongly disagreed: "If I don't fight, I get nowhere. I have to fight."

Notes for Chapter 11

1. Rudolf Dreikurs, "A Case of Functional Disturbance of the Digestive System," 1935; "The Choice of a Mate," 1935; "Certain Factors Effective in Psychotherapy," 1936; "The Problem of Neurasthenia," 1936; "An Introduction to Individual Psychology," 1937; "On Knowing Oneself," 1937.

2. Dreikurs, to his family, Report no. 22, November 22, 1937, Dreikurs Papers.

3. The original Chicago Society for Individual Psychology was founded in 1933 by Dr. A. R. Radcliffe-Brown, professor of anthropology at the University of Chicago, and Dr. Douglas Gordon Campbell, assistant clinical professor of psychiatry at the university's medical school. The *International Journal of Individual Psychology*, with Adler as editor-in-chief, was published quarterly from 1935 to 1937. According to Sydney Roth, who provided financial backing for the journal, it had a distribution of about six hundred copies per issue.

4. Erwin O. Krausz, Ph.D., M.D. (1887–1968). An active associate of Adler's from 1915, he came to the United States in 1935, where he acquired his long-sought degree in medicine. As a practicing psychiatrist, he always based his work on Adlerian theory.

5. Nita Mieth Arnold, M.D., Ph.D. (1898–1952). Born in Argentina and trained in Germany, she was medical superintendent of the Berlin Child Guidance Clinic prior to coming to America in the early 1930s. She left Chicago during the war years and later settled in California.

6. Dreikurs, to his family, Report no. 23, November 24, 1937. Dreikurs Papers.

7. Abraham A. Low, M.D. (1891–1954). Low studied medicine in Vienna and came to the United States in 1921 where he later became associate professor of psychiatry at the University of Illinois Medical School. He is best remembered for his pioneer work in the development of Recovery, an organization to foster self-help among former mental patients. Strongly opposed to psychoanalysis, he was later subject to professional attack by the Freudians, at which time Dreikurs encouraged him greatly.

8. Jacob Kasanin, M.D. (1897–1946). Kasanin was director of the Department of Psychiatry, Michael Reese Hospital, from 1936 to 1939. An ardent psychoanalyst, he came to appreciate Dreikurs's skill as a therapist and wrote the following to Dreikurs in May 1939: "In leaving the Directorship of the Department of Psychiatry my greatest regret lies in ceasing my association with you. Please allow me to express to you my deep appreciation of your help in making our department one of the best in Chicago" (Dreikurs Papers).

9. Otto Saphir, M.D. Saphir was director of pathology at Michael Reese Hospital and clinical professor at the University of Illinois Medical School.

10. Dreikurs, to his family, Report no. 23, November 24, 1937. Dreikurs Papers.

11. Dreikurs-Mackaness interview.

12. In January 1937, Dr. Nita Arnold wrote Kasanin at Michael Reese Hospital informing him that Adler would be coming to Chicago and suggesting that the hospital

might like to schedule a seminar for the staff with Adler. Kasanin's reply: "I have great personal admiration for Dr. Adler, but I doubt very much if I could arrange for a seminar in this hospital. The staff just got through with a seminar in child psychiatry by Dr. George Mohr and Dr. MacDonald, and I doubt that they could swallow more than one seminar a year" (Dreikurs Papers). It was such ludicrous professional behavior by the psychoanalysts that so incensed Dreikurs.

13. Dreikurs, to his family, Report no. 26, December 6, 1937. Dreikurs Papers.

14. Dreikurs-Mackaness interview.

15. Ibid.

16. Dreikurs, to his family, Report no. 27, December 10, 1937. Dreikurs Papers.

17. Dr. Franz Alexander, M.D. (1891–1964). A lifelong psychoanalyst, Alexander trained in Berlin and came to the United States in 1930, founding the Institute for Psychoanalysis in Chicago in 1932. An outstanding theoretician, educator, and therapist, Alexander opposed the rigid and dogmatic attitude among many of his psychoanalytic colleagues. Friendly and open-minded, he maintained good relations with many non-Freudians. While he was a key figure in the shift of American psychoanalysis to an ego-based psychology and briefer therapeutic techniques, he never publicly credited the source of his ideas to anyone other than Freud. Yet, in reviewing his text, *Psychoanalytic Therapy* (1947), Keith Sward wrote: "The modes of therapy reported by Alexander and his co-workers are anything but 'analytic,' in the sense of being 'Freudian.' They are patterned in the main after the thinking of two of Freud's great contemporaries, Otto Rank and Alfred Adler. . . . For their dynamics of *personality*, or their theories of the structure of neuroses . . . the Chicago group would seem to be Adlerian through and through" (*Science* 106 [1947]: 600–601). Dr. Douglas Gordon Campbell, mentioned above, related that Alexander often admitted privately to others that "Adler had made an enormous contribution and was a fundamental influence in his own ego-oriented form of psychoanalysis, but the time had not arrived for such public acknowledgment" (Dr. Douglas Campbell Gordon, personal communication, February 1975).

18. Siegfried Bernfeld, M.D. (1892–1953). Dreikurs's former associate from the Youth Movement and a highly respected psychoanalyst, Bernfeld came to the United States in 1937 and settled in California. Like Dreikurs, he remained dedicated to problems of youth and education all his life.

19. Dreikurs, to his family, Report no. 27, addendum, December 14, 1937. Dreikurs Papers.

20. Dreikurs, to his family, Report no. 27, addendum, December 12, 1937. Dreikurs Papers.

21. Dreikurs, to his family, Report no. 29, December 19, 1937. Dreikurs Papers.

22. William L. Shirer, *The Rise and Fall of the Third Reich* (Greenwich, Conn.: Fawcett Crest, 1959.

23. Herbert Rosenkranz, "The Anschluss and the Tragedy of Austrian Jewry," in *The Jews of Austria*, ed. Joseph Fraenkel, 2d ed. (London: Valentine-Mitchell, 1970).

24. Dreikurs-Mackaness interview.

25. Bronia (Bernice) Grunwald, personal communication, July 1973.

12

Transplanting
the Adlerian Model

In Germany and Austria they closed the clinics, but in
America we will rebuild them.

Alfred Adler
April 1937

If Dreikurs was beset by personal and professional hardships his first year
in the United States, they were small compared with his disillusionment
with child guidance as it was practiced. His dismay was the more acute
because his own pioneering work in Vienna had often been inspired by
American innovations in mental health and child guidance. Somehow,
over the intervening years, the child guidance movement and its clinics
had been transformed and robbed of their capacity to reach the troubled
children that filled our cities. Dreikurs understood then what would take
decades for others to realize—"contemporary clinical services for children
. . . are a failure."[1]

THE RISE AND DECLINE OF THE AMERICAN CLINICS

The "century of the child," a name prophetically coined by Swedish
feminist Ellen Kay, was launched when she and others began championing the child's right to live in a world where his personality could develop
fully and freely. While there have been parents and educators in every
age who believed in the potentiality of the child, for the most part, the
"history of childhood is a nightmare from which we have only recently
begun to awaken."[2] Up until this century, children were generally viewed
as miniature adults and treated as little more than an economic asset or
liability. Likewise, autocratic societies typically attributed criminal or

141

aberrant behavior in children to genetic traits and regarded them as hopelessly incurable.

These attitudes began to change as democratic ideals brought about a critical awakening to the social and environmental influences on the child. These new attitudes were supported by the concurrent founding of the mental hygiene movement, which demanded an end to abusive care of the mentally ill, recognized the need to improve social and environmental circumstances, and began to focus its attention on prevention. In this way the movement was instrumental in fostering a child guidance posture. Mental hygiene, as Walter Bromberg remarked in 1959, is social psychotherapy in the larger sense and could best "originate and flourish in a democratic atmosphere."[3]

The forerunner of the child guidance clinics in the United States was the Chicago Juvenile Court. The court was created in 1899 largely through the efforts of Jane Addams of Hull House and the Chicago Women's Club and reflected the humanitarian spirit of the times.

The Chicago Juvenile Court drew heavily upon volunteers and privately paid settlement-house workers, mainly women, for its probationary program and the operation of its adjunct detention home. The underlying concept of the court was that the community was responsible for the welfare of all its members, and its function was not to determine guilt and mete out punishment but to rehabilitate and guide "as a wise parent would deal with a wayward child."[4]

Despite their zeal and dedication, the court workers found themselves at a loss in handling the individual delinquent. Their sociological orientation pointed to the environmental source of most delinquent or antisocial behavior. What they lacked was a psychological basis for understanding or treating the individual child. To correct this deficiency, an institute and clinic was created in 1909 to conduct scientific research into the cause of delinquency. It was named the Juvenile Psychopathic Institute, and Dr. William Healy, a noted pediatric neurologist, was appointed director. The names reflected the prevalent psychiatric position that antisocial behavior implied serious pathology. It was a view Healy himself soon regarded as incorrect. In his practical work in the clinic, Healy combined psychiatric, psychological, and social approaches that paved the way for other clinics.

Child guidance clinics became firmly established in America in 1922, when demonstration clinics were launched in numerous cities under the sponsorship of the Commonwealth Fund. By that time, a clinic model had emerged that had broadened from Healy's original concept to include children with emotional problems, not only those appearing before the courts. At its heart, the model embraced an interdisciplinary team approach that included a psychiatrist, a psychologist, and a social worker. The goal was to reach the individual child through the widest possible participation of educational and social agencies. By 1930, nearly five hundred such clinics existed.

These early American clinics, with their community orientation, their focus on prevention, and their efforts to integrate the work of the clinics with the public schools were conceptually quite similar to Adler's child guidance clinics that arose at about the same time in Vienna. It is not surprising, then, that Adler and Dreikurs both followed American activities with keen interest. But there were some differences. For one, the Vienna clinics were more deeply and successfully integrated with the public schools. Second, their public character, with parents and teachers participating in the sessions, was a unique Adlerian innovation, one that was never part of American clinical practice.

By the late 1930s, however, the American clinics had changed from their original conception and in the process had diverged from their earlier similarity to the Adlerian model. The major cause of the disparity was the psychological foundation upon which each had become rooted. Within a decade, psychoanalysis emerged as the dominant conceptual basis for the child guidance clinics in the United States. The consequences were profound, affecting both the objectives and the therapeutic methods that were applied to troubled children and their families.

From the psychoanalytic viewpoint, personality development is based upon universal psychosexual stages of maturation—the anal, oral, and Oedipal phases, for example—the route by which the child comes to grips with his conflicting drives of love and aggression. Inadequate gratification and resolution of those conflicting drives gives rise to anxiety, which in turn is seen as the cause of disturbed or delinquent behavior.[5]

Rarely challenged, this paradigmatic model of human behavior was exclusively taught as the "proven" theory of personality development to psychiatrists and psychiatric social workers, both key members of the clinic "team." As a result, child guidance clinical objectives shifted to a narrow psychoanalytic pattern of long-term diagnostic and therapeutic procedures for the child and his family. This approach pictured the child as a "victim" of intrapsychic conflicts. The social, environmental, and interpersonal influences on the child were thereby largely neglected or considered to be superficial.

In time, the focus of the psychoanalytically oriented clinics shifted from assisting the urban poor, where the need was the greatest,[6] to serving the middle class. The poor and undereducated had neither the time nor the patience to follow through with the long-term therapeutic requirements of psychoanalysis. They had concrete problems—children who were habitually truant or constantly in trouble with the law—and they needed immediate and practical help. They could not understand how the way they toilet-trained their child years earlier was the root of their problem, and because they could not find the help they needed, they stopped coming. On the other hand, the intellectual, sophisticated, and fashionable qualities of psychoanalysis made it appealing to educated, middle-class parents, who were anxious to create as perfect a world for their children as possible. They sought the "experts'" advice when any doubts arose in their minds. The therapists, who shared the cultural outlook and values of the middle class, were far more successful working with these families, and they began to disqualify poor families by imposing stringent rules. For example, absurd as it may sound, many families were denied clinical services because there was no male head of the household.

Coincident with the growing influence of psychoanalysis, there waged a proprietary battle over the medical versus nonmedical practice of child guidance and therapy. The innovative clinical team had begun as a broad interdisciplinary approach, with each team member equally valued for his specialized skills. But as each of these disciplines—psychiatry, clinical psychology, and social work—was still in the process of carving out its own professional niche, considerable competition developed concerning who was best qualified to treat the child. By the late 1930s this jockeying for position ended with the medical viewpoint dominant. Thereafter, the clinics characteristically took the position that problem behavior was a pathological condition that only the medical expert—the psychiatrist—could properly diagnose or treat. The clinical team became solidified into a rigid hierarchical structure—the "Holy Trinity," as Leo Kanner dubbed it—with the psychiatrist in control at the top and the psychologist and social worker relegated to subordinate roles.[7]

In the process of standardizing and protecting their own sphere of work, the mental health professions fell prey to "professional precociousness,"[8] the attitude that they and they alone were qualified to provide mental health services. Anyone not possessing the requisite training was viewed as unqualified to help and ran the risk of harming the patient. An increasing estrangement of the mental health professionals from the schools and other community agencies began. The ascendency of the "expert" was accompanied by a growing retreat by others from intervening with or helping their troubled friends or family for fear of doing more harm than good.

This attitude was worsened by the general confusion about child-rearing practices. Thoughtful parents were barraged by a bewildering proliferation of conflicting theories and exhortations. Once again, the psychoanalytic viewpoint became dominant with its image of the helpless child, a passive victim of inner conflicts suffering from inadequate love and pent-up rage. Its prescription was to avoid frustrations to the child at all costs and to encourage the expression of pent-up hostility and repressed emotion. Though few recognized it at the time, this viewpoint, by fostering permissiveness, self-indulgence, and excusing the child from responsibility for his behavior actually decreased rather than increased the child's ability to cope with the demands of life. Ironically, the "century of the child," born in response to centuries of abuse and neglect, was fast approaching the point where the child now assumed the central, often tyrannical, role in the family.

All of these trends had taken hold when Dreikurs began working here, and the reality that there was no tolerance for any other point of view or practice within the mental health realm became obvious. First there was the warning from his Adlerian colleagues in New York, then his unpleasant encounters at Michael Reese. At least he expected that in the realm of child guidance and education, to which Adler had dedicated himself so completely both in Europe and in America, there would be evidence of Adler's great contributions. But there was little of it, as Dreikurs soon discovered.

For instance, Dreikurs looked forward to visiting the famed Institute for Juvenile Research in Chicago (formerly Healy's Juvenile Psychopathic Institute). But as a result of this visit, his enthusiasm plummeted. He described it as:

> a unique institution unlike any other in the world. . . . It is an immense consultation center for children with a staff of about twenty —doctors, psychiatrists, psychologists who do the testing, and social workers. All criminal youth and all social cases, but also parents with difficult children are referred there, taken care of or treated. . . . The only thing is that the people there seem to know very little about children. At a large staff meeting, they discussed the case of a boy

who wet his bed and had thieving tendencies. They talked for about an hour describing every detail of his behavior carefully without having any idea why it occurred. They just described and then finally admitted that they don't understand the child, despite the fact that he has already been under Institute care for four years!

The Director assured me that Adler's teachings had a tremendous effect and were still being used today. But little can be seen of it. They have a totally psychoanalytic attitude, and are concerned only with the sexual interests of the children which is what they seek to explain.[9]

The Freudian standard-bearers, now the lieutenants of the mental health and child guidance movements, were unrelenting in their opposition to any nonpsychoanalytic concept or practice and especially those identified as Adlerian. They dismissed them as simplistic and superficial, incapable of plumbing the depths of the patient to reveal his repressed sexuality and hostility. The Adlerian approach to child guidance, with its open sessions, its treatment of the family as a psychodynamic unit, its view of problems as stemming from interpersonal rather than intrapersonal difficulties, its practice of confronting children in a frank, noncondescending discussion of the purposes of their behavior, was effectively condemned. Lacking support in the professional community and with their appointments in hospitals, clinics, and universities jeopardized, the Adlerian therapists were literally forced to "close the door" in their clinical work with children and families.

An episode that vividly conveyed the message to Dreikurs occurred within days after his arrival in Chicago. Before leaving Europe, he corresponded with Dr. Samuel Plahner, a Milwaukee psychiatrist who founded and directed the Milwaukee Child Guidance Clinic. Trained by Adler, Plahner opened his clinic in 1929 and conducted it along Adlerian principles, with open sessions held weekly in a lecture room of the Milwaukee Public Library for some years. Plahner also lectured extensively on mental health, child rearing, and marital problems from an Adlerian viewpoint throughout the city. Among his colleagues, he was sufficiently esteemed to be nominated head of the neuropsychiatric unit of the Milwaukee General Hospital. In his letters to Dreikurs he was very friendly and seemed eager for him to come to neighboring Chicago.

"As soon as I got here," Dreikurs recalled, "he came to visit me. He pleaded with me, 'Please, Dr. Dreikurs, do not tell anyone that I am an

Adlerian. I don't want anyone to know, because I have a clinic in Milwaukee, and I would lose my position if I declared myself an Adlerian.' "[10]

Dreikurs soon learned that Erwin Wexberg, one of Adler's oldest and closest colleagues in the Vienna clinics, had also succumbed to the pressure and closed the clinic he had begun in New Orleans in conjunction with his work at Louisiana State Medical School. In Baltimore, Sibyl Mandell, an American who had trained with Adler in Europe and America, likewise discontinued the clinic she had established there.

Dreikurs considered this professional coercion shocking, inexcusable, and a clear violation of the scientific spirit. But his Adlerian colleagues who were unwilling to challenge the prevailing attitudes or fight for the right to practice their own legitimate methods incensed him even more. Many stopped mentioning Adler, others adopted various Freudian concepts even though they may actually have conducted their practice along strictly Adlerian lines.

Dreikurs understood what his colleagues were up against—the difficulties that attended the depression, their recent uprooting from Europe, the hardships involved in getting reestablished professionally—he faced all these obstacles himself. Still, from his view, they lacked the courage that the circumstances demanded, and their capitulation to these powerful pressures was, in a way, a betrayal of everything Adler stood for.

Years spent working with adults and children convinced Dreikurs that the Adlerian methods of child guidance were the most effective, practicable, and teachable ones he had yet encountered and that they were particularly suited to America's democratic society. It was impossible for him to compromise what he firmly believed or to placate his professional colleagues, who clung fast to the psychoanalytic bandwagon. The advice that he should sprinkle his Adlerian thinking with a solid dose of Freudian ideas was totally abhorrent to him.

Dreikurs felt compelled to act. Taking strong exception to many of his Adlerian friends, he was convinced that Individual Psychology (as a psychology of *use* and *movement*) could not survive if limited to the lecture platform. Nor could it prove its tremendous usefulness if confined to the printed page. The therapeutic process is an art as much as a science. While one can learn the science from books, the "art" of therapy includes skills gained through experience and practice.

Shocked by the dismal state of clinical services for children, incensed by the professional dogmatism, and spurred by his Adlerian colleagues, Dreikurs resolved to see Adler's guidance concepts and methods reintroduced and established. He needed to have a clinic—a center where he could freely demonstrate and teach what he knew to be lacking in programs for children.

THE EXPERIENCE AT MORTON HIGH SCHOOL

To back his bold plan for an open, group-oriented clinic, Dreikurs first turned to the Chicago Adlerian Society. Given the prevailing medical model of child guidance, it was essential that any such clinic, to be credible, had to be under medical supervision. Besides Dreikurs, only Nita Arnold, the president of the society, was a physician and qualified to run such a clinic. But she and her cautious followers scoffed at Dreikurs's idea, regarding it as foolish if not dangerous to sponsor such a clinic. Other members, mostly educators, were supportive of his idea but were otherwise powerless to help implement it. Dreikurs left no stone unturned in his efforts to see the clinic he envisioned become reality.

The first possibility for a clinic came from a most unexpected source, a public high school, in the fall of 1938. A teacher at Morton High School in suburban Cicero, Illinois, had attended one of Dreikurs's classes. What she learned had led to considerable improvement in her own classroom. Enthused by the results, she enlisted the support of the dean of girls and the acting superintendent at Morton to invite Dreikurs to work directly with the students. Morton High, then the largest technical high school in Illinois outside of Chicago, had a reputation for educational leadership, but with eight thousand students enrolled, it also had its share of problems.

A four-week experimental program was launched in the fall semester involving one afternoon and one evening per week. In the afternoon, Dreikurs met with students for group discussion of general problems, followed by private consultation with students, parents, or teachers. In the evening, he conducted a two-hour discussion with parents and teachers. The students who participated had been specially referred for help by their teachers, and in this four-week period, sixteen students and twenty-four adults (half of them teachers) participated. Although the students who attended did not volunteer, Dreikurs was able to overcome their hostility and resistance.

At the end of the four-week period, a questionnaire completed by the participants revealed that most of the adults noted a great deal of improvement in the behavior or attitude of the youngsters and felt they had benefited in various ways themselves. The students felt they received some or much practical help.

For instance, one parent remarked, "Marie has responded well. She has become more friendly, more alert. She seems to seek carefully the other person's attitude toward the problem rather than forcing her own."[11]

A student commented, "Dr. Dreikurs stated that a child who has been babied all his life usually has a hard time in school. I found a way to combat this only through the help of the discussion." Another noted, "I have found being interested in people's problems, not alone in your own, makes one more friends. At home, instead of not associating with my brother's friends, I have tried to enter into the spirit of the affair and found them anxious to be sociable also." A third remarked, "I was helped in my method of studying. I believe that a great number of students could be helped by lectures of this sort."[12]

Dean of Girls Eunice Prutsman was so impressed by what took place in those few weeks that she proposed that the PTA board sponsor and finance a twelve-week continuation of the guidance clinic beginning in February 1939.[13] She argued persuasively in the clinic's behalf: "(1) I have seen changes in promising and unpromising students and adults, (2) because teachers and parents have reported the reformation still in force, (3) because even yet some students who attended our clinic ask if we aren't going to start again, (4) because I have a list of thirty other students, referred to me by just a few teachers who saw what happened in only a month's experimentation, and whom no teacher has yet helped to succeed here."[14]

The board unanimously approved the proposal, and Dreikurs continued his clinic at Morton for an additional twelve weeks. This series was similar to the first, except that instead of relying upon teacher-referred students, the afternoon session became an open forum with voluntary attendance. Word spread, and interest rose. The forum grew from nineteen or twenty students to as many as one hundred. As the school year drew to a close, the majority of participants registered positive reactions and hoped that the project would be renewed in the fall.

Such was not the case. Over that summer, a new administrator was appointed to Morton High who was opposed the program. The guidance clinic was not revived.

Though disappointed, Dreikurs did not consider this a serious setback but a worthwhile pilot project that only further convinced him that his ideas were both relevant and needed.[15] He had been able to test the waters of American public education and to become acquainted with progressive educational leaders. Carleton Washburne, the superintendent of the Winnetka schools, was one of them. He later played a crucial role in Dreikurs's career.

ABRAHAM LINCOLN CENTER

In 1939 Dreikurs opened the child guidance clinic at Abraham Lincoln Center. It was an obscure beginning. Ahead lay days when nobody would come to learn what Dreikurs craved to teach, when there seemed little chance that his hard-won dream would be welcomed or would succeed.

Located in a lower-class neighborhood, the center was typical of the numerous settlement houses in Chicago. Created and sponsored by All Souls Unitarian Church, the center provided a host of services to the neighborhood, which by the late 1930s was populated by a growing majority of black families newly migrated from the South and a declining white population, many of Irish background. Black or white, all were poor, and 80 percent of the individuals who participated in the center's programs were on relief or WPA employment. A high rate of delinquency, prostitution, and broken homes existed. Racial antagonism caused a vexing problem to the center staff, which was committed to serve equally all segments of the neighborhood.[16]

Growing family disorganization—jobless fathers, parents unable to cope with their children or the demands of urban life, increasingly unruly youths who disrupted the center's programs—all were keenly felt by Elizabeth Hoyt Baker, the center's director of social services. She concluded that a child guidance clinic at the center was needed to aid both her staff and these struggling families. Dr. Ethel Gaal, the gynecologist who ran the birth control clinic at Lincoln Center, suggested that Dreikurs be contacted.[17] After meeting Dreikurs, Miss Baker in turn introduced him to Dr. Curtis W. Reese, a Unitarian minister and dean of Abraham Lincoln Center, the person who would ultimately have to approve the clinic.

Dreikurs's introduction to Reese was a happy meeting of kindred spirits, the beginning of an enduring friendship. Reese was an outspoken social activist dedicated to the cause of human betterment and social democracy. Politically astute and courageous, Reese was an excellent administrator whose idealism was tempered with a strong pragmatism.

Reese spearheaded a universalistic, social-action approach within

Unitarianism and inspired Dreikurs in his views on religion and his involvement with the Unitarian Church. A dedicated Humanist, Reese was a cosigner of the original Humanist Manifesto, and introduced Dreikurs to the movement, where he too played an important role.

Curtis Reese and Elizabeth Baker were impressed with Dreikurs. He was a psychiatrist of a different stripe, unlike most they had encountered. A social activist, Dreikurs not only understood the problems Baker faced but had concrete practical suggestions about what could be done. Moreover, they were intrigued by Dreikurs's steadfast refusal to regard problem behavior as "caused" in the usual sociological sense and by his insistence that behavior could only be understood or corrected when viewed as purposeful. They decided to give Dreikurs's ideas a try.

Dreikurs began late in 1938 by conducting a class for the Lincoln Center staff in the dynamics of child behavior. Dreikurs addressed the staff's pressing concerns. Why did certain children act up? Why did others bully their peers or defy adults? Why did some vandalize the very center that provided recreation and other opportunities not otherwise available? Were these children pathological, destined to be delinquents and social parasites as adults?

To the last question, Dreikurs resoundingly said *no*. These children, he maintained, were discouraged, felt worthless, and had no important place in their world. Their acting up and their defiant behavior only reflected their misguided efforts to feel significant. These were the only ways they had ever found to make others recognize their importance.

For the first time these group workers heard about the *goal* of the misbehavior. They learned how to identify the goal and, most importantly, how they could encourage the child to behave in socially useful ways. Once the staff members tried some of Dreikurs's suggestions and found them effective, they began to understand why he stressed the need to enlist the cooperation of parents and teachers so that all could proceed with a oneness of purpose.

Dreikurs made it clear that the only effective way to accomplish this was through open counseling sessions. Several staff members voiced strong opposition to this idea on the usual grounds that it violated the privacy of the family and could be frightening and damaging to the child. But Baker and others stood behind Dreikurs, and a small budget was set aside to launch the clinic. Accordingly, parents of the most difficult children were invited to attend a special afternoon session once a week along with the so-called problem child and his siblings.

The first clinic session was held in February 1939, and others followed on a weekly basis, each session lasting two and one-half hours. Parents initially were reluctant to expose themselves in this new and revolutionary way, and Baker had difficulty finding willing families. The first families who did come were directed to the fourth floor of the austere but commodious Lincoln Center, where they were interviewed by Dreikurs before a small group of social workers, teachers, and other parents. In addition to the large counseling room, there was a children's playroom supervised by a staff member and a place where parents could wait while their children were being interviewed. A slow-moving elevator, creaking and well worn like the building that housed it, brought families to the clinic, and as Harold Marley, a Unitarian minister who became involved in the work of the guidance centers, remarked, "There was ample opportunity for other children to ridicule those who came in tow with their parents."[18]

An impact was made on the families who came. They reported that their children did change, often dramatically, in the ways Dreikurs had predicted, once they themselves altered their own manner of interacting with their children. They began to understand why one child in their family was bad while the others were good, or vice versa. They began to stop their nagging and realized that they did not need to be slaves to their children in order to be good parents.

The clinic format was almost identical to the one Dreikurs used in Vienna. The client-parent—usually only mothers came in those earliest days—sat with Dreikurs facing the group, who were seated close by in a semicircular arrangement. Dreikurs addressed the parent concerning the particular problems she was experiencing with her children. As the interview progressed, other parents were given an opportunity to describe similar experiences in their own families and how they had handled them. At times, Dreikurs would ask members of the audience what they understood about the problem at hand or the family dynamics; at other times he would launch a discussion on certain issues common to many families. In this way, the parents helped each other in the realization that they were not alone in facing these problems or in making mistakes in managing their children. Frequently, they more readily accepted an explanation or suggestion given to another parent than when it was given directly to them.

The work of the clinic was augmented with services available through the center, including consultations with schools, use of special resources of other agencies, therapeutic groups for children conducted by a social worker under Dreikurs's supervision, and the center's camp located in Milton Junction, Wisconsin, where Dreikurs served as a psychiatric consultant. Apart from the weekly clinic sessions, Dreikurs met monthly with the center staff to discuss cases and conducted a weekly lecture-discussion on child rearing that was well attended by social workers, teachers, and parents.

During the clinic's first season, from February to May 1939, eighteen families were counseled that included thirty-six children and twenty-three adults whose combined clinical visits totaled 184. It was a slow start; on some days not a single family appeared. As the fall 1939 season got underway, the number of families counseled began to increase.

After three years of operation, Baker reported on the clinic's work:

> The Settlement provides an excellent base for the establishment of a child guidance clinic. People are more apt to go for assistance to an agency with which they are already acquainted and which they know is interested in the welfare of their children and themselves. . . . A fairly tangible and fruitful method of parent education, . . . this particular type of psychiatric work, especially the group treatment in the clinic, is uncommonly found in this country and . . . offers a rich field for experimental procedure.[19]

With staff, parents, and children regularly involved in the clinic's activities, attitudes began to change. Before long, the children no longer made fun of those who traveled the elevator to the fourth floor; they too wanted to see the "doctor."

While they were not immediately obvious, there were several important consequences of Dreikurs's first clinic. For one, it vividly demonstrated to a small but dedicated group a totally new way of working with troubled families that differed from the entrenched model in both its assumptions about human behavior and its methods of working with families. Its effectiveness was evident and gave many people cause to reconsider the Freudian assumptions previously accepted without question. The doubt and suspicion raised in many minds by the idea of open group counseling and the treatment of entire families as a psychodynamic unit was dispelled. A few grasped the superiority of this approach for effectively reaching widely into the community. Forty families were counseled in the first three years. That might seem like a small number, but there were at most only eighty-five clinic sessions during that period, totaling no more than 213 hours. These forty families translated into 137 adults and children who were the direct recipients of the counseling, besides many in the audience who benefited from what they saw and heard.

Dreikurs's earliest opportunity to practice his ideas with American families involved him with the most discouraged and problem-ridden families in the city—the poor, undereducated racial and ethnic minorities. Working with poor people was neither new to Dreikurs nor a challenge he sought to avoid. They had been a significant part of all his efforts in Vienna.

The fundamental Adlerian concept of inferiority feelings and compensatory striving provided new insight for fathoming the aspirations, anger, and despair that have characterized minority groups in recent decades. Frantz Fanon, the black psychiatrist who militantly fought the oppression of black people, condemned most psychiatry as irrelevant to the black experience. But, he remarked: "Adler will help us to understand the conception of the world held by the man of color."[20]

Dreikurs was not an elitist, nor did he ever use his expertise to demonstrate a superiority over others. He came from the homogeneous white world of Europe, and candidly admitted to being color conscious. But then who in America, whether black or white, is not, in view of our history of race relations? But he was not racially prejudiced, and he deplored the racial myths and segregationist policies of society. By actions as well as in words, Dreikurs demonstrated a genuine egalitarian attitude.

Commenting on this aspect of Dreikurs's character, Elizabeth Baker remarked: "Since residents, staff and participants in both Lincoln Center and camp were of all races, creeds and national origins, it was particularly gratifying that Dr. Dreikurs had no feelings of rejection to anyone on this basis. This tremendously simplified the work with groups of children and adults since it was [based] solely on their human problems without any overlay of false 'sociology' which is often an impediment to professional people."[21]

With the surge of black militancy in the late 1960s, Dreikurs was occasionally confronted by hostile blacks as he crisscrossed the nation tirelessly lecturing and demonstrating his principles. They challenged his "right" as a symbolic member of the white middle-class establishment to presume to understand the black experience or to offer anything of relevance to them. His response was direct and simple—all human behavior is purposeful. It is directed toward goals in line with the individual's subjective perception of himself in relation to the world. The life style—the unique expression of those convictions for each individual—is understandable whether he be black or white. Adlerian psychology provides a technique for revealing the life style. It does not impose values but exposes the values embodied in it. Dreikurs would invite these militants to stay, watch what he did, and then judge whether it was relevant to their experience.

Those few who worked with Dreikurs in those early years in Chicago witnessed his dedication to and effectiveness with the many black families who sought to raise their children under the most difficult economic and social conditions. These families helped inspire one of Dreikurs's most important contributions in psychology, the four goals of misbehavior in children.

The Four Goals of Misbehavior

First and most importantly throughout his life, Dreikurs was a teacher. He never played the part of an exalted physician who, as if by some special magic, touched the troubled soul and made him well. Therapy or counseling was, in his view, education. While psychoanalysts were pushing mothers into psychotherapy on the ground that children's problems were mostly caused by their mothers' deep, unresolved conflicts. Dreikurs countered: "Mothers don't need therapy, what they need is education. Even a psychotic mother can be a good parent if only she learns what to do." Regardless of whom he worked with, whether a deeply disturbed adult at the hospital, a distressed parent, a rebellious youth, or a young child at the clinic, his primary objective was to educate. His aim was to reveal to the client his fictitious or mistaken goals of which he was only dimly, if at all, aware.[22] Once his goal was revealed, the client could understand how his convictions contributed to his present predicament and see the possibility of choosing different, more appropriate behaviors.

To teach is to communicate. Dreikurs felt compelled by circumstances to recast his ideas in the most systematic and concrete ways possible. To overcome the difficulties imposed by working in a second language, Dreikurs had to sharpen his listening skills, and then quickly translate his concepts from German to English in order to maintain the spontaneity required by the dialectic nature of Adlerian counseling. He was also challenged to help others look at behavior from the standpoint of goals and purposes rather than from antecedent causes. Mechanistic and causal thinking so pervaded people's perception of behavior that it required a reorientation of their reasoning processes to think in terms of goals. Finally, working with underprivileged, poorly educated black families at Lincoln Center forced Dreikurs to express himself clearly and simply.

From these compelling demands, Dreikurs made a significant discovery: that the misbehavior of children, no matter how varied their personality or background, followed one or more of four distinctive goals. These were (1) to gain undue attention (AGM, or Attention Getting Mechanism); (2) to demonstrate power or defiance; (3) to seek revenge or retaliation; or (4) to give up in complete discouragement. Starting from the basic Adlerian assumption that man is a social being whose behavior is purposeful, Dreikurs reasoned that the fundamental goal of the child's behavior is to feel that he belongs, with a sense of social acceptance and contribution. This goal develops from infancy as the child seeks to find his place in his family of adults and siblings, moves outside the family to peer relationships in the school years, and embraces the community-at-large as he enters adolescence and adulthood.

"But," as Dreikurs explained, "even the child who misbehaves and defies the requirements and needs of the situation still believes that his actions will give him social status. He may try to get attention or attempt to prove his power, or he may seek revenge or display his deficiency. . . . Whichever of these four goals he adopts, his behavior is based on his conviction that only in this way can he function within the group. His goal may occasionally vary with circumstances; he may act to attract attention at one moment, and assert his power or seek revenge at another."[23]

The crucial point, Dreikurs discovered, was that the mistaken goal could be recognized by the effects it had on others and by the impulsive reaction of adults. Whatever one is inclined to do to the child when he misbehaves is generally identical with the child's expectation. By giving undue attention, engaging in a power struggle, seeking mutual retaliation, or giving up in despair, the parent's or teacher's reaction always reflects the goal of the child. This was a fruitful discovery because it revealed how and when, in the thousandfold transactions between adult and child, the child's misbehavior is reinforced by the adult's behavior.

Teaching the adult to change his pattern of reacting to the child's provocation forces the child to seek new ways to gain social acceptance. If, simultaneously, the adults are taught genuinely to encourage the child, they are on their way to a new, cooperative, and healthful relationship. The reaction of the adult to the child's provoking actions also offers a definitive clue to determining which mistaken goal the child is pursuing. For example, many typical misbehaviors—laziness, underachievement, lying, stealing, bed-wetting—are all behaviors that can be an expression of any one of the four goals. Knowing which goal is operating for a particular behavior provides immediate insight into the seriousness of the misbehavior and indicates how to handle it.

When Dreikurs revealed to a child his mistaken goal, he did so in a hypothetical manner. This avoided the possibility of sounding accusatory or judgmental and, at the same time, intrigued the child to follow along with the line of reasoning. For example, to a child whose mother complained of continually having to intercede in fights between siblings, Dreikurs might guess from the mother's annoyance that the purpose of the behavior was to gain undue attention. To the child he would ask: "Could it be that you fight with your brother just to keep your mother busy with you?" The child's reaction was critical. If Dreikurs guessed correctly, the child would impulsively say yes or show his affirmation by a curious roguish grin that Dreikurs termed "the recognition reflex." The reflex was the child's spontaneous reaction to the sudden feeling of being understood. If he guessed incorrectly, there was no such response from the child, and Dreikurs then knew he must guess again to ascertain the correct goal of the behavior.

In the decades that followed, Dreikurs claimed that he never encountered a youngster (preadolescent)[24] whose misbehavior did not fall into one of these four mistaken goal patterns, although it might be expressed in some different manner. When challenged on the universality of his claim or asked if there were not other goals of misbehavior, Dreikurs would remark: "I have no scientific proof, but I have found it empirically true in all my clinical work. If someone can ever demonstrate a fifth or sixth goal, I will be happy to incorporate it into my system." Dreikurs also commented that these four goals could be found in Adler's writings about children and that he simply identified and developed them into a systematic conceptual scheme.

The four goals and the recognition reflex were two of Dreikurs's most important contributions for understanding and correcting children's behavior. Countless therapists, counselors, and teachers have benefited from using them in their work with children.

Notes for Chapter 12

1. Murray Levine, and Adeline Levine, *A Social History of the Helping Services* (New York: Appleton-Century-Croft, 1970).

2. Lloyd Demause, *Hist. Childhood Quarterly* 1 (1973).

3. Walter Bromberg, *The Mind of Man* (New York: Harper & Bros., 1959): p. 239.

4. Levine and Levine, *A Social History*, pp. 161–162.

5. Irene M. Josselyn, *Psychosocial Development of Children* (New York: Family Service Association, 1948). There is a certain irony that in America, with its great penchant for eclectic, empirical, and practical considerations, the Freudian model of child development was adopted to such a pervasive degree. Freud's theory of the psychosexual stages of development in children was developed retrospectively from his work with adults and was the weakest component of his conceptual thinking. His first child analysis, the famous case of Hans, was not handled directly by Freud, as he never met the child. Rather, the case grew out of his discussions with the boy's father, who was a student of psychoanalysis. In fairness to Freud, his original theorizing in this area was couched in conjectural terms, but the hypothetical quality was soon converted into "proven scientific laws" by his enthusiastic followers. Nonetheless, the embarrassment caused by the repeated failure of research to find any universal psychosexual stages in children did not result in any serious challenge to Freudian theory until rather recently. By contrast, Adler's concept of childhood development, his ideas concerning inferiority feelings, the impact of siblings on personality development, the origins of the life style in early childhood, and the purposiveness of all behavior grew out of his extensive work with normal as well as disturbed children as part of his practice of general medicine. Likewise, his therapeutic methods with children evolved from his empirical findings with large numbers of children from all walks of life.

6. Robert E. Lee Faris and H. Warren Dunbar, *Mental Disorders in Urban Areas* (Chicago: University of Chicago Press, 1939).

7. Leo Kanner, "Trends in Child Psychiatry," *Journal of Mental Science* 105 (1959): 581–593. In one of the rare cases of agreement between Freud and Adler, both felt that the practice of psychology should not be restricted to the medical profession. Historically, this has held true within the Adlerian school, where there have been relatively few psychiatrists as compared with the number of practicing psychologists and education specialists. The Freudian movement, by contrast, took a sharp turn toward the medical model in 1938, when the American Psychoanalytic Association ruled against authorizing anyone to practice psychoanalysis who was not trained in medicine and, further, laid down stringent training requirements for the medical analysts.

8. Levine and Levine, *A Social History*, p. 5.

9. Dreikurs, to his family, Report no. 25, December 1, 1937. Dreikurs Papers.

10. Dreikurs-Mackaness interview.

11. Eunice M. Prutsman, "Report of Four Sessions of Our Child Guidance Clinic," Morton High School, Cicero, Illinois, 1939, mimeographed. Dreikurs Papers.

12. Ibid.

13. Ibid. Dreikurs received $25 per weekly session for his services. During the four-week experiment, the fees were collected by charging participating adults and students 50¢ and 25¢ respectively for each session attended. In several cases, teachers paid for students out of their own pockets.

14. Eunice M. Prutsman. "Counseling Committee Report," Morton High School, Cicero, Illinois, 1939, mimeographed. Dreikurs Papers.

15. From today's perspective, Dreikurs's involvement might not seem extraordinary. Actually it was quite unusual because psychiatric counseling services in public schools were rare, and the Chicago schools had been particularly uninterested in providing psychological services for students. See Mary J. Herrick, *The Chicago Schools: A Social and Political History* (Beverly Hills, Calif.: Sage Publications, 1971).

16. Elizabeth Hoyt Baker, *The Integration of Case Work and Group Work at Abraham Lincoln Center* (Chicago: Abraham Lincoln Center, 1942).

17. Elizabeth Hoyt Baker (Henderson) to Raymond J. Corsini, June 27, 1967, Dreikurs Papers.

18. Harold Marley, "Beginnings in America," in *Adlerian Family Counseling: A Manual*, ed. Rudolf Dreikurs, Raymond Corsini, Raymond Lowe, and Manford Sonstegard (Eugene, Ore.: University of Oregon Press, 1959).

19. Elizabeth Hoyt Baker, "Child Guidance Clinic at Abraham Lincoln Center," *Individual Psychology Bulletin* 2 (1942): 49–58.

20. Frantz Fanon, *Black Skin, White Masks* (New York: Grove Press, 1967).

21. Elizabeth Hoyt Baker (Henderson), op cit.

22. By being "only dimly aware" of the goals that direct our behavior and attitudes, Dreikurs did not mean that there was a dichotomy between conscious and unconscious motivations. Following Adler, Dreikurs treated *unconscious* as an adjective rather than a noun, thus avoiding reifying the concept. For Dreikurs, that which is unconscious is the nonunderstood, and he drew an appropriate analogy from the characteristic functioning of perception:

> The retina receives visual impressions, but only a small central part of the retina can give us clear pictures of objects, in regard both to shape and color. The further away from the center, the more vague are the impressions. We need a wide field of vision to keep us informed about what is going on around us; if something becomes interesting, important or threatening, we focus our eyes on the object, using the small area that permits clear vision. We can compare this center with conscious perception, and the rest of the vague impressions with the various degrees of awareness. . . . Adler maintained that there is hardly anything in us that we do not know at all, and nothing that we fully know. . . . There is a continuum from the known to the unknown. . . . We operate on a psychological economy principle: we know of ourselves only what we need or want to know. What we do not need to know for our functioning or what we do not like to know, remains totally or partially unknown (Rudolf Dreikurs, *Social Equality: The Challenge of Today* [Chicago: Henry Regner, 1971], pp. 47–48).

The purpose of confronting adults and children with their goals was to bring them into sharp focus, into a state of full awareness and knowledge.

23. Rudolf Dreikurs, "The Immediate Purpose of Children's Mis-behavior, Its Recognition and Correction," *Internationale Zeitschrift für Individualpsychologie* 19 (1950): 70. Dreikurs first mentioned his discovery of the four goals of misbehavior in an article published by *Camping Magazine* in 1940. Over the next few years, he developed and elaborated his ideas and gave a detailed account of how they functioned and could be corrected in his *Manual of Child Guidance* (Chicago: Chicago Medical School, 1945). These ideas were later incorporated in his major books, *The Challenge of Parenthood* (1948), *Psychology in the Classroom* (1957), *Children: The Challenge* (1964), and *Maintaining Sanity in the Classroom* (1971).

24. "Adults," Dreikurs wrote, "have the same fundamental attitudes which they had as children; but in the process of adolescence they learn, for appearance's sake, to

subordinate them to the pattern set by society. The successful accomplishment of covering up one's real intentions and motivations is then called maturity. The child who has not yet reached this stage of 'maturity' . . . openly demonstrates his attitudes. It is possible, therefore, to recognize the goals of child behavior by mere observation" ("The Four Goals of the Maladjusted Child," *Nervous Child* 6 [1947]: 321). Because adolescents are in the process of adopting the mask of adulthood—defense actions, rationalizations, and putting up a front—one cannot confront them with their underlying goals in as direct a fashion as when working with children.

Additional References

John C. Burnham, "The Struggle Between Physicians and Paramedical Personnel in American Psychiatry, 1917–1941," *Journal of the History of Medicine* 29 (1974): 93–106.

Edna Hanson, "The Child Guidance Clinic of Abraham Lincoln Center: History, Purposes, Techniques and Results," *Individual Psychology Bulletin* 4 (1944/1945): 49–58.

Joint Commission on Mental Health of Children, *Crisis in Child Mental Health: Challenge for the Seventies* (New York: Harper & Row, 1970).

Oliver H. Osborne and Helen Nakagawa, "Distortions and Distinction in Community Mental Health," *International Journal of Social Psychiatry* 19 (1973): 121–128.

Sheldon T. Selesnick, "Historical Perspectives in the Development of Child Psychiatry," *International Journal of Psychiatry* 3 (1967): 363–382.

George S. Stevenson and Geddes Smith, *Child Guidance Clinics: A Quarter Century of Development* (New York: Commonwealth Fund, 1934).

Gerald Weinberger, "Some Common Assumptions Underlying Traditional Psychotherapy: Fallacy and Reformulation," *Psychotherapy: Theory, Research & Practice* 9 (1972): 149–152.

13

Hull House

Love is not an emotion—love is a relationship.
Rudolf Dreikurs
Challenge of Marriage

The most unexpected and joyful outcome of Dreikurs's significant but modest venture at Abraham Lincoln Center was meeting Sadie Ellis Garland. Known to friends as "Tee," she later became his devoted wife and partner—his "super-duper ego, severest critic, most trusted friend, devil's advocate, and best-trained student," as he often described her with loving approbation.

A gentle and soft-spoken woman, then in her late thirties, Sadie nonetheless drew attention because of her unusual beauty, her fine features, her slight hint of solemnity and dignified bearing. Graceful and with an artistic aura, she radiated a natural elegance no matter what the occasion.

When they first met, she was married to Leon Garland, who also was an accomplished artist but in failing health. Sadie's background, temperament, and personality contrasted with Rudolf's in every way. No one, Sadie and Rudolf included, could have had the slightest inkling of the rich life they would come to share.

Sadie was born and raised in Chicago, the middle child with an older sister and a younger brother. From her older sister she acquired the childhood nickname Teetaw, which was later shortened to Tee. Her parents were Lithuanian Jews, who migrated to America and settled in a mostly Italian neighborhood. At first they adhered to strict Orthodox Jewish traditions, but as the family became Americanized they became less orthodox, although Tee always maintained close ties to Juadism and a fascination with the history of her people.

The most significant influence on Sadie's development was her friendship with Blanche Magiolli, a girl of Italian background who lived in the neighborhood. When they first met, Sadie was eleven. She fashioned herself after her friend Blanche and decided that she too would be an artist. Blanche studied painting at Hull House when Jane Addams was at the height of her career and deeply involved in all the programs and the people who came there.

"Blanche dragged me along with her," Sadie remembers, "and I mean literally dragged me, because my parents objected to my going. Being in a strictly Italian neighborhood, they feared that if I had Italian friends, then, of course, I would eventually marry one, which just wouldn't do. But they got over their objection once they realized how extremely interested we were in what we were doing. We attended music classes and art classes, but by the time I was twelve, we both switched completely to art. Jane Addams became interested in us because our art teacher thought both of us very talented."[1]

When Sadie was fifteen, she and Blanche, with Addams's help, were awarded scholarships to study at the Art Institute of Chicago. Shortly thereafter, Sadie had to give up her scholarship and go to work when her father's business failed. But at eighteen she was again at Hull House studying art and especially painting. One of her teachers was Leon Garland, a resident at Hull House who designed fabrics and taught batik as well as being a talented painter. For the next several years, Sadie worked, studied, and painted, spending much time at the House among the culturally rich circle of artists and intellectuals who resided and worked there. As a volunteer, she conducted art classes for children and acquired considerable experience trying to help juvenile delinquents work out their problems through group painting and other art techniques.

When she was twenty-seven, she and Leon were married. Jane Addams feted them with a wedding party. It was a marriage Sadie characterized as verging on the idyllic. They worked and painted together at Hull House, jointly exhibited their works, and enjoyed a wide circle of friends. In 1929 they left Chicago to spend two glorious years studying painting in Paris. When they returned in September 1930, they resumed their previous life at Hull House, but the depression intruded, and they found they could no longer make a living working exclusively as artists.

At that time there was a growing demand for social workers. The United Charities of Chicago called Jane Addams asking for help from her residents. Because of her earlier work with delinquents Sadie was considered the best prepared to do social work, and began working with the United Charities. Not long afterward, Jane Addams prophetically advised her,

"You'd better take some courses and really qualify yourself, because it seems you are going to stay in this field a long time."

So Sadie began studying social work at the University of Chicago. Because of her full-time job, she had to take evening and weekend courses and found herself with less and less time for painting.

Then tragedy struck. In 1934, Leon suffered a massive heart attack, from which he never fully recovered. With him no longer able to work and needing constant care, Sadie quit her job as a case supervisor with the Cook County Bureau of Public Welfare and returned to Hull House, where Jane Addams found a paying job for her as a case consultant. It was about this time that Sadie gave up her painting and switched all her energies to social work.

"First of all," she explained, "there was the need of the situation. I became very busy with my work and it took all my time. Second, there was a certain sense of competition between us in art. People began to say, 'You're the better painter of the two.' This I didn't like because Leon was ill, and I didn't want to be in competition with him."

A year later, in 1935, Jane Addams, the indomitable champion of humanitarian causes and one of the rare women ever awarded the Nobel Prize, died at age seventy-five. For those like Leon and Sadie who lived and worked with her at Hull House, the loss was immeasurable.

After her death, Sadie intermittently served as acting director of Hull House until a new permanent director could be found. When Charlotte Carr was appointed director in 1937, Sadie continued to work as director of community services and as a case consultant.

At about this time, the staff at Hull House encountered critical juvenile problems as the neighborhood rapidly changed from Italian and Greek to Mexican and black. Street warfare erupted as the Italian and Greek youths ganged up on the newcomers. Juvenile crime, always a part of the downtrodden neighborhood of Hull House, skyrocketed in quantity and in the level of violence. There were stabbings, vandalism, and larceny. The House became unsafe. The kids broke in, wrecked pianos, and stole whatever they could. As the number of juvenile offenders daily mounted, the juvenile court, not wanting to sentence so many, gave the offenders a last chance: they could go to Hull House and mend their ways.

"It was my assignment," Sadie recalled, "to accomplish this impossible task . . . impossible because we really didn't know what to do. My training at the University of Chicago was the traditional kind in the social services with the obligatory courses in psychoanalysis. I had been fortunate to study with the best, Franz Alexander and Karen Horney. We learned about the Oedipus complex, mother fixations, and the like, but what could we do with this knowledge in individual cases? There was nothing I could apply, no advise I could give my group of workers at Hull House."

In desperation, she consulted with other social workers in the city hoping to find some effective way for dealing with the mounting problems. Elizabeth Baker, her colleague who worked at Abraham Lincoln Center, understood immediately the difficulties she faced and mentioned that there was a Viennese psychiatrist who had recently come to Chicago and was giving a course at her center for dealing with the disturbing child. "Perhaps," she suggested to Sadie, "you would like to join the class."

"Well," Sadie replied,

> I'll join anything if I can find out what to do.
>
> I arrived rather late the first evening I came, and my initial experience of Rudolf Dreikurs as I entered the room was to hear him deliver a tirade against social workers—their inability to understand, their endless fact gathering and not knowing what to do with all their facts, etcetera, etcetera. I was tempted to walk out. I did not come to be insulted. But he caught my eye and stopped his harsh critique long enough to say enthusiastically, "Come in, come in, join us."
>
> I did. The man nearly scared me to death! He frightened me with his aggressive manner, because I'm rather cautious and quiet in my own approach. I also had some difficulty understanding him, as his accent was very thick at that time. I did become intrigued with his dynamic presentation and analysis of a case. But at the same time, I was shocked by his forthright criticism of psychoanalysis, of social workers, of teachers—in other words, the establishment.

The next day, Baker called to ask what impressed her, and Sadie said she was frightened by the man and did not plan to return. Baker urged her to give it another try, and she reluctantly agreed.

At the next session, Dreikurs demonstrated how to understand a case record by reading it a sentence at a time, interpreting each sentence for its meaning in order to discover quickly the dynamic pattern of the behavior.[2] This was a very effective technique discovered by Adler but rarely used as an interpretive strategy by other psychological schools. Most training emphasized the opposite, to keep gathering as much data as possible before attempting any interpretation. Dreikurs wanted to show the value of this strategy, and he asked Sadie to start reading the case.

"I sat down beside him," Sadie recalled,

> and I froze completely. Not one word issued from my mouth. I was so scared, I couldn't speak. He sensed my anxiety and excused me.
>
> After class, he invited me to have coffee with him. I declined because my sick husband was waiting for me at home and I didn't want to take the time. But he persisted, suggesting that he accompany me on the streetcar so that we could talk and perhaps briefly stop for coffee near Hull House. So we did. We found a small Mexican café on Halsted Street, entered, and ordered coffee.
>
> Suddenly, Rudolf spotted a pinball machine in the corner. He got up, went over to it, and proceeded to have a ball playing it. I was offended, said good-night, and left. Later, as I mulled over the incident, I suddenly saw him out of the role of the teacher and expert. I realized that he was also someone who was not only human but almost a little boy thoroughly relishing a new toy. I became fascinated by this multifaceted man and lost my fear of him. Although I still felt like an offended princess. . . .
>
> At the next class, he didn't call on me, and I was able to relax and listen. I became more accustomed to his approach, and once I tried out something he suggested. I brought up a case, he made a suggestion, I tried it, and it worked very well. This completely new approach was a little startling to me. But after I tried one thing and it worked, I became more open to it. My reluctance to speak frankly to children, to jump into a situation, changed immediately, and I stopped my endless pursuit of case material as I had been trained to do.

Charlotte Carr, the capable director at Hull House, got enthusiastic reports about Dreikurs's class from Sadie. Carr then invited Dreikurs to present his ideas to a group of settlement workers who met regularly at Hull House. Dreikurs was delighted to accept. There, his ideas were favorably received. Particularly impressed by what Dreikurs had to offer, Carr invited him to become a resident at Hull House.

Late in 1940, Dreikurs, his sister Bertha, Eric, and Eva moved into a spacious apartment at Hull House and became part of its stimulating community. Reminiscent of the socially and intellectually rich atmosphere of bygone years in Vienna, Rudolf felt at home and thoroughly relished the spontaneous and hearty debates and the treasured interludes of music that were part of life at Hull House. In his apartment, his magnificent hand-carved grand piano, shipped from Vienna, had become the focal point, around which old and new friends regularly gathered for Sunday evenings of chamber music.

Dreikurs consulted daily with the Hull House staff, and especially with Sadie Garland, who was in charge of all social services. A close working relationship developed between them as she studied and implemented his techniques in her work. Together they conducted several experimental programs, and early in 1941, a second child guidance clinic was opened at Hull House in the Mary Crane Nursery Center.

Leon Garland also became Rudolf's friend, although at times he was exasperated by Rudolf's criticism of modern painting. It was amusing to Sadie and Leon that Rudolf, who was a daring pioneer in psychology, was so conservative regarding art and music. With humor and patience, they taught him to appreciate modern art and music.

A Colleague from Vienna

With the opening of a second clinic at Hull House plus his frequent lectures and classes at the settlement houses or in conjunction with the Chicago Adlerian Society, Dreikurs found the demands on his time increasingly burdensome. Fortunately, Elly Redwin (formerly Rotwein), a Viennese colleague, was now able to join him in his work.

She began a career as a piano teacher but switched to social work, training at the Municipal School of Social Work and at the University of Vienna. For four years she studied with Adler, putting his ideas into practice in the children's home and summer camp she operated in Vienna and in three Adlerian child guidance clinics where she served as a counselor. She and Dreikurs shared a touch of the rebel, which gave them the courage to go against the mainstream. Dreikurs was instrumental in getting Elly to Chicago after she wrote to him desperately seeking a way out of Vienna.

"I will never forget," she recalled, "the great relief I felt when his answer came: 'I will get you an affidavit from one of our Adlerian friends here. The beginning will be hard for you. I have no job myself; it is a big struggle. But come. You will find some job, and maybe we can start a child guidance center together.'"[3]

By 1941, Redwin was able to link forces with Dreikurs, working regularly at Hull House and Abraham Lincoln Center and helping to establish a third clinic in 1942 at Marcy Center, a settlement house located in a largely Jewish neighborhood on the near west side of Chicago. Shortly thereafter, a fourth clinic was begun, at the University of Chicago Settlement House, located in a congested Mexican and Polish neighborhood near the stockyards. In addition, she developed mothers' groups and lectured for the local Adlerian Society.

For more than thirty years, until Dreikurs's death and her retirement a year later in 1973, Redwin remained a stalwart, dependable co-worker in the Chicago centers.

In the Lion's Den at Michael Reese

The rent-free accommodations at Hull House helped ease the financial burden Dreikurs still faced nearly three years after his arrival in Chicago. The child guidance clinics and the lectures and classes to which he gave his time and energy so freely were mostly a labor of love that added little to his meager income.

After completing his internship in 1939 at Michael Reese Hospital, Dreikurs was appointed an assistant clinic physician in the neuropsychiatric department at Michael Reese. Much of his energy was spent studying for his medical boards, an onerous task for a foreign-born whose medical training had ended fifteen years earlier. The first time Dreikurs took the exams, he flunked in two subjects; he passed, however, at the next examination. Late in 1939, his license in hand, he opened a small private practice in the heart of Chicago. Since he could not hope to earn an adequate income in the beginning, he continued as a clinic physician at Michael Reese through June 1942.

Throughout the years he spent at Michael Reese, Dreikurs did open battle with the entrenched psychoanalysts who dominated the psychiatric services of the hospital. Of course, Dreikurs often provoked the battle by his searing questions and accurately aimed criticisms. This did not sit well with his Freudian colleagues. He became a nasty thorn in their side, and they in turn did everything in their power to humiliate him and put him in his place. They assigned him the most undesirable patients and relished taking him to task whenever possible.

But in one instance, their efforts to put Dreikurs in his place backfired. He was assigned a number of patients with whom nobody wanted to work, who were regarded as unresponsive to therapy and therefore were routinely treated with drugs to keep them from being a nuisance. Most of them were elderly women who were either totally antagonistic to therapy or who felt hopelessly defeated by their unfavorable living conditions.

"For me," Dreikurs stated, "if a person needs help, I do whatever I can. I started group therapy with these old women who were considered completely beyond psychiatric help. When they got into the group, they began to perk up, to regain hope about their lives, and to get well. . . . Some of the chronic cases made a rather good adjustment. It was quite a miraculous thing."[4]

Later, when Dreikurs wrote about the importance of group psychotherapy, the improvement of these women, referred to him under the most negative circumstances, supported his contention that one great advantage of group over individual therapy is that it can open the door to reaching the most resistant, inaccessible, and rigid personalities.[5]

The enmity between Dreikurs and the Freudians at Michael Reese steadily festered as Dreikurs lectured and worked more widely in the community, attacking psychoanalysis and attracting attention to his Adlerian ideas. This drew the ire of Roy R. Grinker, chief of the psychiatric department at Michael Reese. Grinker, at that time, championed psychoanalysis as the *only* valid form of psychiatry and sought to make his department a bastion of pure psychoanalysis. But there was Dreikurs, an annoying fly in the ointment, audaciously criticizing its methods. In a spate of letters, Grinker tried to stop Dreikurs from claiming any affiliation with the prestigious Michael Reese Hospital.

Dreikurs responded:

> Rudolf Dreikurs, M.D.
> Psychiatrist
> 612 North Michigan Avenue
> Chicago, Illinois
> May 20, 1941

Dear Dr. Grinker:

I have the honor of informing you that the letter confirming my appointment at Michael Reese Hospital, dated July 2nd, 1940, contains the following statement:

> ". . . at the meeting of the Board of Directors of Michael Reese Hospital held June 25th, 1940, you were reappointed Assistant Clinic Physician in the Department of Neuro-Psychiatry. . . ."

I felt and feel that this gives me the right and privilege of regarding myself as a member of the Neuro-psychiatric staff of Michael Reese Hospital in the capacity of Clinical Physician.

Very sincerely yours,

Rudolf Dreikurs, M.D.[6]

For years after he left Michael Reese, Dreikurs tasted the biting sting of retaliation at the hands of the Freudians. With their strong ties to the powerful medical establishment and their esteemed position in the community, they used every opportunity to discredit Dreikurs, to discourage others from having any dealings with him, and to prevent his access to funds and programs in the Chicago area. They rarely attacked him openly; rather, they relied upon subtle innuendo and behind-the-scenes maneuvers.

One example of their powerful influence occurred a few years after the Morton School experiment. In the interim period, Dreikurs assembled the results of that experiment and wrote a report and proposal for implementing such guidance programs in public schools. He hoped to get the paper published and submitted a copy to Florence Hosch, executive secretary of the Illinois Board of Public Welfare Commissioners, for suggestions about an appropriate journal. After considerable delay, she replied: "I have received some comments from others and I will pass them on to you. At the outset since your approach is Adlerian your paper would not be acceptable to the Mental Hygiene organization or the American Journal of Psychiatry."[7]

Such incidents, and there were others, where his ideas were turned down not on their merits but simply because he was identified as an Adlerian, infuriated Dreikurs. Instead of discouraging him, they only steeled his resolve to succeed.

THE WIDENING SPHERE OF INFLUENCE

The years that Dreikurs lived at Hull House, 1940–1943, were filled with ever-widening activities that overshadowed his unrelenting financial hardship and the opposition and resistance he had to overcome as he pursued new ideas and plans. With the establishment of the child guidance clinics, he won the begrudging admiration of his more cautious Adlerian colleagues who earlier had scoffed at him. The old Adlerian

Society, small and largely ineffectual, began to change. Nita Arnold, his former nemesis, left Chicago for the West Coast, and Dreikurs, with his dynamic and visionary qualities, became the unquestioned leader. He attracted a following of dedicated Chicagoans from the fields of medicine, social work, and education. Two of his most remarkable qualities were clearly in evidence by this time—his unflinching optimism and his ability to inspire and encourage others. His optimism was the direct source of his ability to encourage others. "Constructive provocation," his old friend Harold Marley put it. "He was a *pusher* to his everlasting credit and to the profit of those he galvanized into more action and additional education."[8]

Adaline Starr, who later became a specialist in psychodrama and a key member of his office staff, recalled her reaction when she first met Dreikurs in 1940:

> The first time I cast my eyes upon him was when I joined my friends May Simkin and Eve Culper to participate in one of his mothers' study groups. At the time I was a housewife with a daughter three years old. We went to his little office on Michigan Avenue for a weekly afternoon session, for which he charged all of fifty cents. Who were we, just a few young women, really nobody. And here he was, from Europe, an established figure, spending his time with us, devoting as much of himself as he would when he went off for a big lecture. He did our life styles. I was very amazed by it, and good things came out of it. Our studies with him spilled over into social activities, and we often spent evenings with him, our husbands, and some young woman he was currently dating. He invited us to join the IP [Individual Psychology] Association, which I did. My background was in teaching creative dramatics and working in amateur theater productions. Before long, I was working in the child guidance clinics doing creative drama with the children on a voluntary basis.[9]

Now in the prime of his life, healthy and vigorous, Dreikurs developed a pace of life best described as that of a human dynamo. His activities included his work at the hospital, his private office practice with a growing number of patients, his involvement with the IP Association, his counseling at the child guidance clinics and in conjunction with them his training sessions with the settlement-house workers, and his study groups with mothers. In one year, it was recorded that he had delivered ninety

lectures around Chicago on various aspects of Adlerian psychology, ranging from child rearing, delinquency, and marital problems to strictly
psychiatric topics, such as neurosis, and presented to such diverse groups
as PTAs, lodges, colleges, the Jewish Peoples' Institute, and Northwestern
University.[10] Though still relatively unknown and lacking any prestigious
institutional backing, Dreikurs was visible in the Chicago community as
he cast his controversial ideas like so many seeds, hoping that here or
there they would take root and flourish.

He was always a dynamic and forceful speaker, and no one ever felt
bored by or neutral to his lectures. Those who agreed with him felt
inspired, those who disagreed felt angry. In all cases, he sought to disrupt
complacency, to prod, to get under people's skin. "I first heard Dr. Dreikurs in 1938," an admirer wrote, "he was addressing a large audience
sponsored by the Women's International League for Peace and Freedom,
and he held them spellbound with his insightful and revealing explanations . . . opening up new vistas for people."[11] Whether he was talking to
a dozen people or to a crowd of several hundred, his strong voice boomed
into the space with enthusiasm and authority. Nobody ever slept through
a speech by Rudolf Dreikurs.

Humor was his saving grace; his speeches were always peppered with
delightful anecdotes. He firmly believed that humor was one of the best
therapeutic weapons against the frustrations of life. He could turn his
humor to himself, laughing heartily with the audience as he played havoc
with the language with malapropisms such as, "You hit the nail on the
top" and "My books sell like pancakes!" Sadie recalled that when he first
began to lecture on marriage and the revolution between the sexes, he
would begin with a dramatic pronouncement: " 'Today, the positions of
men and women have changed'—which immediately broke up the audience. It took him some time until he finally got that straightened out."

Somehow in this hubbub of activity Dreikurs found time to gather case
materials and research for his future publications on marriage, family life,
and child rearing. He also picked up the pen once again, and his first
articles written in English appeared in 1940.

Busy as he was, he diligently maintained his correspondence with
numerous Adlerians. Outside Chicago, the only other organized Adlerian
group was in New York City and was centered around Adler's widow,
Raissa, whose leadership was limited since she had never been a practicing therapist and could do little more than inspire and encourage others
to keep up their work. In New York, the Freudian domination of the

mental health professions was even more oppressive than in Chicago, and the activities of the New York group were confined to giving lectures and exchanging ideas at meetings attended mostly by fellow Adlerians, with little or no public exposure. In the entire nation there were less than one hundred people who identified themselves as Individual Psychologists. Those outside New York or Chicago had no means for communicating and exchanging ideas, which is so vital to the growth and development of any school of thought.

The letters Dreikurs received greatly distressed him as he grasped the paralyzed condition of Adlerian psychology. In Chicago he fearlessly championed the legitimacy and relevancy of Adlerian psychology at every possible opportunity. But overall, Adlerian psychology was at its nadir and fast disappearing as an actively taught or practiced system.

Dreikurs decided that action was necessary to counteract the debilitating professional isolation his Adlerian colleagues experienced. He needed a vehicle to encourage and inspire them, to convince them of the vitality and crucial importance of their training and outlook. With the backing and volunteer support of the Chicago IP Association, Dreikurs launched the *Individual Psychology Newsletter* in October 1940. It, too, had a humble beginning as a small mimeographed affair that initially provided book reviews, reports of Adlerian activities, and a "Letters to the Editor" section for stimulating and exchanging ideas. Within one year, the *Newsletter* had generated such an excellent response from the far-flung Adlerians that Dreikurs was able to turn it into a quarterly, the *Individual Psychology Bulletin*. The enlarged, now typeset *Bulletin* included original articles on theoretical and applied Adlerian psychology as well as informative articles comparing Individual Psychology with other educational, psychological, and philosophical points of view. Under Dreikurs's skillful editorial leadership, the *Bulletin* became a successful rallying point for Adlerian psychology.

Through his own articles and his "Editorial Comments" section, Dreikurs, with clarity and persuasiveness, addressed the critical issues and obstacles that confronted Adlerians. He pricked the consciences and fired the courage of his demoralized fellow Adlerians and rapidly emerged as a national leader among them.

OUT OF TRAGEDY A NEW UNION

There were other matters that occupied Dreikurs in this period. By the time he moved into Hull House, Europe was engulfed in a war that cast its gloomy pall over the world as one nation after another fell to Hitler's advancing armies. Freedom-loving people everywhere now looked to the United States as the last hope for democracy, and American involvement in the war grew ever more imminent. For Dreikurs it was an agonizing period as he made a desperate, last-ditch effort to save his parents from certain doom at the hands of the Nazis.

It was not until mid-1940 that Sigmund Dreikurs signaled his son that he was at last ready to abandon his beloved homeland. For years, the proud and stubborn father had refused to heed Rudolf's urgent pleas that he and his wife flee Vienna. For too long the elder Dreikurs clung to the hopeless illusion that his privileged status as a prominent, wealthy citizen of Vienna would protect him from the cruel fate that befell his Jewish brethren. His wife harbored no such illusions. As a dedicated Zionist, she had been deeply involved in helping destitute, distraught refugees pass through Vienna since Hitler's rise to power in Germany in 1933. But she could not influence Sigmund's unyielding blindness to reality, nor as his faithful wife could she allow herself to abandon him.

When Sigmund finally wired his son for help, it was perhaps the first time in his life that he acknowledged and trusted his son's wisdom and good judgment. They wanted to flee to neutral Sweden and from there make their way to America. Rudolf carefully assessed the situation. Between April and June of 1940, France, Belgium, Holland, Luxembourg, Denmark, and Norway had been overrun by the Nazis. Once Norway fell, it was considered a certainty that Sweden would inevitably fall too. Believing that Sweden's fall was imminent, he instead instructed them to await their pending United States visas. Reasonable as his advice seemed, it proved to be fatefully wrong. By a strange twist of events, Sweden never did fall to the Nazis, and their American visas were the subject of continual delays and snags.

Dreikurs did not accept these visa delays lightly, and he pursued every possible avenue to hasten the exasperatingly slow process. What he and thousands of other anxious relatives and friends of Jews still in Europe did not, and could not, know was that these delays originated as much on this side of the Atlantic as in Europe. Breckinridge Long, undersecretary of state in charge of the State Department's Visa Division, saw to it that no reform or short-cutting of the cumbersome immigration procedures was permitted on behalf of European Jewry. Inordinate delays were caused by the requirement that immigrant applicants furnish police certificates attesting to their good character, records of military service, birth certificates, and all other public records available. According to Arthur D.

Morse's revealing chronicle of official United States apathy to the plight of the Jews, "the law required these documents only 'if available,' but many American consuls insisted upon full dossiers—and the police certificate in particular. Although the notion of a Jew dropping by police headquarters to receive a certificate of good character from his oppressors strikes a particularly sardonic touch of bureaucracy, State Department files refer repeatedly to this requirement and its importance."[12]

Early in 1941, the U.S. consulate general in Vienna demanded that all who had applied for affidavits to enter the United States should attend in person at the consulate bringing their ship tickets and necessary emigration papers with them—a nearly impossible task given the restrictions and destitute circumstances of Vienna's Jews by that time. Working from both sides of the Atlantic, father and son did everything in their power to meet the requirements. Then came the dreadful news. Dreikurs recalled, "When their American visas finally came through, it was exactly one day too late. There was only one paper they didn't have, and when they finally got it, it was just one day after the American Consulate closed in Vienna. They already had their steamer tickets and everything else, but they couldn't get out. Just one day's difference."[13]

Desperately, Dreikurs turned to his friend Charlotte Carr, the director of Hull House. Wellborn and educated, Carr was an outspoken champion of the have-nots of society. She was a tough, seasoned negotiator who could bargain successfully with the most powerful men in politics and industry. Prior to her appointment at Hull House, Carr had served as New York City's director of relief during the height of the depression, and had a reputation for accomplishing the impossible. She greatly admired Dreikurs and his work and took an active interest in the plight of his parents. She wrote on their behalf to her friend Eleanor Roosevelt:

July 23, 1941

Mrs. Franklin D. Roosevelt
The White House
Washington, D.C.

My dear Mrs. Roosevelt:

I suppose we all think of you as the last Court of Appeal when, through no fault of their own, the various Federal Departments are unable to help in a case that is clearly a good one!

A Viennese psychiatrist who lives at Hull House has been making every effort to have his parents—both Jewish—brought to America from Vienna. Their papers are all in order. They have been told by the American Consulate that their affidavits have been accepted. They had their steamship passage. Their possessions were all packed, and their household goods disposed of. When they went for examination, there was one paper that was incomplete, and they were advised to return the next day. That day was the day the Office of the American Consul at Vienna was closed!

Mrs. Elsa Weinshenk of the National Council of Jewish Women in Chicago tells me nothing can be done about this, and when she says that, I suppose I should accept it, as she really has performed miracles on behalf of Jewish refugees. But I see this doctor and his sister here every day, and I see through their eyes the old couple in Vienna, which has now promised to be free of Jews by 1942, and I cannot quite take Mrs. Weinshenk's view that there is nothing we can do about it. At least, I cannot take this as final, until I have the satisfaction of writing to you. . . . I was one of the sponsors for this family's entrance into this country. Can you give me any suggestion as to what can be done?

Most gratefully,
Charlotte Carr[14]

Upon receiving the letter, Mrs. Roosevelt forwarded it to Undersecretary of State Sumner Welles, who was more sympathetic to the plight of the Jews but who wielded no influence on the Visa Division under Breckinridge Long. In his reply to Mrs. Roosevelt, Welles simply reiterated the impossible requirements for the precious visas, now made all the more elusive by additional procedures:

July 30, 1941

Dear Eleanor:

. . . Unfortunately, the closing of our consular offices at Vienna and elsewhere in Germany means that further difficulties will be unavoidable. . . . Until such time as they may be able to leave Germany and enter a country such as Switzerland, Portugal, or some other, where they can continue their visa applications before an American consular officer, there is no way in which visas might be issued to them.

Under a new procedure which became effective July 1, 1941, the cases of visa applicants must be submitted to the Department of State on certain prescribed forms for preliminary examination before they are given final consideration by consular officers abroad. As soon, therefore, as there is a reasonable expectation that Mr. and Mrs. Dreikurs will be able to leave Germany, the Department should be informed in order that the appropriate forms may be forwarded to Miss Carr for completion in their cases.

I regret my inability to furnish a more favorable reply at this time but you may assure Miss Carr that the cases of Mr. and Mrs. Dreikurs will again be given every possible consideration when they may subsequently be able to leave Germany.

Believe me,
Yours very sincerely,
Sumner Welles[15]

The callousness of the United States position on immigration for the thousands of Jews still trapped in German-occupied nations was especially ominous because of the attitude of the other nations. Since the Evian Conference of 1938, which was attended by thirty-two nations, it became clear that no nation was willing to open its doors to the Jews who fled Nazism. Though the brutal acts, the killings, and the Nazi plans for the Jews were widely publicized in the press, our State Department, as a matter of policy, denied, downplayed, and suppressed his information for years on the grounds that rescuing the Jews from Europe was incompatible with the Allies' principal war aims.[16]

Throughout the summer, Dreikurs and Charlotte Carr pursued the desperate race against time. Late in September 1941, a cable was received from Vienna that the Spanish government was willing to grant visas to the Dreikurs couple provided it received assurances from our State Department that they would receive American visas as soon as they arrived in Barcelona. Charlotte Carr fired off a letter to the State Department requesting such assurances. No answer! A week later, she wrote again:

September 30, 1941

Mr. A. M. Warren, Chief
Visa Division
Department of State
Washington, D.C.

My dear Mr. Warren:

. . . I am writing you again . . . because of new and vital information which has just come to us by cable from the Kultusgemeinde (The

Jewish Community) in Vienna. This agency notifies that definite arrangements have been made with the Spanish government in Barcelona to grant a visa to Fanny and Sigmund Dreikurs as soon as the American Consul in Barcelona receives the quota number and the instructions to grant the visa from our State Department. This cable is enclosed.

. . . I would appreciate your letting me know by collect telegram what actions you are able to take.

Sincerely.

Charlotte Carr[17]

Again, no answer! A week later, Charlotte Carr sent the following telegram to Mr. Warren:

AM GRAVELY CONCERNED LEST SIGMUND AND FANNY DREIKURS LOSE THEIR OPPORTUNITY TO LEAVE VIENNA AT ONCE UNLESS STATE DEPARTMENT CAN SEND APPROVAL AND QUOTA NUMBER TO AMERICAN CONSUL IN BARCELONA. THIS CAUSES ME TO ASK AGAIN IF I MAY HAVE A WIRE COLLECT FROM YOU REPLYING MY LETTERS OF SEPTEMBER TWENTY THIRD AND THIRTIETH AS WHAT WE CAN EXPECT FROM THE STATE DEPARTMENT IN THIS MOST WORTHWHILE CASE.[18]

Once again, only silence from Washington. By then, the message was abundantly clear. There would be no help from Washington. In the weeks that followed, Dreikurs frantically pursued any remaining avenues of escape no matter how remote or costly. He borrowed heavily from friends and his uncle in New York, depositing more than one thousand dollars in advance with the Bank of Havana, Cuba, and another one thousand dollars in a Swedish bank, all on the slim chance that temporary visas might be granted. Each day was an agonizing wait. Then came December, Pearl Harbor, and United States' entry into the war. Once war broke out, there was no more communication, no more hope.

Years later, Dreikurs learned that his father and mother, aged seventy-three and sixty-nine respectively, were arrested on August 20, 1942, by the Gestapo and taken to the Theresienstadt concentration camp, where they perished. He also learned that Steffi, his former wife and the mother of his children, suffered a similar fate.

Reflecting on this period and the tragic loss of his parents, he lamented: "I felt guilty, because, in a certain way, I was responsible for their deaths. If I had sent them to Sweden as they wanted, if I had done what they pleaded with me to do, they would have survived."[19]

Just before Pearl Harbor, further tragedy struck in Hull House. Late in November, Leon Garland died suddenly following a second, serious heart attack. His death was a devastating blow to Sadie, and she grievously mourned his loss. Rudolf, saddened by his own failure after endless months of trying to rescue his parents, extended to Sadie the tender understanding and support she desperately needed in those lonely weeks. Elly Redwin, who was also living at Hull House, poignantly remembered: "I never forgot when she came into the cafeteria after his death. I never saw a sadder face than hers. Rudolf knew how to make her feel better, he was wonderful to her."[20]

Sadie reflected: "Rudolf stood by me and sustained me in my moments of grief and doubt for my future life. About a year later he began to court me."

Their growing relationship evolved steadily. "We had worked very closely together for a number of years," Sadie went on, "and I was dependent upon him professionally. I was so dependent that one day he remarked to me: 'Instead of using the phone to ask me all these questions, why don't we get married?'

"My friend Charlotte Carr and my other professional colleagues noticed his courtship and warned me: 'Don't marry him. He is a fine, capable human being, and you can learn much from him, but if you marry him, he will completely absorb you, and you will stop being you. You are a person with a profession in your own right. Don't become his appendage.'"

Rudolf had not lacked female companions in those Chicago years. He genuinely enjoyed and appreciated women, and they, in turn, found his strength of personality, his zest, and his affectionate manner, with its subtle hint of sensuality, appealing. Those women who counted him a close and trusted friend, experienced a tenderness, warmth, and sensitivity rarely expressed by men. That made him a very eligible partner in many women's eyes. Bronia Grunwald described Rudolf's buoyant *joie de vivre* in those trying years:

He loved parties. Everything he did was with zest and full dedication, just like in his work. When he was at a party, he enjoyed himself like a child, laughing, enthusiastically playing all those party games, and especially his favorite, "Napoleon in the Ice Box." He also loved to dance. Of course, he danced the waltz and fox trot, not the modern dances, but he loved to go out dancing, and he was extremely graceful. We used to have beautiful parties. He would play piano, and we would sing, and we'd dance and play games until late late into the night.

One day, he called me and excitedly said he had to see me, it was urgent. He came over and announced to me, "I met a wonderful, wonderful woman and I'd like to marry her." Then he said something which struck me. He said, "She's forty-one years old, *but* I'm going to marry her," as though somehow her age posed a problem. I remember he asked me what did I think of it, and in his excitement, he didn't even wait for my reaction. Of course, he had chosen to marry the only woman in the whole world for him. How he found this one woman is to me, to this very day, amazing, because I can't imagine anyone with whom he could have been happier, who could have helped him, loved him, understood him more than Sadie. And he found her.[21]

But Sadie needed time. "I was not willing to marry again," she recalled. "A year later, after cautioning him that it would be an impossible assignment to be my husband since I would constantly compare him to my angelic husband now deceased, he assured me that he had no fear, that that would be his problem and he would know how to handle it. And he did."

When they were married, on September 12, 1943, Sadie reflected, "He presented me with his most important wedding gift—two children, Eva, then fourteen, and Eric, twenty-two. He married me with the same ring that Leon Garland used—he merely added his initials and the date. Then he began to work on the problem of being a 'husband' to a very pampered wife who really did not want a new marriage."

Their first night at home, Sadie noticed that the photograph of Leon that she had sadly put away in her dresser drawer was back on top of the dresser again. When she queried Rudolf, he explained, "I know you want to look at his picture, so why go to the drawer to look at it? He was my friend too. I also enjoy looking at him. When you are ready not to look at it, you will put it away yourself."

Sadie did not give up mourning her first husband for some time, and, as a result, she often appeared aloof to Rudolf's friends. At one point, Adaline Starr asked Rudolf why she ignored her. He replied that she was still in mourning.

"Doesn't that bother you?" Adaline asked.

"No," he replied. "So long as I know she loves me, it doesn't bother me at all if she loves someone else."[22]

After they were married, Rudolf and Sadie lived in an apartment on the North Side of Chicago. Earlier that year, Charlotte Carr had resigned from Hull House, and with the resulting conflict between the staff and trustees, they saw no point in staying. Besides, there were few friends for Eva at the House, and the neighborhood schools were a hardship for her. By this time, Eric no longer lived at home but was a member of the United States Armed Forces.

As Charlotte Carr and others had predicted, it was difficult for Sadie to give up all her activities and become an appendage to someone else. "But," Sadie mused, "they did not know that being second to someone was *my* cup of tea. As a middle child and at an early age I learned not to rebel openly. I very cleverly chose an ally to fight my battles; first my younger brother, who did a masterful job with our common enemy, our big sister; then my girl friend, who at eleven introduced me to the life of a painter; then Jane Addams, who championed my causes; then Leon; and then Rudolf. I happily assumed my role of second place to a courageous ally. So you see my choice of a husband in Rudolf Dreikurs was a 'natural,' sort of a marriage made in heaven."

Notes for Chapter 13

1. The material presented in this chapter on the life of Sadie "Tee" Dreikurs was drawn from (1) her speech, "My Life with Rudolf Dreikurs," given at the annual meeting of the American Society of Adlerian Psychology, Toronto, Canada, May 27, 1973; (2) the Dreikurs-Mackaness interview; and (3) numerous interviews conducted with Mrs. Dreikurs between 1972 and 1975.

2. This clinical methodology involved "guessing" to discover the personality structure of an individual in his life space. "In medicine and surgery as in Individual Psychology," Adler wrote, "you have to *guess*, but you have to prove it by other signs which agree. If you have guessed and other signs do not agree, you have to be hard and cruel enough against yourself to look for another explanation. . . . I consider it a prime duty to train my students in the art of guessing" (Alfred Adler, *Superiority and Social Interest*, 2d ed., p. 162). Dreikurs concurred, noting that while this technique was for years considered an "unscientific" approach, "Adler demonstrated that we can learn to 'guess in the right directions.' [He] opened our eyes to the underlying

possibilities of small facts which remain insignificant unless we sense their wider implications" (Ibid., p. 143). The Ansbachers pointed out that such "guessing" is a legitimate form of the hypothetico-deductive method and enables the investigator to be particularly spontaneous and creative in formulating hypotheses (Ibid., p. 141). In discussing scientific creativity, Linus Pauling specifically recommended the study of stochastic guessing, particularly regarding its applicability in the social sciences and its value in training researchers in creative thought processes (see Linus Pauling, "The Genesis of Ideas," in *Proceedings of the 3rd World Congress of Psychiatry* [Montreal: McGill University Press, 1961], p. 46).

3. Eleanor Redwin, personal communication, May 1973.

4. Dreikurs-Mackaness interview.

5. Dreikurs, "Group Psychotherapy: A General Review," pp. 230–231.

6. Dreikurs Papers.

7. Ibid.

8. Harold Marley, "He Provoked to Progress," *Religious Humanism* 6 (1972): 166–168.

9. Adaline Starr, personal communication, November 1972.

10. *Individual Psychology Newsletter* 1 (1940): 2.

11. Esther R. Stangle to Raymond J. Corsini, June 27, 1967, Dreikurs Papers.

12. Arthur D. Morse, *While Six Million Died: A Chronicle of American Apathy* (New York: Random House, 1967), p. 137. See also: Rosenkranz, "Anschluss."

13. Dreikurs-Mackaness interview.

14. Dreikurs Papers.

15. Ibid.

16. Morse, *While Six Million Died*, pp. 130–131. President Roosevelt was ambivalent; he feared that the Jewish question was a political liability, and while he proclaimed America as the asylum for the oppressed, he actually helped doom European Jewry by his inaction and unwillingness to override State Department policies. At the State Department, Secretary Cordell Hull and Undersecretary Breckinridge Long held fast to their belief that they were actually protecting America from an invasion of foreign radicals. So diligent were they in their efforts to uphold the restrictive immigration laws that "during the entire Hitler period the number of immigrants lagged far behind the total permitted under U.S. law. From 1933 to 1943, there were 1,244,858 unfilled places on U.S. immigration quotas. Of these, 341,567 had been allotted to citizens of countries dominated or occupied by Germany or her allies. Each unfilled place represented a potential life exposed to annihilation."

17. Dreikurs Papers.

18. Ibid.

19. Dreikurs-Mackaness interview.

20. Eleanor Redwin, personal communication, May 1973.

21. Bronia Grunwald, personal communication, July 1973.

22. Adaline Starr, personal communication, November 1972.

14

The Professor and the Psychoanalytic Stranglehold

An unfortunate competition had developed between Psychoanalysis and Individual Psychology. Where the first gained ground the latter became ostracized.

Rudolf Dreikurs
"The Last Ten Years," 1947

The academic position that Dreikurs needed and to which he aspired became reality in 1942 with his appointment as professor of psychiatry at the Chicago Medical School. A small and struggling institution, it was not exactly the kind of school he had envisioned for himself. He had yearned to be affiliated with one of Chicago's great schools—the University of Chicago, the University of Illinois, or Northwestern. However, his early emergence as an outspoken, controversial figure made such an appointment unlikely, given the conservative nature of the Chicago medical community.[1]

The smallest of the city's five medical colleges, the Chicago Medical School was ambitiously engaged in upgrading its standing to a first-class training facility at the time of his appointment. Since its beginning in 1912 as an evening medical school, it had labored under its second-class status. Although the school had switched to a full-time training program in 1927, it was still frowned upon by the American Medical Association because it lacked a university affiliation and sufficient clinical facilities. The school finally received full accreditation in 1948 through the skillful leadership of its dean, Dr. John J. Sheinin.

Sheinin was a dynamic exception in the generally colorless world of medical school administrators. He tirelessly pursued his mission, demanding the highest standards of excellence of himself, his school, and his students. Within the bounds of his demands for excellence, Sheinin was also flexible and courageous. He allowed poor but promising students to work in lieu of tuition fees, offered teaching posts to European refugee doctors, and welcomed talented Jewish students who had been denied admission elsewhere due to the restrictive quota system.

When the incumbent professor of psychiatry at the medical school died, Sheinin began an active search to fill the position. Dreikurs impressed him with his well-articulated and innovative ideas about psychiatry, especially as they related to the training of medical students. Aware of the prevailing negative attitude toward Adlerian psychology within medical circles, Sheinin was nonetheless willing to give Dreikurs the chance to show his mettle. He sent Dreikurs to meet Dr. Sigmund Krumholz, the chairman of the joint Division of Neurology and Psychiatry, to work out the details of his appointment. Since Dreikurs had never held an academic post, he anticipated an appointment as assistant professor, possibly as associate professor. But Sheinin and Krumholz had decided to make him full professor. Krumholz then told a surprised Dreikurs that he would be head of the psychiatry section within the division, insisting, "If you take charge of the psychiatry section, you should have the title too."[2]

The psychiatry staff was so small when Dreikurs took charge in the fall of 1942 that, for all practical purposes, he constituted a one-man department. This was the case throughout the war years and gave Dreikurs an unusual opportunity to develop the kind of training in psychiatry and psychology he considered essential to the practice of medicine. Dreikurs's function was to train not graduate physicians specializing in psychiatry but undergraduate medical students, who would then go on to general practice or some specialty.

Dreikurs believed that every physician requires broad psychological understanding of human behavior in order to function adequately as a diagnostician and healer: "A considerable amount of psychotherapy takes place in every medical effort by doctors who are [often not aware] of the actual role they play in the treatment of their patients. . . . Without psychological effectiveness no physician could maintain a practice. In most cases, the medical practitioner relies in his psychotherapeutic endeavors on . . . general principles of conduct, good bedside manner, authoritative role of a father figure, and similar empirically developed approaches."[3]

He set out to teach the medical students an understanding of psychological dynamics and techniques for making a psychological assessment of the patient. He began by introducing required courses in psychiatry in the first two years of the medical curriculum.[4] This in itself was noteworthy because as late as 1940, only 38 percent of the medical schools required first- and second-year students to take courses in psychiatric subjects.[5] Moreover, such courses were generally lacking in coherence, filled with jargon, poorly taught, and otherwise remote from the real needs of future practitioners.[6] By contrast, from Dreikurs the budding physicians received a coherent theory of the psychological aspects of human development, behavior, and interpersonal relations.

Third-year medical students studied psychiatric diagnosis and treatment with special reference to the needs of the general practitioner. In addition, they received a unique outpatient experience by participating in Dreikurs's child guidance clinic at Abraham Lincoln Center. Dreikurs's objective was to provide the students with practical experiences in understanding and handling problem children and their families. Beginning in 1943, approximately fifty third-year medical students and interns each year attended Dreikurs's clinic at the center for a period of six weeks. This program continued through the 1947/48 academic year, when it ended abruptly with the changing character of the psychiatry department at the Chicago Medical School.

The two courses required for fourth-year students, also taught by Dreikurs, were oriented toward practical aspects of psychotherapy for general practitioners and emphasized the importance of accurate social histories in diagnosis and treatment.

Dreikurs's contribution to the psychiatric aspects of medical education was characteristically innovative. He realized that his students would need to deal with the crises in their patients' lives that originally stem from organic problems but that come to be overlaid with psychological factors; they would need an empathetic understanding of their patients and would be called upon for guidance in nonmedical issues. And for the first time since Adler taught at the Long Island Medical College in the 1930s, medical students were exposed to Adler's theories of personality, behavior, and psychopathology.

Dreikurs emphasized the practical significance of Adlerian psychology for physicians in two closely related areas: psychosomatic medicine and what he termed "minor psychotherapy."Adler's theory of compensation for organic and psychological inferiorities was a cornerstone of modern psychosomatic medicine, although it is rarely given credit. His holistic approach resolved the troublesome separation of mind and body that often impeded medical effectiveness. Others shared Adler's conviction about the interrelatedness of mind and body. "However," as Dreikurs pointed out, "references to the unity of mind and body only too often remained empty phrases." That he attributed to looking at symptoms from a causal-mechanistic viewpoint as opposed to a holistic-teleological one. "The unity of the individual can only be recognized through the *goals* which the individual sets himself, [which] . . . bring into play his total assets. . . . The goal . . . integrates the past and present into one focal point of direction toward the future."[7]

From the Adlerian standpoint, neuroses or psychologically induced symptoms serve a purpose for the individual. "Neurosis," Dreikurs contended, "is a human creation built after the image of a disease. . . . Nervous symptoms begin invariably at a moment of personal difficulties in life . . . when the individual decides that the social problems which he has to face are too difficult . . . [and] he withdraws from some life task, either from work or from social relations with friends or relatives, or from love and marriage. . . . However, as the patient believes [that he is] sick, and actually experiences the symptoms which he creates, he really is *sick* for all practical purposes."[8]

Physicians are regularly confronted with the challenging diagnostic task of determining whether a patient's symptoms arise from organic or psychogenic factors. Too often, the diagnosis of neurosis is arrived at by default, that is, when no organic basis for the symptom is revealed in laboratory tests. Dreikurs considered this approach inadequate, unless the physician also asked "the Question," a quick technique for differentially diagnosing whether a symptom is psychogenic or organic. The question posed to the patient is "What would be different in your life if you were well?"

The answer to that question is significant. If the symptom is of neurotic origin, the answer indicates against whom or what condition the symptom is directed. Dreikurs wrote:

> If he were well, the patient might [say that he would] look for another job, get along better with his wife, or perhaps he would get married. . . . Naturally if a patient with a broken leg is asked the Question, he may point out what he would do without the handicap. It is generally easy to judge whether a present lack of function is in accord with the actual physical disability or exceeds it. . . . All such

answers . . . indicate why the patient is sick, if the illness is entirely neurotic, or what use the patient may make of an actual physical ailment. They reveal a psychological superstructure which has to be investigated regardless of any actual organic pathology.[9]

Eliciting and interpreting the answer requires considerable skill and a psychological framework that cannot possibly be fully explained here. However, this approach shows how a purposive orientation to behavior allows the patient to be seen as a total, unified being. The following case study is illustrative:

A 42-year-old man suffered from gastric disturbances. The only clinical finding was hyperacidity, and he was referred for psychiatric attention. It was a year before he consented, in the meantime going to physicians. He was convinced that he was physically ill and considered referral to psychiatry as an insult. However, once he came, he was cooperative. His condition cleared up completely as he began to understand its function and to change his attitude toward life. He was overambitious, tried to please everyone and always tried to make a good impression. He could not say "no" and his stomach "spoke up" for him. If he could not "stomach" a situation, he became ill—but only after the "crisis situation" had developed. Previously, he had been able to get along adequately on his concepts. He did not have to fight, to argue, to assert himself aggressively, because he was a good worker and always able to maintain his superiority over others. Then he came to a point where he realized that any further advance in his position and status was impossible. He did not have the necessary education to get a higher position. At that time his willingness to participate in the give and take of life became impaired. An incidental upset stomach was maintained as a defense mechanism against any threatening situation; he could feel superior only by emphasizing wrongdoings of others. By becoming ill, he escaped tasks that he did not like. He limited his activities and was ill most of the time.

His answer to the question was clear enough. If he were well, he would not get upset so easily, he could get along with his fellow workers, he would meet friends and not stay home all the time. It was obvious that he wished to withdraw from all situations that did not permit him to feel superior, as he had before. He restricted himself to the safety of his own home, where his status was still maintained and even perhaps enhanced through his sickness, which required special attention and evoked sympathy.

In three months of therapy he not only learned to understand what he was doing, but was able to change his basic assumptions, and he developed a new perspective of life. The symptoms disappeared completely.

After several years of well-being he returned to us. The pains had recurred. And he was sure that they were again psychogenic, not only because he felt the same sensation, . . . but because they had first appeared on the train as he returned home from a vacation. Being somewhat familiar with the mechanism of a neurosis, he suspected that he did not want to return home and to go back to work. However, closer scrutiny revealed that he was not "using" the pains in any way. He functioned fully at home and on his job. He did not avoid any participation, nor did he draw attention to his symptoms. Therefore, it was doubtful that the pains were psychogenic since they had no function. He was sent back for a thorough examination. A small tumor in the testicles was found, and upon its removal, the pain subsided.

This case is interesting for several reasons. First it showed how the same symptomatology can be organic or functional and how the answer to the question permits a clear distinction. But it is also interesting to note that the patient was in no position to distinguish between the psychogenic and organic pains. Both were experienced in the same way.[10]

The psychological aspect of illness is important not only in diagnosis but also in therapy. Dreikurs believed that all medical practitioners need some knowledge of psychotherapeutic procedures. Just as a reasonable distinction exists between major and minor surgery, the latter being successfully carried out by general physicians, so a general medical practitioner can learn effective techniques of minor psychotherapy where the emotional disturbance is not severe enough to require the specialized skills of a psychiatrist.

Because the life-style concept provides a rapid approach to understanding an individual's personality, Dreikurs believed that its use as a therapeutic tool should not be restricted to psychiatrists. He contended that it could be effectively applied by general practitioners as minor psychotherapy. Consequently, he taught his students the fundamentals for assessing a life style and demonstrated the technique with actual patients. In so doing, he began to systematize and structure the assessment process, which had been lacking in Adler's writings. Dreikurs's elaboration of the family constellation dynamics and the interpretation of early recollections were among his most important contributions to psychotherapy.

Always seeking to disseminate the Adlerian viewpoint, Dreikurs's professorship opened up a much sought avenue for publishing, the *Chicago Medical School Quarterly*. The student editor of the *Quarterly* in the mid-1940s was Bernard Shulman, who esteemed Dreikurs and welcomed papers by him. Stimulated by his teaching experience, Dreikurs wrote several papers on such psychiatric topics as neurosis, dreams, sexuality, and techniques of psychotherapy, which were published in the *Quarterly*. This helped to break the frustrating logjam Dreikurs had encountered from the Freudian-oriented professional journals, which had routinely rejected his writings.

One article from this period illustrates well Dreikurs's ability to bring clarity where confusion had reigned. In it he distinguishes the structural and functional differences between neurotic, psychotic, and psychopathic personalities. He included an astute prediction: "The problem of psychopathic personalities will probably confront us with great violence after this war [World War II]." In his view, because the psychopath—which includes *indulgent* types (alcoholics, drug addicts, and so on) and *defiant* types (criminals and delinquents)—feels justified in his behavior, he neither feels sick nor is willing to accept therapy. Therefore, prevention is essential. "Psychopathic trends must and can be recognized very early. They cannot be suppressed by force, nor mitigated by indulgence . . . methods predominantly used today with misbehaving children. . . . Once such personalities have been developed, the only therapy that seems to affect them is group therapy."[11]

To his students, Dreikurs was a peppy figure "whose popularity was well attested to by filled classrooms and wide awake psychiatric clinics."[12] Bernard Shulman, a medical student who became one of Dreikurs's closest associates, and later specialized in psychiatry, recalled: "I was in the very first class he ever taught. He strode into the amphitheater briskly and began by announcing that all students in his class would either get an A or a B. There would be no failures. That was unheard of in the intensely competitive atmosphere of medical education, and I interpreted it to mean that if I wanted to 'pass' I would have to get an A.

Only later did I understand his real intention—to remove any obstacles that stood in the way of genuine learning."[13]

Shulman also remembered that at this first lecture Dreikurs described what an Adlerian was. "Up until that time I had read Freud. I began to read Adler and was attracted to his ideas. . . . Dreikurs was able to do some astounding things. He would listen to an early memory from somebody in the class. [Then] he would say [for instance] 'that is the memory of an only child.' He was mostly right."[14]

Most students regarded him as an excellent and dedicated teacher—knowledgeable, stimulating, and lucid. He forthrightly declared his Adlerian orientation, and he never hesitated to criticize what he regarded as the pseudoscientific legacy of Freudian doctrine in psychiatry. His self-assurance, Teutonic accent and manner, and his strong convictions, unconcealed behind a mask of "objectivity," gave him an authoritative image. Some considered him dogmatic. But dogmatic people do not like to be questioned and challenged, which was not true in Dreikurs's case. He relished challenging questions and enjoyed the heated dialogue that followed. While his arguments could be devastating, he did not use his authority to penalize a student who disagreed with him nor did he hold grudges against those who opposed him.

The students who participated at the child guidance clinic were probably unaware of the uniqueness of Dreikurs's clinical approach and that it was an innovative effort in medical education. A number of them were initially opposed to the public counseling model, claiming, under the general impact of Freudian teaching as others had, that children would be traumatized by such an exposure. But watching Dreikurs work with the children allayed their misgivings. Dreikurs was probably correct when he claimed that "for the first time in the history of medical education . . . future physicians received training in child guidance and education."[15]

No doubt it was Dreikurs's genuine hope to train a group of dedicated physicians who would join him in working on a broad, preventive, medico-psychological front in the community. But American medicine, including its students, was marching in a different direction—toward increasing specialization and reliance upon pharmacological treatment to the general exclusion of psychological considerations. In the late 1940s, Drs. Arthur Zweibel, Louis Richmond, Louis Cholden, and Bernard Shulman—all graduates of the Chicago Medical School—worked with Dreikurs in his private practice and at the child guidance clinics. But Zweibel left Chicago, Richmond went on to specialize in internal medicine, and the promising Louis Cholden died prematurely in an auto accident. Only Shulman became a longtime close associate of Dreikurs, his partner in private practice, his successor as medical director to the Community Child Guidance Centers, and a notable Adlerian psychiatrist in his own right.

THE PSYCHOANALYTIC STRANGLEHOLD

Throughout World War II, while many of his fellow psychiatrists were in military service, Dreikurs savored his freedom to practice and teach his Adlerian methods unhindered by Freudian opposition at the medical school. Yet he knew this was not typical, because elsewhere in Chicago and in other parts of the nation the Freudian influence was growing stronger, effectively drowning out all other voices in psychiatry. He opposed this trend and drew upon the prestige and authority of his position to gain visibility for his countering views. Tee was astonished by his fierce attack on psychoanalysis. Not long after they were married, they attended a national psychiatric meeting in New York. During a panel discussion involving the most eminent men in the profession, Dreikurs debunked everything they said.

"I cringed, and afterward admonished him: 'How dare you speak that way to this august body of your own profession? Surely, they can't all be wrong.'"

"You will see," he replied. "In ten to fifteen years they will change their approaches. In the meantime, I'll do my darndest to see the Freudian spook demolished."[16]

Apparently Tee was not the only one to note Dreikurs's lonely stance. Psychiatrist George Saslow remembered that same meeting and, years later, wrote to Dreikurs: "It is hard to communicate to you how encouraging it was for me to discover more than twenty-five years ago that I was not as alone as I had thought in my questioning . . . the extraordinary domination of Boston and American psychiatry by Freudian assertions. Your civil courage in standing up for your differing views heartened me, and, I am sure, others."[17]

But if there were others who agreed with Dreikurs's position in the forties, very few were willing to do more than quietly acknowledge it. The professional risks were too great.

Dreikurs's prediction that the Freudian influence would decline in ten to fifteen years was essentially correct. The psychoanalytic influence peaked in the late 1950s and has declined steadily ever since. What Dreikurs did not foresee was that in the interim the Freudian domination would reach a zenith that would exert a stranglehold on the psychiatric profession.

When the war ended, Dreikurs saw encouraging signs that the profession was beginning to move in the direction of Adler's theories. Wartime experiences impelled psychiatry to shift to briefer therapies and group approaches as well as to a greater emphasis on the social and interpersonal determinants of behavior. This was particularly evident in the rise of neo-Freudianism (or neo-Adlerianism as some prefer to call it) in the 1940s. At the forefront of this group were Karen Horney, Harry Stack Sullivan, and Erich Fromm.[18] All three broke with Freud's fundamental position that behavior is biologically determined and rooted in the sexual instinct and that all problems and conflicts are *intra*psychic in origin. Karen Horney, in particular, took issue with Freud's doctrine on the same grounds that Adler earlier had, and her concepts are remarkably similar to Adler's. Thus, when her book *Our Inner Conflicts* appeared in 1945, it prompted a critic to remark: "The reviewer finds it difficult to think of a single basic 'Horney' tenet, the kernel of which cannot be found in books or papers which Adler published thirty to thirty-five years ago. The two psychiatrists subscribe to a nearly identical theory of personality."[19]

The development of neo-Freudianism was welcomed by the Adlerians, but the silence of these new thinkers in acknowledging their debt to Adler was disturbing.[20]

Dreikurs also found Horney's ideas compatible with his Adlerian stance. Her concept of the functional relationship between "basic anxiety" versus the "feeling of belonging" was nearly identical to Adler's "inferiority feeling" versus "social interest." Unlike Freud—and reechoing Adler—she maintained that "man can change and go on changing as long as he lives."[21] Shulman recalled that during a lecture at the medical school, Dreikurs identified his own theoretical position by drawing a diagram on the board that placed him midway between Adler and Horney. Yet his initial encouragement resulting from the emergence of neo-Freudians gave way to concern when it became clear that Adlerians would neither be welcomed nor integrated with this school of thought. Though Horney formally broke with the orthodox Freudian group, she maintained her identity as a psychoanalyst in "deference to Freud's gigantic achievements."[22] This prompted Dreikurs to state: "It is interesting to note that

Adler's ideas which made a strong impact in American thinking found professional recognition only when they appeared under disguise. Karen Horney, who followed Adler's concepts almost entirely, is acceptable because she calls herself a psychoanalyst and belongs to the dominant group.[23]

The heart of the issue, Dreikurs well understood, stemmed from what psychoanalyst Joseph E. Lipshutz implied when he stated, "Before 1937, psychoanalysis contained no co-ordinated theory of object relations—in other words, no theory of the relationship of the individual to the environment."[24]

What the neo-Freudians were doing was grafting their social-oriented concept of personality onto a psychoanalytic foundation rooted in biologically determined instincts. It was inconsistent and a tenuous link at best, and it muddled even further the confusion among theories that already existed. As Nobel laureate and biologist Peter Medawar later pointed out: "There is some truth in Psychoanalysis . . . as there is in mesmerism and phrenology . . . but, considered in its entirety, psychoanalysis won't do. It is an end-product, moreover, like a dinosaur or Zeppelin: no better theory can ever be constructed on its ruins, which will remain forever one of the saddest and strangest of all landmarks in the history of 20th century thought."[25]

Medawar made his statement in 1969, but Dreikurs understood the trend and, more importantly, had the courage to expose it in the 1940s. Besides the confusion created and the time lost while old discoveries were masqueraded, effective action in the community at a time of growing need was paralyzed. Dreikurs believed that a unified and integrated science of psychology and psychotherapy was imperative and possible. With the backing of the Chicago Individual Psychology Association, Dreikurs launched a novel public forum where theories and methods of various schools of thought could be compared and contrasted. The first series of these "Round-Table Discussions"[26] was held in 1945, with attendance ranging from 150 to 300 people. Participants for the heated debates on fear, dreams, and parent-child relationships included: Drs. Thomas French and Irene Josselyn, representing the psychoanalytic school; Dr. Irene Mead, Jungian psychology; Dr. Ethel Kawin, Meyer's psychobiology; Dr. S. I. Hayakawa, representing the new field of semantics; and, of course, Rudolf Dreikurs representing Adlerian psychology. The following season the topics included psychotherapy, techniques of child guidance, and the psychological problems of veterans.

These seminars lasted only one year, and in all likelihood, Dreikurs's withering attacks on certain psychoanalytic assumptions contributed to their demise. Adaline Starr recalled Dreikurs's concerted effort whenever possible to have people with different points of view sit together and discuss their differences: "He really wanted to create an integration of ideas, a rapprochement. I remember one of these discussions was on guilt feelings [a topic on which Adlerians and Freudians clearly departed in their thinking]. Dreikurs gave his definition, and Dr. Jules Masserman said, 'Well, those are secondary gains.' There followed a big fight between them. There were several more such meetings, and then they stopped. Wherever he could, Dreikurs made efforts to move in and to have his ideas heard and accepted."[27] Though these forums ended, they nonetheless had given an opportunity to bring Adlerian ideas to the fore and to challenge the widespread misunderstanding of Adler that was mindlessly repeated by others.

After reviewing this period in the history of psychiatry, psychoanalyst Dr. Melitta Schmideberg, daughter of the famous Dr. Melanie Klein and a witness to what took place, wrote in 1971: "Psychoanalysis . . . has for over thirty years dominated the American scene . . . [and] has until recently been an almost unchallenged dogma in the U.S.A. It is a strange [phenomenon] that its controversial tenets were suddenly accepted without any attempt at scientific verification and that analysts were in a position to dismiss any criticism as 'resistance.' . . . In the U.S.A., . . . it required courage not to be [an analyst]."[28]

Dreikurs had that courage and knew what he was doing in his lonely attack on the sleeping giant of professional complacency and smugness. He knew it got him into trouble and that it generated criticism from even his most sympathetic and closest colleagues. Still he persisted. He had to make them challenge their own assumptions and to question their acceptance of the Freudian picture of human nature. "Truth and popularity are seldom bedfellows; therefore, let the truthseeker beware,"[29] commented Dreikurs's friend Emily Thorn, as she reflected on his role and its consequences. Dreikurs understood. "There are two kinds of persons in the world," he once told a colleague. "Those who get ulcers and those who give them. I give ulcers."[30] So he did, but in the process he paid a price, one that nearly cost him his coveted professorship.

In the decade following the war, as psychiatry departments across the nation grew in number, they became staffed and directed mostly by men with solid psychoanalytic credentials. Conditions at the Chicago Medical

School followed suit. With the death of Dr. Sigmund Krumholz, the joint Department of Neurology and Psychiatry was left without a chairman. Krumholz had served as head of the neurology section and chairman of the joint department, while Dreikurs served as head of the psychiatry section. Psychoanalyst Dr. Harry H. Garner was chosen to fill the vacant position. Fair-minded and tolerant, Dreikurs believed that different points of view should be represented on the staff and agreed to Garner's appointment. Garner became professor of Neurology and head of the joint department. An ardent Freudian, Garner was critical of Dreikurs's teaching and especially the way he conducted the psychiatric clinic at the hospital. This is not surprising, because from the orthodox Freudian standpoint there was only one real therapeutic method—psychoanalysis. Anything else was, from that view, superficial, nonscientific, and wrong. Before long, Garner asked if he might teach some psychiatry courses as well.

"I did not refuse him," Dreikurs reflected, "because I wanted to integrate my work with the psychoanalysts through staff meetings and the like. But he objected; he didn't want any integration." Dreikurs regarded Garner as a poor theorist but a shrewd individual who quickly "filled the department with psychoanalysts."[31] The record shows that the department staff mushroomed from a low of seven in 1946 to thirty-one in five years. Dreikurs protested Garner's growing encroachment and soon found himself isolated and outnumbered within his own section. The few staff members who knew him and respected his work as a therapist and teacher—including several former students on the staff—supported him, but they were outnumbered by the analysts loyal to Garner.

The question arises why Dreikurs was not selected to succeed Krumholz. While he was an excellent teacher and an able organizer, Dreikurs was not well suited to be an administrator. His unadorned directness was not conducive to the diplomatic and political finesse required for the job, and while he believed that opposing views should be represented on the faculty, he was too staunch in his beliefs to provide the even-handed, moderating stance of a good administrator. Furthermore, he had never taken his national specialty boards in neurology and psychiatry, and department chairmen were rarely appointed who were not board-certified in their specialties.

Perhaps because Dreikurs was apolitical and uncompromising in his beliefs, he missed the opportunity to build a diversified psychiatry section that was resistant to the Freudian hegemony. When Garner moved in, he aggressively enlarged the department and enhanced it by securing hospital clerkships and other liaisons. In the process, as an ardent Freudian, he had no tolerance for Adlerian psychology and saw Dreikurs as an obstacle. Indirectly, he tried to force Dreikurs out altogether. Dreikurs reflected with chagrin, "An unfortunate competition had developed between Psychoanalysis and Individual Psychology. Where the first gained ground the latter became ostracized."[32]

Dreikurs did not resist Garner's efforts to take control of the psychiatry section as strongly as he might have. No doubt his widening activities beyond his academic position kept him from exerting all his energies at the medical school. "I then decided—and it was foolish on my part—to take a year's leave of absence, and let Garner settle the whole situation."[33] That was early in 1949, by which time the number of courses Dreikurs taught had already been reduced and he was no longer in charge of the psychiatry dispensary at Mount Sinai Hospital, the clinical affiliate of the Chicago Medical School.

When he returned the following year, he realized that Garner was not about to restore his position as head of psychiatry. Moreover, "the psychoanalysts tried to petition my removal from the faculty! I was not removed, because I had tenure, and they had nothing against me. . . . Then they threatened to resign if I resumed teaching."[34]

No matter what they tried, Dreikurs drew the line at his professorship. He clung to it tenaciously, even during the painful experiences that occurred in the next decade, when psychoanalysis reigned supreme. He fought back and never gave an inch, maintaining that the Freudian doctrine was wrong, a hindrance rather than an asset to the public need. Dreikurs described the highly charged atmosphere:

> Because I was still a staff member, I came to the regular staff meetings, which sometimes resulted in very unpleasant arguments. One time, the staff was discussing the teaching of the unconscious and complaining that the students had too much anxiety, too much reservation about it, and couldn't comprehend it—for which I didn't blame them at all. So I said, "I will tell you how I discuss the unconscious," and I gave my example of the analogy to the eye, the degree of awareness, etcetera. With that, one of the aggressive, belligerent Freudians got up and said, "We don't want Dr. Dreikurs's kind of nonsense. . . . We want a scientific approach to psychiatry and none of this!" I retorted, "Since when do you have the right to

assume that only what you are doing is scientific, and that someone who disagrees with you is not scientific?" He snapped back, "But Dr. Dreikurs, don't you realize that in a school of homeopathy, they would not let a chiropractor teach? In our school, we don't want anyone teaching something other than what we are doing."[35]

Garner stood by and said nothing. By his refusal to defend Dreikurs's rightful place on the faculty, his utter discourteousness, and his routinely "forgetting" to inform Dreikurs of staff meetings, the message came through loud and clear: Dreikurs was there against their will—he had no place at Chicago Medical School anymore. But no matter how unpleasant the atmosphere, Dreikurs refused to leave. Buttonholing Garner one day, he challenged: "You can't force me out. I will stay in this department until this monopoly is broken, and other views will be included again!"[36]

But after 1950, Dreikurs found himself with his title of full professor and no classes to teach. What an insult, especially since he had virtually served as a one-man department during the war years and had proven to be a popular teacher and a uniquely capable therapist. Though he was no longer allowed to teach, his very presence around the school kept alive the interest of students and other faculty in his work, which Dreikurs capitalized upon and which, in turn, only hardened Garner's opposition to him.

Some of Dreikurs's non-Freudian colleagues elsewhere did not fare as well. Shulman summarized the state of psychiatry in those years: "At this particular time in psychiatry anyone who was not a psychoanalyst was under severe attack. This was when Abraham Low, the founder of Recovery, Inc. was very severely attacked by the psychoanalysts. He attacked them back. Dreikurs supported Low and Low supported Dreikurs. . . . There was a psychiatrist named Haase, a Viennese psychiatrist, and another, Samuel Kraines, who had been forced out of teaching at the University of Illinois because he was not a psychoanalyst. They all stuck together and helped each other."[37]

Dreikurs never regained a significant role at Chicago Medical School. However, in the late 1950s, the man in charge of psychiatric training for residents arranged for Dreikurs to teach an elective course in Adlerian psychotherapy, which he continued doing until his retirement in 1967. By then, the psychoanalytic stranglehold had been broken in American psychiatry, which in turn began to move in new directions, often discovering ideas that Dreikurs had advocated years earlier. In that same year Dreikurs retired as emeritus professor of psychiatry.

Reviewing those painful years, Dreikurs said, "Kasanin warned me about what would happen if I fought the psychoanalysts. The Adlerians warned me. They were absolutely right. I came near to being professionally killed in Chicago. I think the history of our department is characteristic of many incidents which happened all over the United States where people who opposed psychoanalysis lost their positions. I think I am one of the very few who opposed Psychoanalysis and managed to remain a member of a department that had become totally psychoanalytic."[38]

Notes for Chapter 14

1. Thomas N. Bonner, "Social and Political Attitudes of Midwestern Physicians, 1840–1940," *Journal of the History of Medicine and Allied Sciences* 8 (1953): 133–164.

2. Dreikurs-Mackaness interview.

3. Rudolf Dreikurs, "The Psychological Interview in Medicine," *American Journal of Individual Psychology* 10 (1954): 108–109.

4. According to the *Chicago Medical School Bulletin*, 1942–1948, first-year medical students were required to study "Medical Psychology," a lecture course on understanding human nature, the development of personality and character, social adjustments to the problems of life, and psychological approaches to patients in general. Second-year students were required to attend a lecture course on child guidance that covered parent-child relations, understanding the child, maladjustment, and educational and guidance techniques; plus a lecture course on the theory of neurosis and psychosomatic medicine.

5. Group for the Advancement of Psychiatry, *The Preclinical Training of Psychiatry*, Report no. 54 (New York, 1962).

6. Sidney L. Werkman, *The Role of Psychiatry in Medical Education: An Appraisal and Forecast* (Cambridge, Mass.: Harvard University Press, 1966).

7. Rudolf Dreikurs, "Adler's Contribution to Medicine, Psychology, and Education," *American Journal of Individual Psychology* 10 (1953): 83–84.

8. Rudolf Dreikurs, "Psychological Differentiation of Psychopathological Disorders," *Individual Psychology Bulletin* 4 (1945): 39, 38.

9. Dreikurs, "The Psychological Interview," p. 105.

10. "A Reliable Differential Diagnosis of Psychological or Somatic Disturbances." *International Record of Medicine* 171 (1958): 241.

11. Dreikurs, "Psychological Differentiation," pp. 48, 47.

12. "Faculty Notes," *Chicago Medical School Quarterly* 2 (1942): 23.

13. Bernard H. Shulman, personal communication, May 1974.

14. Joan C. Truitt, *A Legacy for the Future: The Historical Development of "The Open Educational Model" of Adlerian Child Guidance (1920 to the Present)* (Ann Arbor, Mich.: University Microfilms, 1974), p. 269.

15. Rudolf Dreikurs, "Our Child Guidance Clinics in Chicago," *Individual Psychology Bulletin* 3 (1943): 18. More than a decade later, in 1956, the Committee on Medical Education of the American Psychiatric Association called for instructing medical students "in the use of psychotherapy under supervision," and regarding "a variety of minor behavior problems of children such as sleeping and feeding diffi-

culties, aneurosis, temper tantrums and negativistic behavior." Werkman commented that with the Committee's recommendations: "for the first time childhood emotional experience . . . was given a major place in teaching" (*Role of Psychiatry*, p. 15). See also: T. Lidz, "Outline for a Curriculum for Teaching Psychiatry in Medical Schools, *Journal of Medical Education* 31 (1956): 115–122.

16. Sadie "Tee" Dreikurs, "My Life With Rudolf Dreikurs."

17. George Saslow to Rudolf Dreikurs, January 17, 1967, Dreikurs Papers.

18. Other prominent neo-Freudians include Franz Alexander, Thomas French, Freida Fromm-Reichmann, Abraham Kardiner, and Clara Thompson. The emergence of neo-Freudianism prompted Fritz Wittels to write: "The field of 'social' etiologies was the exclusive object of Alfred Adler's research, and although his heirs rarely quote him, the 'new' discoveries in this field are based on his theories. For this reason I call this school which is now in formation, the Neo-Adlerians" ("The Neo-Adlerians." *American Journal of Sociology* 45 (1939): 433. See also: Heinz L. Ansbacher, " 'Neo-Freudian or 'Neo-Adlerian'?" *American Psychologist* 8 (1953): 165–166.

19. Keith Sward, "Review of Karen Horney, *Our Inner Conflicts*," *Journal of Abnormal and Social Psychology* 41 (1946): 496.

20. Alexandra Adler, "New Ways?" *Individual Psychology Bulletin* 2 (1942): 77.

21. Karen Horney, *Our Inner Conflicts* (New York: Norton, 1945), p. 19.

22. Karen Horney, *The Neurotic Personality in Our Time* (New York: Norton, 1937), p. ix.

23. Rudolf Dreikurs, "The Last Ten Years," *Individual Psychology Bulletin* 6 (1947): 2.

24. Joseph E. Lipshutz, "A Brief Review of Psychoanalytic Ego Psychology," *Social Casework* 45 (1964): 5–6.

25. Peter Medawar, "A Reply" [to "Misunderstanding Psychoanalysis" by Anthony Storr], *Encounter* 33 (1969): 94.

26. "From Our Friends: The Chicago Group," *Individual Psychology Bulletin* 4 (1944/1945); *Individual Psychology Bulletin* 5 (1946): 30.

27. Adaline Starr, personal communication, November 1972. The social consequences and the purposes served by a neurotic illness were considered "secondary gains" by Freud because of his insistence on a more basic, sexually rooted intrapsychic conflict, whereas for the Adlerians the social consequences and interpersonal conflicts are foremost and the motivating factors in the neurotic illness. See Dreikurs, "Psychological Interview."

28. Melitta A. Schmideberg, "A Contribution to the History of the Psychoanalytic Movement in Britain," *British Journal of Psychiatry* 118 (1971): 61–67.

29. Emily Thorn, personal communication, August 1973.

30. Helene Ray to Raymond J. Corsini, June 24, 1967. Dreikurs Papers.

31. Dreikurs-Mackaness interview.

32. Dreikurs, "The Last Ten Years," p. 3.

33. Dreikurs-Mackaness interview.

34. Ibid.

35. Ibid.

36. Ibid.

37. Truitt, *Legacy for the Future*, p. 269.

38. Dreikurs-Mackaness interview.

15

To Reach the People: A Bold Attempt at Community Psychiatry

> If mankind survives at all the terrific upheaval of our days,
> it can never be as it was before. . . . Either we shall perish
> or we shall establish real equality, which is the basis of
> democracy. There must be a new order that will give
> meaning to this word so often used for a principle so little
> practiced.
>
> Rudolf Dreikurs
> *The Challenge of Marriage*, 1946

Just as World War I led to Adler's concept of "social interest," so World War II marks the point when Dreikurs first expressed his prophetic theme that a *psychological* revolution toward social equality was taking root at all levels in society. The war seemed to have evoked in Dreikurs this new focus that would be stamped upon everything he would do in succeeding years.

"The world is aflame, violence is rampant over the earth—men, women, and children perish in agony and misery,"[1] Dreikurs cried out in a wartime editorial reflecting the anguished state of the world in 1942. No one knew then whether America could halt Hitler's advancing armies: Europe had fallen; England was under imminent threat; only the Atlantic Ocean gave scant breathing space as an unprepared America raced to mobilize its forces. Never before in history had there been such a clear-cut confrontation between the forces of tyranny and the forces of democracy. Mankind's future hung precariously in the balance.

As fear and uncertainty swept the nation, Dreikurs was concerned that America, from sheer necessity, might succumb to the tantalizing but illusory efficiency of dictatorial methods. But if the times were gloomy, he was not. Rather, he steeled his determination to do whatever he could to strengthen freedom and the democratic principles he had championed since his days in the youth movement.

It was fortunate that the nation's leaders were equally dedicated to awakening the American people to what was at stake. Calling America the "arsenal of democracy," President Franklin D. Roosevelt fired the nation with his stirring speeches. Wartime propaganda provoked a ringing debate on the issues of democracy and freedom not heard since the days of the Founding Fathers. Dreikurs was inspired but nonetheless felt something was lacking in these lofty discussions that seemed only to consider the political or economic aspects of democracy. What he found missing was the psychological component of democracy and its relationship to beliefs and actions. This led to his earliest paper[2] in which he described the psychological consequences of a political doctrine, namely, the "four freedoms" proclaimed in the Atlantic Charter and their implications for the education of children.

Churchill and Roosevelt had created the Atlantic Charter as a blueprint for the conduct of the war and for the future that lay beyond. In it they pledged that their respective nations would seek no aggrandizement in victory and would respect the right of all people to choose their own form of government. Projecting beyond the war, they pledged to create a world order founded on four essential freedoms—freedom of speech, freedom of religion, freedom from want, and freedom from fear. Dreikurs believed this document might become "as outstanding an event in modern American history as the Bill of Rights [and] the Gettysburg Address. . . . These four freedoms seem to form the basis for the development of democracy. We have as much [real] freedom as we possess these four freedoms."

Regarding freedom of speech, he observed that there is more of it in the political life than in the daily routine within the family. "We must recognize the necessity of bringing up our children in such a way that expressing their opinions is natural and does not require either rebellion or aggressiveness. Otherwise only those children will express their opinion freely who are impertinent or hostile. . . . We cannot start teaching democracy at a certain age after we have first suppressed with force and intimidation the natural inclination of the child to take a stand and express an opinion in a constructive and cooperative way. . . . Parents must become aware of how important the atmosphere of the family is for the community and the whole country. . . . There is no freedom of speech so long as talking frankly means hostility and so long as many refuse to talk at all."

Freedom from fear seemed the most challenging of the four to Dreikurs:

> Fear is very often not caused by real dangers; even death loses its terror for those who have developed courage. . . . Courage, [the] confidence in one's own strength, is the only antidote for fear. . . . Freedom from fear cannot be accomplished by merely economic or political measures. Persecution and oppression are consequences of fear as well as causes. Only frightened people suppress others. Worse than famine or disease is the fear of losing social status, of being less than the next fellow. This fear engulfs children competing with [siblings] and rebelling against parents who either pamper or oppress them. Bringing up children without fear might prove to be more important even than teaching them to read or write. . . . How far from developing freedom from fear are educators who deliberately use fear as an educational method, who are convinced that only fear of punishment, fear of humiliation, fear of the consequences can prevent children from misbehaving? . . . [Such a teacher] wears only the title of educator without being one.

The following year, he organized a lecture series on the "psychological preparation for democracy," in which he stressed that democracy remains an empty theoretical concept unless it rests on a firm psychological belief in the equal worth and dignity of each individual. In Dreikurs's view, the psychological obstacles to regarding others with the dignity and respect required for democracy were the prevailing educational methods, personal insecurity, and attitudes about competition, as well as fear and distrust between the races and between the sexes.[3]

The gap between the promises of democracy, so boldly championed for the war effort, and the reality of entrenched racial discrimination and social injustice did not escape his attention. Early in the war, he sensed that the rising expectations of those groups who had been treated as inferior or as second-class citizens, would quickly grow to a demand for full equality.

Never content to be the armchair psychologist who sits back and reflects on the shortcomings of society and what others should do about it, Dreikurs linked his beliefs to action. He joined forces with various activist groups dedicated to the promotion of social justice and better under-standing between peoples. These groups included the Humanists, the Quaker's American Friends Service Committee, and the Co-op Movement. Long before the civil rights movement got underway, Rudolf and Tee hosted and attended gatherings in which blacks, whites, and orientals discussed their common interests and explored ways to overcome the debilitating effects of a discriminatory society.

Spared from military participation, Dreikurs spent the war years on the Chicago home front, where he witnessed firsthand the tremendous social upheaval that was precipitated by the war. Today it is difficult to imagine the tumultuous conditions that prevailed. The nation was turned topsy-turvy by the withdrawal of 15 million men to fight overseas, the reorientation of hundreds of thousands of women who entered military service or took skilled industrial jobs that previously had been the exclu-sive province of men, and the vast migration of people from farms and small towns to the teeming cities. The fabulous salaries for war produc-tion work that came on the heels of the depression lured adolescents to quit school in droves and strike out on their own. Family life rapidly dis-integrated as a consequence of these chaotic conditions.[4]

In Chicago, as elsewhere, the incidence of juvenile delinquency and mental illness soared, while the ranks of physicians, social workers, and teachers were sorely depleted. Knowing that the psychological health and courage of the home-front community would be critical to the war effort and the character of American society that would emerge thereafter, Drei-kurs offered his assistance in many areas. Family life and education—the molds in which the developing generation's attitudes, values, and courage are shaped—were the targets of his especial concern.

The confusion that characterized American family life was particularly disturbing to Dreikurs. Our child rearing and educational practices had become a chaotic mix of tradition, myth, and conflicting theories. Chil-dren received a strangely inconsistent message: Often they were required to give unquestioning obedience at the same time that ideals of freedom, justice, and rugged individualism were given the highest praise. The di-versity of theories preached by the experts only heightened the chaos. Permissiveness, spawned by the psychoanalytic movement, was a growing phenomenon aided by an unfortunate amalgamation with John Dewey's philosophy of democratic education. Psychoanalysis, with its emphasis on shielding the child from frustration and, in effect, from facing the prob-lems of life, fostered a self-indulgent, egocentric attitude that made social responsibility and cooperation seem contrary to the pursuit of individuality. Behaviorism was also gaining strength. It viewed the developing child as a simple *tabula rasa,* a bundle of stimulus-response reflexes to be molded by reward and punishment according to the grand design of its psychological engineers. For Dreikurs, both views were mistaken doctrines that were not only inappropriate but counterproductive to the principles of democracy.

More than ever before, Dreikurs felt an urgency that bordered on missionary zeal to see Adlerian psychology brought to public attention and its methods given an opportunity to be practiced and tested widely. "It's not a question of whether Individual Psychology is accepted or rejected," he lamented, "but how few know it at all or are aware what could be done with it."[5]

The genuine kind of broad community programs in mental health that Dreikurs advocated was supported by a critical exposé of Illinois mental health programs written in response to the war situation. Documenting the soaring financial and social costs of mental illness, the report[6] castigated the professioal leadership for its failure to meet the community's staggering needs. It called for massive new programs aimed at prevention of mental illness through public education and the establishment of local clinics on the neighborhood level. Dreikurs could not have agreed more; his child guidance clinics, situated in neighborhood centers, were a start in precisely that direction. Lacking an opening in the broader professional literature, Dreikurs presented his ideas in his own journal, where he delineated the functional purpose of his child guidance clinics and gave his definition of community psychiatry. This concept was "discovered" in the mid-1960s and hailed as a great breakthrough in the mental health field. But in 1943, he wrote:

In what ways are our clinics different from others? First: They are decentralized. They approach and serve the parents, the teachers, the group workers, and churches of a small community. The technique which we use makes our clinics efficient only within a limited locality. . . . The type of disturbance handled at the clinic changes with the community. We have not found that the prevalent nationality in the community makes so much difference. Economic conditions seem to have a certain influence. Although we find identical problems and conflicts in all brackets of the population, the ways and means of expressing defiance or opposition on the part of children change with the cultural and economic level of the parents. This is . . . why child guidance clinics should be decentralized and can best serve the needs of the immediate community in which they are located. . . .

Second: Our psychological approach is decidedly different . . . in dealing with "problem children." . . . For us, the child's problems are not intrapersonal conflicts, disturbances created by ambivalent and contradictory emotions, by Oedipus complexes, by castration fears or guilt feelings. Such things . . . are not causes, but merely symptoms of disturbed social relationships between the children and their environment, represented mostly by parents. We cannot accept [as do] many leading child psychiatrists. . . . that the same psychotherapist should not treat the child and the mother at the same time. If the conflicts actually were just intrapersonal, then this position would be correct. But if . . . all problems are conflicts of relationship, then the problem of the child and that of the mother is identical and can . . . be [better] handled by the same psychiatrist. And that is exactly what we are doing—and it works!

Third: We use group therapy as the most effective method. . . . By group discussion parents and children realize how much their own private problem is like that of their neighbors. This feeling of belonging together, like being in the same boat, increases the social feeling and diminishes fear and apprehension, the feeling of failure and shame in every participant. . . . We are really one great family, we all—we children, we parents, and we workers and teachers. We all have similar problems and conflicts, [and] make similar mistakes to an astonishing degree. Our clinics represent really a cross section of our community life.[7]

Dreikurs and his colleague, Elly Redwin, maintained the child guidance clinics, with their free services to the community, throughout the war years. He thought the time was ripe for his innovative ideas in child guidance and, in his optimistic fashion, began to envision their rapid growth throughout Chicago. But the support and backing from the professional community was not forthcoming. His ideas were too radical and contrary to entrenched practice and only won the establishment's ridicule and disdain. Such reactions never defeated him. Tee regarded his expectations as unrealistic in those years, "I thought it was a hopeless endeavor, knowing that he had nothing to work with, no funds, no institutional support—plus the strong opposition. I soon learned that he refused to recognize a situation as hopeless. No matter how tough things got, no matter the hardship or disappointment, he kept plugging away, and always found some advantage, some constructive meaning in these setbacks."[8]

In the treatment of juvenile delinquency, which was an escalating problem in the war years, Dreikurs was able to see his ideas practiced on a limited scale. He advocated remedies designed to compensate for the ineffectiveness of the courts in handling delinquent youth, and he was instrumental in the establishment of a youth bureau within the Chicago Park Police in 1945. Appointed special examiner for the park district, he selected and trained personnel to administer the corrective programs for predelinquent and delinquent youths. He utilized the coordinated services of several social agencies. The objective was to avoid stigmatizing these youngsters with police records and to prevent them from becoming hardened criminals. Dreikurs's major concern was to train the park police officers to understand and to work effectively with the young offenders. According to reports issued by the Chicago Park District, the program was effective, and only 21 percent of the 1,880 youths processed through the bureau in 1948 later appeared before the juvenile court.[9] Of Dreikurs's contribution, the director of the Park Police Training School, Robert V. Keleher wrote:

> It was the first time that a whole police force received systematic training in understanding and handling children. . . . Before the training course started, there was some apprehension in regard to the reaction which the policemen, who had never been exposed to psychiatry before, would have to such a program. The unexpected receptiveness and enthusiastic response can be attributed to the down to earth and common sense approach of Individual Psychology. . . . In a poll of the officers, taken afterwards, this series . . . was named as one of the most useful courses ever given in the police training school.[10]

Another area of family life that drew Dreikurs's concerted attention was the escalated sexual and marital confusion that accompanied the stresses of war. "Every war accelerates change,"[11] he contended, and this one was bound to profoundly affect the status of women as a consequence of their unprecedented entry into military service and the industrial work force. In the process of counseling women daily, he learned firsthand of their despair, loneliness, and fear and also of their doubts and guilt relating to sexual morality. Responding to their need for sound psychological guidance, Dreikurs, assisted by free-lance writer Sylvia Pass Martin, wrote a book, "Marriage for One," that provided understanding of their problems and encouragement for coping with them. The book was completed early in 1943, but efforts to find a publisher were unsuccessful. Presently only of historical interest, the manuscript included an astute prediction: "The changes taking place today will probably not continue after the war when new economic conditions might change the picture in favor of men. However, such profound changes . . . cannot be undone completely. The implications which even a transitory episode of this magnitude has for . . . women . . . for relationships between men and women, [and] for attitudes toward family life . . . are certainly not reversible."[12]

Years later, historians would reflect on the war years and recognize the tremendous impetus they gave to egalitarianism. "The homefront," historian William Manchester recently concluded, "was in reality a battleground of ideas, customs, economic theory, foreign policy, and relations between the sexes and social classes. Rosy the Riveter, like Kilroy, was everywhere, and she would never be the same. . . . Every great war is accompanied by social revolution and the very dimensions of this war were bound to alter America greatly. Few realized it then."[13]

Dreikurs was one of the few. From his varied experiences on this homefront "battleground," he perceived a fundamental change in people's attitudes toward themselves and in their relationships with others. It was a subtle change but one that he recognized as a growing pattern with far-reaching consequences. He identified it as a pervasive revolution toward social equality—the demand by each individual that he be treated with the dignity and respect accorded a sovereign. That revolution, he predicted, would profoundly alter social interactions and relations between the sexes. It would be accompanied by chaos and marred by discord, and while its progress might be stalled now and again, its momentum would steadily increase. In the years that followed the war, Dreikurs elaborated on the concept of social equality, exposing its fast-rooting psychological underpinnings.[14]

THE CHALLENGE OF MARRIAGE

After the war, Dreikurs felt thoroughly optimistic about the future, both his and that of Adlerian psychology. His private practice was growing, and the child guidance clinics now had the steady support of a small but enthusiastic group of people. His efforts to launch a journal had passed the critical early stages, and the journal now seemed established. It had renewed interest among the Adlerians, who resurfaced after the war isolated and widely scattered throughout America and the world. His activities on the home front had brought him into close contact with a variety of people and organizations in Chicago and elsewhere. He truly felt at home in America and that he no longer was an outsider.

As 1945 drew to a close, Dreikurs's expectations rose as his first American book, *The Challenge of Marriage*, was published. A decade earlier, while in Vienna, he had begun to develop his manuscripts on marriage and childrearing, but since his arrival in America, he encountered only frustrating difficulty in securing a publisher. This deadlock ended when Dreikurs met C. Halliwell Duell, the president of Duell, Sloan & Pearce in New York, who was willing to publish the book. The inordinate difficulty Dreikurs had in getting a publisher is curious. His books are not literary masterpieces, but his writing is clear, highly readable, and non-technical. This publishing delay, similar to those encountered in getting his earliest papers published in professional journals, was largely due to the influence of Freudianism in the publishing world, especially in New York, which made it exceedingly difficult to get an "Adlerian" book published.

In *The Challenge of Marriage* Dreikurs took a sweeping look at sex, marriage, and family life from a psychological and sociological viewpoint, especially in light of the newly emerging cultural trends. Contrary to the widely held notion, he maintained that sexuality is determined by social factors more than by biological instincts and emphasized that all emotions, including love, are selected by the individual to maintain and to promote his life style. Many of the ideas expressed were prescient of things to come. Especially so was his analysis of women's changing role— in progress but far from complete—which would shake the age-old dominance-submission equilibrium between the sexes. He saw difficult years ahead in the area of sexual relationships. Throughout the book, he emphasized the responsibility of each individual, who through his attitudes not only determines his own marital happiness but also influences the development of the group in which he lives.

Now in its sixteenth printing, the book was favorably reviewed when it first appeared and has maintained a steady popularity. After thirty years it is somewhat dated, a quality that Dreikurs hoped to correct in a revised edition. But he never found time before he died. Nonetheless, its ideas are still cogent and rewarding. Writer Colman McCarthy, in a 1973 review of Dreikurs's contributions, commented: "*The Challenge of Marriage* is written without the flashy language common to current books on sexuality —always illustrated as if people forgot what they looked like—but contains every shade of meaning needed to understand marriage. Dreikurs has a certain wit as when he wrote that getting a divorce is often the first cooperative effort between husband and wife."[15]

Dreikurs advocated the creation of marriage counseling centers, which had been pioneered in Vienna by the Adlerian group but which were practically nonexistent in America. With the increasing rate of divorce and the growing confusion in relations between the sexes Dreikurs saw a need for professional services for "normal" people as they encountered the "normal" problems and frustrations of living together. Whether a troubled couple eventually decided to divorce or not was not the foremost issue. Rather, it was the consequences for each party if he or she never gained personal insight about what had made the marriage go sour. That is why he urged that both psychological and legal counsel were needed to assess the advisability of divorce. Too often, what looked like hopeless incompatibility dissolved when insight brought changed attitudes. Dreikurs often spoke of the offended party being "logically right, but psychologically wrong," as he explained with the following case:

> A typical example of contradictory interests and their detrimental effect upon marital harmony is the case of Mrs. D. She is a young woman with wide and liberal interests. She married the brother of her best girl friend. As she and her friend were very congenial in their interests and likes, she expected the brother to be like his sister. During a short courtship he was very attentive, sharing her activities. They married while he was in the Army, shortly before he left for overseas duty. When he came back, they really got acquainted with each other—and then her disappointment began. She found that he had little interest in classical music, only in light operettas, and that his political beliefs opposed those held by her and her family. She felt cheated and hurt; the more she argued and criticized him for his reluctance to enjoy a concert, the stronger he stuck to his guns. Their arguments and frictions affected shortly their sexual relationship. She lost interest—he demanded more; she felt abused and ceased responding. At this point, when she came for advice, she had begun to give serious consideration to obtaining a divorce.
>
> After listening to all her complaints, I suggested an interview with

both of them present. In the following three-way discussion, it became apparent that he was very much in love with her, was himself happy, and could not understand why she was not. He expressed willingness to do whatever was necessary. But she maintained that he had promised cooperation before and had failed to keep his promises. He admitted that he did not know why he could not refrain from antagonizing her, why, though he wanted to comply with her wishes, he by no means always did so.

It became clear that she was completely right in her complaints; on the logical level he was wrong. But psychologically she was the cause of all their conflicts. Her resentment, her pressure and disapproval were the real causes of the friction and endangered her marriage. As she was the key person, as the whole fate of this union depended upon her attitude alone since he was willing to get along, I suggested that she was the person in need of help.

After only a few consultations the situation changed completely. As she came to recognize her own part in the dirty game, she stopped provoking and resenting. The first effect was an immediate improvement of their relationship. They became friendly and mutually affectionate again. Since she again responded sexually, he ceased demanding so much. From then on she learned to approach her husband in a different way. She realized that she could just as well sympathize with his difficulties in sitting through a heavy program when they went to a concert, instead of arguing with him and assuring him that he did not understand the beauty of the music. In political discussions she could call on him to express his points of view, appreciating the fact that she had an expert from the other side of the fence, instead of scolding him about his wrong views. She recognized that, while she accused him of undemocratic attitudes, her own attitude of intolerance toward his political outlook could certainly not be considered democratic. With such an attitude of appreciation on her part, it could be expected that his own opinions and tastes would gradually change and approximate hers, since her violent and humiliating disapproval was the main force that kept him in opposition for the sake of his pride and self-esteem.

The decisive factor in the rehabilitation of this marriage was Mrs. D.'s recognition that logical right is not enough, that she had first to accept him as he was—and she had to start with herself, considering only what she could do.[16]

In later years when Dreikurs was traveling around the country conducting training seminars, he frequently demonstrated his techniques of marital counseling. California psychologist Loren Grey recalled one such marital counseling demonstration in Oregon when a young couple was brought to "Dr. D" (as he affectionately came to be known to thousands of people). A therapist had been working with them a whole year with little result, and now the couple was on the verge of breaking up:

> Dr. D.'s condition for taking the case was that the initial interview be a demonstration in front of the group who were studying at the seminar. At first the husband was unwilling to proceed under these conditions. Dr. Dreikurs put it to him in what might be considered his characteristic manner under such circumstances. "Do you want to save your marriage or do you want to break it up?" To those of us trained in the more traditional and less directive methods of therapy, this was heresy, but it worked. The young man ended his resistance at that point and was cooperative for the rest of the demonstration. In the space of an hour, without any prior knowledge of the background of either of the two clients, Dr. D. had revealed to them their styles of life, how these corresponded and how they could learn to make the diverse styles more fitting to each other. One had only to look at the expressions of the faces of the two to be aware of the insights they had attained. At first they expressed bewilderment and not a little resentment at what they heard. This changed to absorption, then to what seemed almost a sheepish acknowledgment of what had taken place, then almost dramatically to feelings of relief, as if they were saying to themselves, "Now, why hadn't *I* thought of that before?"[17]

Dreikurs's early efforts in conjoint marital counseling prompted Dr. David R. Mace to write to Dreikurs in 1960 that his ideas "on marriage counseling, written so many years ago, showed remarkable insight, because the whole process of marriage counseling has developed pretty well along the lines you predicted."[18]

RETURN TO BRAZIL

When the invitation came to return to Brazil in 1946 to lecture at the university and to give the faltering Adlerian group a solid Dreikursian shot in the arm, he enthusiastically accepted. Tee was excited but at the same time distressed because they could not afford such a financial undertaking, especially since it would require four months of leave from his private practice. But Dreikurs never permitted anything to stand in the way when he wanted something badly enough. So he borrowed money for the trip and persuaded Tee that he would earn more than enough in consulting fees to cover the entire cost of the trip. Tee agreed, having already discovered that, "He lives like a rich man, but he isn't. He has no respect for money or aggrandizement for material things or wealth. If anything, he has an antipathy to such things, but he likes to live well for the sheer enjoyment of it. He shocked most of my family by claiming it isn't necessary to save money. Money to him was simply there to live for today."[19]

Professionally, the trip turned out to be a mixed experience. Teaching at the University of Rio, demonstrating his techniques at the hospital, and lecturing before the medical faculty, he was able to teach more comprehensively than before. But in the nine years since 1937, the psychoanalytic viewpoint had risen to ascendency in Brazil as elsewhere, and the bitterness left by Dreikurs's stunning attacks was not forgotten. "On this second visit, I was really effective," Dreikurs explained. "Then the opposition started. Suddenly, there was some kind of ill-feeling and a rumor floating around. I finally found out that some of the psychoanalytically oriented people claimed that I was neither a professor nor a member of the psychiatric society, and not even a psychiatrist. We had to go after them. I got hold of an American Psychiatric Association directory which proved I was a fellow, and my books had the imprint that I was a professor of psychiatry. So, we squelched that."[20]

He succeeded in revitalizing the small Adlerian group in Brazil. There was also an important breakthrough with his publications. Through the recommendation of his old friend da Silva Mello, Dreikurs treated the troubled, illegitimate son of a prominent newspaper publisher. The father, a man of great wealth, was so influential that he was able to get a special law passed to legitimize his son. Greatly impressed with Dreikurs's results in counseling his son, he saw to it that all of Dreikurs's books were quickly translated and published in Brazil.

Personally for Tee and Ru (as she endearingly called him), the trip was like a honeymoon. Brazil presented a splendid and relaxing interlude away from the struggles of Chicago. Eva, shortly to enter college, joined them for the trip and treasured the long strolls on the beach in the moonlight, the closeness, and the fun, as all three, arm-in-arm, singing as they walked, soaked up Rio's exotic atmosphere. When they returned to Chicago, Tee seemed to lose the sadness she had borne since Leon's death and began to shed her self-woven cocoon of timidity.

When they were first married, Tee gave up her full-time position to take on a role she had always cherished—motherhood. Eric was already an adult and was away from Chicago in the army. Eva was fourteen, and there were only a few brief years before she too would be off on her own. However, Tee did not completely abandon her professional activities. During the war years she served as head of a crippled children's camp, as director of a day camp, and as consultant to the Chicago Board of Education. While she was running the camps, her husband helped her with the problem children and staff training and even brought some of his medical students along for training. After the war her activities became subordinated to her function as chief collaborator for his wide-ranging activities. Tee was quickly drawn into his many writing projects; she functioned as an active sounding board for his ideas and edited his manuscripts. Frequently she served as a volunteer social worker at the child guidance clinics, but most often on the sidelines, observing, reacting, sensing the audience's mood, and commenting rarely but with great perspicacity. As one longtime associate commented: "I observed her quiet, continuous support. She was always there—enabling him to do what he wanted to do. She appeared to be the launching pad from which he derived the strength to fly."[21]

A Grass Roots Program

Dreikurs returned from his trip to Brazil invigorated and determined to see his expanding goals for the child guidance clinics become a reality. By the early postwar years, only two clinics were still functioning. Dreikurs had won support from individuals in the community who were convinced of the centers' important and unique contribution. Nevertheless, the programs faced serious difficulties. The essential problem was organizational and was due to the lack of adequate funding and the need for administrative structure. So long as the clinics were sponsored by the settlement houses, their continuation was dependent upon the annual reapproval of their hosts—the directors and board members who ran the settlement houses. These directors were often remote from the work of the clinics, and Dreikurs was called upon to reargue the cause of the clinics when settlement-house funds ran low and when pressures mounted in opposition to Dreikurs's methods.

An effective solution was found when the Individual Psychology Association (IPA)—not formerly involved with Dreikurs's first clinics—entered the picture. Previously IPA's activities had been concerned exclusively with lectures and classes in Adlerian psychology. But at the suggestion of its vice-president, Harold Wheeler, the association decided to concentrate its energies on the organization and development of the centers. A fresh infusion of enthusiastic volunteer workers stabilized and broadened their base of support. Where "previously each clinic was conducted by a psychiatrist or psychologist and social worker," Dreikurs recalled, "now each had a large staff of volunteer workers provided by the membership, who supported actively and efficiently the work of the professional staff."[22] These volunteers performed a variety of important functions, including those of maintaining liaisons with the community, keeping clinic records, and assisting the counseling work as recorders, playroom workers, and through activities like art and story telling.

This change of direction of the Individual Psychology Association led to the formal establishment of a nonprofit corporation, the Community Child Guidance Centers (CCGC), which provided the necessary stable organizational base for the centers. It had its own board of directors drawn from the community. They assumed the task of fund raising, the development of new centers, and the routine coordination of professional and volunteer staffing for the centers. Dreikurs served as the overall medical director and director of professional services for the centers. "As far as I know," he commented, "it was the first Adlerian organization in existence consisting entirely of lay people. Other Adlerian groups had accepted lay people as members, but they were led by professionals, which was not the case with the Community Child Guidance Centers. These were completely independent from the Adlerian counselors whom they contracted for services."[23]

It was at this juncture that Dreikurs reemphasized and clarified the essential educational character of his guidance work. "The centers are not intended to provide psychiatric services, but educational facilities. . . . Their main function is not to heal but to instruct parents and children in new patterns of family relationships, leading to a better understanding and a more efficient resolution of problems and conflicts. . . . [The] improvement of the child and of the family relationship in general is the result of a learning process."[24] As part of this defining process, he re-placed the word *clinic* with the word *center*. It was meant to convey the idea that the centers were not designed to deal with "sick" children and adults but with the lack of sound training techniques on the part of parents and the misdirected goals on the part of children. "Mothers don't need therapy—they need education," Dreikurs often repeated. Similarly, to the widely held notion that misbehaving children were "emotionally disturbed," Dreikurs countered, "There is nothing wrong with their emo-tions, only their intentions."[25]

Under the sponsorship of the new organization, a third child guidance center was begun in 1947 at Henry Booth Settlement House, located in a blighted area off Halsted Street, in Chicago. The neighborhood was popu-lated by predominantly poor black families, newly migrated from the South, ill adjusted to the tough Chicago ghetto life, and wary of "do-gooder" whites. Like the earlier centers, it, too, experienced a slow start and initially had difficulty getting local families involved. The staff and volunteers understood and waited patiently. In time the families began to come, and the center was successfully underway. Because the sessions were conducted on Saturdays, it became feasible for fathers and working mothers to attend. This increased the effectiveness of the guidance work by revealing significant conflict areas, not only between child and parent but also between mother and father. This added another dimension to the therapeutic effort.

The following year, the North Side Child Guidance Center was begun at Temple Sholom on exclusive Lake Shore Drive. Dreikurs's friends ex-pressed doubt as to whether the group approach would be acceptable to a middle-class and upper-middle-class population. Competitiveness and concern with prestige, they anticipated, might prevent the participation of such families. Their doubts proved to be unfounded, as did the notion that wealthier, better educated parents behaved fundamentally differ-ently toward children than did their less educated, poorer counterparts. Dreikurs's favorite remark, "No two mothers are alike in personality, abil-ity, or background, but all mothers make identical mistakes in dealing with their children," reflected this realization. As it turned out, attendance at the North Side center was greater and more involved than ever, and Dreikurs claimed, "Within a short time, the entire community became aware of the amount of help needed by almost every parent. Schools in the area took a more active part, since the parent-teacher relationships in the area were cordial and close."[26] To enhance the educational effort, he started his first project at training discussion leaders for parent study groups in areas where child guidance centers were located.[27]

But organizational support itself was not sufficient to launch Dreikurs's ambitious plan to establish twenty child guidance centers in the Chicago area. Funding was the other critical ingredient necessary to the development and operation of these centers, and to staff them with trained personnel. In mid-1947, Dreikurs and Sydney Roth, president of the board of the Community Child Guidance Centers, made their first bid for membership in the Chicago Council of Social Agencies in order to qualify for community-chest funds. The tricky politics of community funding quickly proved to be a subtle but potent arm of the dominant Freudian outlook in the mental health field. Like the insidious developments at the medical school, which occurred at this same time, a solid wall of opposition arose to Dreikurs's psychological viewpoint and methods.

When application for membership was made, the Council of Social Agencies turned to the liaison committee of the Illinois Psychiatric Association and the Chicago Neurological Society for its advice. They asked whether the Adlerian approach had something to offer in child guidance and also about the professional qualifications of the centers' staffs. Based upon the committee's confidential report,[28] the council denied membership to the Community Child Guidance Centers and suggested that the contributions in personnel and techniques from the Individual Psychology Association be disbursed through existing agencies.[29] Dreikurs was incensed: "We received an amazing letter which said that the Adlerian approach is a recognized one and that I am a qualified psychiatrist. However, any service which uses only one school of thought would not deserve public support. That was complete nonsense, because the Psychoanalytic Institute, Michael Reese Hospital, and other institutions which only used the Freudian approach received public funds. They could qualify, but not so anyone else. Our negotiations with the council failed continually."[30]

The denial of membership in the council had consequences that went far beyond the lack of access to community-chest funding. It severely hampered funding grants from private charitable foundations and gave the centers a dubious image. "When people wanted to make contributions to the centers," Dreikurs recalled, "they would be advised by the Chicago Association of Commerce (the local chamber of commerce) not to give money to us because we were not a bona fide agency."[31]

With the centers, as at the medical school, Dreikurs experienced the bitter fruit of an earlier insight: "We Individual Psychologists have to bear the whole brunt of this opposition [to] any one school [of thought] because we do not represent as yet the majority. . . . The difference between a 'sect' and a publicly accepted opinion is, unfortunately, still determined by numbers and not by the value of the contribution. . . . Partisan opinion rules politics, economics, morals—and science."[32]

In his characteristic fashion, Dreikurs refused to be discouraged by this setback although in the long run, it so crippled his plans that the child guidance centers were never able to develop to the degree he once envisioned. Obviously, he had to find other sources of financial backing for the centers—wealthy individuals and fund-raising schemes that were time-consuming, exhausting, temporary in nature, and all too frequently interfered with his zealous commitment to the centers. This intricate story of the child guidance centers cannot be adequately explained here.[33] But for the time being, Dreikurs realized that he had to get beyond Chicago, to break out of the restrictive professional cocoon that enveloped the city and find a receptive audience for his ideas elsewhere.

The Challenge of Parenthood

Dreikurs's book *The Challenge of Parenthood* was published that same year, 1948, and provided a suitable vehicle for conveying the theory and practice for the study groups and for the broader dissemination of his child-rearing philosophy. Since the start of his first center in 1939, there had been a growing demand to have Dreikurs's ideas available in print. The long delay was not due to lack of effort on Dreikurs's part. Like his book on marriage, his book for parents originated in Vienna in the mid-1930s. A German manuscript containing the basic principles of his child-rearing philosophy was then under contract for publication by the Sensen-Verlag Publishing House in Vienna,[34] but it was never released because of the fascist takeover. However, as described earlier, Dreikurs managed to get a copy of the manuscript to Holland, where it was translated into Dutch and published in 1936. After Dreikurs arrived in the United States, he needed the German manuscript in order to continue his work and so wrote to his sister, then still in Vienna, to try to retrieve it from the publisher. Because the publisher, Josef Schwarz, was Jewish and therefore forbidden to publish anything, his activities were closely watched. Through clandestine and dangerous maneuvers, he managed secretly to pass the manuscript to Bertha at a prearranged rendezvous.

She, in turn, smuggled it out of Austria to Dreikurs.[35] By 1939, an English translation had been made, and although Phyllis Bottome, a well-known British author and Adler's biographer heartily endorsed it in writing,[36] no American publisher accepted it. In the meantime, Dreikurs continued to work on the manuscript, adding new case materials from his Chicago child guidance centers. He also incorporated his important discoveries of the four goals of misbehavior in children and the "recognition reflex."

Dreikurs managed to get the Chicago Medical School to underwrite the publication of a mimeographed version entitled *Manual of Child Guidance*. When, some three years later, Duell, Sloan & Pearce finally published his long-awaited book, the public reaction was most favorable and in some cases enthusiastic:

> This book is one of the most sensible and practical of publications . . . not so much a cold scientific analysis as an expression of warm understanding of the problems of childhood . . . [with] countless valuable suggestions.
>
> —*Journal of the American Medical Association* 137 (1948): 1563

> Those who read it—and their number should be countless—will remove themselves from the ranks of amateur parents.
>
> —*National Parent Teacher*, April 1948, p. 34.

> [It] probes deeply the problems of parent-child relations . . . [and] shows how democracy can be established in the home and children taught to take on responsibilities without being dominated or coerced.
>
> —*New York Times*, March 28, 1949, p. 31.

In the introduction to the book, Dreikurs pointed out the difficulties and pitfalls parents face in a rapidly evolving democratic society: "Many of you may have tried to grant your children freedom and self-expression, but . . . you are inclined to confuse freedom with anarchy, self-expression with indulgence, liberty with license. . . . When you fail with your ideas of freedom and liberty, then you feel compelled to revert to the old methods of authority, severity, and force. Most . . . contemporary parents vacillate between indulgence and suppression, with damaging effects on their children. . . . This book attempts to show you how you can . . . prepare your children for life in a democracy."[37]

Natural and logical consequences, techniques of encouragement, and the family council were the distinctive principles Dreikurs introduced to help guide parents to a new middle course—a democratic one—between the extremes of authoritarianism and anarchic permissiveness. Natural consequences and encouragement, he contended, were genuine and efficient alternatives to the outdated traditions of reward and punishment. "Natural consequences" is a learning technique drawn from experiencing the results of behavior. The child quickly learns the inherent order and reality of the physical and social environment from the natural consequences of his acts: "If I touch the hot stove, it hurts"; "If I fail to get my dirty clothes into the hamper, they don't get washed."

Natural consequences occur all the time, and parents should allow the child to experience them without interference, except when health or safety is threatened. Logical consequences are contrived by the parent but are otherwise the same as natural consequences. To the challenge that natural consequences and encouragement are only semantic coverups for reward and punishment, Dreikurs countered, "Reward is meaningful only if given for *accomplishments*; in contrast, encouragement is *always* necessary, and particularly when the child has *failed*. . . . Punishment is imposed upon the child for past transgressions; the consequences, which must be natural and logical to the disturbance of order, are self-evident. . . . It is order and reality . . . not the arbitrary power of adults, which brings about the unpleasant consequences."[38]

Dreikurs also advocated the family council, a regularly scheduled meeting for all family members in which each has a chance to express himself freely in all matters pertaining to the family and each participates in decisions and responsibilities. The family council constitutes education for democratic living and provides each member with a sense of equal status in regard to both rights and obligations.[39]

"His Organizational Genius"

By the late 1940s, three geographic centers of Adlerian activities had emerged in the United States.

In Los Angeles, a small Adlerian group developed with Dr. Lydia Sicher as its central figure. She had been Adler's closest colleague in Vienna in his last years. Besides the group in Los Angeles and the one in Chicago under Dreikurs's dynamic leadership, there was the New York group, which centered around the Adler family. Adler's widow, Raissa, was its inspiring leader and figurehead. In addition, Adler's daughter, Dr. Alexandra Adler, had settled in New York to practice psychiatry after earlier associations with Duke and Harvard Universities. Kurt A. Adler, the only son and next to youngest of the four Adler children, already had a Ph.D. from Europe and would soon complete medical and psychiatric training and take up practice in New York City.

Other important members of the New York group were the educator-psychologists Willard and Marguerite Beecher, who wrote several excellent books; Dr. Sofie Lazarsfeld; Dr. Helene Papanek; Ernst Papanek; Leonhard and Danica Deutsch; Drs. Frederick Feichtinger, Alfred Farau, and Asya Kaydis; and educator Nahum Shoobs, who made a pioneering effort to introduce Adlerian ideas and psychodrama techniques into high school guidance work. Ernst Papanek did distinguished work as executive director at the Wiltwyck School for Boys in New York, where his Adlerian approach to juvenile delinquents was later credited by Claude Brown, author of *Manchild in the Promised Land,* and prizefighter Floyd Patterson as having been an important influence in redirecting them to useful and rewarding careers.

Nearby, at Brown University, and later at the University of Vermont, were psychologists Drs. Heinz and Rowena Ansbacher, who, with great patience and exacting scholarship, brought a new awareness to the profundity of Adler's contribution through their outstanding books, *The Individual Psychology of Alfred Adler* (1956) and *Superiority and Social Interest* (1964). In these works, the Ansbachers brought together Adler's unsystematic and scattered writings into a coherent conceptual system that brilliantly reflected the depth, originality, and prescience of Adler's thinking. Not surprisingly, because of their totally different outlooks, Dreikurs and the Ansbachers—who were academic, not clinical psychologists—frequently clashed on issues over the years. Dreikurs, the brilliant pioneer, always provoking, teaching, demonstrating, pushing ahead into new frontiers, did not devote himself to exacting scholarship, which often vexed the Ansbachers. Yet, in later years, Heinz Ansbacher came to appreciate Dreikurs's role in his own development: "During my early days of writing on Adler the *Individual Psychology Bulletin,* which Rudolf Dreikurs started, . . . offered me an opportunity to formulate my thoughts."[40] After sixteen challenging years guiding the Adlerian journal as editor-in-chief, Dreikurs stepped aside in 1956, and Heinz Ansbacher assumed the editorship of the journal, now renamed *Journal of Individual Psychology.*

By the late 1940s, because of his role as editor and his untiring efforts to inject Adlerian principles into American consciousness, Dreikurs emerged as a potent leader, the central figure in the communication link between the various Adlerian individuals and groups. He forever prodded others to defend their right to practice Adlerian psychology, to open clinics (as he had done in Chicago), and to aggressively seek out opportunities to teach. Soon there emerged the glimmering of a struggle between the New York group and the Chicago group. The New York group was the more conservative and did not openly challenge the psychoanalytic domination of the profession there but instead sought peacefully to coexist and to do their own thing quietly. Dreikurs, by contrast, was always an activist— forthrightly criticizing the Freudian posture and its monopoly of the psychiatric professions. He was always heralding Adler's ideas, pushing new programs, and seeking to enlarge the scope and therapeutic techniques in which he so firmly believed.

More orthodox in outlook, the New York group, which included many long-established Adlerians who had worked directly with Adler in Europe, as well as the Adlers themselves, was critical of Dreikurs's enlargement of Adlerian principles. They had formed their own interpretations of what Adler said and were not about to regard Dreikurs in any way as an authority on their common mentor. Those who had known Dreikurs in Europe saw him differently. There he was one of many younger colleagues and by no means a chief lieutenant within the movement. They objected to what they considered to be Dreikurs's oversimplification of Adler's concepts. While it is true that Adler's writing and manner reflected his special talent for painting the subtle nuances of human behavior and motivation, that very quality made the translation of Adler's ideas into guidelines for concrete actions very difficult. Dreikurs's foremost concern was to make Adler teachable, and if in the process he exaggerated a point or left out some of the subtle nuances or ramifications of the ideas, it was because he wanted to get people moving and doing, rather than simply theorizing. "Only when you take action, try something, can you find out for yourself if it works and is useful," he often commented. In sum, Dreikurs's bold initiative and assertive leadership were at best begrudgingly acknowledged by his contemporary, but more traditionally rooted, Adlerian colleagues.

The founding of the American Society of Adlerian Psychology (ASAP) in 1952 was also largely due to Dreikurs's initiative and organizational ability. Three years earlier, he and Louise Herst, an active member of the Chicago Individual Psychology Association, had drawn up a proposal outlining the steps to be taken for the purpose of establishing a national organization and, following that, an international organization. Dr. Alexandra Adler was elected ASAP's first president. She acknowledged at the inaugural meeting that "it was, as so often, the organizational genius of Dr. Dreikurs, which is basically responsible for our being here today."[41] He succeeded her as president for the years 1954–1956 and was always an active, vocal member of the board of directors. Nonetheless, within the organization he came to feel that his vision and role were considerably hampered.

Outside the Adlerian group, his books, his professorship, and his role as editor of a professional journal aided him in his quest to propagate Adlerian psychology. Of value also was his growing involvement in a number of national organizations. These included the National Committee for Mental Hygiene, the Association for the Advancement of Psychotherapy, the American Society of Group Psychotherapy, and the American Humanist Association. Like Adler, he considered himself a psychologist as well as a psychiatrist. That is, he was interested in a general theory of psychology, personality, and motivation, and not simply with the treatment of pathological aspects of behavior. Yet, in practice, these overlapping disciplines were often remote from each other, and professionally antagonistic, and their leaders were anxious to safeguard their exclusive functions in society. This only enlarged the obstacles for Dreikurs as he tried to get beyond the limitations of Chicago and draw greater professional attention to the theory and practice of Adlerian psychology.

An interesting episode involving Dreikurs, Abraham Maslow, and the American Psychological Association is illustrative. Dreikurs had written to Maslow, whose psychological ideas were developing along the lines of Adlerian psychology, to invite him to submit his papers to the *Individual Psychology Bulletin* for publication. This was early in 1949, and Maslow replied:

> Of course I am interested in your bulletin and . . . shall certainly keep it in mind for possible papers. And I shall be glad to read your books of which I have heard.
>
> I shall soon send you some papers that may interest you. I couldn't call them "Adlerian" and yet they represent, as do *all* my writings, an attempt to fuse Adler's great insights with those of other great psychologists especially Wertheimer, James, etc.[42]

Some time later, after Maslow had read Dreikurs's books, he wrote to Dreikurs again:

I was delighted with your books. I shall certainly recommend them to my students since I think them the best of the "adult education" books I have read in these fields. I hope they get the popular success they deserve.

My one criticism, or rather, suggestion is probably what you would expect, i.e., a more empirical-scientific attitude synthesized with the medico-clinical attitude. . . . Why don't you join yourself to the researchers as well as the clinicians? I'd be very glad to sponsor you for membership in the American Psychological Association.[43]

Following Maslow's suggestion, Dreikurs submitted an application for membership in the APA and was summarily turned down in a routine form letter.[44] When Maslow learned of this, he wrote to Dreikurs:

Your letter shocked me beyond words. I had never expected this degree of arrogance from these people although I had recently heard of similar incidents—a kind of general anticlinical drive within APA by the "experimenters"—mostly animal psychologists.

I must apologize profoundly for the insult to which I exposed you and can plead only that a very large majority of psychologists feel as I do about liaison. As for "distinguished" I consider your book on parenthood *easily* the best one in existence. I am quite convinced that it outweighs a thousand rats in a thousand mazes.

With sincerest apologies for my foolish colleagues,
A. H. Maslow[45]

Dreikurs often voiced strong objections to the prevailing scientific model of research adopted in psychology. He certainly recognized the value of solid empirical research but at the same time felt that the overwhelming preoccupation with statistical research and animal studies that characterized academic psychology had become more hindering than advancing to the development of psychological understanding. His chief criticism was directed at the inadequacy of the research design, but he also deplored the delays brought about by pursuing research rather than providing much-needed services to the community. Once, at a meeting on juvenile delinquency, it was argued that to gain respectability, research was needed. "Nonsense," Dreikurs retorted, "What we need to do is work with the knowledge we have at the moment. We cannot wait for research." He knew that most research findings are rarely implemented to any great extent. He had also discovered that professionals generally followed their own convictions regardless of research findings.

Notes for Chapter 15

1. Rudolf Dreikurs, "Dear Friends," *Individual Psychology Bulletin* 2 (January 1942): 1.
2. Rudolf Dreikurs, "The Educational Implications of the 'Four Freedoms,'" *Individual Psychology Bulletin* 2 (1942): 68–71.
3. "The Chicago Group," *Individual Psychology Bulletin* 3 (1943): 27–28.
4. Charles A. Beard and Mary R. Beard, *The Beards' Basic History of the United States* (Garden City, N.Y.: Garden City Books, 1944), pp. 474–476.
5. Rudolf Dreikurs, "Organizing Distribution of Knowledge," *Individual Psychology Bulletin* 2 (1942): 38.
6. Stuart K. Jaffary, *The Mentally Ill and Public Provision for Their Care in Illinois* (Chicago: University of Chicago Press, 1942), pp. 206–207.
7. Dreikurs, "Our Child Guidance Clinics in Chicago," pp. 15–16.
8. From a tape-recorded interview with Sadie "Tee" Dreikurs by William H. Mackaness, 1961.
9. Chicago Park District, *Annual Reports*, nos. 11, 12, 13, 14, 1945–1948.
10. Robert V. Keleher, "Individual Psychology Used in Police Training," *Individual Psychology Bulletin* 6 (1947): 61–64.
11. Rudolf Dreikurs and Sylvia Pass Martin, "Marriage for One," 1943, Dreikurs Papers.
12. Ibid.
13. William Manchester, *The Glory and the Dream: A Narrative History of America, 1932–1972* (New York: Bantam Books, 1975), p. 289.
14. In Adler's later writings, he alluded to the notion of social equality. His "ironclad logic of social living," which Dreikurs often quoted as a point of departure, indicated that equality was the only stable basis for harmonious living. But Adler's hopeful prophecy was more idealistic than realistic given the social and political conditions that prevailed during his life. Adler understood that fact well enough and predicted more than sixty years ago that it would take two generations before women would rise to demand equality with men.
15. Colman McCarthy, "Child-Parent Wars," *Washington Post*, October 9, 1973; also his *Inner Companions* (Washington, D.C.: Acropolis Books, 1975).
16. Rudolf Dreikurs, *The Challenge of Marriage* (New York: Duell, Sloan & Pearce, 1946), pp. 181–183.
17. Raymond J. Corsini, "Rudolf Dreikurs: A Consensual Appreciation on His 70th Birthday," *Journal of Individual Psychology* 23 (1967): 176.
18. David R. Mace to Dreikurs, June 5, 1960, Dreikurs Papers. Dr. Mace is a founder of Parents Without Partners and former executive director of the American Association of Marriage and Family Counselors.
19. Sadie "Tee" Dreikurs–Mackaness interview.
20. Dreikurs-Mackaness interview.
21. Shirley Gould, personal communication, August 1973.
22. Rudolf Dreikurs, "Report on the Community Child Guidance Centers of Chicago," *Individual Psychology Bulletin* 7 (1949): 35.

23. Dreikurs, "Guiding, Teaching and Demonstrating," p. 152.

24. Rudolf Dreikurs, "Fundamental Principles of Child Guidance," in *Adlerian Family Counseling*, p. 17.

25. Rudolf Dreikurs, *Understanding Your Children: Study Guidebook*, ed. James A. and Neysa M. Peterson (Winooski, Vt.: Vermont Educational Television Network, 1969), p. 49.

26. Rudolf Dreikurs, "Family Group Therapy in the Chicago Community Child Guidance Centers," *Mental Hygiene* 35 (1951): 296. In this paper, which grew out of a speech before the American Group Therapy Association in 1950, Dreikurs emphasized the various group approaches embodied in the work of the Chicago centers. His description of "family group therapy" later prompted Dr. Robert MacGregor to write to Dreikurs: "I find the term 'family group therapy' to be yours rather than John E. Bell's" (July 12, 1968, Dreikurs Papers). Bell is often credited with having initiated family group therapy. Clearly, Dreikurs's work either preceded or was parallel to that of other pioneers in group approaches to family therapy.

27. "The Chicago Group," *Individual Psychology Bulletin* 6 (1947): 196.

28. Illinois Psychiatric Society, Liaison Committee, "Confidential Report," May 10, 1947, Dreikurs Papers. The report was signed by psychiatrists David B. Rotman, R. P. Mackay, Meyer Solomon, and Francis J. Gerty (chairman).

29. Council on Social Agencies of Chicago to Dreikurs, July 7, 1947, Dreikurs Papers.

30. Dreikurs-Mackaness interview.

31. Ibid.

32. Rudolf Dreikurs, "The Present Position of Individual Psychology," *Individual Psychology Bulletin* 2 (1941): 13.

33. For a detailed history of the Chicago Community Child Guidance Centers, see Truitt, *Legacy for the Future*.

34. Josef Schwarz of Sensen-Verlag to Rudolf Dreikurs, November 21, 1936, Dreikurs Papers.

35. Bertha Dreikurs Simkins, personal communication, May 1974.

36. Phyllis Bottome, July 24, 1939, Dreikurs Papers.

37. Dreikurs, *Challenge of Parenthood*, p. xi.

38. Rudolf Dreikurs, "The Cultural Implications of Reward and Punishment," *International Journal of Social Psychiatry* 4 (1958): 177.

39. For a practical guide to the family council, reflecting many years of experience by numerous families, see Rudolf Dreikurs, Raymond J. Corsini, and Shirley Gould, *Family Council: The Dreikurs Technique for Putting an End to War Between Parents and Children (and Between Children and Children)* (Chicago: Henry Regnery, 1974).

40. Theodore S. Krawiec, ed., *The Psychologists*, vol. 2 (New York: Oxford University Press, 1974), p. 34.

41. "Proceedings of the Inaugural Meeting of the American Society of Adlerian Psychology," *American Journal of Individual Psychology* 10 (1952/1953): 82.

42. Abraham H. Maslow to Dreikurs, [1949?], Dreikurs Papers.

43. Maslow to Dreikurs, [1949?], Dreikurs Papers.

44. American Psychological Association to Dreikurs, April 13, 1949, Dreikurs Papers.

45. Maslow to Dreikurs, [1949?], Dreikurs Papers.

16

The Art and Science
of Psychotherapy

> I deal with each patient as if it were the last time I would
> see him. . . . In each session one has to see the total situa-
> tion and do something about it. . . . I am not afraid of
> making a mistake nor do I feel that the patient may be
> harmed. I have too much confidence in him to be appre-
> hensive. And this may be my most revolutionary procedure
> in contrast to the prevalent caution and patronizing prac-
> tices in the field of psychotherapy.
>
> Rudolf Dreikurs,
> "Guiding, Teaching, and Demonstrating," 1967

By the time most men reach the age of fifty, the ambitions of their youth
have been tempered by the ups and downs of life. Reassessing their aims,
some are content with their lot, others grow bitter with disappointment, or
retreat in defeat. A very few seem recharged with enthusiasm, and ready
to embark on new adventures. When Dreikurs turned fifty in 1947, he
entered the most prolific and energetic phase of his life. In this period he
branched out in so many different directions—each with significant
consequences—that it has been nearly impossible to re-create this part of
his life story with the coherence with which he actually lived it. By the
late 1940s, the following activities were ongoing simultaneously: work
with the child guidance centers, professional writing and the demanding task of editing a journal, teaching and the continuing adversity
at the medical school, growing involvement at the leadership level in a
number of national organizations, new ventures into the sphere of education, and private practice. Despite this impressive schedule of work and
achievement, he once commented to Bernard Shulman, "Until I was fifty,
I felt like a failure."

In the face of the continuing opposition to his theories and methods—

and much to the chagrin of his adversaries, who opposed his legitimately practicing what he believed—Dreikurs was determined to argue his case. This resolve stimulated him to move beyond the parochialism of the mental health professions. His approach was twofold: to spend increasing amounts of time away from Chicago traveling and lecturing while searching for more receptive audiences; and to shift his emphasis from psychiatry to education. "By this time," he wrote, "I had decided to concentrate my work, apart from the practice of psychiatry in my office, to the field of education and guidance, training educators and counselors, and through them teachers and parents for their difficult job of raising and influencing children."[1] This decision reflected his steadfast belief in what he could accomplish and also precipitated important innovations in his practice of psychotherapy. These innovations were the fruition of an ambition from his youth to link his intuitive art with the science of psychotherapy.

PSYCHODRAMA

Adaline Starr recalled that in 1946, after his first book was published, Dreikurs was buoyant, "He thought the whole world would open up for him." But he knew he could not do it alone and that he would need to involve others in his private practice. Ever seeking to incorporate new therapeutic methods that were compatible with Adlerian principles, he became interested in psychodrama, the promising therapeutic approach created by Dr. Jacob L. Moreno. Dreikurs proposed to Starr, "Why don't you go to Moreno and train in psychodrama? Because I will be so busy, I won't be able to go it alone."[2] She had already been involved for several years as a volunteer in the child guidance clinics doing creative dramatics, and Dreikurs saw her warmth, empathy, spontaneity, and humor as valuable therapeutic talents.

Dreikurs's fascination with psychodrama actually began when he read a paper by Nahum Shoobs,[3] an American educator who had trained under Adler. Shoobs experimented with psychodrama in the New York public schools and found it an effective method for helping children to understand their behavior and to solve problems.

Moreno, the father of psychodrama, was Viennese like Dreikurs, and for a time, had some affiliation with Adler. However, Dreikurs and Moreno only met in America and not until the late 1940s. Theirs was an infrequent but testy relationship. Yet both worked together in conjunction with the American Society of Group Psychotherapy and Psychodrama, where Dreikurs succeeded Moreno as president in 1954.

When Starr completed her training with Moreno in 1947, she returned to Chicago and began to integrate psychodrama into Dreikurs's private practice and the work of the child guidance centers. In time, she became a consultant to many Chicago hospitals and emerged as a leading psychodramatist. From this beginning in Chicago, psychodrama became a potent adjunct to Adlerian therapy, in contrast to Moreno's view of it as a complete therapy in itself. While Moreno emphasized spontaneity and catharsis, Adlerians held that spontaneity without insight was not enough, nor was catharsis (emotional release) an end in itself.[4]

Starr defines psychodrama as the "dramatic enactment of the *self*—'the self in action.' A synthesis of analysis and action, it focuses on the individual, using significant life situations and the information about the 'actor's difficulties to design a play which will allow him to experience his conflict in a new light." In the child guidance centers, Starr explains:

> psychodrama is designed to give the child an insight into his action patterns and to help him to learn other, more acceptable roles in meeting social situations. . . . At the centers, the psychodramatist invites some children to come with her into the psychodrama room, . . . [and then] either encourages a spontaneous situation to develop in the group or she assigns roles. . . . Since acting is a form of play for children, it is rarely difficult to get something going. . . . The counselor and psychodramatist work together. The psychodramatist reveals through role-playing the normal interactions of the child while the counselor uncovers the life style and purposes the action serves. . . . The episodes are designed to help the children find positive ways of solving problems and behaving.[5]

Incorporating psychodrama in his psychiatric practice was a radical departure from standard procedure, and Dreikurs approached it with caution at first. Starr recalled that he made clear that her role would be strictly limited to counseling. She was not to do interpretations of early recollections or dreams or to act them out with psychodramatic techniques:

> He was careful at first, not so later on. I remember I was with him when there was a meeting for doctors and others, and I used the

word "hostility." One psychiatrist looked at me and said, "Are you a doctor? That's an interpretation I don't think you are qualified to make." No question, having a psychodramatist in the office was revolutionary, and while at first he put a fence around me, gradually that too disappeared. It wasn't too long ago that the Chicago State Hospital wouldn't allow nonmedical people to work with medical people. Dreikurs was one of the first to break down that barrier. He met resistance and opposition for doing it. I think the only ones who appreciated what he did were the psychologists.[6]

MULTIPLE PSYCHOTHERAPY

It was Dreikurs's trip to Brazil in 1946 that led to one of his most important contributions to psychiatry—multiple psychotherapy. In anticipation of his four-month absence, he began to train an assistant, Dr. Arthur Zweibel, a young associate from the Chicago Medical School, to take over his private practice while he was away. Instead of simply describing his patients to his associate, he had Zweibel attend each therapy session along with Dreikurs and the patient. "The ensuing double interviews . . . proved so effective, both for the training of the therapist and for the therapy of the patient, that we decided to keep the system . . . as a regular procedure. Although I was cautioned that assigning patients to an associate would be impossible in psychiatry and would ruin my practice, this dire prediction proved to be false. . . . My numerous trainees and longstanding co-therapists work together with our patients, both in double interviews and in group therapy. Multiple therapy . . . clearly makes therapy an educational process."[7]

When a new patient would come for help, Dreikurs, as consultant therapist, would assess the patient's need for therapy in a diagnostic interview. If they agreed that therapy was appropriate, the patient would be assigned to one of the associate therapists for a life-style assessment. Thereafter, at a joint interview, the associate therapist would present his findings to Dreikurs, and together they would discuss the issues in the presence of the patient, who was encouraged to correct or add to the discussion. The associate would then see the patient for two or three individual sessions, and then there would be another joint session. Because the patient was able to observe a discussion of his problems and because the co-therapist reduced the emotional relationship between the therapist and the patient, there was a more objective atmosphere. The patient therefore learned more quickly, and the treatment period could be shortened.

A more detailed discussion of multiple psychotherapy is not possible here, but an example might prove more valuable:

> Patient E. was a depressed young woman who was extremely ambitious and felt "stupid" in spite of her above average accomplishments in her own profession. She could stand no criticism from her husband, responding to his slightest remark with feelings of inferiority and consequent angry outbursts. Her competitiveness with men extended itself to the active therapist, who reacted by feeling irritated by the patient and being disinclined to work with her. The consultant therapist could show the active therapist the nature of his reactions, and the therapists switched roles. The former active therapist, now in the role of consultant, no longer responded to the rejection by the patient, and the therapy could proceed.[8]

Since Dreikurs's whole approach to psychotherapy and family therapy was so different, or contrary to traditional practice, it was not easy to find suitable colleagues to join him. Even those who might have claimed an ideological kinship to Adlerian viewpoints (such as students of neo-Freudianism) were by training so steeped in traditional therapeutic modes and viewpoints that they lacked the flexibility even to try Dreikurs's methods to see if they worked. So it happened that the key people he assembled in his private practice came from a variety of backgrounds and training experiences and were characterized by an openness to new ideas and the courage to try them, adopt them, and defend them. With his innovative technique of multiple therapy, Dreikurs had an effective mechanism for training his associates and for increasing the number of patients who could adequately be treated within a given period of time. Bernard Shulman, Harold Mosak, Elly Redwin, Bina Rosenberg, Ray Corsini, Adaline Starr, Robert Powers, and others were such individuals. They became the core professional associates who carried on the important work of the practice and of the Community Child Guidance Centers while Dreikurs ventured in and out of Chicago.

As a medical student, Bernard Shulman had admired his audacious psychiatry professor but had planned to pursue a career in internal medicine, not psychiatry. While he was studying for his medical boards, a friend mentioned, "I know you don't want to be a psychiatrist, but Drei-kurs needs help." Shulman went to see his former professor and learned that Dreikurs was contemplating a trip to Europe and needed an associate who could commit himself to the practice for a full year.

So, Shulman recalled, "I went to work for him one day a week for a month—that was April of 1949. In May . . . I started working three days a week . . . and discovered I really liked the work. In July, Dreikurs went to Europe and left me with his patients. When he returned . . . he was pleased to see that I had been able to hold on to them. . . . In December of 1950, I . . . went to work [full time] for Dreikurs. [He] asked me if I was willing to be identified with an Adlerian and I had said yes."[9]

The next year Shulman began a psychiatry residency at the Hines, Illinois, Veterans' Administration hospital, and apart from the years he served in the army in the early 1950s, he was a permanent associate in practice with Dreikurs.

Harold Mosak became another of Dreikurs's talented colleagues, and together they helped to break down the barriers that existed between psychiatry and psychology. Mosak was a student of psychology at the University of Chicago at a time when clinical psychology, previously restricted to administering and evaluating tests, was expanding to include psychotherapy. He recollected:

> In 1942, experimental psychology was taught in the psychology de-partment, biological psychology was taught in the biology depart-ment, social psychology was taught in the sociology department, child psychology was taught in the education department, and the home economics department offered a course in the counseling of adults. I decided to take the course in the home economics depart-ment and the first night we were assigned a textbook called *Counsel-ing and Psychotherapy* by Carl Rogers. . . . After reading his book I realized that at least somewhere a psychologist was actually practic-ing psychotherapy.[10]

After the war, during which he served in an army-hospital psychiatric unit, Mosak returned to the University of Chicago to continue his doctoral studies. In the meantime, the Veterans' Administration, which took over the care of military patients, was drastically lacking in manpower to treat the psychiatric casualties. In response, the VA initiated a clinical intern-ship program for psychologists in conjunction with certain universities.

The University of Chicago was one of these, and there, Carl Rogers, a member of the faculty, supervised the first group of trainees. Mosak was one of them, and consequently his training at the University was Rogerian (client-centered), while his practical training at the VA hospital in Hines, Illinois, was Freudian. Because of the duality of his training, Mosak recalled, "we were being taught one thing and asked to practice another, although some trainees, including myself, did practice nondirective therapy with the VA patients. However, nondirective therapy did not sit well with me—at least not with the population I worked with at the hospital. It worked better with university students than it did with a schizophrenic who wouldn't talk to you. Being nondirective, I had to respect his wishes, and we would sit and look at each other for an hour. I suspect it didn't make the schizophrenic uncomfortable, but it did make me uncomfortable."[11]

For pioneering psychologists who were about to become psychotherapists, it was considered essential to undergo a personal analysis. "The Rogerians didn't do analyses," Mosak commented, "but a Freudian analysis was supposed to be tops."[12] The difficulty was that the Chicago Institute for Psychoanalysis would not take nonmedical people for training analyses. Besides, Mosak remarked, "I was a graduate student getting ready to do my dissertation, and I couldn't see how I would find the time or money to get myself analyzed—and I wasn't really sure I wanted to be a Freudian."[13] He described his dilemma one day to E. H. Porter, Jr., who was the chairman of his dissertation committee and Rogers's right hand at the University of Chicago.

Rogerians were not favorably disposed to Freudian psychoanalysis, and Porter, who had recently been impressed with a life-style demonstration by Dreikurs, suggested that Mosak see Dreikurs, who he said "was really supposed to be quite good." Shortly, Mosak began a didactic experience with Dreikurs, and what he learned gave direction to his subsequent career as an Adlerian psychotherapist.

When Mosak expressed his interest in working with children, Dreikurs lost no time involving him with the newly opened Henry Booth House Child Guidance Center. There Mosak did some testing and began to co-counsel families. After receiving his doctorate, and following a brief but unsatisfying experience working with the VA in Denver, Mosak wrote to Dreikurs asking for a job. Dreikurs replied affirmatively, and Mosak returned to Chicago to join the private practice and to counsel at the child guidance centers.

In taking Mosak into his private practice, Dreikurs broke again with established tradition. When clinical psychologists began to practice psychotherapy, they intruded upon what had previously been the exclusive domain of psychiatry. The psychiatric profession vigorously resisted this intrusion. Dreikurs was perhaps the first psychiatrist in America to engage a clinical psychologist as a coequal psychotherapist.[14] From the first day, Mosak functioned as a therapist, learning Adlerian techniques while working with patients in multiple psychotherapy. "The first thing that impressed me about Dr. D. when I came to work with him was his courage," Mosak stated. "He felt good therapy was good therapy. He didn't care what kind of degree you had in order to do it." Like other Dreikurs innovations, it was a daring move that drew criticism. "The next thing I knew," Mosak continued, "I was being charged with practicing medicine without a license. For about seven or eight months we fought that battle through, as we fought through a good number of other battles after that."[15]

Mosak elaborated on the difficulties they faced in their first decade together:

> When we were invited to appear on panels or in a symposium, the psychoanalysts on the program would withdraw from participation. Part of it was anti-Dreikurs, but it was also anti-Adlerian. We had, for instance, refused to adhere to the team approach. Our feeling was that instead of a psychiatrist treating the child, a social worker treating the parent, and a psychologist doing the testing, anyone with the requisite competence could do any of these, independent of type of degree. . . . And the fact that we saw a whole family at once was outrageous. Our public demonstrations were considered unethical. The chairman of my department at Roosevelt University where I was teaching at the time, even got a call from the Chicago Association of Commerce and Industry asking if I was qualified and if so, why did I work for a quack outfit like the CCGC. . . . Perhaps Dreikurs did overreact at times, but this still does not minimize the fact that between 1947 when I became acquainted with Dreikurs and let's say 1957, we took a terrible beating.[16]

One such incident that provides a sad commentary on the entrenched and petty thinking that dominated the mental health field occurred when Dreikurs applied for membership in the American Orthopsychiatric Association (AOA) in 1958. Since its creation in 1924, the AOA has been dedicated to fostering a multidisciplinary approach to the prevention and treatment of delinquency and the broad problems of mental illness. Despite its professed openness to new ideas and its eclectic image, the AOA helped to fortify the psychoanalytic viewpoint as well as the medical model with its hierarchical team approach in child guidance. Dreikurs submitted information on his extensive work in this field gathered since his Vienna years. But after "careful" processing, his application was refused on the grounds that he had "inadequate experience in an approved clinic setting." This was especially outrageous considering that the AOA prides itself on its multidisciplinary perspective and a membership that includes teachers, social workers, anthropologists, lawyers, and lay workers.[17]

While Dreikurs suffered the enmity of the Freudians, he won the admiration and respect of the Rogerians at the University of Chicago Counseling Center, who became acquainted with Adlerian psychology through Mosak. "Since they were not on the Freudian side, and in some sense, they were just lesser devils than we were in the Freudians' eyes," Mosak remembered, "we shared a community of interest politically. And since our psychological theories are quite alike, we could at least talk with each other."[18] This cooperative atmosphere led to some joint research between the Rogerians and Adlerians.[19]

When the newly incorporated Community Child Guidance Centers celebrated their first anniversary in 1950, Rogers was among the featured speakers. In a letter a few years later, Rogers acknowledged Dreikurs's tireless efforts: "You have made a real contribution to the city of Chicago through your Community Child Guidance Centers, and I hope you are able to continue your work for many years."[20]

As the practice grew, Dreikurs added more associates, who either worked in the office for a limited period while they were training or became longtime associates. Among the latter were Drs. J. W. Klapman, who wrote the first text on group psychotherapy, Eric Sacks, and Bina Rosenberg, who switched from a Freudian orientation after she became acquainted with Dreikurs.

For nearly a decade, Ray Corsini, a clinical psychologist who had trained first as a Rogerian therapist at the University of Chicago, was associated with Dreikurs. They met in the fall of 1953 when Corsini gave a talk on his concept of "immediate therapy" before the Midwest Group Psychotherapy and Psychodrama Association. Afterward, Dreikurs approached Corsini. "My immediate impression of him," Corsini mused, "was a stage image of the Viennese psychiatrist—a little, fat guy, bald, very intense."

"Vat is your name?" Dreikurs demanded. Corsini identified himself. "You are very good—do you know that?" Dreikurs continued. "I am Dr. Dreikurs. Have you ever heard of me? I am an Adlerian. Do you know about Adlerian psychology?" Much to Dreikurs's surprise, Corsini said yes, that he had once heard Adler lecture and was acquainted with another Adlerian, Regine Seidler.[21]

Dreikurs then surprised him. "I want to offer you a scholarship to study at my Institute, the Alfred Adler Institute. Would you like to come and work with me?"[22] Corsini had never heard of Dreikurs before that day, but he accepted, so eager was he to learn whatever he could that would be useful in his practice. So, while Corsini completed his studies for his Ph.D. at the University of Chicago, he also enrolled at the new Adler Institute founded by Dreikurs in 1950.

A year later, Corsini became Dreikurs's co-counselor at the North Side Child Guidance Center in Evanston, Illinois. A facile writer, he also assisted Dreikurs in editing the Adlerian journal and worked part time in his office for nearly ten years. Looking back on that time, he remarked, "I was very excited by it. He was such a genius, and I learned so much in those years. He was very easy to work with—actually a delight, because his mind was so quick and insightful. It made everything very exciting."[23] In the mid-1960s, Corsini moved to Hawaii and created a nucleus of Adlerian activities there.

THE ALFRED ADLER INSTITUTE

Denied the opportunity to teach his theories at the medical school, Dreikurs sought other ways to train professional people in his methods. Once Mosak and Shulman joined him in his work, the possibility of creating an Adlerian training institute began to take shape. Mosak and Shulman were important, in part, because they were American born and educated, were well regarded by their colleagues, and because of the various academic posts they held in the Chicago area. Mosak was a staff member of the University of Chicago Counseling Center, a member of its Committee on Human Relations, and on the faculty of Roosevelt University. Shulman became a consultant in psychiatry for state hospitals and a professor of psychiatry at Northwestern University Medical School. Their teaching attracted a growing number of students who became interested in Adlerian psychology.

Beginning in late 1951, the Chicago Individual Psychology Association sponsored an Institute of Adlerian Psychology, offering two courses taught by Dreikurs, Mosak, Shulman, Redwin, and Starr. By 1954, the institute was sufficiently developed that it was formally incorporated as the Alfred Adler Institute. It offered introductory and specialized courses for psychotherapists and teachers. The leadership of the institute rested firmly with Dreikurs, who, as the founder and director, was, as always, the dramatic, powerful showman with a host of therapeutic gymnastics and daring concepts. Mosak and Shulman provided the essential backup —steady development, scholarship, structure, and administrative follow-through. The institute was effective and slowly won the respect of the Chicago professional community.

By 1955, a postgraduate program in psychotherapy was offered to qualified candidates, and a year later a joint research program with the University of Chicago Counseling Center was initiated. As the number of students, faculty, and courses increased, a certification program was developed in the fields of psychotherapy, counseling, and child guidance. In April 1959, the institute certified its first graduate, Charles Brudo (Ph.D., Northwestern University). By then, the institute was firmly established. Its home was a bustling suite of offices in the heart of Chicago at 6 North Michigan Avenue, where Dreikurs also conducted his private practice.

Robert L. Powers became another major figure of the Chicago Adlerian team. He came to the institute through Charles Brudo. An ordained Episcopal priest serving in an Elkhart, Indiana, parish in the late 1950s, Powers was often called upon by his parishioners for counseling in all manner of personal problems. He felt ill-equipped to advise them but did the best he could until one man whom he was counseling attempted suicide. "I could tell," Powers related, "that he was psychotic. That much I knew. After that I was concerned enough that I felt I had to talk to somebody because I couldn't get this man to go to a doctor even though he had great confidence in me. I asked my friend Charles Brudo for advice. He had a Ph.D. in clinical psychology, and even though he ran a little clinic in Elkhart, he told me his training in psychology was not any more useful in understanding and helping people than my B.D. in theology. He then told me about the Adler Institute and said that he had begun training there and asked if I might want ot come along and take the beginning course. So I traveled from Elkhart to Chicago one day a week and commenced studying at the institute."[24]

Dreikurs was out of the country when Powers began studying at the institute, so they did not meet until some time later. Powers recalled:

> Of course I had heard about him—he was the great man—and there was a great flurry of excitement in anticipation of his return to the offices. I watched him come bursting through the door, like a shot out of a cannon, and I was fascinated to follow his movements. I stood to be introduced to him. Being very tall and skinny, I had a stovepipe look, which was accentuated by my all-black clothing. Moreover, I'm a firstborn son, and a firstborn grandson, and I have all the characteristics that are applicable—including rather formal manners. So I stood, and when I was introduced to him, I bowed. And when I bowed, he bowed. I knew at once that he was teasing me, but he did it in such a way that I couldn't possibly take offense. I was at once impressed by the forcefulness and playfulness of the man. He was unignorable when he came upon the scene, and at the same time he was delightfully perceptive. I felt he saw me quickly as a whole—he saw the pretenses and the games that are involved, I suppose, in all manners and customs.[25]

Dreikurs regularly involved his students and close colleagues with the family counseling efforts of the child guidance centers. The centers provided vivid experiential training that enabled the student to see for himself the correlation between theory and the actual behavior of children and families.

One counseling experience, as Powers put it, was the great turning point in his education with Dreikurs:

> A young couple came to the class at the Adler Institute one night to discuss their problems with their six-year-old daughter, who was an absolute tyrant. After conducting his usual interview with the parents, Dreikurs asked them to leave the room and that the daughter be brought in. I went to get her. She was standing outside waiting with her grandmother. Brought to the door, she clutched grandma round the legs and began to wail. She was not about to come in, and I told Dreikurs so. He, in a matter-of-fact tone that was so characteristic at times, said, "Well, pick her up and bring her in." I was most reluc-

tant, because I had the feeling that this was a violation of the child—
to pick her up and carry her in. I did it as a blind act of faith, thinking to myself, "All right, this is going to be his problem."

I brought in this kicking, screaming, wailing youngster and really it
made my heart break. I thought I was doing violence to the child. I
put her down next to him, and he took her by the hand. Just held on
to her, with an attitude that said, "I can wait. . . ." He looked to us
and said, "It's very important to take the position . . . I can wait."
Then he said to her, "Want to sit down or want to stand up?" And
you know she was not about to be taken in by any of these ruses.
Instead, she played her trump card. She put her feet apart and wet
herself. The water streamed down her legs and puddled all over the
floor and splattered on her shoes. She stamped in it, and it splattered
on his shoes and on his pants. He never budged—he never was
the least bit impressed or distressed. "I can wait" was his attitude.
Well, the change in that child was something. She couldn't believe
what she had run across! Here was somebody who was not impressed
by her suffering, nor intimidated by her tantrum, nor put off even by
her urine. He just couldn't be budged. He could wait and he did
wait, and you could see her studying him like he was a creature that
didn't fit any category of her understanding. She studied him up and
down. Finally he had a conversation with her.

He talked to her awhile and asked her whether she wasn't really
boss in her house. "Could it be you know how to make Mummy do
what you want?" And the little girl understood. It was one of those
marvelous interviews with a child. When the interview ended, she
went out to her grandma, who had suffered many deaths. I don't
know how many deaths, many more than I did, and I felt like I had
died a few. So the child scampered out, and the parents came back in
and witnessed, of course, what their daughter had done and were all
apologies. But Dreikurs didn't want to talk about the urine on the
floor. He just wanted to talk about the daughter and to make some
recommendations, which he did.

Among the students present that night were psychiatric residents
from the Illinois State Psychiatric Institute. One resident asked Dreikurs, "How do you think that child felt?" (suggesting that she was
crushed and defeated). Dreikurs answered, "I will tell you something
even though you won't believe me: 'Zat' child loves me!" There was a
stunned silence in the room, and I must confess, I was among the

dubious. I felt Dreikurs was overstating things (which was not unusual).

This was not the end of the drama, however. When the session ended, the door opened and we got up to go home. Dreikurs was saying good-night to the parents, and the little girl ran into the room, ran up to Dreikurs, threw her arms around him, and kissed him. Here was the first person that ever really respected that child, was neither intimidated by her nor fought with her nor suffered over her but treated her like another human being. He won the child, and she ran to him and kissed him.[26]

Years spent working with Dreikurs convinced Harold Mosak that he was as inventive a strategist as he had ever seen. "He could move patients that nobody else could move." Doing public demonstrations sharpened his skill. Time and again, he would suddenly be confronted with a patient-subject whom he didn't know, and on the spot, he had to invent a strategy for whatever came up."[27]

Shulman's reflections were similar. "He was the best diagnostician I have ever seen. More important, he could also *teach* others how to diagnose. In his training approach, he reversed the usual order and operated on the premise—learn to practice first, then study theory. He genuinely believed that anyone was capable of learning his concepts and methods."[28]

This, by the way, did not mean that he was an easy teacher. Quite the contrary. As the Adler Institute grew in courses and students, Dreikurs insisted that each student demonstrate his skills before others just as he did. Psychotherapist Marvin Chernoff, who studied with Dreikurs for four years, recalled the awesome feeling when called upon to demonstrate what he had learned in the large amphitheater at St. Joseph's Hospital.[29] Dreikurs would sit next to his student, who would proceed to interview the subject. "He was very impatient, and if he felt you were going off the track at all, he was on you, holding you, touching you, and finally breaking in with, "Where are you trying to go with [that question]?" It was a terrifying experience. I had had my Ph.D. for five years before I went into training with him and I felt as if I were starting all over again. And I was."[30]

Although tough as a teacher, Dreikurs cared deeply about his students. He could also admit his mistakes, and he once made a colossal one when Achi Yotam came to Chicago from Israel in the mid-1960s for graduate training at Roosevelt University. He was asked by Dreikurs to present a life-style demonstration with a volunteer patient as part of the practicum training. It took place in the amphitheater of St. Joseph's Hospital, which seats about three hundred people:

> We were on the platform, Dr. D., the girl, and I, and I proceeded to present the case—what the problem was, the family constellation, etc. Dr. D. interjected, "Now I want to hear the early recollections." I read the first one, and he stopped me. "Achi, Achi, after all your studies with me, how could you do something like that?" "What did I do?" I asked. "Don't you know?" "No." And he blurted out, "How stupid can you be?" This he said to me on a stage in front of three hundred people. I was getting angry and blocked. He kept on, "Don't you know the difference between an early recollection and a report? This is a report!" And I thought to myself, "That's it, I'm going to teach him a lesson once and for all." "OK," I said, "I'm going," and I took my papers and got up to leave. "Where are you going?" he asked. "To the bathroom!" I said, and I left to go home.
>
> Two hours later, I got a phone call from him. He said, "Achi, are you mad at me?" "Yes," Achi replied and hung up. I didn't want to talk to him—He was terribly unfair to me and shouldn't have embarrassed me in public like that.
>
> Two hours later came another call. "Achi, are you still mad at me?" "Yes," I said angrily. "How long will it last?" he asked. "I don't know" was my reply, and I hung up and went to sleep.
>
> The next morning around seven, he called again. "Achi, are you still angry with me?" "I don't know," I grumbled. "I just woke up . . . you woke me up!"
>
> Then he called again, the fourth time. And I just couldn't carry on with it. I saw how important it was for him to talk to me, and I realized how sorry he felt. When he asked if I was still angry, I said, "No, no, I'm not angry anymore." "Good," he said, "that's enough. And I want you to know that I'm sorry for what I did. I am going to apologize to the class. I want to apologize in front of everyone for what I did . . . is that OK?" I said yes, and my anger was over. The next week he got up before the class and apologized.[31]

Through the years, these colleagues, with their professionalism and dedication to Dreikurs and the principles of Adlerian psychology, formed the mainstay of the practice, the child guidance centers, and the institute. Their supportive work enabled him to venture beyond Chicago and extend himself to other realms.

The quality and dedication of their work is indicated in the report of the North Central Association's Commission on Higher Education recommending accreditation of the Alfred Adler Institute in 1976. It reads, in part: "The courses are conducted by experienced clinicians and are of high quality. The supervision of practicum is in the hands of accomplished professionals who provide a frequency and intensity of consultation which is equal to that in the very best training programs in graduate departments of traditional universities. . . . The Institute is permeated by a regard for high standards of achievement as well as for Adlerian principles of interaction. The faculty is more than merely competent . . . and the zeal of the students for learning is a joy to behold."[32]

Dreikurs as Therapist

Dreikurs was primarily a healer, with the legendary devotion of the old-time family physician. Patients could telephone any time of the day or night. Many a dinner or social plan was canceled because a patient needed him. Tee drew the line early in their marriage when he wanted her to open their home to patients. For a while they did consider establishing a residential treatment center for adults and children, but they were never able to afford such a project, and Dreikurs always regretted not being able to combine his therapeutic and training methods under one roof.

In his approach to people, Dreikurs was most generous in giving of himself and was a genuine friend. He went out of his way to counsel those in need, and he frequently gave therapy without receiving a penny and without ever mentioning it. To him that was only natural. This did not always suit his associates, because he sometimes offered their services for free as well. Shulman mused that "he could never say no to a patient who he felt needed his help. I finally told him I wouldn't let him give me any more free patients."[33]

As a therapist, Dreikurs practiced what Ray Corsini calls "immediate therapy":

> That is, for him to diagnose was to treat. Describing the person to himself uncovers the heart of his problems, exposes the basic errors

of the private logic, and this was for Dr. D. the heart of therapy. . . . In my thirty years of experience as a clinical psychologist, I have had an opportunity to work very closely with a great many clinical psychologists and psychiatrists and in my judgment no one has come even close to Dr. Dreikurs in his genius for seeing a situation as it really is and for putting the problem or the solution simply and fully. . . . I constantly marveled how awkwardly he phrased his comments and questions—and yet what results he obtained in responses or changes.[34]

Coincident with and at times superseding his role as a healer was Dreikurs's desire to teach. "Psychotherapy, regardless of what individual therapists may consider it to be, is always a learning procedure. A learning procedure is more than an emotional experience. Any learning or any experience, if it is strong, like anything else that is strong and impressive, has some emotional impact. As I see it, all learning is a formation—or change—of concepts or beliefs."[35] The basis of all psychotherapy, from faith healing to psychoanalysis, he contended, involved the patient's changing some concept about himself, or life, or what he is doing.

In his work with patients, Dreikurs distinguished four phases of psychotherapy, which often overlap and are not necessarily successive: (1) establishment and maintenance of a proper relationship; (2) assessment or analysis of the patient, his problems, and personality; (3) provision of insight in order that the patient understand himself; and (4) reorientation —change.

Establishing and maintaining a proper relationship was a foremost consideration, but Dreikurs strongly rejected the psychoanalytic notion that the therapist achieves results through transference (the redirection of feelings and desires, especially those unconscious sexual thoughts retained from childhood, toward a new object, that is, the analyst).[36]

Of course, a friendly, positive relationship was important, but as an Adlerian, he found that maintenance of a proper therapeutic relationship was dependent upon the congruence of goals between the therapist and the patient. Any resistance whatsoever, he believed, was due to the fact that the respective goals did not coincide. For example, a patient

comes because he wants help. He wants to get well but he doesn't actually expect that he ever will get well. He comes only because it is the right thing to do and he wants to try everything; but he is pretty much determined to prove to you that he is hopeless. The therapist naturally wants to show him that he is *not* hopeless. This is a clash of goals. . . .

Most patients are pessimistic. If they weren't discouraged and rather pessimistic, they wouldn't come to therapy. One of the most frequent underlying mechanisms of resistance in psychotherapy is that the patient doesn't believe he can get well. A neophyte may be inclined to assure the patient that others with similar conditions had been helped, and that there is no reason for his pessimism. But there is no chance to convince the patient at the beginning that he could get well. However, one can offer him an exploration of the reasons [for] his doubts. He may well accede to that or to an exploration of his personality. But without an open discussion of this predicament, the patient would not give up his reservation, or [might] even sabotage progress.[37]

Dreikurs discussed another example of incongruent goals—the patient who does not trust the therapist:

It would not be very useful to say, "Now, I am a decent guy. You can trust me." That would be futile. On the other hand, if I don't say anything about it, he still wouldn't trust me. I bring it into the open and say, "You seem not to have much confidence in me. Maybe you have had some experience that justifies it. I don't know whether I can gain your confidence but will you give me a chance to see what I have to offer? Maybe you will find out that you can have confidence in me; I don't know." At this moment we have our goals synchronized. It is not a question whether he can trust me now or not, but he is willing to see whether we can work it out together so that he may perhaps be able to trust me. We have at least made some kind of plan for a concerted effort, and that's all that is needed. Now, what if the patient gets angry or becomes unhappy when we don't make progress? Our work is clogged up somehow, but our therapeutic relationship can remain positive, because we always talk about our aims.

In our relationships the patient is free to voice his feelings about the therapist, and the therapist to voice his feelings about the patient. But this does not imply the kind of permissiveness which characterizes contemporary psychotherapy. . . . There is too much concern with fear of weakening the ego, of suppressing the patient. There is a fear that the patient can't take it, that he isn't ready yet. And the psychiatrist sits in self-glorified superiority determining what the patient can take, which is degrading and shows lack of respect and confidence in the patient as a human being.

If I get angry, I get angry and the patient may respond as he feels. I don't recommend getting angry, but I recommend very much not being afraid of getting angry. I *can* be human. Anything which could detract from the sincerity of a spontaneous reaction would be detrimental. I even prefer to make a mistake rather than to be so cautious that the poor patient should not be abused by me. I do it with children, with adults, with anybody. It creates a much better therapeutic and human relationship. I don't mind the patient criticizing me. I don't mind admitting that I have made a mistake—I very often make mistakes.

We should not be afraid of making mistakes. . . . It is more important that we are human. It is unfortunate that one has to emphasize that today, because it is not the customary practice in psychotherapy to be human. Some psychiatrists wouldn't go into the elevator with the last patient of the day for fear of coming too close to him. They have to wait until the patient has gone down. "Don't come too close because that interferes with the therapeutic relationship." This is just the opposite of what I am saying. I want to function and to be recognized as a fellow human being.[38]

In the second phase of psychotherapy, Dreikurs contended that one should start with the patient's present field of action, and then proceed to his general movement through life to his life style. He made an important distinction at this point between psychotherapy and counseling. In counseling—whether vocational, marital, or child guidance—he believed that, in many cases, people could be helped to overcome their difficulties without going deeper than the present level of functioning. For example, he pointed out, even parents who are not emotionally disturbed have conflicts with their children. When mothers do not know what to do with their children to resolve these conflicts, they feel defeated and then become emotionally disturbed. When they learn to deal with their children effectively, the emotional disturbance, in most cases, disappears. Thus, if a woman came complaining about her husband or child, Dreikurs did not immediately recommend psychotherapy. He would first pinpoint the diffi-

culty by examining specific incidents and try to resolve it. Only people
who did not respond to counseling in terms of clarification of the current
situation were then referred to therapy. "When we try to deal with an
immediate situation, with a current problem . . . that is counseling. . . .
The object of [psycho]therapy is not the immediate situation, but the
total personality structure, the life style."[39]

> If psychotherapy is indicated, we have to examine the patient's per-
> sonality structure—the life style. . . . The technique requires first the
> examination of the formative years of the person in his family constel-
> lation. Within the family constellation, within his early childhood
> group, each of the children develops his personality through inter-
> action with all of the others. We have a method by which we can
> make a sociogram of early childhood relationships through the per-
> sonality differences of brothers and sisters. We can distinguish how
> the first child moved in one direction, the second in another, and the
> third in still a different direction, how they formed alliances and
> competitive struggles, and how they formed subgroups. In this way,
> we can see how an individual was exposed to a number of influences
> and in turn provoked the others to certain behavior. The individual is
> never the passive recipient of environmental influence, but always an
> active participant in establishing his relationship with the others. The
> child influences his parents at least as much as the parents influence
> the child. . . . In each case, after we have the family constellation
> established, we write a summary and then we have the material
> which we need [to see how the person] moves, the field of action in
> which [the personality] developed.
>
> The second thing we do is to collect early recollections. Adler's
> discovery of the significance of the early memories was not utilized
> until recently, because Freud considered them as mere screen mem-
> ories which cover up the really important childhood incidents which
> were repressed. Consequently, nobody except the Adlerians con-
> cerned themselves with early recollections until recently. . . . We
> remember from all the millions of experiences from early childhood
> only those which fit into our concept of life. Whatever we remember
> from early childhood indicates how we look at life. This is so reliable
> that when the patient changes his concept of himself and his life, his
> early recollections change also. . . . One of the things for which
> recollections are analyzed is what I call "Basic Mistakes" because

these are the mistakes which we have to correct when we want to help the patient.[40]

The third phase of psychotherapy is designed to give insight to the patient, not by telling him what to do or not to do but by showing him what he is doing in his life, on what principles he operates, by confronting him with his goals.

With the life-style data and insight, Dreikurs could proceed effectively to the fourth phase—reorientation. The essential ingredient is *encouragement*, a term that is, he maintained, widely used yet little understood. Encouragement, he wrote, is

> a very complex process. . . . At the root of all deficiencies lies discouragement. As long as somebody has confidence in himself he will function. Only when he has become demoralized, discouraged, doubtful of himself, doubting his chances, doubting his place in the group, only then does he switch, as we call it, to the "useless side," becoming deficient and maladjusted and psychopathologic. . . . Whenever the patient believes in himself, he will improve, because functioning presupposes his conviction of his ability.
>
> Thus encouragement is one of the essential factors without which no improvement is possible, but with which improvement is almost automatic. This encouragement can come from . . . the realization of the patient's responsibilities, which he cannot assume without realizing his own strength. By making him aware of how he makes himself sick, we give him the realization that he can also make himself well. We show him what he is doing. He may not like it because he doesn't want to feel responsible for what he is doing; but he can't escape eventually from finding out that not his emotions, his complexes, his nature, his constitution, nor even his parents are responsible, but he himself; and only he, not they, can save himself. In my mind such realization implies becoming a free man. Realizing the tremendous power which we have, we know that we can make ourselves well and sick, that we can play weak when it suits our purposes, and play strong when we prefer to do so. We can create our own fears for whatever advantages may lie in withdrawal, or for putting others in our service; or we can free ourselves of fear. This kind of reorientation is . . . a moral rehabilitation, a spiritual one.[41]

At all times Dreikurs's approach to psychotherapy followed the dictum "to diagnose is to treat." Diagnosis, in his hands, was merely to establish a working hypothesis. He had no interest in labeling people with medical jargon, and he refused to engage in prognosis. How much therapy was enough? Dreikurs would not predict. Sometimes the change of one basic misconception was sufficient to help a client function more effectively and cooperatively in the human community. He did not believe that a fundamental change in the life style was often necessary, because each person's life style has within it the capacity for both useful and useless behaviors that are consistent with the fundamental goal of the life style. The goal of therapy is to help the client learn to accept himself, his emotions, even his mistakes. Freed from fears of inadequacy, of loss of status, he or she could utilize previously unrecognized potentialities for important and useful tasks.

TECHNIQUES AND INNOVATIONS

Adler's concept of the life style was one of his most brilliant contributions to modern psychology, and it was a concept he regularly taught to his students. Yet, as Dreikurs recounted, "During his lectures and demonstrations in Vienna, we were frustrated because Adler often did not explain what he meant by some of the terms he used nor how he functioned as a therapist or counselor. We were always aware that *he* knew, but could not understand why what was clear to him we didn't see as well. It was right there that I resolved to always have a logical explanation for anything I did or said."[42]

Through his keen diagnostic skill and analytical mind, Dreikurs refined Adler's concept of the life style into a systematic assessment process that was highly reliable in its results. Moreover, he made it a teachable concept that could be applied not only by the most experienced therapists but also by social workers, vocational counselors, guidance personnel, and in later years, by trained paraprofessional counselors.

In addition to formalizing the method for characterizing the childhood family constellation and atmosphere, Dreikurs made a major discovery regarding early recollections (ER's). He delineated an essential difference between an "early recollection" and a "report." Recollections are valid indications of the life style only if they describe one-time occurrences and entail visual recall. For that reason, the client is asked to pinpoint the moment within the recollection that is most vivid, and to describe its concurrent emotional tone. Early recollections are recorded verbatim, because Dreikurs found that changes, often very subtle, may occur in the early recollection when they are redescribed at a later time. Such changes in content or tone provide one of the few objective indicators of change in the life style, and therefore, of the effectiveness of therapy. By 1954, Dreikurs had worked out his basic refinements of the life style and published a questionnaire form for eliciting the life-style data that has been widely adopted.[43]

Another innovation developed by Dreikurs in his continual effort to increase the efficiency of the therapeutic process was his concept of "two points on a line." He used an analogy from geometry applied to the life-style concept. "One needs two points to draw a line, and once a line is drawn, one knows an infinite number of points." If a client reveals two apparently independent and contrary facts, a line of logic can be drawn to delineate a picture of a unified, self-consistent life style. The counselor attempts to find the line of logic through intelligent guessing, and if correct, the answer will resolve the puzzle and indicate the basic life style. For some, this appears to be little more than a clever analogy, but the following example demonstrates its usefulness:

Keith Wiggins, a psychologist in Dayton, Ohio, described an incident that took place at West Virginia Medical College in the late 1960s when Dreikurs spent two weeks there lecturing and demonstrating his methods to students. Dreikurs was to demonstrate a life style. The subject of the demonstration was a schizophrenic, brain-damaged woman who had been in and out of hospitals all her life. Using his concept of two points on a line, he understood her life style in five minutes and then used the remainder of the hour to counsel her.

Before he even got one early recollection, he discerned two contradictory facts about her. She was (1) the good child in the family, and (2) at the same time, the most punished. From this obvious contradiction, he sought to make a consistent line of logic. He looked at her and said, "I can understand. You were so good even your family couldn't stand you, and they punished you for being so good." She immediately understood and her eyes lit up as the insight swept over her. Until that point she had been acting crazy, but afterward she stopped the bizarre behavior. At the end of the session, she said to Dreikurs, "You're the first person who really understood me."

Deeply moved by the demonstration, the psychiatrists in the audience gave Dreikurs a standing ovation. In a discussion that followed, one psychiatrist got up and exclaimed that he did not think the demonstration was very effective because Dreikurs did not make her angry. Dreikurs retorted, "That is stupid—the idea that you have to make someone angry to help them!"[44]

Dreikurs cautioned therapists who were hesitant by showing that "the easiest way to fail is by your conviction that you cannot help the patient anyhow. The next best is to tell him that you are sure you can help him. Then he will be honor-bound to prove to you that you can't. Other fool-proof means for achieving a therapeutic failure are either by talking too much or by not talking at all; both approaches seem to be rather popular today. Next comes the inability or unwillingness to understand what the patient wants, and, therefore, impressing him with what you want. And when he and you work at cross purposes, then you can attribute his lack of response to his 'resistance.' This will certainly prevent any therapeutic progress."[45]

REASON AND EMOTION

Perhaps nothing was more indicative of the refreshing alternative perspective Dreikurs brought to psychotherapy than his position on the function and relationship of reason and emotion. Contrary to prevailing views, he argued that they are not in opposition to each other: "Reason and emotion are like our two hands, they always work together—even when they seem to move against one another." In his view, emotions are not irrational, and they do not dominate nor drive man—rather they are his tools and function in line with the goals of the individual just as the ability to reason does. The purpose of emotions, he wrote, is to "provide the fuel, the steam, so to speak for our actions, the driving force without which we would be impotent. . . . They make it possible to carry out our decisions." Deploring the tendency to blame antisocial behavior on emotions, he continued: "Certain schools of thought . . . describe man as being besieged by animalistic drives and urges which prevent him from adequate social functioning. A new mysticism, clad in scientific language and using mechanistic formulation, degrades man by assuming the existence of a cesspool within each individual containing all the repressed urges and drives—which then interfere with all good intentions and cause undue hostility and aggression. . . . Their findings are . . . acceptable to the general public as most people have not yet learned to deal with their own emotions effectively."

Dreikurs explained this elusive quality of emotions: "Their strength lies in the fact that their purpose is not recognized. . . . We feel driven by them, while we actually create them. But we do not want to admit this to ourselves; so we set our emotions up as masters, when they actually are our slaves. . . . If one realized for what purpose one stimulates one's own emotions . . . such admissions would deprive the emotion of its powerful drive."[46] When people challenged his view, insisting that we cannot control our emotions, Dreikurs reminded them of how easy it is to shut off heated emotions and postpone an argument when the doorbell or phone rings.

Dreikurs believed that in many cases guilt feelings are a face-saving stratagem. Oftentimes a person will evoke guilt feelings when he believes something he did was wrong, as a means of salving his own conscience and consoling himself that he really is a well-intentioned person. Dreikurs enjoyed recounting the story of a three-year-old girl who was observed sneaking into the cookie jar, taking a cookie out, and eating it. She then slapped her hand and said, "Bad girl!" Having made retribution, she then took more cookies, repeating the same self-reproach after each one.[47]

He emphasized the value of helping the patient recognize his own mistaken attitudes by involving him in action situations where his goals would be revealed by his movements in a social setting. This is why he advocated a variety of action-oriented therapeutic modalities: music therapy, dance therapy, and art therapy along with his earlier innovations of multiple therapy, group therapy, and his use of psychodrama.

Music Therapy

Given his love of music, it is not surprising that Dreikurs enlisted it as a therapeutic bridge to help troubled humans. He was a founding member of the National Association for Music Therapy in 1950 and wrote numerous papers on music therapy. Music has a profound effect on human emotions and also the capacity to bring people together. Dreikurs believed that music therapy is an effective means for drawing aggressive children and social isolates—even autistic ones—to the group and thereby giving them a sense of belonging.[48] Music was for him another level of communication—a language which, though nonverbal, was nonetheless real. Whenever verbal communication fails, as with some psychotics who resist the common logic of words, music can reestablish communication without provoking defensive reactions. Music pulls people together, uniting a group and integrating each individual into the whole. It sets an emotional tone for group activity while producing an equalizing effect on all those under its spell.

THE GOAL OF THERAPY

Psychotherapy, as we see it, is a learning process. The object to be studied is the individual. Nobody knows himself. As long as he is functioning adequately, he does not need such knowledge. But if he does not function well, if he becomes deficient or maladjusted, then he cannot change unless he first knows what to change. Everybody knows when he does something wrong, but he does not know why he is doing it. Psychotherapy permits uncovering the motivation of the individual and the nature of his difficulties. It remedies the mistakes made in the natural learning process by which the child developed his personality.

This process of learning implied in psychotherapy does not concern itself with personal qualities nor with feelings, assets and deficiencies, but with social values. . . . His inferiority "feelings," which are a wrong judgment of self, express the contemporary social contention that everybody who is not superior is necessarily inferior. Psychotherapy cannot avoid discussion of the value systems which have formed guiding lines for the patient. It attempts to replace wrong social values with those more beneficial. It tries to instill in the patient a sense of equality to all others, in a society which speaks about equality and grants it to none.[49]

Overcoming the individual's inferiority feelings in turn profoundly affects his behavior. Social interest is the antidote for inferiority feelings. It grows in inverse proportion to feelings of inferiority. An increase in social interest necessarily increases the social and emotional adjustment of the individual. It allows the individual to cope in his relations with others and successfully to confront the ups and downs of life without feeling frustrated, discouraged, demoralized, or sick.

Notes for Chapter 16

1. Dreikurs, "Guiding, Teaching, and Demonstrating," p. 152.
2. Adaline Starr, personal communication, November 1972.
3. Nahum Shoobs, "Psychodrama in the Classroom," *Sociometry* 7 (1944): 152–169.
4. Walter E. O'Connell, "Psychodrama: Involving the Audience," *Rational Living* 2 (1967): 22–25.
5. Adaline Starr, "Psychodrama in the Child Guidance Centers," in *Adlerian Family Counseling*, pp. 75, 76.
6. Adaline Starr, personal communication, November 1972.
7. Dreikurs, "Guiding, Teaching, and Demonstrating," p. 154.
8. Rudolf Dreikurs, Bernard H. Shulman, and Harold H. Mosak, "Patient-Therapist Relationship in Multiple Psychotherapy. I. Its Advantages to the Therapist," *Psychiatric Quarterly* 26 (1952): 223.
9. Truitt, *A Legacy for the Future*, p. 268.
10. Ibid., p. 270.
11. Harold H. Mosak, personal communication, May 1973.
12. Truitt, *A Legacy for the Future*, p. 271.
13. Mosak, personal communication, May 1973.
14. Knowing this was an unorthodox move, Dreikurs wrote to the AMA for its policy on the matter. The Bureau of Legal Medicine and Legislation of the AMA replied that so long as the psychologist did not engage in activities that constitute practicing medicine, there was no objection ethically or legally to such an arrangement. AMA to Rudolf Dreikurs, December 20, 1950, Dreikurs Papers.
15. Mosak, personal communication, May 1973.
16. Truitt, *Legacy for the Future*, pp. 272–273.
17. American Orthopsychiatric Association to Rudolf Dreikurs, April 14, 1958, Dreikurs Papers.
18. Mosak, personal communication, May 1972.
19. John M. Shlien, Harold H. Mosak, and Rudolf Dreikurs, "A Comparison of Client-Centered and Adlerian Therapy," *Counseling Center Discussion Papers* 6, no. 8 (1960). Also: "Effect of Time Limits: A Comparison of Two Psychotherapies," *Journal of Counseling Psychology* 9 (1962): 31–34.
20. Carl R. Rogers to Dreikurs, February 4, 1957, Dreikurs Papers.
21. Dreikurs, "Regine Seidler (1895–1967)," *Journal of Individual Psychology* 4 [1967]: 70. Seidler worked with Adler in Vienna, and together with Ferdinand Birnbaum and Oskar Spiel helped to organize the Adlerian Experimental School there. Arriving in the United States in 1939, she continued her training at Syracuse University, and after 1947, served as senior psychologist at the Des Moines Child Guidance Center, where she was an esteemed figure.
22. Raymond J. Corsini, personal communication, May 1976.
23. Ibid.
24. Robert L. Powers, personal communication, October 1973.
25. Ibid.
26. Ibid.
27. Mosak, personal communication, May 1973.
28. Bernard H. Shulman, personal communication, May 1974.
29. Dreikurs was appointed a courtesy member of the medical staff of St. Joseph's

Hospital in 1964. That same year Shulman became head of the psychiatry section of this new hospital on Chicago's Lake Shore.

30. "In Memory of Rudolf Dreikurs, 1897–1972," *Journal of Individual Psychology* 29 (1973): 11.

31. Achi Yotam, personal communication, July 1973.

32. "Excerpts from the North Central Association Evaluators' Report," *Alfred Adler Institute Newsletter* 14 (1976): 1.

33. Shulman, personal communication, May 1974.

34. Corsini, "Rudolf Dreikurs," pp. 174–175.

35. Excerpts from Rudolf Dreikurs, "The Adlerian Approach to Therapy," reprinted with permission of Macmillan Publishing Co., Inc., from *Contemporary Psychotherapies*, by Morris Stein © 1961 by The Free Press, a Corporation, p. 80.

36. Concerning the issue of transference and resistance, Dreikurs wrote:
> Freud is of the opinion that this "resistance" is always directed against the uncovering of "unconscious" sexual thoughts and experiences. He believes that this shows itself most in the "transference" [which] according to Freud, is the patient's love for the analyst, who is for him the symbol ["Imago"] of all the persons he loved before, especially those he loved in his earliest childhood. Freud makes a distinction between a "positive transference" of affection and a hostile "negative transference," the latter originating in the revolt against this love, in hatred of the analyst. . . . Do we need the hypothesis of an erotic attraction or rejection between physician and patient [to explain resistance]? . . . When the patient resists us we know for a certainty that we are expecting something from him which he does not like. When he rejects an insight, he does so, not because of some embarrassing sexual revelation or because he hates us, rather . . . he expects from this revelation a burden on his life which he does not feel strong enough to bear. . . . Is it not understandable that he should resist? ("The Technique of Psychotherapy," *Chicago Medical School Quarterly* 5 [1944]: 4–7, 35).

37. Dreikurs, "Adlerian Approach to Therapy," pp. 83–84.

38. Ibid., pp. 85–87.

39. Ibid., p. 89.

40. Ibid., pp. 90–91.

41. Ibid., p. 93.

42. Loren Grey, "What Dr. Dreikurs Has Meant to Me," June 28, 1967, Dreikurs Papers.

43. Dreikurs, "Psychological Interview." For more extensive accounts of the life-style concept, see *The Counseling Psychologist* 3, no. 1 (1971) (whole issue devoted to Individual Psychology). See also Harold H. Mosak and Rudolf Dreikurs, "Adlerian Psychotherapy," in *Current Psychotherapies*, ed. Raymond J. Corsini (Itasco, Ill.: Peacock, 1973), pp. 35–83.

44. Keith Wiggins, personal communication, May 1975.

45. Rudolf Dreikurs, "Hesitant Therapist," *Voices* 3 (1967): 17.

46. Rudolf Dreikurs, "The Function of Emotions," *Christian Register* 130, no. 3 (1951): 13.

47. Rudolf Dreikurs, "Guilt Feelings as an Excuse," *Individual Psychology Bulletin* 8 (1950): 18–21.

48. Rudolf Dreikurs, "The Dynamics of Music Therapy," *Music Therapy* 3 (1953: 15–23.

49. Rudolf Dreikurs, "Goals in Therapy," *American Journal of Psychoanalysis* 16 (1956): 18–23.

17

To Teach the Teachers

Naturally, the teacher is a psychological manipulator; so are the children. Everyone who interacts with someone else is a psychological manipulator who tries to evoke reactions which are favorable to him and to change those which work against him. The teacher uses psychology to influence the children's cooperation. If you don't want to influence their thinking you can neither teach them— which means to change their thinking about the subject matter—nor can you help them or correct them.

Rudolf Dreikurs
Dreikurs-Mackaness interview, 1961

Dreikurs's decision after the war to focus his considerable energy on education had far-reaching consequences. Entering the field of American education was a bold move, especially for a foreign-sounding, imposing figure like Dreikurs. American public education is a most formidable and entrenched institution and does not typically condone meddling from other professions such as psychiatry. Dreikurs knew it would be a most challenging task and that his integrative approach—an amalgamation of educational, psychological, and guidance principles—ran counter to the characteristic specialization of American professionalism.

He pointed out that Adler too had bucked the system:

He went out to teach and open the eyes of all whom he met so that they could realize the need of their fellowmen and learn how to assist, that is, how to cooperate. Adler's [approach] did not always find general approval. Especially America, with its general conception that proper organization demands strict demarcations, regarded with distrust and distaste Adler's neglect to acknowledge any limitation in teaching and helping. His simplicity . . . was not ignorance but real wisdom. For him, the truth was always simple, and complicated were only the tricks with which men tried to escape the truth and its logic. . . . For Adler, actions revealed truth, and actions are always simple facts, clear and unequivocal in their direction and in their consequences.[1]

Like Adler, Dreikurs sought to bring a refreshing simplicity to a host of human issues that had become suffocated by a tangled web of complexities.

It was nearly a decade after Dreikurs's first involvement with education at Morton High School that the opportunity to move into the arena of public education finally became a reality. The goal was always there, and in the interim years, Dreikurs quietly pursued his educational interests, waiting and hoping for a chance to put them into practice. For example, in the late 1930s, he encouraged Bronia Grunwald to become an educator because he felt that he would need her to introduce and test his ideas later. Grunwald pursued her teaching career in the Gary, Indiana, public school system, and Dreikurs's counsel and instruction in Adlerian ideas provided the foundation for the notable success she experienced. She stood out from the other teachers and was soon assigned the most difficult children because of her special skill.

The child guidance centers provided a perennial liaison between families and the educators and schools. The centers drew steady interest, participation, and support from a variety of local schools, principals, and teachers who found guidance for improving their understanding of children. In any one year as many as five hundred teachers attended child guidance sessions. Yet no matter how enthusiastic these individuals became, their dispersion among the various school systems minimized the impact of Dreikurs's educational techniques. Therefore, any systematic implementation or real test of his ideas was prevented, and his methods remained relatively unknown to the larger educational community in Chicago.

Dreikurs persistently sought to put his educational theories into practice. He therefore did not hesitate to offer his expertise when, as editor of the *Individual Psychology Bulletin*, he received an intriguing request for help from the Margaret Hall School in Versailles, Kentucky.

Sister Rachel, the principal of the Episcopal boarding and day school for girls, had written for professional guidance regarding a crisis that had befuddled the school's administration. It involved the seventh grade, normally intelligent and cooperative girls, who individually never did anything outstandingly "wicked." But as a group, they were hostile, uncooperative, disruptive, and constantly flaunted the rules both in and out of class. They were also failing academically, especially in arithmetic. The faculty imposed extra study hours—but the girls' grades continued to worsen. Social restrictions were ordered, but still the grades and behavior worsened.

The faculty's frustration led Sister Rachel to seek outside advice. Since 1935, she had regularly subscribed to the Adlerian journal. She was attracted to Adler's psychology, because "here was a body of helpful knowledge about human difficulties, and especially about children, based on a philosophy which had, apparently, many affinities and sympathies with Christianity."[2] She recognized that unlike Freud, Adler did not denigrate religion as a neurotic symptom and that he expressed no hostility to religion in his writing. The Adlerian system with its premise that man is a social being who is healthy only when integrated into society also appealed to her, as did its concern with normal development and ordinary problems.

She admitted that "we awaited our first visit from our Adlerian psychiatrist with great hopes and a few fears. Some children and some parents were disturbed at the idea. They were afraid we would be stigmatized as a school for queer people."[3]

Dreikurs arrived at Margaret Hall in November 1946 and immediately began to visit the classes, interviewing each seventh-grader and discussing the problems with faculty members. He participated in all the school's activities—from religion classes to dining and social events. After a few days he met with the faculty to discuss his findings. He told them, "The whole seventh grade is in total revolt. You are fighting a war and you are losing!" He saw the seventh grade as analogous to the typical middle child. They were neither the youngest nor the oldest group in the school and had none of the privileges of either. They felt laughed at, that everyone was against them, and that they were unfairly blamed and punished. They were in absolute opposition to authority.

Dreikurs found that the staff was completely intimidated by the girls and their bad acts. He told the faculty that adults who are afraid in dealing with children often overreact by taking excessive measures of reprisal. Sister Rachel recalled, "When we realized that we were afraid of these kids, something clicked and we chuckled."[4] To eliminate the tension and hostility between the staff and the seventh grade, he suggested that the group be given some kind of project of their own to prove that they could do something others would appreciate. "The children want to prove they are smart," he observed, "and it is always a bad thing if the only possibility for heroism is by doing something bad."[5]

The rebellious group, he noted, was generally operating on the "goal 2" level of misbehavior—power.[6] They resist authority and fight back. Some of the leaders operate on "goal 3"—revenge. They are in effect saying, "We are not liked. We don't care, and we have nothing to lose." He recommended that the school initiate regular, frank group discussions to listen to what the children had to say. This would be the best way of directing them into constructive channels.

Dreikurs shocked the faculty when the subject of reward and punishment was raised. "We were told that punishment and bribery are utterly inadequate as educational methods," Sister Rachel recalled. "Their good results are only apparent. If you punish a child severely enough, you get what you want and you increase your sense of power. But you teach the child that force is necessary, with the result that he will not listen to you unless you force him, and he in his turn will copy you in his dealings with those who are weaker. . . . When we punish them, we do not teach them to correct their faulty behavior. We teach them that power counts and they learn that it is wise to get and keep power over others."[7]

"If punishment were abandoned, what *then* would we do? We can't let the kids run wild!" the faculty members demanded.

Dreikurs told them that he was not advocating a free-for-all. Children need training to develop properly and, instead of being punished, should be allowed to experience the logical consequence of their disorderly behavior. The best way to train children, he explained, is to win their trust and encourage them.

"We put his suggestions into effect at once," Sister Rachel remembered. "We withdrew the restrictions, we gave the seventh grade a project—they wrote and produced a play for the whole school. . . . [Weekly] discussion groups for each class . . . were begun. . . . When we stopped trying to force them to do arithmetic and began to convince them that they could do constructive things for others, their attitudes changed and they became more cooperative—about arithmetic as well as other things. It was a dramatic experience for all of us."[8]

While Dreikurs gave advice for working with the disruptive group as a whole, he also gave very concrete insights about the individual girls and specific suggestions for dealing with each—especially the provocative leaders. Spending about twenty minutes with each student, he quickly produced "mini life styles" that revealed the genuine humanity of the man and that demonstrate the cogent insights of the life-style technique. Two of these are reproduced here (with fictional names):

[*Helen M:*] She is an overambitious child who is trying to get a place in her family. She is the oldest of the second group of children and is in conflict with her youngest sister. She feels pushed down. She also feels that Kathy is smarter than she is, whereas she is probably the smartest of the whole bunch. She has an inferior feeling with regard to Pat (an older sister) and also to her mother and to Kathy. She is eager to show her smartness, but can't find useful outlets. She can't take it when she is pushed down. An early memory reflects her life style. When she was three years old she remembers having a wonderful time in a pink dress at a party and was allowed to stay up exceptionally late. This shows her ambition. She wants privileges and position.

She is a leader in the group and the girls accept her leadership because her feelings coincide with the group feeling. She came here to school because this was a better school, and she wants to be high up.

She is frank and objective and ought to be easy to handle. It would help if we could give her a sense of responsibility and recognition. Otherwise she will use her leadership for something wrong. The more you punish her, the more you discourage her. It would be good if she could go back to the ballet class, for that is something which she does well, and she needs the experience of excellence.

[*Jane C:*] When she came in for her interview a certain sexiness was apparent about her—a lot of bracelets, etc., and her first response was "Why, everything is fine." She fights a little, she likes the Sisters best. "I don't know," is her answer for everything.

I asked about her family constellation and she said she had an older sister and a brother "who died November 12, 1932, one day after he was born."

[I] asked her how she knew, because she wasn't born yet herself. She said she found it in the Bible of her mother. [I] asked her if her parents ever told her that they wanted another boy and she started to cry. [I] said to her, "Has your mother hurt you?" That was the end of the interview. The child just sat and cried and cried.

Jane feels that she has no chance, that she is lost, that she couldn't be good. The reason why she is a leader in the group is that she responds to the need of the group. The group situation is a background for her action, which you might call violent passivity. She doesn't know why she should not hurt others. She has been hurt so why shouldn't she hurt other people? There is some sexy indication in her behavior. Perhaps she thinks that the one chance for her is in sex. She is pretty and may say to herself, "Sex is no good. I am no good, maybe sex will get me somewhere and make people like me." Now what should we do with such a child?

A child who acts like that must first be convinced that she can be liked. They have to learn that there are no bad children; only unhappy children, and we must find a way to help them. They are part of the great suffering mass of mankind. Often such people cover up their real feelings with flippancy just as Jane does. We have to break through to the girl, and we can if we realize that she is suffering.

In dealing with her, make as little issue of her misdeeds as possible and try to gain her confidence and make her feel that she has a chance.[9]

Dreikurs maintained his advisory position at Margaret Hall until 1959, when Sister Rachel left the school to assume other duties.

NORTHWESTERN UNIVERSITY

The breakthrough Dreikurs was seeking in the field of education came in 1947, when Carleton W. Washburne introduced him to the education department at Northwestern University. "He did me a tremendous service," Dreikurs reflected, "since it was one of the most important leads in my life."

Washburne was one of America's outstanding educators. As superintendent of the Winnetka, Illinois, schools for a quarter century, he introduced numerous concepts, including early childhood education, elementary school guidance, individualized and programmed instruction, and a mental hygiene approach, that were subsequently widely adopted into educational practice. The Winnetka schools were, in effect, an educational laboratory, and the impressive educational research conducted there led to their national reputation for excellence. In his persistent search for better educational methods, Washburne traveled widely and visited Vienna in the 1920s to observe the reforms instituted there. It was then that he became acquainted with Adler's work.

Washburne's incorporation of a mental hygiene approach into the educational process led to the creation of a Department of Educational Counsel, which by 1939 included a psychiatrist, a psychologist, a pediatrician, and psychiatric social workers. They had "by far the most extensive child guidance clinic . . . in any public school system anywhere."[10] Dreikurs and Washburne became acquainted through their mutual interest in promoting child guidance in the public schools in the Chicago area.

Washburne was impressed with Dreikurs, especially with his goal-directed approach to understanding behavior, and told him that his "four goals" were a major contribution that would be most useful to teachers.[11] Thus, when the position of psychiatrist for the Winnetka schools fell vacant, Washburne urged Dreikurs to apply and was prepared to hire him, but only if, upon consulting with the principals of the district, he met with a favorable response. However, the principals were not enthusiastic about Dreikurs, and he was not appointed. One participant at that meeting later commented: "Old-fashioned discipline was still in high favor in the community and the mental hygiene program was having enough difficulty in making its way without being identified as a foreign import. Also, [Dreikurs] seemed somewhat of a forbidding personage for a faculty to readily approach about their problems of discipline and adjustment."[12]

Washburne's support did not diminish, and not long afterward, Washburne took Dreikurs to Northwestern to introduce him to the School of Education faculty. Dreikurs recalled with a certain pride that Washburne told them, "You try to get Dr. Franz Alexander of the Psychoanalytic Institute to teach here, but I think you would be better off if you take Dr. Dreikurs."[13] Some years later, Washburne described what he admired about his Adlerian colleague: "Dreikurs had a sane common sense approach to problems as well as a great skill and psychological insight. He knows how to talk to parents and teachers in a way that is positive and helpful. I have great confidence in him and whole-hearted respect for him and his work. Any person, group, or child guidance center that can have his services is, in my opinion, exceedingly fortunate."[14]

As a consequence of Washburne's support, Dreikurs was invited to lecture at summer workshops for guidance personnel sponsored by Northwestern's Education Department in 1940 and 1944. Then came the invitation from Dr. Shirley Hamrin, director of the Guidance Department, to teach a postgraduate course in child guidance at the university summer session of 1947. Dreikurs accepted and taught there during that and successive summer sessions, through 1951. He generated some controversy and a mixed reception from the faculty and students, which stemmed as much from his personal style as from his ideological position.

His appearance on campus caused something of a stir in those lazy, summer days in Evanston. Sporting a black beret jauntily poised on his bald head, he would abruptly pull up in his sleek, red convertible, sometimes accompanied by Tee. He would dismount and move across campus to and from the old Education Building as if propelled by some invisible force.

What made him so controversial was the anachronistic image he presented as the autocratic Germanic professor lecturing to the assembled multitude on the absolute necessity for establishing equality and democracy in the home and at school. Ray Lowe, then a graduate assistant, recalled his first encounter with the "autocrat of democracy":

> My office was just outside the door of a large lecture room. I recall the booming voice with a foreign accent lecturing with an air of certainty—and volume. Each lecture was like a major address at Madison Square Garden. One day the lecture room door was ajar and I peeked in. There he was lecturing . . . totally absorbed in what he was saying, with but seven students in the class. I was greatly impressed and lingered a bit, almost entranced with his powerful being. . . . I continued to peek [in] for the few lectures remaining. While I found much of what he was saying most fascinating, it wasn't until several years later that I could bring myself to approach him.[15]

Perhaps it was an overanxiety to succeed at Northwestern that led Dreikurs to assume his puffed-up, professorial air. He modeled his approach on the professors he had known in Vienna. Germanic professors were famous for their absolutist manner, arbitrarily setting rules and insisting that students defer to them. He copied that as well as their disdain for the day-to-day bookkeeping details regarding attendance, grades, and course work, which offended some of his American students. "In the European tradition, he always had an assistant—one of the chosen," a student remembered. "He or she, upon his insistence and in some instances with extreme embarrassment, would sit beside him 'facing' the class for the entire session and never have or was permitted to express a word. We resented it. There was God in his Heaven, and St. Mary or St. Peter there to hand him his pencil or his chalk."[16]

Dreikurs's "professorial mannerisms" softened after his initial experience at Northwestern. Later, in Oregon, for example, though he presented his ideas in a highly authoritative fashion, he was relaxed, and dressed and acted informally—hardly the "Herr Doktor Professor" image of his earliest years at Northwestern. Tee explained that Northwestern represented an immense challenge, a first opportunity to teach at a major university. Just as he was about to start his first classes there, Tee recalled, Frederick and Muriel Reed, both educators and close associates of Carleton Washburne who were also instrumental in bringing the child guidance centers to the North Shore suburbs, joined her and had a discussion with Dreikurs. "We warned him not to antagonize the people there. We told him, 'This is the chance you've been waiting for for years. Don't mess it up.' He agreed, and because it was not his nature to be polite or diplomatic, he felt inhibited. That inhibition, in turn, resulted in his being very formal and proper. It was not his normal way of functioning, but a pose to help keep himself in line. He dropped it when he felt comfortable in his teaching role."[17]

The following summer, Lowe again did not take his course, but he participated in a guidance workshop where Dreikurs gave the keynote speech. "I was fascinated again, listening to the flow of this man's ideas," he recalled. "They were sequential and developmental, and if he didn't substantiate them, I could from my own experience. I saw the merit in what he was saying."[18]

Finally, in the summer of 1950, Lowe signed up for Dreikurs's course. Ever since he first heard Dreikurs, he had recommended the course to others. "I remember," Lowe mused, "he said to me, 'O-o-oh, you're the person who sent me all those students.' Immediately there was a euphoric positive feeling toward me. It was part of his hunger for approval, for recognition. People who recognized him were something special in his life."[19]

At Northwestern, as elsewhere, when Dreikurs taught, the strength of his instruction rested not only on the coherent conceptual framework he presented but also on his demonstration of techniques with people in real-life social interactions. Thus, students at Northwestern often attended the child guidance center in Evanston that Dreikurs conducted. He also arranged for his students to visit a kindergarten. There, they were to observe the children playing and interacting and to determine their goals, but without talking to them. Teaching others to look at behavior in a goal-oriented fashion was perhaps the most difficult task Dreikurs faced, because causalistic thinking is so deeply ingrained in traditional approaches to behavior.

An anology Dreikurs used to help change the students' perspective showed the teleological thinking involved in day-to-day situations:

> When you drive a car on a highway, how is it possible that there are so many cars moving together without colliding? You communicate to each other only your intentions. The guy on the right of you will indicate to you that he wants to pass, and you indicate to him whether you'll let him or not. Do you give a hoot why he wants to pass? Whether its because he's an old meanie, has a conflict with his mother-in-law, or has a problem at work? It doesn't make any difference *why* he wants to pass. The crucial point is his indication of his intentions. You are responding to that. So in practical life we are all teleo-analysts, but we don't know it.[20]

Many of the experienced teachers in his classes were surprised and impressed by the results of looking at behavior from the perspective of its purpose. They wondered why nobody had ever taught them that before. Their traditional training had taught them to look for the causes of mis-behavior in genetic or environmental influences and then to apply an appropriate label—aggressiveness, hyperactivity, inability to concentrate, brain-damaged, culturally deprived, and so on.

Their puzzlement and surprise was understandable. As psychologist James E. Royce humorously noted: "Although the child fairly early in life discovers he has a will (or at least a won't)—the notion hardly ever appears in textbooks and the 'will' practically never, except perhaps in derision."[21]

Another important person to emerge from the Northwestern experience was Manford Sonstegard. A Ph.D. candidate with considerable experi-ence in public school teaching and administration, Sonstegard enrolled in the Dreikurs course in 1950, the same summer as did Ray Lowe. How-ever, he did not fare as well in his initial encounters with Dreikurs.

"In fact, our first verbal interchange was rather stormy. We got into conflict almost immediately. . . . It was not my first conflict with college professors," Sonstegard reminisced, "however, this one was vastly differ-ent. Whereas previously my conflict with authority figures had led to alienation, with Dr. 'D.' it did not seem to make any difference. I was accorded the same respect and privileges as other students. For the first time in an interaction in a group situation, I learned that friction and a clash of interests can take place without disrupting or destroying the relationship."[22]

Sonstegard was intrigued by Dreikurs's interpretation of behavior as goal-directed, with its orientation toward the future rather than the past. The future allows for the possibility of change, the past can only describe what took place; it cannot be altered. Using his considerable experience as an elementary school teacher and principal, Sonstegard began making astute interpretations of behavior that caught Dreikurs's attention. As the course drew to a close, Sonstegard realized "that it was one of the most important and revealing courses [in] which I had ever enrolled." He continued, "Dreikurs asked the students what they planned to do when they returned to their teaching positions. When he questioned me directly, I replied that I planned to go back to Iowa State Teachers College and form a Child Guidance Center such as [those] in Chicago. This brought a ripple of ill-concealed mirth from the other students in the class. However, this did not deter me. . . ."[23]

A quiet, independent man of few words but strong determination, Sonstegard did as planned. Returning to the college, where he was a faculty member, he succeeded, by 1952, in launching and directing four child guidance centers in the Waterloo–Cedar Falls area, sponsored by the Malcolm Price Laboratory of Iowa State Teachers College. Conducted on the Adler-Dreikurs model, they were well integrated into the community and drew their organizational strength from local parents who served on the board of directors.[24] These centers were a significant milestone for Dreikurs. For the first time, he saw his model of child guidance established and maintained outside of Chicago. It was a challenging undertaking for Sonstegard, and he returned to Chicago during a brief leave of absence to study Dreikurs's methods more intensely. He commented on the experience:

> I was practically worn out after one week's work . . . keeping up with this human dynamo as he went about his daily work of consulting with private patients, counseling at the Centers, lecturing in the evening and conducting a class. . . . Even with my youth . . . and good physical condition from outdoors activities, I was on the point of exhaustion at the end of each day. Nevertheless, it was worth it. I returned . . . much inspired and with new courage for an approach to child guidance which was openly criticized by my colleagues.

Those first years were rough and it was, I believe, the confidence and courage that Dr. 'D.' exhibited that gave me the spirit to push ahead against opposition.[25]

Dreikurs gave selflessly of his time to promote his ideas, and when others described him as an egotist, Sonstegard disagreed. "He did what needed to be done, regardless of the consequence to himself personally . . . without any thought of his well-being or expenses, to say nothing of monetary reward."[26]

Shortly after the centers got underway, Sonstegard invited Dreikurs to come to Cedar Falls to advise the group there on further developments. Dreikurs accepted, boarded a train in Chicago at eleven in the evening after teaching class from seven to ten, rode the train all night, and arrived in time for breakfast. He spent the entire day in meetings with students, in a discussion with the faculty at the college, and addressing a dinner meeting. That night, Sonstegard attempted to press a small amount of money into his hand that had been raised from ticket sales to the dinner. Dreikurs refrained, querying, "Is that out of your own pocket?" Assured that it was not, he accepted a sum so meager that Sonstegard was reluctant to press it upon him.[27]

Sonstegard remained at the Iowa college until 1963, with the exception of a two-year period spent in Ethiopia. The community support of the centers was more dependent on his leadership than he realized, and when he left for a new post, the centers closed. Later he realized how he had failed—he had restricted his training in counseling techniques to graduate students at Iowa State Teachers College and had neglected to train the local community people served by the center who would be left to carry on the work in succeeding years. Thus, when his students graduated and went elsewhere to pursue their careers, and when he himself left for Southern Illinois University, there was no one in the community trained to continue the work of the centers, and they ceased functioning.

In succeeding years at SIU, at West Virginia University, at the College for Graduate Studies in West Virginia, his current affiliation, and as a visiting professor here and abroad, Sonstegard made training community leaders and paraprofessionals the hallmark of his approach.

Sonstegard's soft-spoken, easy-going, and modest demeanor contrasted sharply with Dreikurs's bold, powerhouse approach. Antagonistic as Dreikurs could be, Sonstegard was as remarkedly unantagonistic. This contrast proved useful in succeeding years. When Dreikurs was invited to talk to a new group, he would characteristically start by dropping a bombshell: "Teachers [or psychologists, or social workers, or whomever it was that he was addressing] don't understand anything about children!" This would immediately raise the hackles of some in the audience, who could be seen walking out in a huff and ever after cursing under their breath when Dreikurs's name was mentioned. As many as were angered, others were intrigued by Dreikurs's refreshing ideas and were ready to put them into practice. Frequently, Sonstegard would provide the follow-up training and consultation in Adlerian techniques after Dreikurs had sparked the interest. When Sonstegard would arrive to begin working with the new group of school personnel, he would find a hostile atmosphere generated by those who had been antagonized by Dreikurs. With his modest, understated style, he would sooth the ruffled feathers, and with his own effective demonstrations he would win a new group to Adlerian principles of educational psychology.

For a time, Sonstegard, like other close colleagues of Dreikurs, was upset by Dreikurs's imprudent approach and tried to convince him to tone down his provocative statements. But it never had any discernible effect. Later, Sonstegard concluded, "There is a definite place in [the] scheme of things for Dreikurs's approach. There is a need for someone to shake people up, . . . to point out dramatically, and perhaps in an exaggerated form, the crisis in education which we are facing. However, . . . [he] needs to be followed . . . by someone who is slightly more temperate in his approach, more flexible in his dealings but nevertheless, not compromising the principles for which we Adlerians stand."[28]

Another Northwestern student, Don Dinkmeyer, incorporated and developed Adlerian principles in his teachings and writings in the then emerging field of elementary school guidance. He also coauthored with Dreikurs a valuable book on the encouragement process, *Encouraging Children to Learn* (1963). He was the first of many students who eventually coauthored books with Dreikurs.

Dreikurs's teaching career at Northwestern ended after the summer of 1951. The following year, Dr. Hamrin, his sponsor, who had admired him and supported his appointment in the face of perennial opposition, fell seriously ill and was not present when the 1952 summer program and faculty were planned.[29]

The Teachers of Gary, Indiana

Just as the Northwestern experience came to an end, a new opportunity emerged for Dreikurs in neighboring Gary, Indiana. This time it involved working directly with classroom teachers. Although his good friend Bronia Grunwald had taught in the Gary schools and made an impact because of her success in using Adlerian principles, it was Mark Roser, director of child welfare for the Gary schools, who brought Dreikurs into the system.

They first met in the mid-1940s, when Roser happened upon an announcement of Dreikurs's summer workshop at Circle Pines Camp near Kalamazoo, Michigan. "For some reason, or intuition," he recalled, "this announcement appealed to me, although I had not heard of Dr. Dreikurs before." Professionally trained in psychology and social work at Harvard and the University of Chicago, with additional training at the Institute of Psychoanalysis and at Indiana University, he found "none of these disciplines seemed adequate or realistic for the challenge of teachers and educators." Dreikurs convinced him that the commonsense concepts and methods of Adlerian psychology "could readily be grasped by the teachers and social workers under my supervision."[30]

A few years later, Roser proposed that Dreikurs be invited to work with the teachers of Gary. But before his supervisors were willing to hire Dreikurs, they wanted to see if he could stand up under the test of fire. Dreikurs recalled with amusement:

> One day I got an invitation to talk to about two hundred junior and senior high school students. As I was about to enter the auditorium, I spotted a dozen or so husky fellows pass me by. They looked rather suspiciously at me as if they were sizing me up and then filed into the room. When I entered, I immediately saw what was up. In the last two rows, far away, were the husky fellows, and sitting in the first rows were all the neat, clean-cut girls. I could see the whole sociometric structure, and I knew I was in for trouble. So, the first thing I did was to ask the last two rows to change seats with the first two rows. There followed considerable commotion, and finally, three boys came forward and said, "We represent the last two rows." I replied, "I did not ask for representation, I asked the last two rows to come forward." Then I told them why. "You have seated yourselves as far

back from me as possible so you can make your remarks and stir up trouble. And I won't start my talk until you change seats." Still they did not come forward. So I said, "It's OK with me, I can stand here all day, but I won't start until you move." I didn't scold, I didn't nag, I didn't impose my will on them. I just stood there. They were taken by surprise. They didn't know what to do, and finally, they made the switch. No sooner than I began talking than I spotted certain troublemakers making a commotion here or there. Each time I asked the youngster to come sit to the left or right of me at the front. By then they knew it was something more than an invitation. I wouldn't continue until they came up. I was told afterwards that I had spotted and isolated every single troublemaker.[31]

Though the teachers and guidance personnel were present, the students were rather outspoken in their views. One girl mockingly asked, "Why do I need a piece of paper [meaning the marriage certificate] in order to make love to a boy? Why is it immoral if I don't have the paper and moral if I do have it? All these social conventions are for the birds!" To Dreikurs this was a typical example of how teen-agers challenge adults, and you have to be a match for them:

This is very crucial with these kids. You must avoid getting into a fight with them, because if you do, you are lost. To help these kids think, you have to be flexible and imaginative, otherwise you wind up covering up with empty moralistic phrases. I pointed out to her that social conventions are never logical, but they do mean something. "Would you be willing to wear a swim suit on the beach?" "Yes, of course," she answered. "Now, would you wear that same bathing suit in a restaurant downtown?" She said she would not. "Isn't that silly?" I said. "If it's proper at the beach, why not in the restaurant?" Then she realized the reason for social conventions—we get certain benefits from them. There followed a very candid discussion.[32]

Afterward, Dreikurs learned that this invitation had been designed to test him. Another psychiatrist, who was also being considered as a consultant, had spoken before the very same group two weeks earlier, and pandemonium had broken out, with nobody able to get the group under control. So Dreikurs passed the "test," and shortly thereafter he began teaching social workers, counselors, and teachers in Gary under the joint sponsorship of the public school system and the Gary Extension of the University of Indiana Department of Psychology.

For nearly two and a half years, from 1951 to 1954, Dreikurs worked with the teachers of Gary. Roser remarked that his lectures and demonstrations were met with enthusiasm, and there were numerous indications of the concrete help that teachers, parents, and case workers experienced at school and at home. But there also emerged a growing opposition among certain faculty members of Indiana's Psychology Department. Roser believed that "their security [was] undermined as they faced these new, and . . . somewhat radical ideas. Finally, the local director of the university informed me that the class could not be continued, although he knew and I knew that they were the most helpful and popular in the history of the schools. Why? I was informed that the basic concepts of psychology [were] being violated, that the approach was not scientific, and [that] it was not being supported by the university professors."[33]

Many teachers who had participated in the classes rose in opposition to the decision and sent letters to Bloomington calling for the course to be continued, but to no avail.

Many months later, at a dinner honoring Dreikurs's contribution to the Gary system, Mark Roser, seated next to Dreikurs, expressed his regrets and apologized for the abrupt turn of events. Dreikurs reassured him, "Actually, it turned out to be a blessing in disguise. If I had not been thrown out, I probably never would have written my book for teachers. As it turned out, I had all this material from the classes and the free time to work on it."

Free time was a rare commodity in Dreikurs's hectic life, yet the pressure to write, to get his ideas in print was continual. He approached the writing process in a characteristically unique way, one that intimately involved Tee, who helped formulate ideas, typed, and edited. The usual setting for this work was their apartment.

By the mid-1950s, they had settled into a spacious and comfortable apartment on Chicago's lake front. Located on the sixth floor, above the trees in Lincoln Park below, it faced east with a lovely, unobstructed view of Lake Michigan. Tee's artistry was evidenced by the tastefully chosen modern furnishings of muted complementary colors that were comfortable and inviting. The walls in the living and dining rooms were filled with marvelous paintings by her first husband, Leon Garland, and herself, done in well-executed cubist and abstract styles. Toward one end of the spacious living room, in a window-filled alcove, was Dreikurs's hand-carved grand piano, and sofas and chairs were arranged in a conversational setting around a cocktail table. The adjoining dining room, which frequently doubled as a guest room, also served as a library with crammed bookshelves that included numerous *objets d'art* and a stereo music system that filled the rooms with classical music whenever Dreikurs was home. There was a tiny kitchen, where with grace and aplomb, Tee always managed to come up with food and drink for an abundance of guests. Adjacent to the kitchen was a small room that served as Dreikurs's private study. The desk and bookshelves and spare chair were always overflowing with papers, in no apparent order. Here he retreated to work on his stamps, a lifelong hobby, which had grown to a very substantial collection. Stamps were his tranquilizer—no matter how overtired, tense, or provoked he might be from a long, demanding day, a short time spent alone with his stamps was enough to clear the fatigue, and he would emerge refreshed, ready to tackle whatever lay ahead.

Picture then, in the alcove section of the living room overlooking the lake, a card table with a portable typewriter and scattered piles of loose paper on top. That was the center for Dreikurs's prolific writing activities. Tee would sit at the typewriter and begin typing drafts as he dictated his thoughts. Remarked Tee:

> Ru never sat when he wrote, and he never stood. Rather, he paced from one end of the apartment to the other tracing a random route by the bedroom or into the dining room to adjust the stereo, which was going full blast at the same time. It was quite remarkable, what with the clatter of the typewriter, plus the music, plus his booming voice that faded in and out as he moved about. The more interesting the topic, the more animated he became—he was always in motion. That sometimes made it difficult to hear. But that was how we worked together. He used to call me his "super-duper ego," because as we worked together I often tried to get him to tone down any stridency or harshness that might antagonize the reader. He generally followed my advice, but reluctantly, believing that his writings would make a greater impression if all the acid and anger he felt about a situation was left intact. I always disagreed.[34]

The origins of *Psychology in the Classroom* (1957) go back to 1951, when Dreikurs put together a mimeographed version containing his basic principles for teachers. But the bulk of the book, the many valuable case studies and examples, were derived mostly from the actual classroom experiences of the Gary teachers. Dreikurs's course emphasized the application of principles such as group discussions, methods of encouragement, and the use of natural and logical consequences. The teachers wrote brief accounts of their experiences in applying his techniques and then presented them to the class for analysis. Suggestions were then given to the teachers to take back to their respective classrooms. Tee was present for all the Gary classes, and at the end of five semesters they had acquired reams of examples, which had to be culled and edited for the book Dreikurs intended to publish. Time was what was needed to complete the task.

JAMAICA

Shortly after Dreikurs's work in Gary came to an end in 1954, he received an unexpected phone call from his old friend Harold Wheeler, who had moved to Jamaica, British West Indies. He suggested that Dreikurs drop everything and come to Jamaica because he had a rare opportunity to offer. Wheeler had previously lived in Chicago and had been a keen supporter of the child guidance centers for years until he resettled in Jamaica. There he had dear British friends whose twelve-year-old son had suddenly developed signs of serious disturbance, and the parents were distraught and uncertain about what to do for their boy. Wheeler proposed that Dreikurs come to Jamaica for two months. The family would pay all expenses and would make available a lovely home, where Dreikurs could write while he also worked with the boy. It was too enticing to resist. Dreikurs canceled plans to attend the International Congress of Psychotherapy in Vienna and went to Jamaica instead. "There," he reminisced, "I worked with this boy in a beautiful setting called Paradise, and wrote my book, *Psychology in the Classroom*."[35]

Much was accomplished on the book that summer, and little thought was given to doing anything beyond it and counseling the boy. Dreikurs was concerned, however, to find a suitable school for the youngster for the following year. He then remembered that he had corresponded some time earlier with the Reverend Lewis Davidson, who was headmaster at Knox College, a boarding school high in the mountains near Spalding, Jamaica.

Davidson, a Scotsman, and Right Reverend of the Presbyterian Church, who also held a master's degree in psychology, had become acquainted with Alderian psychology through his friendship with Phyllis Bottome, Adler's biographer. He had fashioned his school on Adlerian educational principles. So Dreikurs was curious to meet Davidson and to learn more about his school. He described his initial impressions of the school in a letter to his colleagues in Chicago: "We went up and up the road into nowhere, [through] deep valleys and steep hills. . . . We finally came to a small bumpy sideroad and, on top of a mountain, we found it. . . . Davidson had built out of nothing, almost without funds, the most beautitful and modern school on top of the wilderness, overlooking the hills and valleys. . . . His auditor told him he had known many who never knew where their money went, but none before him who never knew from where the money came. Davidson is a . . . most energetic, idealistic and resourceful person . . . a convinced Adlerian, . . . and is now groping for more detailed knowledge."[36]

Davidson was originally sent to Jamaica by the British Colonial Education Service and gained experience in educational administration and in research and consultation in social, economic, and religious affairs. From meager beginnings in 1948, with fourteen students and 100 pounds sterling, he developed Knox College into an outstanding educational facility. His goal was to provide jobs and training that would then enable the people to earn a living. "We are dedicated to the care of the individual— the development of the capacity to live and work together."[37] To that end, Knox had a community development program with a large printing plant, a food production unit, a food processing plant, and a construction company. During the academic year, Knox functioned as a progressive, coeducational high school. But each summer Davidson ran a two-week seminar or school for adults on specialized topics that drew people of all professions from Jamaica and nearby islands.

The initial encounter between Davidson and Dreikurs was a happy, enthusiastic meeting of minds, not unlike that with da Silva Mello in Brazil. They made plans to use the printing and distribution facilities of Knox College as a much needed avenue for getting Dreikurs's materials into print and more widely distributed. Davidson also asked Dreikurs to return to Jamaica at the first opportunity to conduct the summer school on issues of child guidance. When Dreikurs returned, in 1956, to conduct the Knox College summer school, Davidson remarked: "He was a fantastic success. . . . There were morning seminars, afternoon demonstrations, and evening lectures open to the public. He really wowed the people of the district. They came from far and near for the evening lectures, and ranged from simple peasants to quite sophisticated characters from far away who drove up in their cars. Many speak of it, remember him still."[38]

Dreikurs, in Davidson's view, was one of the most effective lecturers and demonstrators he had ever met. "I saw him do really fantastic things; he excelled in the drama of these demonstrations."[39] One in particular stood out in the memory of Davidson and many others who attended the summer school. A mother approached Dreikurs in a general discussion concerning her son, a three-year-old boy who did not speak and who had been designated as retarded and physically incompetent. From the exchange between them, Dreikurs learned that the boy had two normal but much older siblings and had been "an afterthought." The parents had split up, and the mother, overanxious for the welfare of her baby, indulged him, spoiled him, and anticipated his every need. She continually repeated, "He's so helpless, poor thing." Dreikurs had a hunch that there was nothing physically wrong with the boy. He confronted the mother, "Do you realize how he runs your life—you are his slave!" She was shocked, angered, and refused to accept it. She stormed out. That seemed to be the end of that.

But a few days before the summer school ended, the mother returned, much to everyone's surprise. She was desperate and willing to find out if this strange, yet intriguing man could help. Before the large group of assembled professionals, the mother came into the room, carrying her "helpless" child.

Dreikurs signaled the mother to join him on the platform and told her, "Leave the boy there." She did, and as soon as she was out of the child's grasp, he started bawling. Dreikurs said to the boy (who was not supposed to understand anything), "When you want, you can come up here and join your mother." He then turned to her and began his counseling dialogue. The child screamed, tears streaming down his cheeks, his bewildered eyes riveted on his mother and Dreikurs. The audience grew uncomfortable; the urge to stop this cruelty welled up. Slowly the boy began to make his way to the platform, and succeeded—on his own. Still Dreikurs went on, finishing the dialogue with the mother. He then asked her to leave the room so he could talk to the boy. She did so, and a new round of bawling began. Dreikurs tried to talk to the child, who seemed frantic and said not one word. Dreikurs's voice grew louder—he seemed impatient. He attacked the boy with a steady barrage of questions in an unrelenting confrontation. The audience was shocked. This is no way to treat such a pitiful child. The boy's face grew red with anger, and suddenly, to everyone's amazement, he blurted out, "I want to go to mommy."

"It is very, very dramatic," Davidson remarked. "He demonstrated without question that there was no organic disorder at all. He made the boy so angry that he responded out of sheer defense. Dreikurs was a bully. And I don't know any psychiatrist who isn't—when push comes to shove. He was a bully. And I don't use the word disparagingly—you could say a surgeon is a sadist because he cuts you up with a knife. And I mean that in the exact same sense. He knew when to apply tremendous pressure to get what he wanted done, and he did."[40]

A public-health nurse who sat in on the same session and who later went to Chicago to train with Dreikurs recalled the emotional drama. "It was unforgettable and made a deep impression on those present. He took a calculated risk to do what he did, and he was right. People talked about it for years."

In succeeding years, Dreikurs returned to Jamaica, and his impact on the Jamaican society and government was significant because of his extensive work with the police, probation officers, social workers, teachers, and educators. Plans were made to form a Jamaican Society of Adlerian Psychology, and several Jamaicans came to Chicago for additional training at the institute. The Jamaican experience encouraged Dreikurs and gave him a clear indication of his potential for extending the influence of Adlerian psychology internationally.

However, nothing gave him greater pleasure than the new, more active role Tee began to play in his work: "What Knox did to Tee was most memorable. She looked better and felt better than I have seen her for many a year. She was very active in her participation . . . taking the position of the Devil's Advocate, and expressing her feminine caution, to the delight of all the other cautious souls in the group. . . . She began to paint for the first time after twenty years. Of course, she did not want to do it and was pressured by me . . . , and, of course, she felt utterly frustrated— but what she produced was just wonderful."[41]

Lew Davidson also noted Tee's contributions to the sessions and described what became the characteristic way Rudolf and Tee worked together in the years that followed: "She was full of insight and able to counsel him directly. She could gauge the temperature of an audience— how he was getting across to them. And I have seen him change in midstream. For instance, at a session at the university, I remember him going full guns, fighting everybody at the drop of a hat. Then he caught Tee's eyes, and he changed just like that. In a nonverbal way she communicated, and he understood perfectly. That was the kind of influence she had."[42]

Dreikurs's extensive visits to Jamaica revealed another side of the man that both captivated and vexed his Jamaican host. "He was a perfectly delightful guest," Davidson remarked,

> Of course, he had this quality of being a big spoiled boy. . . . And there was a certain innocence about him. He was rather like a little boy who is very determined. For instance, he just loved to play the piano. More than playing one piano he liked to play duo-pianos. Once, during the summer school, the "urge" to play duo-pianos came over him. He told me, "I vant to play two pianos." I replied, "Well, Rudolf, we've only got one piano in the building." He was very downcast with that. About a half an hour later, having done a lot of homework, he said, pointing with his finger, he had found another piano, down there. That is to say about a quarter of a mile away. "But Rudolf," I said, "that's a long way, and you know, pianos don't move very well." He thought about that and said, "But, I vant to play two pianos." I refused to help, and so he went off, very annoyed with me.
>
> Shortly, he came and said, "Some of the students—they say they will move the piano for me." So what could I do. I said, "Fine, take the piano!" Having got the two pianos, he had yet to find someone to play with him. We had a music teacher, who by this time, having been quizzed by Rudolf, was terrified of him. She didn't like him at all. But she was the only musician available. So, he set to work on her, and before I knew it, he had turned her around and persuaded her to play the other piano. And they had a very good time.[43]

PSYCHOLOGY IN THE CLASSROOM

Dreikurs returned to Chicago after his second visit to Jamaica, in 1956, more buoyant and optimistic than ever, not only because of the great success of the Knox summer school but also because, while there, he and Tee had revamped and polished the text for teachers, and a publisher had been found.

When Harper and Row undertook the publishing of *Psychology in the*

Classroom, an advance copy was sent to Dr. Henry Clay Lindgren, professor of psychology at San Francisco State College, for his professional assessment of the book. He replied to the editor at Harper & Row:

> I was very much interested when you told me that you were sending me the proofs of Dr. Dreikurs' book, *Psychology in the Classroom,* because he and I had discussed the problem of the use of techniques in improving the relationship between adults and children, and I wanted to see how his ideas looked in print. I must confess that I had some doubts as to the validity of his method. As a result of having read this book, I still have some reservations, but I think I have swung a good many degrees toward his position.
>
> Perhaps this modification in my orientation comes about because Dr. Dreikurs is such a lucid writer. There are very few in the psychology profession who can equal him in this. But I think even more credit must be allowed to what he has written rather than how he has written it. . . . Exciting and stimulating . . . it is one of the few books in the field of educational psychology that I can tell teachers to buy and read without making any reservations and qualifications. . . . It could bring about a much-needed revolution in teaching.
>
> *Psychology in the Classroom* is an advice-giving book that will, I am sure, go far toward restoring the confidence of the teachers that will read it. And as Dr. Dreikurs implies, discouragement pervades the educational scene, infecting both pupils and teachers, and it is this discouragement that underlies the pupil misbehavior and teacher mismanagement that are unfortunately so widespread in our schools. Hence you can see why this book is badly needed.[44]

The success of the Jamaican visits and the prospect of the forthcoming book were offset for Dreikurs by the realization that there were no longer any doors open for him in education in and around Chicago. After the Gary experience, he taught for two years at Roosevelt College, where he had won the admiration and support of Dr. George W. Hartmann. But his appointment at Roosevelt sparked a bitter feud within the faculty, a number of whom, defenders of the Freudian viewpoint, had opposed him. When Hartmann suddenly died, Dreikurs was not reappointed.

He reflected thereafter, "It looked pretty bad about that time. I was out of Chicago Medical School, out of Northwestern, out of Indiana, and out of Roosevelt. It looked almost like I was out for good."[45]

Notes for Chapter 17

1. Rudolf Dreikurs, "In Memoriam—Alfred Adler," *Individual Psychology Bulletin* 2 (1942): 76–77.

2. Sister Rachel, O.S.H., *Notes on Dr. Dreikurs' Meeting with the Lower School Faculty, November 23, 1946.* Mimeographed report, p. 1. This report was kindly supplied by Miss E. V. Freeland, academic head, Margaret Hall School. See also: Sister Rachel, O.S.H., "Individual Psychology in a Church School," *Individual Psychology Bulletin* 9 (1951): 156–166.

3. Sister Rachel, *Notes on Dr. Dreikurs' Meeting*, p. 3.

4. Sister Rachel, personal communication, March 1973.

5. Sister Rachel, *Notes on Dr. Dreikurs's Meeting*, p. 2.

6. Reference is made here to two of the "four goals of misbehavior" in children that Dreikurs had earlier discovered (see chapter 12). For an elaboration of the psychological dynamics of these four goals, see Rudolf Dreikurs, *Psychology in the Classroom* (New York: Harper & Row, 1957), pp. 27–32; idem, "Four Goals of the Maladjusted Child."

7. Sister Rachel, *Notes on Dr. Dreikurs' Meeting*, p. 2.

8. Ibid., p. 3.

9. Ibid., pp. 3–5.

10. Carleton Wesley Washburne and Sidney P. Marland, *Winnetka: The History and Significance of an Educational Experiment* (Englewood Cliffs, N.J.: Prentice-Hall, 1963), p. 112.

11. Dreikurs-Mackaness interview.

12. Mackaness, *Biographical Study*, p. 183.

13. Dreikurs-Mackaness interview.

14. Mackaness, *A Biographical Study*, p. 184.

15. Ibid., p. 187.

16. Ibid., pp. 189–190.

17. Sadie "Tee" Dreikurs, personal communication, September 1976.

18. Raymond Lowe, personal communication, October 1973.

19. Ibid.

20. Rudolf Dreikurs, "An Interview," *Counseling Psychologist* 3 (1971): 50.

21. James E. Royce, "Historical Aspects of Free Choice," *Journal of the History of the Behavioral Sciences* 6 (January 1970): 48. Royce pointed out that for decades, under the impact of quantitative methodologies in the sciences, final cause (the goal) or motive, not being capable of measurement, was counted as nothing, and "the tide is beginning to turn in the area of volition. Rogers, Maslow, Cantril, Allport, Rollo May, Nuttin, some of Festinger's followers, and . . . others . . . have discovered that inner subjective variables can be experimentally investigated including the self as a part-determiner of behavior" (p. 50). Shortly thereafter, reporting the results of an extensive study, Joseph F. Rychlak commented, "Psychology is now sufficiently mature to readmit theories which rely upon a human teleology" ("Causality and the Proper Image of Man in Scientific Psychology," *Journal of Personality Assessment* 5 [1971]: 403. Rychlak concluded, "The true scientist is he who knows precisely where he stands, where his meanings emanate from as he paints his portrait of events. . . . The climate of professional repression for the humanist and others who would put intentions back into behavior is dissipating at an increasing tempo" [p. 419]).

22. Manford Sonstegard, "What Doctor 'D' Has Meant to Me," 1967, Dreikurs Papers.

23. Manford Sonstegard to William H. Mackaness, October 11, 1961, Dreikurs Papers.

24. Manford Sonstegard, "A Center for the Guidance of Parents and Children in a Small Community," *American Journal of Individual Psychology* 11 (1954): 81–89. See also his "How a Center Is Organized," in *Adlerian Family Counseling*, pp. 101–109.

25. Sonstegard to Mackaness, October 11, 1961, Dreikurs Papers.

26. Manford Sonstegard, "Dreikurs' Contribution to Community Mental Health, Social Psychiatry, and Community Involvement," *Proceedings of the Rudolf Dreikurs Memorial Institute*, ICASSI 1973, *Espinho, Portugal, July 1973*, p. 3.

27. Ibid.

28. Sonstegard to Mackaness, October 11, 1961, Dreikurs Papers.

29. Mackaness, *Biographical Study*, p. 190.

30. Mark C. Roser, personal communication, January 18, 1973.

31. Dreikurs-Mackaness interview.

32. Ibid.

33. Mark C. Roser, personal communication, January 18, 1973.

34. Sadie "Tee" Dreikurs-Mackaness interview.

35. Dreikurs-Mackaness interview.

36. Dreikurs, to family and office staff, July 9, 1954, Dreikurs Papers.

37. The Reverend Lewis Davidson, interview conducted by Manford Sonstegard, Summer 1973.

38. Ibid.

39. Ibid.

40. Ibid.

41. Dreikurs, to family and office staff, August 12, 1958, Dreikurs Papers.

42. Davidson-Sonstegard interview.

43. Ibid.

44. Henry Clay Lindgren to Ordway Teague, January 17, 1957, Dreikurs Papers.

45. Dreikurs-Mackaness interview.

PART III

A MOVEMENT IS BORN

18

Oregon: Gateway to the World

The progressive evolution of mankind is inseparably linked
with the improved spirit and technique of child-rearing.

Rudolf Dreikurs
Challenge of Parenthood

Dreikurs's options in the field of education—at least in working directly
with teachers and educators—appeared to have run out. Then, in 1957,
came another providential call. This time it was from Ray Lowe, his
former student at Northwestern. Lowe wanted to know if he was willing
to teach at the eight-week summer session at the University of Oregon in
Eugene. One hardly need guess the answer—"Yes."

The one brief course with Dreikurs at Northwestern had left a lasting
effect on Lowe. Critical of the trends in public education and the quality
of teacher education, he commented, "I had been grasping for a democratic basis for my work. I was intrigued with Dreikurs's ideas." Following the summer course at Northwestern, Lowe attended some of the first
classes of the fledgling Alfred Adler Institute in Chicago. After receiving
his Ph.D. at Northwestern, in 1951, he left the area for a position as
associate professor of education and assistant to the president at East
Montana College. He became frustrated with the politics of academic
administration and decided to use his sabbatical to return to Chicago and
see, as he put it, "if Dreikurs was for real." En route, he stopped in Cedar
Falls to observe Sonstegard's successful child guidance centers there.

"Dreikurs gave unselfishly of his time and made every effort to help me
grow and learn," Lowe commented. "I spent five and a half days each
week—all day and evening—with him, watching him work. He had
unique abilities. He could, in a counseling session, make relationships to
things that had surfaced three sessions previously. He was always on
target. He was a genius in his own right, because he was able to relate so
many different areas—ideas from history, science, sociology, art, and

music—into a meaningful whole. In Chicago, they didn't appreciate his greatness."[1]

Dreikurs's educational ideas—especially the solid link between the theory and its practical applications—were appealing to Lowe. "One needs but to attend a teacher's convention, teach a class of experienced teachers, or visit a school to realize that the gap between theory and practice in working with children is all but irreconcilable. . . . Many teachers are becoming alarmed at their inability to cope with children who misbehave or refuse to learn."[2]

When Lowe joined the education department faculty at the University of Oregon in 1956, he introduced a new course, "The Maladjusted Child." An outspoken, flamboyant teacher, Lowe based his course on Adlerian theory and particularly on Dreikurs's extensions and refinements of the principles for the classroom teacher. The course was enthusiastically received both by undergraduate teachers-in-training and by experienced teachers who had returned to the campus for graduate work. A touch of the rebel runs deep in Lowe, and he took a certain pleasure in stating that his educational principles for the classroom came not from the field of education but from a psychiatrist from Chicago, a man named Rudolf Dreikurs.

Lowe's course was particularly well received, because at that time there was a critical need in Oregon public education for teachers and counselors skilled in handling special-education problems—dyslexic readers, the mentally retarded, underachievers, and a growing assortment of disruptive behaviors in children. Oregon was later than other states in introducing guidance counselors to their junior and senior high school programming, and there were too few trained to fill the need. Though there was an impressive psychology department at the university, it was heavily oriented toward either academic research or experimental work with animals. The psychology department was not even prepared to train counselors to fulfill its own needs at the psychology clinic for students of the university. They had to bring people in from other regions to staff their own clinic.[3]

The following year Lowe began to explore with his university colleagues the long-range possibility of initiating a family counseling program modeled after Dreikurs's centers in Chicago. Dr. Robert Leeper, chairman of the psychology department, supported Lowe's suggestion that Dreikurs's firsthand involvement would be beneficial. Thus came the invitation for the 1957 summer session. Dreikurs's visiting professorship was a joint appointment of the psychology and the education departments of the university.

Knowing Dreikurs's tendency to antagonize people and provoke opposition, Lowe set out to smooth the path for his arrival in Eugene:

> I took every opportunity to talk to students, faculty, and particularly physicians in the community, about the kind of person he was. As I look back, I now realize I practically had a speech memorized. It went something like this: "He has more to offer about how to deal with children than anyone I know. But, he can't stand to have his position challenged; he takes such a challenge personally. He is most eager to explain his ideas but not justify them. If you are interested you can learn a lot if you listen and ask for clarification, but if you want to argue, it will be a most unpleasant experience." I know many helped me in this regard. . . . They didn't argue.[4]

Dreikurs arrived in Eugene prepared for the anticipated opposition. Opposition was a spark that ignited him, sharpened his keen wit, and evoked a bottomless reserve of energy. Adler once wrote, "No advance is ever made without the consciousness of a hindrance. It is the thing which appears to be a deterrent which acts as the incentive whenever there is a courageous struggle for success."[5] That certainly applied in the case of his indefatigable disciple.

Contrary to expectation, there was no concerted opposition to Dreikurs's view. He taught three courses that summer. One was Leeper's regular class, "Theories of Personality," for the psychology department. Though only six students registered for the class, there were never less than forty or fifty people in attendance. Mostly they were faculty members from other departments—philosophy, biology, sociology, as well as psychology. That in itself was a rare phenomenon—faculty members are not generally known to sit in on other classes. But Dreikurs created a flurry on campus, and they were curious to learn about this man who had sparked so much interest and controversy. Lowe mused, "The psychology people came because they anticipated a blowup between Dreikurs and Abe Luchins. Luchins was a brilliant psychologist and an indelible character who marched around the campus in a trench coat and hat in the middle of summer. He had the sharpest of minds, and many feared him because no matter what position you might take, he would take the opposite position for instructional purposes, but in such a way that you felt torn apart—destroyed."

Well, Dreikurs knew of Luchins and anticipated his opposition: "I understand he's going to go after me," he said to Ray Lowe. Lowe deflated the issue, "No, I don't think he will. He has a lot of respect for you, and you have a lot of respect for him." Nonetheless, everyone came from the psychology department to see Dreikurs and Luchins draw each other out. "They didn't like Luchins at all, and they didn't like having this 'outsider' psychiatrist from Chicago either," Lowe recalled. "Hell," he chuckled, "they fell in love with each other. Luchins was very supportive—both he and his wife."

Dreikurs wrote about the experience in a letter to his colleagues in Chicago:

> The situation at the university is beyond my grandest expectation. Ray Lowe did a remarkable job in selling me to the university and to the community. . . . My seminar is actually slanted toward the faculty members who will participate. [Lowe and Leeper] think that my greatest contribution can be made to them. I have never had such an experience before . . . and am almost overwhelmed.
>
> What impressed the seminar group more than anything else was the friendly and supporting attitude of Dr. Luchins. . . . Nobody ever saw him agreeing with anyone, nor refraining from tearing into everyone. I seem to be the first exception. . . . He found my theoretical premises perfectly acceptable and . . . is the only one who is not mechanistically oriented and is groping in the same direction as I do. . . . [He and his wife, a Ph.D. in mathematics] both happen to be interested in my pet subject, namely, the possibility to apply mathematics to psychology. . . . It seems that [Ivan] London at Harvard is already speculating about the same problem, the psychological uncertainty principle.[6]

Subsequently, Dreikurs began corresponding with London at Harvard, and, stimulated in his thinking by Luchins, delivered the paper "The Psychological Uncertainty Principle," at the Fifth International Congress of Psychotherapy in Vienna in 1961.[7]

The other courses Dreikurs taught that first summer were Lowe's regular course, "The Maladjusted Child," and a practicum in family counseling. Regarding the former, Dreikurs wrote, "The teachers . . . are most receptive. . . . It is almost unbelievable how much they learned in two or three weeks, and how well they could explore and analyze the case materials. Fortunately, I have hardly any psychology students in the class, because they . . . have a hard time understanding what I am doing, and accepting it. I run into no such difficulties with teachers who already had classroom experience. . . . Some of the students are quite advanced and already trained by Lowe."[8] Two of the "advanced" students alluded to were Oscar Christensen and Harold Kozuma. Both would become important in training others in Adlerian psychology in later years.

In the practicum courses and in the seminar on personality theory, Dreikurs began to demonstrate his techniques, doing life-style analyses and family counseling. A number of public demonstrations were also arranged that enabled the audience to see Dreikurs at work. They witnessed his facility at establishing a relationship with the client, his penetrating questions, his ubiquitous "could it be?," that he posed to children as he confronted them with their goals and noted the unmistakable "recognition reflex" that followed when he was on target—which was most of the time.

While Dreikurs had been doing public demonstrations of counseling for years, it was a new phenomenon in Oregon, and in regard to history, he was, even at that time, perhaps the only therapist to attempt such a daring method of teaching and bringing an understanding of psychodynamics to the public. The word soon spread through the small, quiet university town that the best show going, filled with human drama, humor, excitement, and insight, was taking place on the campus. Soon audiences were sitting on the floor and standing in the back. Smaller rooms were soon filled to overflowing and had to be exchanged for larger ones. Dreikurs was at his best—a convincing teacher and dazzling salesman for his ideas. He was, as Ray Lowe liked to say, "in his area, limitless."

Naturally, much controversy was generated, and a certain amount of opposition followed. Unquestionably his self-assurance and his seeming lack of scholarly humility led numerous individuals to challenge the correctness of Dreikurs's far-reaching conclusions. The effect was stimulating. After class or in the evenings, the discussions spilled over into freewheeling, exciting debates among the students who evaluated, attacked, or defended Dreikurs's positions. "They trailed after Dreikurs like he was the Pied Piper," Lowe recalled. "Every time you'd see a bunch of people gathered, or moving en masse across the campus, you could be sure he was at the head of the line."

Several notable incidents occurred that summer. One took place in the advanced seminar which was heavily attended by other faculty members. For years, while psychoanalysis reigned supreme, Dreikurs longed for a genuine opportunity to vividly demonstrate the difference between how a Freudian and an Adlerian would handle the same case. In Chicago, no psychoanalyst had been willing to be a party to such a "test." But in Oregon, a psychiatrist from the VA Hospital in Portland who claimed he was an "eclectic" with a psychoanalytic orientation agreed to come to class and offer his interpretation of a real case. The subject was a young woman who was having difficulties in her marriage and in her job. The case was seemingly complicated because she had been sexually molested by her father until the age of eleven. She tried to stop him by wearing heavy clothes at night and by forcefully resisting him. Dreikurs gave his version of what happened:

> The discussion was most dramatic. Not only did it show clearly the differences of our two approaches; but the sequence of events was [such] that at any one time [each] of us seemed to be supported by the data which came up. [When he came to the interpretations,] Dr. _____ maintained that her difficulties with her husband were due to the fact that she felt married to her father and did not want to be unfaithful to him, and [that] she resented her first child because it was an expression of her faithlessness to her father. It is hard to believe that such nonsense, not supported by any evidence or statement, could be presented seriously by a scientifically minded, reasonable and intelligent person. It was equally shocking when he refused to see the obvious pathological reasons for her fear of typing tests which was due partly to her overambition and perfectionism, partly because she was afraid of giving up her husband and standing on her own two feet. For [my colleague] the fear of typing was merely a symbol for her concern with masturbation, or playing with her father's penis. . . . Overall, it was a most frightful experience for me and for most of the faculty members present. Here was a man, intelligent, competent, well versed with the literature, who considered himself an eclectic . . . and who [even] agreed with some of my criticism of Freud and the orthodox analysts. . . . It was very courageous of him to come and expose himself to such a discussion; but in

doing so, he helped me immeasurably to have my point of view fortified on the campus.[9]

One day especially stands out from that summer. It was July 25, 1957. In the afternoon of that day Dreikurs gave one of his worst demonstrations, and that same evening returned to give what some consider his most memorable presentation ever.

According to Lowe, the afternoon session was arranged by a faculty member who was also the chairman of a loosely federated group responsible for child guidance clinics in Oregon. Dreikurs wrote his impression of the afternoon session and the two demonstrations he gave: "We had about forty people from the Child Guidance Clinic, the State Hospital and the Medical School, besides all my classes, one class of teachers from the Oregon State Teachers College, the representatives of the PTA and whoever wanted from the faculty, plus the family—in a room to hold 200, we had almost 300 crowded together, with people sitting on the floor and standing around. It was TERRIFIC. But I don't believe that the people from the Child Guidance Clinics could [even] understand what I offered. One social worker in the first row was so violently furious and hostile in her facial expression that she created a public nuisance."[10]

Lowe saw it a little differently: "I never saw him try so hard and do so poorly. Many of the psychologists and psychiatrists of the state were there. He hadn't been talking ten minutes when he said—I shudder now as I recall it, 'Psychologists and psychiatrists don't know anything about children.' For a few moments I wished he hadn't accepted our invitation."[11]

Dreikurs felt justified in his position and probably realized how much opposition he had incurred that afternoon. But from that day on, whenever he talked to Lowe, his first question was, "What's new?" and his second question, "And what about the opposition?"

Nevertheless, he came back to the Student Union that evening and gave a speech to a capacity crowd of more than seven hundred people. It would be reprinted and widely distributed and quoted thereafter. In his best black suit with bow tie and tailor-made white shirt with cuff links, he looked the part of a humble though triumphant maestro as the crowd made way for him and Tee in her chic, long dress.

Dreikurs had long since discovered how to captivate an audience and the value of sending people home with a few potent phrases that rocked the boat—challenging the current myths—and that would stimulate later discussion. He seldom formally prepared a speech. He would jot down a few key words on a scrap of paper and then never glance at his notes.

He chose for his title "The Courage to Be Imperfect."[12] Maybe he was speaking out about his own recognized imperfections, so glaring that very afternoon. He pointed out:

> Perfectionism is rampant today . . . and it is in this competitive drive to accomplish a moral and intellectual superiority that making a mistake becomes so dangerous. . . .
>
> People who try so desperately to avoid mistakes are endangering themselves. The reason for this is twofold. First, when you think about the mistake which you might make, you do yourself the greatest of harm by discouraging yourself. We know that discouragement is the best motivation for doing something wrong. In order to do something right, one has to have confidence—self-confidence. When you think about the mistake you might make, you express your lack of faith—in yourself, your lack of confidence—in yourself. And, consequently, out of this discouragement we are more prone to make a mistake. . . .
>
> There is no sense in crying over spilled milk, but most people who make mistakes feel guilty. They feel degraded; they lose respect for themselves; they lose belief in their own ability. And I have seen it time and again—the real damage was not done through the mistakes they made but through the guilt feeling and discouragement which they had afterwards. Then they really messed it up for themselves. As long as we are so preoccupied with the fallacious assumption of the importance of mistakes, we can't take mistakes in our stride. . . .
>
> It seems to me that our children are exposed to a sequence of discouraging experiences, both at home and at school. Everyone points out what they did do wrong and what they could do wrong. We deprive the children of the only experience which can really promote growth and development—experience of their own strengths. We impress them with their deficiencies, with their smallness, with their limitations, and at the same time try to drive them on to be much more. . . . If we want to institute in children the desire to accomplish something, a faith in themselves and a regard for their own strengths, then we have to minimize the importance of the mistakes they are making and emphasize all the good things—not [what] they could do, but [what] they *do* do. . . .

And so this mistaken idea of the importance of mistakes leads us to a mistaken concept of ourselves. We become overly impressed by everything that is wrong in us and around us: "If I am critical of myself, I naturally am going to be critical of the people around me. If I am sure that I am no good, at least I have to find that you are worse." That is what we are doing. Anyone who is critical of himself is always critical of others. . . . To be human does not mean to be right, does not mean to be perfect. To be human means to be useful, to make contributions—not for oneself, but for others—to take what there is and to make the best out of it.

He closed his relatively short speech that evening by saying, "We have to realize that we are good enough as we are; we never will be better, regardless of how much more we may know, how much more skill we may acquire, how much status or money or what-have-you. If we can't make peace with ourselves as we are, we never will be able to make peace with ourselves. This requires the courage to be imperfect; requires the realization that 'I am no angel, that I am no superhuman, that I make mistakes, that I have faults. But I am pretty good because I don't *have* to be better than the others'—which is a tremendous relief. . . . If we learn to function—to do our best regardless of what it is—out of the enjoyment of the functioning, we can grow just as well, even better than if we drove ourselves to be perfect."

Applause exploded. He mopped his brow with his handkerchief, waving to his audience with his other hand, then stepped off the platform where Tee awaited him with tears of pride.

Whatever mistakes Dreikurs made that summer, whomever's pride or sense of scholarship he offended, was overshadowed by the positive sense of purpose and the momentum he injected into the community. He wrote:

People get more and more excited. Particularly the teachers have already found out that they will not be able to continue what they have learned here in their own systems where our ideas hardly fit in. So they decided to organize, to publish a newsletter with discussion of cases and situations, to give them the moral support they will need when they are back home and on their own. They even think about a national group with my former students of other parts of the country, and Lowe wants to organize that as a section of the American Society of Adlerian Psychology. The interest of the faculty is continuing. . . . Ray will be in charge of the Guidance Department next year and is a guidance consultant for all the state PTAs. . . . He is under considerable pressure to start his counseling center as soon as possible, and intends to do it within one year, on the campus as part of teacher training. It has been agreed that he and Luchins . . . will start a seminar on Adlerian Psychology without any pretenses or cover-ups. Leeper . . . is quite in agreement.[13]

Lowe succeeded in his plan to open a counseling center the following year. It was the first university-sponsored Adlerian counseling center and provided a direct link to the academic curriculum for training teachers and counselors. It is still operating today. The three other sponsors of the Community Parent-Teacher Education Center are the Oregon State System of Higher Education, the Eugene Public School District, and the PTA of the Frances Willard School, where the weekly sessions are held.

Dreikurs returned to Eugene as visiting professor at the university in the summers of 1959, 1961, and 1963. During these summers, he taught Ray Lowe's regular course and conducted the Saturday morning counseling sessions. Often more than two hundred people would attend when Dreikurs was in town.

The Saturday sessions were characterized by a warm, congenial atmosphere created by the volunteer staff who welcomed the many families, teachers, counselors, psychologists, and even physicians who came. An ambience of excitement and humor emerged as all shared in the drama of learning during the counseling sessions. Dreikurs's image had softened considerably since his early days at Northwestern. His appearance and dress in class were informal, and some people thought he seemed like an oversized elf with an ever-present twinkle in his eyes. Others found him reminiscent of Humpty Dumpty, as he characteristically perched his corpulent trunk on the desk, his legs swinging free beneath.

Ray Lowe beamed with delight the first time he took Rudolf and Tee to see the setup at Frances Willard School. Dreikurs exclaimed, "The counseling center is something to behold. It is located in a beautiful new building, overlooking the hills with their fir trees—an almost Hollywoodian setting. . . . There are dozens of workers, many student teachers. Everything is splendidly organized—the game room and the reception [area]. The sessions are held in the large auditorium. For the first session we had more than 300 people."[14]

A condensed transcription of a typical family counseling session that took place one Saturday morning at the center follows. The family counseled by Dreikurs included Mrs. Brown and her two sons, Bruce and Barry. (The counselees' names have been fictionalized.)

Dr. D: Do we have Mrs. B. here? . . . How do you do? . . . I have heard that you have never been to one of our sessions before. And you have heard that we do not, as a rule, counsel a mother until she has sat in on some sessions. If you had sat in a few times, you would know that other mothers have exactly the same difficulties that you have. And you soon lose any shyness as you realize that all are in the same boat and make the same mistakes. So now, how do you feel about being here?

Mrs. B: Scared. But I hope I can answer your questions without being too nervous.

Dr. D: Tell me, is there any reason why you shouldn't be nervous? What is wrong with it if you want to be nervous?

Mrs. B: (*smiling*) Nothing, I guess.

Dr. D: You can answer questions even if you are nervous. You will find after a while that you can decide whether you want to be nervous or not. Then you have no reservations about talking with me in front of all the other parents sitting in?

Mrs. B: No.

Dr. D: Good. Now let us hear about your problem. You have two children?

Mrs. B: Yes, I do. Their names are Bruce, who will be six next week, and Barry, who will be three tomorrow.

Dr. D: Tomorrow!
I want to use my interview with you for teaching purposes. Will you mind if, from time to time, I interrupt interviewing you to discuss some points with the group? Or any objection if, from time to time, I have a little discussion with the trainees on why I do certain things in the interview?

Mrs. B: No, I don't.

Dr. D: Now, tell us about your problem. What is the reason you came here?

Mrs. B: We did not recognize Bruce's speech hesitation until about two years ago.

Dr. D: Will you elaborate on that?

(*to students*) This gives us an opening to learn more about the details.

Mrs. B: He does not seem to be able to speak it out.

Dr. D: Does he stammer? Does he hesitate? What is he doing?

Mrs. B: Sometimes he stammers but mostly he just hesitates. He thinks faster than he can speak it out.

Dr. D: (*to students*) And what is the next thing to ask?

Student in audience: What did you do about it?

Dr. D: (*to Mrs. B.*) What do you do about it?

Mrs. B: I wait for him.

Dr. D: You wait until it comes out?

(*to students*) What would this response of the mother indicate? Does anyone have an idea? . . . Isn't it amazing how well a boy can train his mother?

(*to Mrs. B.*) And I feel you are a well-trained mother.

Mrs. B: That's right.

Dr. D: What else?

Mrs. B: That is the main problem. Like most children, he has to be urged on in the morning to get dressed.

Dr. D: Are you sure that "most" children of six have to be hurried a bit? Do you think he could have dressed himself without being urged on?

Mrs. B: Yes. But, he might have been late—and he was for about three mornings.

Dr. D: Now that is another area where we will want some discussion. What else? When you applied for the interview, you wrote down that you want to know whether Bruce is happy. What do you mean by that?

Mrs. B: I visited him in kindergarten, and he did not seem to be happy. He did not smile. He never seems to be. . . .

Dr. D: Did the teacher say anything about his not being happy?

Mrs. B: No. She didn't.

Dr. D: Tell us more about it.

Mrs. B: He came home from kindergarten one day and said his hand stinks. I did not see anything. When he kept insisting, I told him to wash them. He came back and said his hands still stink. Soon after that he started bawling—that sometimes he did not write his name right. I looked at it, and it was spelled fine. But the teacher had meant for him to put it in the upper left hand corner of the paper. And when I talked to the teacher, she said they had been working on that for about a week and a half. And Bruce had not seemed to be happy in kindergarten from about that time.

Dr. D: Without any reason?

Mrs. B: Because he figured the teacher thought he wasn't spelling his name right, that he was not doing it like the other children.

Dr. D: (*to audience*) Do you have any idea what this picture would make us suspect?

Member of audience: I see the picture of a boy who has to be perfect.

Dr. D: You are on the right track. (*to Mrs. B.*) How does he respond to criticism?

Mrs. B: Do you want me to answer that?

Dr. D: Yes.

Mrs. B: The other day he went to his little cousin's. Outside, the city was pouring cement, and the two made marks on it. The cousin's father came out and told them to stop. His little boy is used to it and didn't pay it much mind. (*chuckle*) The next day my cousin asked me if Bruce had told me about the trouble. He had not told me at all, and yet, when questioned, he was very sensitive about it. All the children he plays with are a year younger than he. He acts as if he did not have to bother to listen to what—

Dr. D: —other children have to say?

Mrs. B: He is way ahead of them and then he gets real short with them.

Dr. D: (*to students*) The indications that he is overly ambitious would have come out. The first one came when mother said he was unhappy about not having written his name in the right place. That made me suspect that this ambition was one of the problems. Now I suspect that it is the major problem—to do everything right and to be first.

(*to Mrs. B.*) How does he get along with Barry, who is three years younger?

Mrs. B: Fine for the first year, until Barry learned to walk. Then he was through with him.

Dr. D: He could enjoy him only as long as he was helpless.

Mrs. B: That's right. After that he did not like to share things with Barry, or teach him different things, and they fight a good bit.

Dr. D: You had the feeling he wanted Barry to remain a dumb infant?

Mrs. B: Yes, but he wanted a girl.

Dr. D: Oh!

Mrs. B: But now he is proud of Barry. He wanted Barry to come and visit his school. That has been a remarkable change.

Dr. D: But only last year? And for two years he was angry at you for not having given him a sister.

Mrs. B: Yes. He still wants a girl, but he never says anything about taking Barry back anymore.

(*laughter*)

Dr. D: This is quite an interesting story.

(*to audience*) What impresses you when you listen to that?

Member of audience: I see the boy as put out over having a younger brother to compete with, until he went to school and again found something else to be superior about.

Dr. D: You are quite right, but there was another aspect that is significant, I think. What else is characteristic about their relationship? It looks almost as if he had the feeling that it was mother's obligation to do what he wanted. That he had a right to punish her when she dared to give him a brother instead of a sister. And mother does feel apologetic, implying that she would have done it if she could.

(*to Mrs. B.*) Did you ever have such discussions with him?

Mrs. B: No.

Dr. D: Were there any indications that you felt bad that he did not have a sister?

Mrs. B: Well . . . yes . . . in a way. I probably did tell him that one day, maybe. . . .

Dr. D: (*to audience*) You see. She already promised for the future!

(*laughter*)

Dr. D: What can we learn from this? When you find a child with definite ideas of superiority, the question arises: how did he become like that? We supply him the justification for his mistaken concepts by our reactions to him—so subtle that we are not even aware of them! We are looking at a typical example—in your efforts to be a good mother, his accusations forced you to acknowledge his right to make demands. We can learn to become sensitive to how the child uses his demands. It is far less important how he got the idea, originally. When he asks these supposedly innocent questions, we can not assume that a child does not have purpose or plan. It is one of the prime objectives of our work in child guidance to train parents to become a better match for their children, and not their innocent victims. Do you understand what I am trying to say? I am using this subtle illustration to show you, and the other parents in the room, that all that the child does has a meaning and can be understood. You may find that all of Bruce's problems are tied in with this one—that he is the only one to judge what is right and wrong. Let us return now to the development of speech on the part of Bruce.

Mrs. B: He made baby sounds at the usual age but did not speak clearly until late. Barry does not talk clearly even now.

Dr. D: Why did he not talk? He did not have to! Mother was so anxious to do the right thing that she did what he wanted without his saying a word. Is that right?

Mrs. B: Yes. And with the younger, I have done the opposite for about two weeks, and it is remarkable what words he has come out with since.

Dr. D: When you have a three-year-old boy and a grown mother, who is training whom?

Mrs. B: I think the boy is training me.

Dr. D: He does not have to bother with talking, and you just did not realize what was going on. The better the children have trained mother, the less they will do. When did Bruce begin to talk?

Mrs. B: About three. No matter what I said to him, he said "me" for "I" until he started kindergarten. Like, "Me want more milk."

Dr. D: How often did you correct him?

Mrs. B: Right after he got through saying it.

Dr. D: Each time?

Mrs. B: Almost every time.

(*laughter*)

Dr. D: Who trained whom, do you think?

Mrs. B: He trained me, I guess, to keep repeating after him.

Dr. D: Right.

Mrs. B: My husband says I am a slave to the children.

Dr. D: That is bad. . . . And when I say it, you will not believe me, either.

(*laughter*)

Mrs. B: When father is with them, they let him sleep or join into what he is doing.

Dr. D: What do you think about his notion that you are a slave to the children?

Mrs. B: I don't mind it to a certain extent, unless it is inconvenient at the time.

Dr. D: Do you think that we will mind if you are a slave to them?

Mrs. B: Yes, you do. And the teachers do, too. I have gathered from this discussion that it is too hard on the children.

Dr. D: It's not good for them, when you spoil the children and deprive them of their proper functions.

(*to audience*) What we see here is part of the tragedy that is characteristic of our times. Like millions of others, this sincere, loving, and good mother ruins her children with her efforts to do the right thing. The desires of mothers to be so good will be doing much damage to all of our next generation. In part, our so-called experts are at fault. They tell parents to give their children more love. Is there a mother who gives her children more love than Mrs. B? And what comes from this? You ruin them! They cannot even talk!

(*to Mrs. B.*) I am in the unfortunate position to make you a bit uncomfortable by showing you the things that you are doing wrong. But I cannot blame you, you did the very best you could. It was the very concern for the welfare of the children that led you astray. But still, I have to make you aware that you have done harm.

Mrs. B: I understand.

Dr. D: How do you feel about this discussion?

Mrs. B: I have learned a lot. But it will be hard. If you don't talk to your children, how are they going to learn to talk?

Dr. D: If you talk to them the way you did, they won't learn.

Mrs. B: Are you suggesting that mothers should not love their children?

Dr. D: You can be led astray by love as readily as by lack of love. Love that is warm is fine, and is necessary, but there is one quality that I consider even more important than love: *respect*. If the children, as individuals, have your respect—only then will you encourage and help them. While we cannot expect every teacher to love all the children—that would be impossible—every teacher can learn to respect every child. The best combination is, of course, when love and respect go together. Love, and the feeling of warmth, is the consequence of a good relationship—not its cause.

(*Dreikurs then proceeded to get a description of a typical day in the family from Mrs. B. It showed that Bruce manages to get service from his mother about getting dressed and that mother feels sorry for him. Then the discussion turned to mealtimes.*)

Dr. D: Let us go on. How about mealtimes?

Mrs. B: That is a bit complicated. The children do not have dinner with their daddy.

Dr. D: Does everyone feel sorry for the children for not having dinner with father? If they can, it is advisable for the family to eat together. But one does not have to feel sorry for the "poor" children who don't get the chance. I am always in favor of doing what is possible, but it is no cause for grumbling or other destructive acts over what cannot be helped. I always say that people who cannot take it always have to put up with even worse. The greater your limit of what you can endure, the better will you cope with things as they are. What is the problem with the eating situation?

Mrs. B: The problem is with the baby. Bruce eats well, but Barry does not. All he wants is milk and bread.

Dr. D: What's wrong with milk and bread?

Mrs. B: Nothing. But that is practically all he will eat.

Dr. D: And what are you doing about it?

Mrs. B: I have taken away those two articles of food.

Dr. D: What else have you done?

Mrs. B: I have tried to persuade him to eat his other foods.

Dr. D: In other words, you are talking!

Mrs. B: I am talking to him.

Dr. D: Constantly!

Mrs. B: I also try to make the food attractive.

Dr. D: How? Paint the toast? (*laughter*) How did you make the food attractive?

Mrs. B: I got his baby bowl out again. It has three sections, and I thought that would fascinate him. That did not seem to work. He still wanted his bread and butter. If he didn't get it, he would just take a few bites and then go to bed having eaten hardly anything.

Dr. D: (*to audience*) What is going on here?

Member of audience: She is being kept very busy. I also have another question.

Dr. D: Go ahead.

Member of audience: How many people consider a three-year-old a baby?

Dr. D: (*to Mrs. B.*) What do you think about that question?

Mrs. B: As a rule I do call him Barry.

Dr. D: You may refer to him as "baby" more than you think, and he does have a point that you have to be careful that you don't treat him like a baby. Right?

Mrs. B: Yes.

Dr. D: Tell me, who wins out in the struggle over food?

Mrs. B: Well, Barry does.

Dr. D: Once I cured a boy of wanting nothing but hot dogs. He got nothing but hot dogs (*laughter*)—and after just three days, was he fed up with hot dogs. We have to learn to handle the child on more even terms. We have to learn to pit our wits against his. Can you guess what I have in mind?

Mrs. B: Feeding him bread and milk. (*laughs*)

Dr. D: That you make an agreement with him that he will get bread and milk for a whole week, and nothing else. No matter what the others eat, he doesn't get a bite of it.

Mrs. B: I've tried that on him.

Dr. D: For how long?

Mrs. B: Not very long. I try to persuade him to eat his dinner.

Dr. D: You talk, persuade, and bribe. We are trying something else: that you have just one talk with him—and if you want, I can have that talk with him—and tell him as I have told you that for the rest of the week all he gets is bread and milk.

Member of audience: Aren't you punishing him?

Dr. D: No. I am calling his bluff by doing what he says he wants. (*to Mrs. B.*) What do you feel about it?

Mrs. B: If it will help . . .

Dr. D: There is no guarantee. The only thing is, what you have been doing so far certainly has not helped. Are you willing to take a chance on something new?

Mrs. B: Yes.

Dr. D: Would you be able to stand firm when he wants just a bit of what the others eat?

Mrs. B: It would be hard.

Dr. D: From now on, you will have an agreement, either he eats just milk and bread, or he eats everything, and not just what he likes. After a few days he will be fed up and will agree to eat everything. You go right back to milk and bread again the first time he reneges. Either he joins the rest of the family, or he gets his own diet.

Member of audience: Do we have a right to hold a three-year-old responsible to such an agreement?

Dr. D: (*to audience*) We have no right. But does he have the right to tyrannize mother? There is only one issue: either she fights with him each time, or she learns to arrange things to make him think better of it. This is a matter of order, not a matter of agreement. It is our procedure to give concrete advice. Not the cookbook variety, but always designed to change the personal relationship. In this instance, the aim is to break the tyranny of Barry. This is not a matter of right or wrong. Our sole objective is to allow mother to realign the relationship. I would like to talk with the boys now.

(*Mother leaves the room and the boys enter.*)

Dr. D: Hello! Will you come in? What is your name?

Bruce: Bruce.

Dr. D: I am Dr. Dreikurs. Want to shake hands with me? (*Bruce shakes hands with Dr. D.*) And what is your name?

Barry: Barry. (*They shake hands.*)

Dr. D: Barry! Come on, sit down! Do you know what all these people are doing here? What do you think?

Bruce: I don't know.

Dr. D: They all are parents and teachers who want to find out what to do with children. Do you have an idea why mother came?

Bruce: Because.

Dr. D: Because of what?

Bruce: For us.

Dr. D: For you. You are quite right. But why for you? Do you have any idea? Because mother does not know what to do with you. You know what to do with mother, don't you? (*no response, but a sheepish grin appears on Bruce's face*) When you want something, you know how to get it. But mother does not know how to get it. Do you have an idea what bothers mother? . . . Shall we discuss what bothers her? (*no response*) . . . You don't want to talk any-

thing over? Wouldn't you like to talk with me? I would like to help
you. I would like to help Barry, too. Is Barry doing something that
mother does not like? What is Barry doing that mother does not
like.

Bruce: Saying "me."

Dr. D: You are quite right. Do you know why he does that all the
time? (*pause*) Because he wants mother to keep after him and
correct him. Do you think that Barry can say "I"?

Bruce: I don't know.

Dr. D: I am sure he can. What else is Barry doing that mother does
not like? How about his eating?
(*aside to audience*) He looks well nourished.
Does he eat everything?

Bruce: No.

Dr. D: And mother does not know what to do about that either. You
know what I told her? What does Barry like to eat?

Bruce: Bread.

Dr. D: Barry, what do you like to eat?
(*silence*)

Dr. D: (*to audience*) Here you have a typical example: Barry looks
away in disinterest. He looks only where he wants. He only likes
to eat bread and milk. Right? And I told mother to give him nothing else, if he wants just bread and milk. He might like that. Barry
wants to show mother that he will eat only what he wants.
(*to Bruce*) Do you talk well?

Bruce: Uh-huh.

Dr. D: Do you talk quickly, or very slowly? (*pause*) What do you
think? (*pause*) Could it be that you always want someone to come
and help you?

Bruce: I don't know. (*another recognition reflex*)

Dr. D: Can you tie your shoes?

Bruce: Uh-huh.

Dr. D: Do you always tie your shoes? (*pause*) Sometimes you don't?
(*Bruce nods.*) Do you know why not? (*no response*) Could it be
that you want mother to do it for you? (*Bruce exhibits recognition
reflex*) Do you cry, sometimes, and feel sorry for yourself? (*pause*)
And do you know what happens when you feel sorry for yourself?
Could it be that when you do, mother feels sorry for you, also, and
you like that? Then she tells you how good you are and how she

loves you. When something does not go your way, you let her know that you don't like it. Then she comes to apologize and tries to make up for it. Do you know what has been the consequence of that? That you are very unhappy. You feel miserable if something does not go the way you want. Like right now. I tell you a few things that you don't like and you feel miserable. It would be much better that when you don't get your own way, that you wouldn't be miserable. Right? (*pause*) But you are a big boy, and can help Barry a great deal. Help him do things, so that he can do them well. Right? Is there anything you want to tell me at this point? Fine, then. Thank you very much for coming.[15]

Loren Grey recalled what took place when the session ended and everyone began to leave the school grounds:

We discovered Barry standing in front of the auditorium by himself, screaming at the top of his lungs. A few yards ahead of him was Dr. D. Across the steep narrow street, where cars were beginning to move along, was the frantic Mrs. Brown, and the older boy who was also crying. Every time she made a motion as if to rescue Barry, Dr. D. waved her back. Finally, when he was convinced she had gotten the message not to come back and get Barry, Dr. D. walked slowly back and asked Barry if he needed some help to get across the street. The little boy put his hand in Dr. D.'s and together they slowly went down the walk toward the street. I think I will always remember the sight of the two of them walking together hand in hand, the old man and the little boy—a symbol of the bridge that we need to cross so often in learning to truly relate with other human beings.[16]

Later, Dreikurs explained that this was the first time that Barry's power had been challenged by anyone. By the follow-up session two weeks later, Mrs. Brown had effected a remarkable restructuring of the family relationship. Highlights of that session follow:

Dr. D: I remember, Mrs. Brown, that you were surprised when we told you what was going on. What was your reaction after that first interview?

Mrs. B: I thought it would be impossible to do, but I found a remarkable change in my baby. I don't want to keep calling him "baby."

Dr. D: Aha! (*laughter*) And last time mother said that it was unusual. But now you are inclined to catch yourself when you call him "baby." What happened since last time?

Mrs. B: He wanted a drink of water when we left, and I told him to wait until we got home. He doesn't usually take no for an answer, and we did have a time getting him to the car. But I walked on, and he cried, "You are leaving 'baby!' "

Dr. D: That was quite a dramatic scene.

Mrs. B: Half the way home he cried and stormed, but I saw no reason to repeat what I had told him.

Dr. D: Good for you. (*laughter*) Am I correct that earlier you would have repeated it several times?

Mrs. B: Yes.

Dr. D: So this was a complete departure, and an important lesson: if a mother can learn to keep her mouth shut she can learn anything else. (*laughter*)

Mrs. B: That evening he got up from the table to get bread, so I took his dinner away. I told him then: if he wanted bread and milk that was all he was going to get; that I wasn't going to tell him again, and that he would have bread and milk for a week. So he went ahead and ate his bread and milk. Before bedtime, he wanted a cookie and a glass of milk, so I gave him bread and milk. (*laughter*) And he didn't like that too well. So he went to bed without talking back at all because he was mad at me. The next morning he again got his bread and milk, and Bruce had his regular breakfast. So Barry cried and left the table, and I took his milk and bread away. He got back to the table and I said that it was just too bad. He stormed around a bit, and then went outside to play. At lunch he got his bread and milk. (*laughter*) This went on for days. And we all ate something yummy as you had suggested (*laughter*). Later he begged food from his daddy, but his daddy went along with me. Since then he has eaten everything! He will eat anything that's served. (*laughter*)

Dr. D: (*to audience*) Keep in mind how much fighting had gone on before. Talking and punishing didn't accomplish anything. But when you knew what to do and acted accordingly, how simply the problem was resolved.

Mrs. B: He used to say "me" instead of "I" . . .

Dr. D: (*to audience*) That had been a major problem with both children. When the oldest finally started to say "I" she had the problem all over again with the younger one.

Mrs. B: That's right. But as he started begging for food, he began to say, "I want . . ." In one week. He likes ice cream, and when I didn't answer his "Me wants ice cream," he started to say "I want ice cream."

* * * * * *

Dr. D: Two weeks ago you talked of Barry as uncooperative, determined, defiant. Is that still the case?

Mrs. B: No. He's not very defiant anymore.

Dr. D: (*to audience*) It is hard to believe that such a change could come about in two short weeks. Can you tell how calmly and effectively she goes about things? No scolding, preaching, or explaining. She now has a warm and quiet way of handling the children.

Mrs. B: There was an interesting episode with Bruce. One time he did not come when I called him for lunch, and he wanted his lunch two hours later. He stormed around when I told him he could not have it. He threatened what he would do if I didn't give him his lunch, but I ignored it. At the time, Barry was sitting on my lap, and Bruce said that I didn't like him anymore.

Dr. D: He threw that at you to catch you off guard.

Mrs. B: I said that I did like him and that I was sorry he did not come for lunch. Because he would not come in when I called him, I refused to let him go back outside afterwards. He grumbled and groaned, but I still would not let him out and play. Now he has the feeling of not being wanted or loved. Last evening for instance, I got tired of his splashing his clothes whenever he took a bath, so I let him put his wet ones on again. He wanted to know where his clean pants were, and I said he could not have them. He wanted to know why. I said it seemed that he liked to get them wet. I didn't explain or anything. He finally managed to put the wet ones on and announced that some day he would leave here. (*laughter*) He took me by surprise. So I said he might as well get started right now—which was wrong. (*laughter*)

Dr. D: Yes, that was a bit too strong.

Mrs. B: But he yelled back that he had told me "some day" and not now! (*laughter*)

Dr. D: (*chuckling*) Can you see how smart the children are?

Mrs. B: Later, we were watching two cute little girls acting on TV, and I said I wouldn't trade these two cute little girls for our two boys. When Bruce heard that, he just looked at me and grinned.

Dr. D: That was good. Love not by giving in or feeling sorry. But show love in other ways so the child does not have to tug at your heartstrings in order to feel loved.

Mrs. B: I see.

Dr. D: Anything else that bothers you right now?

Mrs. B: No.

Dr. D: Is there any difference in your relationship to the children?

Mrs. B: I feel closer to them, because I have more time—I don't spend all my time being nervous and upset. Now I have time to talk with them, to enjoy them. . . .

Dr. D: When parents learn to avoid the conflicts, they discover that they enjoy the children. . . .[17]

When Dreikurs returned to Oregon in 1959, there were, owing to Lowe's excellent teaching, twelve students ready for advanced training in theory. In the succeeding years, Dreikurs devoted most of his time in Oregon to advanced training, refining the counseling techniques of a number of interested graduate-level and postgraduate-level students, while Lowe took over teaching the introductory courses. "Lowe and his associates can do it much better," Dreikurs chuckled. "After all, they have read my book and . . . follow [it while] I improvise. This is good for the most advanced students but not so good for the beginners."[18]

Through these advanced students, Dreikurs's ideas began to be carried to other parts of the state and to other states as well. Oscar Christensen, after completing his Ph.D., became consultant and supervisor of guidance for all Oregon public schools. He trained teachers and counselors throughout the state through in-service workshops and training seminars in Adlerian approaches for the classroom. Later he became professor of psychology at the University of Arizona in Tucson, where he has created a solid training program for teachers and counselors based on the Adlerian model.

Dreikurs's 1959 summer session brought Loren Grey from Los Angeles to the Eugene campus. He had just completed his Ph.D. program in educational psychology but had long been acquainted with Adlerian psychology through Lydia Sicher, one of Adler's closest colleagues in Vienna. But Sicher, a brilliant therapist, did not pursue the kind of training programs and child guidance centers that became the hallmark of Dreikurs's work. Grey was most impressed with what he learned that summer and enthusiastically returned to the Los Angeles area to start a center and to begin training teachers in the methods.

A few years later, Grey coauthored a book with Dreikurs, *Logical Consequences* (1968).[19] It provided an enlarged and practical guide to Dreikurs's alternative approach to discipline in child rearing. Dreikurs condemned equally the autocratic technique of reward and punishment and the habit of permissiveness. "Trying to impose one's will on the child violates respect for him, and makes him rebellious, while permissiveness and indulgence violates respect for one's self and produces tyrannical children and anarchy in the home," he often pointed out. Logical consequences, that is, allowing the child to learn directly from the results of his own actions is the alternative, and is more suitable to a democratic social order. "Logical consequences express the reality of the social order; punishment, the power of a personal authority." Dreikurs traced the conceptual origins of logical consequences to Herbert Spencer, Alfred Adler, and Jean Piaget.[20] In the book, more than a hundred concrete examples of the use of logical and natural consequences in a variety of different circumstances make it, like others by Dreikurs, lofty in purpose, yet down to earth in practicability.

Ray Lowe also made a determined effort to acquaint physicians in the Eugene area with the Adlerian approach to family and childhood problems. During the 1959 session, Dreikurs began meeting for a weekly breakfast with pediatricians in the Eugene area. "I was an active skeptic," recalled pediatrician Bill Pew of his first meetings with this man who challenged the major psychological principles that were widely accepted without question. Dreikurs proposed that he and the others come out to the Frances Willard School and see for themselves if what he said did not make sense. "I accepted the challenge and along with my pediatric colleagues, was greatly impressed."[21] Pew's wife, Mim, went along, and both were so stimulated that they began to study with Lowe. As Dreikurs's ideas gained momentum in Oregon, Mim Pew took an energetic and creative role in the development of a "study group" format that set the pattern for the successful and expanding roles of these groups in communities all over America. They subsequently left Oregon for the Minneapolis–Saint Paul area, where they helped create the first Alfred Adler Institute outside the Chicago or New York areas. Today, such institutes are developing in other parts of the country in response to demand for Adlerian training.

Others inspired by the Oregon experience were Floy C. Pepper and Harold V. McAbee. Pepper, who did important work with retarded children, later became coordinator of instruction for a Portland, Oregon, school district and jointly authored *Maintaining Sanity in the Classroom*

(1971)[22] with Dreikurs and Bronia Grunwald. In the late 1950s, Harold McAbee was an assistant superintendent for one of the Eugene area school districts and became interested in Adlerian psychology through Lowe and then Dreikurs. He introduced the principles in his work with the Job Corps program and eventually made his way to the East Coast in the late 1960s, where he became dean of graduate studies at Bowie State College, near Washington, D.C. In conjunction with the local Adlerian laymen's organization and the help of William H. McKelvie, who trained with Sonstegard at West Virginia University, the Adler-Dreikurs Institute of Human Relations was established in 1975 as part of Bowie State's graduate program.

Dreikurs realized that in Oregon there was no entrenched Freudian stronghold in professional thinking. Professional people on the West Coast generally prided themselves on their nonadherence to any particular school of thought and their commitment to eclecticism. But Dreikurs also discovered that if you scratched the surface of an "eclectic," out popped an "unaware" Freudian. This pattern was revealed in his earliest classes at Oregon: "We had the child psychiatrist of the local mental health clinic at our last session," Dreikurs wrote in June of 1957. "He was one of those who had described himself to Lowe as an eclectic. But then it turned out that he was most concerned with the psychosexual development of the child, with transference and free association—but he is not a Freudian, mind you."[23]

The Freudian model of development was not limited to the thinking of psychiatrists and psychologists but had permeated educational theory as well. A study by Ray Lowe of textbooks in educational psychology written in the 1950s revealed that 95 percent presented psychoanalytic theory, though not exclusively, in their description of psychological development of the child, and not one of them made reference to Adlerian theory.[24]

The impact of Dreikurs's alternative approach is evident from what happened to Theodore Grubb, who attended Dreikurs's class at Oregon in 1957 and then left for the San Francisco area, where he became chief psychologist of the Castro Valley school system. Dreikurs commented:

> He wrote to me telling me the following story. During my class two years ago, he was quite a nuisance since he had strong Freudian leanings and was not willing to see anything else. Apparently he was well aware of that, as he wrote in his letter. He reminded me that I told him at the end that he would have to [find out] for himself. And

he did. He wrote that he had compiled five years work for his doctor's thesis all based on the Freudian approach. But after my class he
could no longer follow this trend. It did not make sense to him any
more after he experimented with our approach. So he finally decided
to scrap five years of work and start a new thesis on an Adlerian
basis.[25]

Dreikurs realized that the growing disenchantment with psychoanalysis
that began to be expressed widely by the late 1950s and early 1960s had
brought many professional people to regard adherence to any school of
thought as a sign of their lack of "objectivity." They were anxious to make
clear that they were really eclectic in outlook—they took a little from this
theory, a little from that theory, and tailored their approach to the particular case before them.

Ironically, at a time when everyone was anxious to get on the bandwagon of eclecticism, Dreikurs was advocating that there was still a need
for "schools" of thought and that eclecticism only beclouded the real
issues confronting psychology. In his mind, to be genuinely eclectic, one
has to have some basis for judgment. That could only come from solid
training and understanding in a particular framework. Learn something
well, then you can judge its merits and workability. In a speech in 1959,
Dreikurs pleaded for a continuation of particular psychological schools of
thought as necessary to the further development of psychology:

> The fact that scientific validation of any school of personality theory
> and psychotherapy is presently impossible, far from discrediting
> schools as such, is the very reason for their existence, and should not
> prevent psychiatrists and psychologists from taking a stand on the
> basic, unsettled issues. Clarification, exemplification, and delineation
> of basic assumptions about man can only be accomplished within a
> well-defined theory. Thus, schools can contribute to the progress of
> knowledge and practice by permitting free comparisons about and
> controversy between the proponents of well-defined and declared
> assumptions. The emphasis of their differences is perhaps even more
> important than the recognition of their similarities. This would seem
> the most fruitful procedure until such time as scientific approaches to
> complex phenomena are developed, and the basic laws regulating
> individuals and groups in their interactions have been discovered.[26]

Dreikurs's article prompted the following response from George A. Kelly, the distinguished psychologist and personality theorist: "I am in hearty agreement with your thesis. It is only when adherents of a school of thought try to close out discussion that they do a dis-service to our discipline."[27]

Dreikurs considered his Oregon experience to be one of the most rewarding of his career. After decades of lonely struggle against unrelenting opposition to the ideas he believed in so completely, he could, at last, see them adopted and put into practice. They were used not by a few isolated individuals here and there but by a significant number of people with a wide variety of backgrounds and roles in the community. Because Adlerian theory penetrated into these various levels of the community— family life, schools, medical practice, social work—it grew beyond a mere school of thought to become a movement. The first glimmerings of an Adlerian movement came from the Jamaican experience, but it was in Oregon that a genuine, organized, and concerted effort arose not simply to teach but to practice Adlerian principles in daily life and activities. It quickly spread beyond Eugene to Corvallis, Portland, and throughout the entire state. Of course, it was not Dreikurs alone who made it happen but many people.

A major force behind the development of a statewide Adlerian society in Oregon was Maurice Bullard, director of guidance for the Corvallis school system, who for years has edited, with his wife, an informative newsletter for the statewide Adlerian society. Lowe was personally uninterested in organizations and movements. He devoted himself to his courses at the university and his regular Saturday morning counseling sessions, which he is still running. But he has trained many students who have settled in Oregon and others who have carried Adlerian ideas to other states and even to other nations. Dreikurs always credited Lowe and the Oregon experience as having marked the starting point of an international Adlerian movement. For among the students who attended his classes in Oregon in 1961 was Ruth Bickel Holger-Nielsen a psychologist from Copenhagen, who began planning with Dreikurs an international summer school for Adlerian psychology in Denmark for the following summer.

In Oregon, rejoiced Dreikurs in 1959, "one can say that one is an Adlerian without any embarrassing reaction—with considerable pride."[28]

Notes for Chapter 18

1. Raymond Lowe, personal communication, October 1973. Additional quotes from Lowe, unless otherwise identified, are from this interview.

2. Raymond Lowe, "Teacher Education Through Child Guidance Centers," in *Adlerian Family Counseling*, p. 89.

3. Harold V. McAbee, personal communication, November 1976.

4. Mackaness, *Biographical Study*, p. 204.

5. Alfred Adler, *Problems of Neurosis: A Book of Case-Histories*, ed. P. Mairet (New York: Harper Torchbooks, 1964), p. 66.

6. Dreikurs, to family and office staff, June 16 and July 9, 1957, Dreikurs Papers.

7. Rudolf Dreikurs, "The Psychological Uncertainty Principle," *Proceedings of the 5th International Congress of Psychotherapy, Vienna, August 1961, Pt. 2. Topical Problems in Psychotherapy*, vol. 4 (New York: S. Karger, 1963), pp. 23–31.

8. Dreikurs, to family and office staff, July 9, 1957, Dreikurs Papers.

9. Dreikurs, to family and office staff, August 8, 1957, Dreikurs Papers.

10. Dreikurs, to family and office staff, July 27, 1957, Dreikurs Papers.

11. Mackaness, *Biographical Study*, p. 205.

12. Rudolf Dreikurs, "The Courage to Be Imperfect," in *Articles of Supplementary Reading for Parents* (Chicago: Alfred Adler Institute, 1970).

13. Dreikurs, to family and office staff, July 27, 1957, Dreikurs Papers.

14. Dreikurs, Report no. 2, July 5, 1959, Dreikurs Papers.

15. Adapted from a transcription by Dr. Eric Dreikurs, Dreikurs Papers.

16. Loren Grey, "What Dr. Dreikurs Has Meant to Me," June 28, 1967, Dreikurs Papers.

17. Adapted from a transcription by Dr. Eric Dreikurs.

18. Dreikurs, Final Report [from Oregon], 1959, Dreikurs Papers.

19. Rudolf Dreikurs and Loren Grey, *Logical Consequences: A New Approach to Discipline* (New York: Meredith, 1968).

20. Rudolf Dreikurs, "The Cultural Implications of Reward and Punishment," *International Journal of Social Psychiatry* 4 (1958): 171–178.

21. W. L. Pew, lecture to Oregon Society of Individual Psychology, Eugene, Oregon, Spring 1961, Dreikurs Papers.

22. Rudolf Dreikurs, Bernice Bronia Grunwald, and Floy C. Pepper, *Maintaining Sanity in the Classroom: Illustrated Teaching Techniques* (New York, Harper & Row, 1971).

23. Dreikurs, to family and office staff, June 23, 1957, Dreikurs Papers.

24. Raymond Lowe, "Teacher Education," p. 91.

25. Dreikurs, Final Report [from Oregon], 1959, Dreikurs Papers.

26. Rudolf Dreikurs, "Are Psychological Schools of Thought Outdated?" *Journal of Individual Psychology* 16 (1960): 3–10.

27. George A. Kelley to Dreikurs, May 12, 1960, Dreikurs Papers.

28. Dreikurs, Final Report [from Oregon], 1959, Dreikurs Papers.

19

Social Equality:
A Blueprint for the Future

> Among the laws that rule human societies there is one
> which seems to be more precise and clear than all others.
> If men are to remain civilized or to become so, the art of
> associating together must grow and improve in the same
> ratio in which equality of conditions is increased.
>
> Alexis de Toqueville
> *Democracy in America*, 1862

The decade of the 1960s was especially significant and rewarding to
Rudolf Dreikurs. Following his experience at Oregon, there came a surge
of invitations and requests for lectures, workshops, and demonstrations of
his ideas at universities and communities throughout the country. In the
early 1960s, in addition to his ongoing activities, his efforts included:
workshops for the faculty members of the public schools of Racine, Wisconsin; participation as delegate of the American Humanist Association to
the White House Conference on Children and Youth in Washington,
D.C.; a workshop at the Eighth National Institute of Crime and Delinquency at Atlantic City, New Jersey; and three presentations before the
American Personnel and Guidance Association. He also gave workshops
or summer school sessions at the University of Delaware, Southern Illinois
University, Texas Technological College, the University of Illinois, Loyola
University of Chicago, Duquesne University, and Iowa State College. His
growing recognition was attested to by his election as vice-president of
the American Academy of Psychotherapy in 1959 and his appointments to
the editorial boards of both the *Journal of Existential Psychiatry* and
Psychosomatics in 1960.

Wherever he taught, a characteristic pattern of activity would follow.
His workshops, seminars, and summer courses—and especially the pro-

found impact of his demonstrations—generated enthusiasm in others to continue studying Adlerian concepts. Through his public presentations, many lay people also became acquainted with his ideas on child rearing and the effects of democratization on family relationships. Oftentimes a single lecture or demonstration only whetted the appetite of parents to learn more. When these parents approached local professional psychologists for additional guidance in Adlerian principles, they received scant assistance. Few professionals were trained in Adlerian psychology to fulfill this need, others were uninterested, since the principles were so contrary to their own training. Consequently, these parents often united to pursue the study of Adlerian principles and practices on their own. The favorite vehicle was a study-group format. The book studied was *The Challenge of Parenthood.*

Dr. Milton M. Tyler, the district psychologist for Lawndale City School District in Los Angeles described to Dreikurs the effect of his lecture there in 1959:

> You had made a presentation at the Culver City School District in Los Angeles, which I did not attend. I did acquire a transcript of the tape recording made of your presentation. I asked my secretary to make a number of copies, though I was not sure just how I would use them. Unbeknown to me, the secretary passed a few copies out to the other secretaries in the office, and I soon had on my hands a spontaneous luncheon discussion group. Not being one to let a good thing go to waste, I soon had two teacher and four parent groups going. Since that time, I have carried your approach to parent-child, teacher-child, and child-authority relationships wherever I have been—San Diego County, Germany, Spain, Morocco, and Lawrence, Kansas.[1]

The increasing interest on the part of parents and teachers reflected the growing awareness of what Dreikurs referred to as the bankruptcy of our educational systems—both in the home and at school. It indicated the failure of the traditional, autocratic ways of human relationships. They no longer worked. Children who defied parents and teachers as never before became increasingly problematic. To Dreikurs this was not surprising. Since the war years, he had predicted an accelerating social revolution toward equality and that it would wreak havoc on our traditional institutions. The decade of the 1960s ushered in the civil rights movement, student revolt on the campus, violence in the community at unprecedented levels, the drop-out society and the drug culture, and the rise of the women's movement. The complacency and indifference of the 1950s were shattered—confusion, frustration, anomie, and fear of what was becoming of society arose from the fragments.

Dreikurs first began to teach and write about the democratic evolution toward equality in the 1940s, but his ideas were little noted. He said:

> Equality is the most pressing problem of our times . . . the prize for which mankind is struggling today. The world is a battlefield where two forces meet: the most powerful seeking to retain their power and the weaker seeking to gain influence. The powerful need the conviction that there always will be rulers and servants, that the world never experienced equality, and that culture and order can be maintained only by force and threat. The weaker reject this ideology. They fight for equal rights for all human beings—for the general establishment and recognition of human dignity and mutual respect and mutual assistance. . . . Those who have no faith in human nature and wish to subdue and to regiment it are opposed to progress and try to turn back the wheel of time. They believe in [masculine superiority], . . . in spanking their children. . . . They look down on other nations and races, they scorn the masses and recognize as intelligence only their own minds. They ridicule any idea of equality as an illusion of dreamers, with no prospect of materialization. Their "realism" is powerful because they represent those who are in power.[2]

Democratization, Dreikurs claimed, was more than a political development. It involved a radical alteration of human relationships. In the autocratic past, all relations between individuals and groups were those between superiors and inferiors. But with the growing belief in the democratic ideal, equality became a reality in peoples' minds and no longer only an abstract principle. The sense of equality is based upon a belief in the right to decide for oneself, to be self-determining, to refuse to submit to coercion and domination by others. That sense of equality, he continued, would lead all those to whom equal status is denied to rebel openly.

Dreikurs recognized that even the most powerful autocracy cannot eliminate rebellion completely, even though the power of authority is well entrenched and upheld by the community. People behave properly regardless of whether they like or dislike the given situation or the person who gives the orders. Proper behavior and adequate performance is an obligation imposed by the authorities, who see to it that the rules and standards are observed. Those in authority have little concern for how the subordinate feels or what he thinks. What rebellion is exercised is difficult and rarely succeeds. Subtle means of defiance are employed instead, such as acting dumb, feigning submissiveness, or performing in a minimal fashion. Those courageous few who choose to rebel openly have to pay the full consequences without anybody coming to their rescue.

But in a democratic atmosphere, rebellion can be openly expressed because authority is diffused, and suppression is no longer supported by society at large. Even children sense this social atmosphere and rebel against adults who try to impose their will upon them. In an autocratic social order, society upholds the right of parents to use every conceivable method to enforce submission, even if it means severe beatings. Today, the tables have turned, and parents and teachers experience the open rebellion of children. In America, society now sides with the child and declares a brutal father or mother as unfit to parent.

When Dreikurs first wrote about social equality back in the 1940s, only a few of his friends in Adlerian circles and in the Humanist movement agreed with him. Most people reacted with indifference—it was just another dreamer's theory, so what else is new? And of course, some few objected strongly, feeling that his idea of equality would be a threat to the continued growth and achievements of society.

During the postwar years, Dreikurs became active in the American Humanist Association, serving as national vice-president from 1949 to 1957 and frequently contributing articles to the *Humanist* magazine. From the reactions to his articles and speeches he quickly learned that the issue of social equality was discomforting even to the most liberal minds. Upon his election as vice-president to the association late in 1949, he proposed a ten-point humanist philosophy of life. Published in the *Humanist* and widely distributed as a broadside, it created quite a reaction, both pro and con. Most of the negative response centered on article eight, which reads:

Man[3] is the ruler in democracy; therefore, every member of society is entitled to the same dignity and respect which is accorded to a sovereign. Fundamental human equality is not affected by any incidental individual characteristic like race, color, religion, sex, age, social and economic position, education, physical or mental health and beauty, moral or intellectual development, skill or personal achievement. Any assumption of superiority or inferiority on the basis of such incidental factors·is arbitrary and fallacious.[4]

Dreikurs answered his critics in his *Humanist* column: "The concept that human beings are equal and all individual differences only 'incidental' met with strong objection. There is even in the most liberal and progressive minds a great reluctance to abandon the superior-inferior structure in human relationships. On this one issue our fundamental attitudes toward each other become apparent; a truly humanist philosophy . . . hinges on the acceptance of the assumption of human equality." That professed humanists objected so strongly amazed Dreikurs: "One even went so far as to call the assumption of human equality a sign of ignorance and arrogance. People obviously feel deeply hurt when you question their superiority over their fellowmen!" In response, he agreed that we cannot "subtract" any of the incidental factors, because they do characterize each individual: Every person "*has* a race, color, sex, age, etc. But do these factors make him superior or inferior?"[5]

Throughout the 1950s, Dreikurs continued to enlarge and develop his ideas concerning the meaning of social equality and its impact on our attitudes and in our interactions. Most importantly, he developed concrete principles of human interaction and conflict solving that enhance democratic living and can be practiced in the home and in the school. His objective was to bridge the void between ideology and what really goes on in many daily interactions.

Dreikurs's ideas rested upon what he considered to be a fundamental law of human social life, Adler's "ironclad logic of living together," which implies a relationship of equals as the only basis of harmonious and stable living conditions. The idea of fundamental human equality evolved from its first expression by the Greek Stoics, through the early Christian sects, and the late Roman lawyers. It was sidetracked by medieval feudalism, but resumed its evolution with the Renaissance. The French and American Revolutions were historic milestones in the evolution of democracy. But the biggest advances, Dreikurs contended, came in the aftermath of World War II, in the United States when: "Negroes [began] gaining equality with white men, management yielded more rights to labor, [and] masculine superiority, unchallenged throughout many thousands of years, [began] crumbling."[6] But the problem, as he saw it, was that we had no tradition of living as social equals, only the old, anachronistic model of inferiority-superiority. "The proximity of equality is responsible for our conflicts and tensions becoming more intense and violent."[7]

Dreikurs's claim that children feel and act as social equals is perhaps the most difficult notion for adults to accept. Are children not small, inexperienced, and incapable, without education and judgment? Their own sense of equality is evidenced by the inability of parents and teachers to force children to behave, to learn, and to be responsible. The rampant rise of juvenile delinquency, the growing number of students who are labeled as underachievers or unable to read, or who are dropping out of school in defiance of parents and teachers was increasing but went unrecognized in the 1950s. For that was essentially a calm decade— women had retreated into suburban domesticity, and feminism had hardly a spokeswoman; the old masculine/feminine roles of dominance and submission had been reasserted.

But beneath the surface calm and apparent satisfaction of the 1950s, a new attitude was fermenting that broke through with a vengence in the upheavals of the 1960s. A precipitating event was the monumental 1954 Supreme Court decision in *Brown* v. *Board of Education,* which ended the legal segregationist doctrine of "separate but equal" educational systems. The crux of the decision was: "To separate [Negro children] from others of similar age and qualifications solely because of their race generates a feeling of inferiority as to their status in the community that may affect their hearts and minds in a way unlikely ever to be undone. . . . In the field of public education the doctrine of 'separate but equal' has no place. Separate educational facilities are inherently unequal." The majority report continued, citing the lower court's findings: "The policy of separating the races is usually interpreted as denoting the inferiority of the Negro group. A sense of inferiority affects the motivation of the child to learn."[8]

The full impact of the court's decision would not be felt for another decade, but it immediately ratified Dreikurs's claim that equality and relationships built upon the inferiority-superiority model were incompatible. Equality was no longer the idyllic dream of philosophers—it was fact. The most rewarding aspect of that decision for Dreikurs was the obvious role of Adlerian thought in this historic advance toward racial justice and equality. Psychologist Kenneth B. Clark, who assembled and prepared the social science brief submitted to the court for the case, acknowledged that "the unifying theoretical theme which made the findings from the various studies cited in this report coherent and eventually useful was that of Adlerian psychodynamic theory. . . . I do not believe that it is an unpardonable exaggeration to assert that this finding reflects a major contribution of Alfred Adler to man's endless struggle for justice and dignity."[9]

The following year, on December 1, 1955, an incident occurred in Montgomery, Alabama, that epitomized what Dreikurs called the sense of equality, when the individual awakens to his inherent right to dignity and self-respect and refuses to submit to the disrespect and unjust demands of an arbitrary superiority. Eldridge Cleaver referred to the incident as the moment when "somewhere in the universe a gear in the machinery had shifted."[10]

That day, Rosa Parks, a forty-two-year-old black woman, boarded a bus at the end of a tiring day and found a seat. In the southern custom, blacks were expected to yield their seats to whites if so demanded, and when the bus was filled, the driver told her to surrender her seat to a white man. To refuse was against the local law. After some thought, Mrs. Parks said that she would not move. She was arrested at the next stop and fined. This incident triggered the Montgomery bus boycott that brought national attention and fired the courage of black people to demand dignity, respect, and equal rights even in the face of hardship, threats, and potential danger to themselves.

Dreikurs had long acknowledged the inevitability of this igniting event somewhere, sometime, and he also saw that the civil rights movement would not be an issue for blacks alone. "His greatest frustration," Tee reflected, "came when he could see things so clearly and others did not heed his advice." As the civil rights movement gained momentum, "he desperately tried to sound the alarm. Said he: 'You will see how this is only the beginning; all groups who were previously treated as inferiors will rebel, the children against their parents, women against men, there will be a sexual and marital rebellion. His greatest frustration came when he could not convince the various groups that they should all join together as one, since they are all striving for equality."[11] He further argued that "in a process of polarization each group fights its own battles, and does not realize that all parties are fighting to be recognized as equals, even though in doing so they deny equality to everybody else. Each group is unwilling to grant to its opponents the dignity and respect which it demands for itself."[12]

Addressing a workshop on minority counseling in Portland, Oregon, in 1961, Dreikurs took exception to the growing trend to create new, specialized counseling approaches to deal with the problems of minority youth. "We have to realize that today every counseling situation is always with a minority group, because in each situation the counselor represents society to somebody who is, for whatever reason, against society by not functioning, by rebelling, by defying. . . . Each one of us in this world constitutes a minority group. . . . Each of us has some kind of notion of 'myself' pitted against the rest of society. . . . None of us is aware of the fact that we ourselves constitute the rest of society. That is part of our neurotic culture in which we are living, where the feeling of belonging is restricted in everybody because of this doubt of our status, of our worth, of our value, of our adequacy."[13]

Dreikurs found it difficult to convey the concept of social equality. He once remarked, "When I am asked, 'Please explain what equality is?' I understand your discomfort. But I am in a tough position. How can I explain the color red to a color-blind person? There are certain axiomatic beliefs. Even if I talked with the tongue of angels, . . . there will be some . . . who will understand and . . . others who will have difficulties."[14]

He pointed out that the fundamental mistake people make is to assume that equality means similarity and, if practiced, would reduce everyone to a common denominator of mediocrity that would eliminate individuality and excellence. This mistaken idea he traced to the poverty in language. In English, *equality* has several meanings, whereas in other languages there are different terms for the concepts of equality as an expression of quantitative sameness and of equality as an expression of equal value. Equality does not mean sameness, Dreikurs repeatedly argued. On the contrary, only when one is assured of his or her place and equally valued, can one dare to be different and avoid the lockstep of conformity. Every individual is different and has different assets, intellectual capacities, talents, and opportunities. But a democracy implies that all individuals *have* equal value, just as they have equal rights before the law.

In a democratic social order, proper (that is, harmonious) relationships are characterized by *mutual* respect. There can be no equality without it, and there can be no democracy when equality is denied to any member. If only *one* is respected, then that one becomes superior to the other, who feels put down and resents openly or subtly the imposed inferiority. There is no harmony or long-term stability in the relationship, and no equality. When mutual disrespect prevails, Dreikurs quickly pointed out, there is no equality either, because disrespect indicates that one looks down on the other.

Dreikurs was always a step ahead of his time. Though he enunciated the principle of social equality, he also knew what would be the likely outcome when those who had felt inferior began to assert themselves— overcompensation:

> We see now a strange development which Adler first described in the process of a child's overcompensation for an innate deficiency. The child does not merely try to compensate for it; he overcompensates. This is also a biological principle. Nature also provides for over-compensation. When one kidney takes over because the other is removed, the remaining kidney overdevelops as if to safeguard adequate functioning. This process is true for social inferiorities as well. Whenever one tries to compensate for an inferiority, he overcompensates. So women, not satisfied with being equal, tried to be superior, to be better than men. Now our women try to be so good that neither husband nor children have a chance. The image of a good mother is often the reason for her difficulties with her children. It prevents her from giving responsibility to them. She takes it on herself.
>
> An intensification of warfare takes place between all groups where one was previously dominant and the other submissive. Labor rebels against management and often tries to dictate. The same occurs in the relationship between the races. The blacks, . . . in order to have status as equals, . . . seek the same overcompensation, looking down on the "whities." While these struggles have been recognized, the most insidious warfare between adults and children has not been understood. Here, again, children who want to declare their independence overcompensate for their assumed inferiority. As a consequence, in the United States and in other countries where children experience their equality through self-determination we are raising a generation of tyrants.

As with his earlier books on marriage and family life, Dreikurs began assembling material on the theme of social equality long before it was published as a book. The nugget of many of these ideas was included in *The Challenge of Marriage* and in a series of lectures named *Cultural Upheaval and Modern Family Life*, which were published in pamphlet form in 1950. In 1961, he published *Social Equality: The Challenge of Our Times*, in mimeographed form, through the Alfred Adler Institute.

In it can be found his most complete statement of his philosophy and insights into man's biological, social, and cosmic feelings of inferiority; the meaning of social interest and the sense of belonging; the useful and detrimental aspects of competition in the evolution of contemporary society; and the role of religion. It also includes his view of the future of mankind, when the individual's potential for social cooperation, for creative decision making, and for self-determination will no longer be hindered by a society that pits one against the other as rivals for superiority and focuses on mistakes and humiliation in the developmental stage of childhood and youth.

Dreikurs struggled for years to find a publisher for this work, and when *Social Equality: Challenge of Today* was finally published in 1971, it was in a truncated form compared to its mimeographed precursor.

CHILDREN: THE CHALLENGE

"It is part of our difficulty that we have become equal to each other without the tradition or knowledge of how to live with each other as equals," Dreikurs remarked almost every time he addressed a group. The chaos, rebellion, and disharmony that characterize most American families stem from what he saw as the transition of our culture from its autocratic relationships of the past to new ones based on equality and mutual respect. "Each generation of parents is the foundation of the future. . . . [Do] we need first, better individuals to form a better society, or a better society to produce better individuals? The two factors work hand in hand: the training of children influences the future social order, just as existing living conditions determine the form of upbringing. The progressive evolution of mankind is inseparably linked with the improved spirit and technique of child-rearing."[15]

Dreikurs regarded social equality as part of the evolutionary development of mankind. "We are compelled to go through this process of democratization," he believed. "The ills of democracy can only be cured by more democracy. Whatever difficulties we have in living together as equals cannot be resolved by reverting to the old power structure of dominance. We have to learn to live together as equals."[16]

The dilemma, however, is that adults, themselves raised in the traditional mode of superior-inferior relations with its stress on competitive striving for superiority, do not know proper techniques for raising children in a democratic social order. They do not know how to foster self-reliance, inner motivation, a sense of responsibility, or the spirit of cooperation:

> Adults find it . . . difficult to accept the assumption of equality with their children. . . . Children are the last ones whom we could possibly consider as our equals. They are small, limited in their abilities, weak and helpless. All our [propensities] for feeling superior are met here. This assumption of adult supremacy led to a widespread, but mostly unrecognized "prejudice" against children. . . . Relatively few adults are capable of establishing a "proper" relationship with them. Listen to the tone of voice—particularly mothers—use in their interaction with children! They either coo, drip with sweetness, or are critical, impatient, threatening or domineering. Very few use respectful tones with children. . . . And the tone of voice reveals the character of any human relationship.[17]

"The family is the laboratory of human relationships," Dreikurs often taught. "The family sets the pattern for what goes on not only in the family but in society." For that reason, he regarded the need for providing new principles for raising children in a manner appropriate to a democratic social order the most challenging issue of our time.

Dreikurs sought to answer this need in all his books for parents and teachers. *Psychology in the Classroom* (1957); *Encouraging Children to Learn* (1963), coauthored with Don Dinkmeyer; *Maintaining Sanity in the Classroom* (1971), coauthored with Bronia Grunwald and Floy Pepper; and *Discipline Without Tears* (1972), coauthored with Pearl Cassel, are specifically oriented to teachers and provide direction and concrete suggestions for creating a democratically functioning classroom. Parents also needed a new approach that was addressed to the daily challenges and issues of raising children.

In *Children: The Challenge* (1964), coauthored with Vicki Soltz (Statton), Dreikurs succeeded admirably. Soltz, a nurse by professional training, first became acquainted with Dreikurs while researching a series of newspaper articles she wrote concerning the child guidance centers in Chicago. As a mother seeking solutions to parent-child problems, she learned firsthand the ideas and methods Dreikurs taught.

Dreikurs and Soltz provided what they considered a primer, a self-help book designed to reach as large an audience as possible.

The basic Adlerian premise of mankind's inherent social nature led Dreikurs to assert that the young child's strongest motivation is the desire to belong. His security or lack of it will depend upon his feelings of belonging in the family group. From infancy, everything he does is aimed at finding his place. From his observations and successes, he draws conclusions—not formed in words, but definite nonetheless—"Ah! *This* is how I can belong. This is how I can have significance." He chooses the method by which he hopes to achieve his basic long-term goal. This method is reflected in his immediate goal such as "to be the center of attention," and becomes the basis for his behavior. The desire to belong is a person's basic goal, but any one of a variety of immediate goals may be chosen. A person's behavior is always goal-directed.

In Dreikurs's system, nothing is more important in child rearing than encouragement. A child cannot develop and acquire a sense of belonging without encouragement. The lack of it is the fundamental cause for misbehavior. *Children: The Challenge* is full of illustrations that show how well-meaning parents actually *discourage* their children despite their good intentions. A common practice regarded as beneficial to children is the use of rewards. Dreikurs contended that "the system of rewarding children for good behavior is as detrimental to their outlook as the system of punishment. The same lack of respect is shown. We 'reward' our inferiors for favors or for good deeds. . . . Children don't need bribes to be good. Good behavior on the part of the child springs from his desire to belong, to contribute usefully and to cooperate. When we bribe a child for good behavior we are in effect showing him that we do not trust him, which is a form of discouragement."[18]

Moreover, the system of rewards no longer works, because in a democratic atmosphere, children who get rewards regard them as a "right" and refuse to perform unless some rewards are forthcoming. Rewards foster the notion of "what's in it for me?" which is contrary to the satisfaction that comes from simply doing a job that needs to be done.

He recognized that children are exposed to a sequence of discouraging experiences. They are first discouraged by their parents, who unwittingly deprive them of the realization of their ability, either through overprotection, overanxiety, or indulgent service, or through all the forms of humiliation common in our present-day methods of raising children, a residual from an autocratic tradition. Scolding, nagging, threatening, and punishment are almost a daily routine in most families. Parents take it for granted that that is what they should do. They do not recognize the detrimental effect of these methods on the morale of children, and so undermine their self-respect. "Every child needs continuous encouragement just as a plant needs water." Without encouragement, no beneficial influences can be exerted.

Most parents sincerely want to be democratic in their dealings but instead, vacillate between anarchy and autocracy. *Children: The Challenge* addresses the frequent mistake parents make by confusing freedom with license, and democracy with anarchy. If a child refuses to behave and defies authority simply because he assumes that he can do as he pleases, this is not democracy, but anarchy. The freedom to do what one wishes is part of democracy, but only when it respects the rights of others. Without respect for the rights of others, there can be no order. Freedom and democracy require order:

> Parents have [shouldered] the disastrous consequences of the excess freedom assumed by their children; they have covered up for them, taken the brunt of punishment for them, borne their insults, endured their multiple demands, and thereby lost their influence over their children. The children, without knowing what bothers them, sense the loss of order because there are no restrictions to guide them. They become more concerned with getting their own way than with learning the principles and restrictions necessary for group living. As a result, the ever present capacity for social interest, or interest in one's fellow man, remains stunted and underdeveloped. This has resulted in a sense of confusion and has increased the maladjustment of children. Well-defined restrictions give a sense of security and a certainty of function within the social structure. Without this, a child feels at a total loss. His ever renewed efforts to "find himself" take the destructive course we see manifest in our many unhappy, defiant children. . . . To help our children, then, we must turn from the obsolete autocratic method of demanding submission to a new order based on the principles of freedom and responsibility. Our children no longer can be forced into compliance; they must be stimulated and encouraged into voluntarily taking their part in the maintenance of order.[19]

Dreikurs maintained that democratic principles provide a middle ground between autocracy and anarchy, and he showed parents how they can be firm and provide limits while maintaining respect and avoiding domination. This is well illustrated in the following example from *Children: The Challenge:*

As Mother drove, Judy and Jerry, five-year-old twins, merrily romped in the back of the station wagon. They became more and more noisy. The distracted mother asked them several times to quiet down. They would stop for a minute and then return to their roughhouse play, which became wilder and wilder. Suddenly Jerry pushed Judy in such a fashion that she was thrown against Mother's head and shoulders. "This is the utter end," she screamed as she stopped the car at the curb. Both children looked panic-stricken and frightened. Mother gave each a sound spanking. The twins were completely astounded, since Mother rarely used violence.

Mother is very lenient with the lively spirits of the twins who in turn feel that "anything goes." If we permit violation of order at one time and blow up at another, we teach our children to mind us only if we get violent.

A car is not the place for wild play at any time. Mother can establish order in the car without any force; she can be firm without dominating. How can this be done? The secret lies in knowing *how* to be firm. Domination means that we try to impose our will upon the child. We tell him what he should do. If Mother attempts to impose her will upon the twins, she will succeed only in evoking their rebellion. Firmness, on the other hand, expresses *our own action.* Mother can always decide what *she* will do and carry it out. She simply will not drive while the children are unruly. Every time that they cut up, she stops the car. She may say, "I will not drive as long as you misbehave." Then she sits quietly until they are orderly. No other explanation is necessary. Mother has taken her stand and is firm in her decision.[20]

In *Children: The Challenge*, as in his other works, Dreikurs demonstrated a genius for formulating complex ideas in a very simple way. His books are excellent popularizers and are very readable. But because he refused to convey his thoughts in a specialized, learned jargon, they have not made a great impact on professional people—especially in academic settings. That is why scholars tend not to give much recognition to Dreikurs's books. However, anthropologist Ashley Montagu recently remarked that Dreikus's books on child rearing are the finest he has ever encountered.[21]

Because of the simplicity and concreteness of the ideas and principles in the book, there were those who denigrated them as "cookbook" techniques. Dreikurs countered: "We bring a practical method together with a philosophy. When we show parents, teachers and professionals what we do, we do not operate on a cookbook method. All our recommendations aim at a change in human relationships and the basis of all our efforts to reduce conflict rest on social consciousness, the logic of social living, and the equality of all people."[22]

Children: The Challenge, because it fuses philosophical insight with practical application, is remarkably well suited to generate lively discussion. It has become an excellent vehicle for study groups, and interest in parent participation has mushroomed because of it, although such groups have been underway to a limited degree since the late 1940s. Vicki Soltz worked with parents and leaders in Oregon; Chicago; and Wilmington, Delaware; and thereafter wrote a manual for organizing and leading study groups aimed at helping parents apply the ideas through shared experiences and encouragement. Within a year or two after the book was published, study groups for parents, averaging ten weeks in length, were functioning in cities everywhere. Soon a fledgling movement of Adlerians was promoting and practicing Dreikurs's refinements and contributions to Adler's philosophy of parenting. By 1970, an estimated twenty thousand people were engaged at any one time in these study groups.[23]

As Dreikurs traveled around the country and as the study groups spread, he knew that there was a growing audience eagerly searching for better, more effective ways to understand and correct misguided behavior. That growing audience indicated that the long-standing, deeply entrenched Freudian-mechanistic model of child development was at last breaking down. For years, owing to its pervasive influence on the professions, the media, and the literature, Freudianism had so distorted people's perceptions that they could not, or were unwilling to, look at behavior from any other perspective. Freudianism crumbled under the weight of its repeated ineffectiveness—that is, its inability to be translated from theory into a coherent, understandable, workable set of practices for daily life. The ineffectiveness of the more entrenched approaches for dealing with interpersonal conflicts led to paralyzing confusion, demoralization, and pessimism that so characterize most of the adult population's attitude toward children. The defeatism it generated has infected our whole society. "Nothing expressed this widespread defeatism as pathetically as the reaction of a mother or teacher who [had come] to discuss a problem and [was] given a definite suggestion of what [she] could do," Dreikurs explained. "[She] comes the next time with an expression of utter surprise, 'It really worked!' . . . Who ever heard of something that works with a child? 'I tried everything,' they say. 'Nothing works.' You find such attitudes in almost every mother. That is the sad story."[24]

This pervasive defeatism in adults explains the great enthusiasm that is generated in parents and teachers when they encounter Dreikurs's ideas and methods, try them in their homes or classrooms, and discover that they work. The effect of these new ideas is an astonishing, eye-opening experience, because what Adlerian theory does is to demonstrate with great clarity how the most complex and common everyday experiences can be perceived from an entirely different slant. For many it is an exhilarating experience, a "natural high." Its quality is akin to the joy that accompanies a discovery, a bridging of the gap between knowledge of the facts of human behavior and an understanding of their underlying connectedness.

But the ideas generate skepticism, even among those who want to believe them. "How dare any adult feel self-assured, and positive about dealing with children or students?" is the standard defeatist reaction of those caught in the morass of demoralizing experiences. Oddly enough, there is nothing mysterious or esoteric about what these teachers and parents are learning. Actually, it has been part of our lives, and of our daily experiences, but we have neither seen it for what it is nor appreciated it because we are not trained to look for it.

No doubt Dreikurs could have turned his special insights and skills into a clever mystique reserved for an elite few and turned himself into some sort of worshiped guru. He probably could have made a fortune in the process. But nothing would have been more abhorrent to him. His integrity was impeccable, which testifies clearly to the genuineness of his goals and to the fact that his certitude stemmed mainly from the depth of his belief in what he could contribute, in what Adlerian psychology has to offer, and in the ability of others to learn, practice, and, in turn, transmit that knowledge. Beneath his brilliant showmanship, his search for recognition, his desire to be the center of attention, even his propensity for arrogant attack was an untiring devotion to help people learn to live more fully and harmoniously in their relationships with others. "He did not guard zealously his own contribution to protect his exclusive right to be recognized," Bronia Grunwald said. "His ultimate goal was to train others so that they could carry on the work on their own. He encouraged people to write of their experiences, often insisting that we write because we owe it to others. When someone told him he was not ready to undertake such a task, he would say, 'You will never be ready until you start.' "[25]

Helene Rae, a woman who worked in the Chicago Child Guidance Centers for years and became an active supporter of Dreikurs's principles, perhaps summed up his contribution the best:

> There is no yardstick to measure the value of Dr. Rudolf Dreikurs . . . either as a man . . . or as a major contributor to . . . psychology and psychiatry. . . . What did he contribute? He *taught* and shared his knowledge with teachers, yes! . . . with students, yes! But have you any idea what he gave to mothers, fathers, children—the non-professionals whose lives were saved from chaos and resentment? No parent or child thrives on quiet desperation or open rebellion, and the whirlpool of this kind of living echoes all over the world today. . . . He threw a lifeline to the desperate—led us to a ladder where each step taken offered self-respect, personal dignity, and awareness of the privilege of changing our attitude."[26]

Notes for Chapter 19

1. Milton M. Tyler to Rudolf Dreikurs, February 3, 1971, Dreikurs Papers.
2. Dreikurs, *Challenge of Marriage*, p. 252.
3. Dreikurs probably meant "every" man, implying the common man.
4. Rudolf Dreikurs, "Ten Premises for a Humanist Philosophy of Life," *Humanist* 9 (1949): 19.
5. Rudolf Dreikurs, "Humanism—a Philosophy for Human Living," *Humanist* 10 (1950): 73–74.
6. Rudolf Dreikurs, *Cultural Upheaval and Modern Family Life* (Chicago: Community Child Guidance Centers, 1950).
7. Ibid.
8. *Brown* v. *Board of Education*, 347 U.S. 483 (1954).
9. Kenneth B. Clark, "Implications of Adlerian Theory for an Understanding of Civil Rights Problems and Actions," *Journal of Individual Psychology* 23 (1967): 181–190.
10. William Manchester, *The Glory and the Dream*, p. 740.
11. Sadie "Tee" Dreikurs, "My Life with Rudolf Dreikurs."
12. Rudolf Dreikurs, "Equality: The Life-Style of Tomorrow," *Futurist* 6 (1972): 154.
13. Rudolf Dreikurs, "Rationale of Counseling," in *Proceedings of the Delta Workshop on Counseling Minority Youth, June 14–16, 1961* (Portland, Ore.: Oregon State System of Higher Education, 1961), p. 1.

14. Rudolf Dreikurs, *Human Patterns in a Changing Society* (Jerusalem: Israel Civil Service Commission, 1970), p. 26.

15. Rudolf Dreikurs, *Coping with Childrens' Misbehavior: A Parent's Guide* (New York: Hawthorn Books, 1972), pp. 149–150.

16. Rudolf Dreikurs, "The Realization of Equality in the Home," *Individual Psychologist* 9 (1972): 46–55.

17. Rudolf Dreikurs, "How Do We Get Moral Values?" 1964, Dreikurs Papers.

18. Rudolf Dreikurs and Vicki Soltz, *Children: The Challenge* (New York: Duell, Sloan & Pearce, 1964), pp. 72, 74.

19. Ibid., p. 10.

20. Ibid., pp. 86–87.

21. Ashley Montagu, personal communication, 1974.

22. Rudolf Dreikurs, "Rudolf Dreikurs: 1897–1972." In *Psychotherapie in Selbstdarstellungen*, ed. Ludwig J. Pongratz (Bern, Switzerland: Hans Huber, 1973), p. 121.

23. Mark R. Arnold, "Let 'Em Fight," *National Observer*, January 1, 1972.

24. Dreikurs, "Rationale on Counseling," p. 4.

25. Bernice Bronia Grunwald, "Rudolf Dreikurs' Contributions to Education," in *Proceedings of the Rudolf Dreikurs Memorial Institute, ICASSI 1973, Espinho, Portugal, July 1973*, p. 10.

26. Helene Rae to Raymond J. Corsini, June 24, 1967, Dreikurs Papers.

20

The Roving Ambassador
of Adlerian Psychology

It is necessary that Adlerians keep their identity . . . not for
the sake of tradition or loyalty to Adler, but to preserve . . .
the discoveries . . . made by Adler and his co-workers so
that they may not get lost in the violent competition of
schools and systems and have to be rediscovered again, to
the detriment of science and all who can benefit from them.
                                         Rudolf Dreikurs
          "The International Picture of Individual Psychology"

In 1950, thirteen years after his departure from Austria, Dreikurs returned
to Europe and his native Vienna. The event-filled intervening years
seemed more like a century than like little more than a decade. This trip
was but the first of many to Europe, which in succeeding years included
Greece and Israel. All of his extensive travels to Europe, Jamaica, Oregon,
and Israel were well documented through his lengthy, descriptive letters,
which are filled with delightful accounts of geography, people, and the
overwhelming numbers of his activities. Nothing tells more about this
man, his self-declared mission to spread Individual Psychology, his per-
ceptivity, and his unflagging optimism than these letters, which in themselves could amply fill a book. It is not possible within the scope of this
biography to begin to do justice to the richness and detail in these extensive letters, covering the period 1950–1971, and only the most exemplary
issues and events can be touched upon here.

Ostensibly, the trip in 1950 was to attend two international meetings,
the Mental Hygiene Congress and the First International Congress of
Psychiatry, both in Paris. But a side trip to Vienna was not to be missed.
It was only five years since the end of the war, and Europe was just

beginning to rebuild. Evidence of the human pain and cultural destruction was everywhere. Vienna was a shock for Dreikurs. "When we walked through the streets, I got more excited and upset. The destruction of the buildings, of all the well-known places which were gone, was in line with the deterioration of the people. . . . No old, well-known types, no intellectuals. A ghost town amongst the ruins of the past."[1]

About the congress in Paris, Dreikurs reported that his Adlerian ideas seemed completely new to others and that the monopolistic influence of the Freudians was very evident. He considered the trip important because it brought together for the first time since the Hitler years the surviving remnants of Adlerian psychologists in Europe. He noted with some pride, "Our Adlerian friends seem to look to me for leadership." He was pleased by how many people knew of him through his books. He generated enthusiasm, and firm plans were laid for reactivating an international Adlerian society.

At the Paris congress, he presented a penetrating analysis of the origin and meaning of the newly emerging field of group psychotherapy (G.T.). He commented:

> We recognize more and more the emotional isolation of the individual in our modern competitive society as one of the foremost causes of social maladjustment, neurosis and emotional distress. The integration of the individual into a whole, indispensable as it is for the adequate functioning of a human being, is greatly restricted today. Orthodox religion lost its appeal to many; the modern family is permeated with the competitive strife, characteristic for our era, setting father against mother, parents against children, sibling against sibling, and thereby depriving each of them of a true feeling of belonging to a group. G.T. provides such an inspirational group experience, whereby the individual can be sure of his social status even if he lets his fellowmen know how he feels and what he is. Normally nobody can let his hair down, so to speak, without fearing disapproval, criticism or ridicule. The experience in G.T. is foreign to any other social experience in our time.
>
> For this reason we may well have to think in terms of organizing therapy groups not only for our emotionally sick but for the normal population which is emotionally unbalanced in a world of unrest and suspicion, hardly anywhere permitting sincere cooperation. Social and emotional maladjustment characterizes our present family rela-

tionships, our community life, our national and international relations. Individual psychotherapy is no answer for a culture problem of
this proportion. G.T. in one form or other will be necessary to supple-
ment merely educational efforts on a logical and intellectual level.[2]

The international Adlerian association that Dreikurs envisioned and
enthusiastically helped to create became a reality in 1954. But the IAIP
(International Association for Individual Psychology) proved to be a
great disappointment to him because of the way it evolved through the
1960s. What disturbed him was the basic conservative posture of its con-
trolling members, the "older" Adlerians, who, though contemporaries of
Dreikurs in terms of age, were, in his mind, satisfied merely to reiterate
what Adler had said without enlarging the theory or the practice. They
were reluctant or ill prepared to train others, and largely confined their
interests to private practice. They neglected that entire realm of teacher
and parent education that Adler and Dreikurs advocated so tirelessly.
Unhappy with what he saw as the undemocratic power structure of the
new organization, Dreikurs chose to go to Jamaica rather than attend the
fledgling society's first meeting in Zurich in 1954. However, three years
later, he was elected vice-president of the IAIP and thereafter worked
vigorously to have his ideas heard within the organization.

Rudolf and Tee returned again to Europe in 1958, stopping off first for
a week in England. There he lectured widely, at the universities of Edin-
burgh, Aberdeen, Liverpool, and London, and was sponsored by the
prominent Adlerian social psychiatrist, Dr. Joshua Bierer. Dreikurs found
the remnant groups of Adlerian psychologists in England, which originated in the 1930s, to be in a weak, ineffective state. "They all talk in
favor of Adlerian psychology," he wrote, "but are in no position to train
physicians, psychologists, and psychiatrists."[3] At the Marlborough Day
Hospital, where Bierer as medical director had instituted innovative reforms in the care and treatment of mental patients, Dreikurs did a demonstration with a woman patient. "It was obvious that during the two
years of treatment there she had found none who was a match for her,
although she did improve and people have tried very hard to help her.
When I explained at the end that I had probably 'spit in her soup,' Bierer
added, 'And probably in that of many others too.' "[4]

Nonetheless, Bierer genuinely admired Dreikurs and acknowledged his
contributions in a letter a few years later:

Marlborough Day Hospital
London, NW 8
December 13, 1966

My dear Rudolf:

It seems like only yesterday that I listened to your interesting lectures in the twenties on the various topics of individual psychology and group psychotherapy!

Every pioneer in history has been accused of being aggressive, decisive, and sometimes paranoid, wondering why the world is not prepared to accept his ideas. I would like to remind you of the wise words of Lord Balfour who in 1904 said that people who were too far advanced for their times were called mad charlatans and not taken seriously.

You had a difficult task on the one hand and a great privilege on the other, to be in certain things far in advance of your time, and in others, just leading the reconnaissance platoon. In your first role you must accept being treated as too far in advance—as visionaries and dreamers have been treated throughout history—and in the second, in psychiatry and especially Individual Psychology, as a great pioneer with a unique contribution.

The modern "Zeitgeist" owes you a great debt. . . .

I remain as ever,
Yours,

Joshua Bierer, M.D.
Medical Director[5]

Following England came a brief stop in Switzerland, where Dreikurs savored the opportunity to speak at the famous hospital Burgholzli. Again, as in England, he found the Adlerian group a puzzle. In Switzerland there were only four Adlerian-trained professionals, and of them, Dr. Victor Louis was not in regular practice and Professor Hans Biasch, the director of the Institute of Industrial Psychology, did not want to be identified as an Adlerian for political reasons. Dreikurs thought the weak state of Adlerian psychology was pitiful, and there seemed to be little new blood to change this condition.[6]

Returning to Vienna had a strong effect on Dreikurs, who visited all the places in Döbling where he had lived and worked many years earlier. He gave three lectures while there and remarked, "It was rather peculiar to talk at the same places, in the same lecture room where I went as a student and later gave lectures. It was the same experience everywhere, this peculiar coexistence of foreign strangeness and yet intimate knowledge and experience. Something is unreal about it. . . . The Adlerian position here is one of the most mixed up I ever saw." The older, well-trained Adlerians seemed unwilling to have any dealing with the younger Adlerians:

> Professor [Hans] Hoff pointed out that the old clash between Adlerians [and Freudians] does not exist in Vienna where the first assistant [at the clinic] is a Freudian . . . and the other two are the leading Adlerians. That sounds wonderful, only . . . the alliance between the Adlerians and the Freudians at the clinic may perhaps be less the result of a real mutual understanding than of a common plight. Both the school authorities and the department of psychology at the University [are] against any form of dynamic psychology and . . . the rebellion against Freud includes rejection of Adler as well. Both [are] officially regarded as foolish although everybody bows to their names when they are mentioned. . . .
>
> The most heated discussion . . . was about my reference to the psychologists who become better trained in psychodynamics [than the psychiatrists] in the States. The psychiatrists were . . . outraged. . . . No one would even dream about preparing [psychologists] for psychotherapy or letting them practice. . . . My statement that times will eventually also catch up with Vienna was taken with great incredulity. . . . You can clearly see that the Prophet is not only not heard in his own country, but in a foreign country either.[7]

This visit evoked a personal and emotional impact on Dreikurs. "Somehow, I found the link to the past. Since I [moved to] the States, I realized that I had no past. Other people could talk about their friends from school and [their] young years; I had none and did not want to have any, because Vienna, . . . the past, was gone forever. And suddenly it appeared again while I was here just a few days. The streets took on familiar hues, the people spoke again in the same language, the friends thought I was again Viennese—and to my own surprise, I myself felt I was. . . . It was exciting and gratifying, as if an empty space had been filled—the past."[8]

Dreikurs's experiences with the older Adlerians in Europe as he traveled about were all too reminiscent of the way he had found the Adlerians in America in the late 1930s—a dedicated enough group but clearly getting older and confining their work to their private practices, some clinic work, and occasional meetings and lectures. It was not only the lack of skilled Adlerian therapists in Europe as in the United States, but that they were isolated, dispirited, and unwilling to identify with Adlerian psychology, or actively teach it to others, that disturbed him. It was frustrating for him, and his anger was exacerbated by the lack of action within the newly reconstituted international society, which met every three years but amounted to little more than a tiny gathering and reading of papers. Dreikurs was by then in his sixties, robust and healthy, but painfully aware that there were a limited number of years in which he could continue teaching and working at his breakneck pace. Perhaps his impatience was also aroused by his growing impact in America, where the demand for his lectures and training seminars had begun to multiply beyond his own expectations. Yet, at times, the older Adlerians seemed to impede his vision as much as any partisan Freudian. Dreikurs's singular missionary sense prompted Lewis Davidson to remark that "he was a lone bird, but he needed an army."[9] That army was growing, but it did not include many who were his contemporary Adlerian colleagues.

He returned to Europe again in 1960 to attend the third meeting of IAIP and remarked:

Now, the situation is much clearer to me in my own field. Here we find a whole group of psychiatrists playing the role of progressive leaders in the field. They hold the presidency of International societies, and organize International Conventions, and talk big—but what are they doing? This I know, it is worse than it was thirty years ago when I left here. The Mental hospital [in Vienna] is a snake pit as it was before with some new trimmings of words. In the City which was the cradle of psychotherapy, we find today a small group of well organized psychoanalysts, and besides that, nobody who does or knows anything about psychotherapy, except Frankl, who has altogether two associates who practice his method, and that is all for the City of Vienna.

I had a long session with fifteen of the twenty members of the Viennese Adlerian Society. It was most interesting. First they all told me about their rich activities, how much they are doing, [what] important positions each one had, how they [as] Adlerians, . . . further the movement. Only at the end did it become clear that they give a training seminar once every five years, and the last one could only be given for one semester because there are not sufficient students. No classes are given for teachers, . . . Nobody is prepared yet to really do group psychotherapy, they have no trained personnel for what should be done, etc. etc.[10]

After leaving Vienna, Rudolf and Tee took a relaxing cruise to Greece and thoroughly enjoyed all the great antiquities and sights. Little did he suspect that the disheartening prospect for Adlerian psychology he found in Vienna and elsewhere in Europe was about to change dramatically. The limited activities of his first visit to Athens in 1960 only hinted at what would follow in later years. He gave a series of lectures at the Goethe Institute, at the invitation of Erik Blumenthal, which drew large and enthusiastic audiences. In addition, he gave a demonstration of family counseling, arranged by Mrs. Frosso Keni, a psychologist who had studied for a time with Dreikurs in Chicago while completing her professional training. Mrs. Keni took the role of co-counselor during the demonstrations, translating the dialogue between the Greek parents and Dreikurs. "I was actually amazed how good she was," Dreikurs wrote. "She was excellent in her approach with parents and children."[11] What particularly struck him as he listened to the problems of the Greek family that volunteered for the demonstration was that they faced exactly the same problems as those confronting parents in the United States. It was for him another example of the growing impact of the democratic ideal that was steadily altering the nature of human relationships. That it was already evident in Greece, a far more traditional and autocratic society where the paternal figure was still a genuine authority, convinced him that Greece would also be faced with an increase of disobedience, conflict, rebellion, and the host of behavioral problems that had emerged in the United States so rapidly and pervasively after World War II.

Many Europeans scoffed at his ideas in those early years of the 1960s. After all, they read about all those crazy kids in America who do not learn, do not want to learn, drop out, become hippies, delinquent, or whatever. But not in Greece! In the "cradle of democracy" a repressive autocratic regime was in power, traditional family structures were a matter of pride, and what was happening in America was, to most Greeks, like something taking place on another planet. Yet Dreikurs was, as usual, correct. With each successive visit to Greece—there were eight in all, the last in 1969—he saw the despair, perplexity, and confusion grow as parents, teachers, and husbands and wives discovered that the traditional, unchallenged obedience of old was gone. Rebellion against domination, both in its subtle and in its more open forms, was disrupting human relations.

What happened in Greece would be repeated experiences in Germany, Switzerland, Denmark, and Israel. The initial scoffing and cynicism of those who heard Dreikurs in the early years ended when they realized that what he had predicted had become so unerringly—and frustratingly—true.

But back in 1960, on his first visit to Greece, this disquietude seemed very remote indeed. Juliet Cavadas, a high school teacher by training but later a journalist, covered Dreikurs's lectures and demonstrations in Athens. A sister-in-law to Frosso Keni, who assisted Dreikurs in the counseling, she was intrigued by him and invited him and Tee to stay at their home while in Athens. This enabled him to see some private clients who came to him for help. "I really didn't know that much about his ideas then," she reflected, "but I was immediately impressed by his personality—his drive, his eagerness, his authenticity. There was a power about him—a self-acceptance, a total lack of pretense."[12]

Dreikurs was likewise impressed by Cavadas, an intelligent, versatile young woman with an engaging personality who was adept at expressing her ideas—a real leader. He lost no time in involving her in his work. "He asked me if I would be his interpreter. He challenged me, encouraged me, complimented me on my sensitivity and awareness toward others," she later remembered. "I was happily married with two young children. He was always seeking to find people who were still searching for a direction or meaning in their lives, and he sensed that quality in me. As he was almost to leave, he challenged me: 'Who will work with these parents and teachers and children who need help after I leave?' 'Well, not me—I'm not trained—what could I do?' was her response. 'Whatever you would do is better than doing nothing. If you and Frosso don't do it, nobody will.'" After he left, she began to study his books and to work with mothers and teachers in study-group settings.

"On his second visit," Cavadas reflected, "we gathered together a small group, mostly psychologists, to train with him. We did each other's life styles in the group as part of the training and also for self-knowledge. He did my life style. While I admired him and thought his ideas about parenting and teaching were superb, I wasn't sure how sophisticated he was as a therapist. The Adlerian principles seemed almost too simple. I thought, 'I'm too complicated for him, he'll never figure me out.' But he was so good, so accurate, so subtle—it was a revelation to me. Thereafter I plunged into study, went to the United States to get a master's degree in psychology, and studied with Dreikurs and all the people connected with the Adler Institute in Chicago."[13] Back in Athens, Cavadas became the leader of a growing group of professional and paraprofessional workers who tirelessly taught Adlerian principles of human relations to parents, teachers, and adolescents in a time of growing need for help. She also translated all of Dreikurs's major books into Greek, after which they enjoyed much popularity.

Professional psychologist Frosso Keni reflected:

> When I first met Dr. Dreikurs and assisted in one of his counseling sessions I immediately felt: "This is what I am looking for." . . . I learned from him all I know that is really valuable and so different from the sterile scientific terms . . . or the clichés of the so-called dynamic psychology.
>
> He was my great discovery and I made every possible effort to bring other people in my country to know him; and his work in Greece was quite remarkable.
>
> When he first visited Athens the mere fact that he was an Adlerian made professional people quite reluctant to listen to him. But one demonstration of Child Guidance was enough to change the atmosphere. The impression was so great that even people from very different psychological orientations became interested and a great number of them felt that they could find in Dr. Dreikurs's method a realistic and practical approach to meet the problems of today's youth. In his short visits in this country, he accomplished what would take years for others to achieve. . . .
>
> Dr. Dreikurs belongs to this high class of teachers who teach not only by their word, but also by their action and mainly by the whole of their personality.[14]

Summing up the Greek experience, Cavadas wrote, "In a country where traditional ways of childrearing and the myth of antithetical roles for man and woman are still in existence, though more and more devastating, the role of a counselor is often to work toward demystifying such myths—one of [being] a cultural modifier. . . . The conviction that adequate information about child education and the dynamics of human relations is as necessary . . . to every particular individual in a community as mass vaccination, and [must] not be the monopoly of a minority of professionals, was a deeply rooted belief, innoculated in all of us . . . by Rudolf Dreikurs."[15]

On his trip to Greece in 1962, Dreikurs received from his Greek friends a "beautiful ancient Athenian silver coin as a 'genuine souvenir from the City of Democracy to the man who promotes genuine democracy.'"[16]

Erik Blumenthal, the man who invited Dreikurs to speak at the Goethe Institute in Athens, was also to play an important role in introducing and spreading Dreikurs's ideas. However, this did not take place in Greece but in Germany and Switzerland, where Blumenthal lives and works. When he first met Dreikurs that year, he was already a trained Adlerian psychologist. Blumenthal changed careers in midlife, after a successful start as an industrial manager. His professional training was Jungian and took place in Switzerland. During his studies, Blumenthal became curious about Adler, whose name was often mentioned but always in a critical or demeaning manner. "Oh, Adler, they would say—he's only interested in the power drive." But Blumenthal, a soft-spoken man with a deep spiritual nature and inquiring mind, began to read Adler's writings and switched his orientation to Adlerian psychology. He studied with Dr. Alexander Müller at the Institute of Applied Psychology in Zurich and began his private practice in the mid-1950s. "My training as an Adlerian was quite different from the way Dreikurs worked. I was very cautious, not very directive, not very open, and I had not been trained in how to formulate the life style, but waited and let it unfold slowly in the process of therapy until the patient discovered bits of it himself. Therapy took a rather long time that way," Blumenthal mused.[17]

His first realization that Adlerian psychology could be approached in a more active way came when he first encountered Dreikurs's *Challenge of Parenthood*. This launched a correspondence between the two men, culminating in their meeting at the Vienna congress in 1960. Blumenthal found Dreikurs's ideas very appealing and began introducing his methods of working with parents and teachers when he resettled in Germany. On later trips to Europe, Dreikurs lectured and trained widely in Germany, and Blumenthal steadily carried on the work in the interim periods. His translations into German of *Children: The Challenge* and *Psychology in the Classroom* have been great successes, selling even faster than their American editions and helping to spearhead a rapidly developing Adlerian movement in contemporary Germany and Switzerland.

With dedicated colleagues like Cavadas and Blumenthal and numerous others from Europe and Israel, Dreikurs was able to accomplish what he could not do through his older conservative colleagues and the international society. He succeeded in reawakening an interest in Adlerian psychology among a whole new generation of psychologists and educators who, in turn, began introducing Adlerian concepts in homes and school in various parts of Europe.

A major vehicle for this development and one that brought Dreikurs great satisfaction was the International Summer School, which was launched in 1962. It grew, from its unpretentious beginnings in the early 1960s, to be a major international gathering place for the advancement of Adlerian psychology by the mid-1970s.

Ruth Bickel Holger-Nielsen, a Danish psychologist, first encountered Dreikurs through his book *Psychology in the Classroom* and set out deliberately to meet him at the Vienna congress in 1960. The following year she and her husband traveled to Oregon specifically to attend the summer school there. It was then decided to hold a two-week summer school for interested Europeans the following year in Denmark. Perhaps no more than twenty-five to thirty people attended that first International Summer School, sponsored by ICASSI (International Committee for Adlerian Summer Schools and Institutes) in 1962. Holger-Nielsen recalled that Dreikurs predicted, that summer, that within the decade European families and schools would experience all the disruptions and difficulties that had already occurred in the United States, in the wake of increasing democracy and the demand for equality. The Europeans did not believe him and scoffed. "He gave us a warning of ten years," Holger-Nielsen chuckled, "but it took only six,"[18] before his prediction came true.

Following Denmark in 1962, ICASSI Summer Schools were conducted biannually as a vehicle to introduce Adlerian psychology to various countries. Since 1973, they have been conducted annually and generally attract three hundred to four hundred people. Sites for the summer schools have included Crete, Germany, Greece, Israel, Holland, Portugal, and Austria. The objective is to provide intensive training for teachers, counselors, psychiatrists, pastors, physicians, psychologists, social workers, and others concerned with mental health who seek to learn how to apply the democratic principles of Adlerian psychology to their particular field.

Notes for Chapter 20

1. Dreikurs, to his family, August 29, 1950, Dreikurs Papers.
2. Dreikurs, "Group Psychotherapy: General Review," pp. 223–239.
3. Dreikurs, Report no. 3, March 28, 1958, Dreikurs Papers.
4. Dreikurs to family and staff, March 15, 1958, Dreikurs Papers.. "Spitting in her soup," refers to an Adlerian psychotherapeutic strategy designed to modify behavior by changing its *meaning* to the person. It probably derived its name from the old boarding school technique of wrestling another's rations from him by spoiling it with spittle. See Thomas W. Allen, "Adlerian Interview Strategies for Behavior Change," *Counseling Psychologist* 3 (1971): 41.
5. In Dreikurs Papers.
6. Dreikurs, Report no. 3, March 28, 1958, Dreikurs Papers.
7. Dreikurs, to family and staff, April 2, 1958, Dreikurs Papers.
8. Dreikurs, to family and staff, April 10, 1958, Dreikurs Papers.
9. Davidson-Sonstegard interview, 1973.
10. Dreikurs, Report no. 3, September 16, 1960, Dreikurs Papers.
11. Dreikurs, Report no. 7, October 16, 1960, Dreikurs Papers.
12. Juliet Cavadas, personal communication, July 1973.
13. Ibid.
14. Frosso Keni to Raymond J. Corsini, July 7, 1967, Dreikurs Papers.
15. Juliet Cavadas, "Introducing Adlerian Principles in a Conservative Community: Rudolf Dreikurs' Contribution to Greece," in *Proceedings of the Rudolf Dreikurs Memorial Institute, ICASSI 1973, Espinho, Portugal, July 1973*, p. 1.
16. Dreikurs, Report no. 5, September 28, 1962, Dreikurs Papers.
17. Erik Blumenthal, personal communication, July 1973.
18. Ruth Bickel Holger-Nielsen, personal communication, July 1973.

21

Israel: Vision into Reality

"You will never know what you can do until you do it."
Rudolf Dreikurs
Tel Aviv, March 1963

The final destination of that momentous 1960 trip, which was already filled with the contradictions and surprises of Vienna and Athens, was Israel. As the El Al airliner made its landing approach to Lod Airport, the passengers spontaneously began singing "Hatikva," the national anthem of Israel. Tee was surprised to see tears roll down Rudolf's cheeks. Though a spiritual man, he felt no particular religious identity with Judaism. He had turned away from organized religion as a young man in Vienna, as part of the antireligious, assimilationist atmosphere that prevailed in the intellectual circles there. He never denied his Jewish origin, but spiritually his identification was more universalistic.

Tee's faith in Judaism was unfailing and a source of comfort and inspiration. Religion was one of the few areas in their marriage where their philosophical viewpoints differed, and no amount of discussion seemed to move either party. Dreikurs was interested in religion, but more from the standpoint of its philosophic meaning and role for humanity than from a personal feeling for it. He considered religion to have the potential to make an important contribution to social living. He speculated about a new religion for a democratic era in several papers and his book *Social Equality*. Whenever asked his religious affiliation, he would say, "By birth I am a Jew, by choice a Humanist."

Dreikurs's interest in the Humanist movement grew out of his friendship with Curtis W. Reese, which began in 1939. Reese was an important leader and a national president of the American Humanist Association (AHA) and attempted to make his Unitarian ministry the embodiment of the Humanist philosophy. He belonged to that branch of the Universalist Unitarian Association that is nontheistic and yet uses religious forms to promote distinctive human values. When Dreikurs became active in the Humanist movement, he occasionally lectured at Reese's church.

In a speech Dreikurs delivered there in 1949—in which he also laid down his ten premises for a Humanist philosophy of life—he traced the evolution of his attitude toward religion: "Before I came to America, before I had a chance to meet my Humanist friends, I had a rather dubious stand in regard to religion. I didn't agree with religious concepts which regarded the individual as a feeble, stupid, irresponsible being who had to rely on the reward . . . grace or punishment of a superior force which would keep him in line. I rebelled against that [and] did not move for many years, until recently, to the realization that religion has a function to perform in all our lives."[1]

Dreikurs never felt a sense of religious belonging with Judaism, and since he found nothing that could convince him of the existence of a supernatural being, he concluded that by definition he was not a Jew. He believed in Humanism as the expression of his spirituality and religion.

That is why he maintained, "By birth I am a Jew, by choice a Humanist." But it was an attitude that Tee could not share, and when he cried at the singing of "Hatikva," Tee nudged him, asking, "What's the matter with you? You're not a Jew. Why are you crying?" He replied, "I would cry if I landed in the midst of any young nation which is working out a new life." Tee did not accept that, she was not satisfied with that explanation at all. The same thing happened again when they were present at the opening concert of the beautiful new Mann Auditorium. Rudolf was always deeply moved by music and concerts, but when the audience rose that night to sing the Jewish national anthem he cried once again. Again, Tee challenged him, "Why are you crying? You're not a Jew." "But I feel part of this," he replied. "This is part of me." That was his acknowledgment, Tee reasoned, not directly as a Jew, but as an "Israeli."

Israel moved Dreikurs profoundly, and he soon came to feel as much or more at home in Israel as any place on earth.

One of the most moving experiences for Dreikurs occurred during a visit to Jerusalem on his and Tee's second trip to Israel. That day, they decided to climb Mount Zion to visit the tomb of David and the room of the Last Supper. Dreikurs thereafter wrote:

> For me the climb up the hill, over the valley and to the wall was almost more awe-inspiring than the shrines. . . . There was the loftiness of Mt. Zion crowned by the ancient wall with innumerable

vestiges of ancient times, walls of ancient synagogues, and Arab and Christian cemeteries, left and right of the path, which goes . . . to a dilapidated ancient stairway up the mountain. The whole atmosphere is one of wonderment, of silence and veneration . . . almost emerging from the ground on which you stood or walked. I really never had experienced anything like that before. (Tee's proof of my collective unconscious—another of our occasional disagreements). . . . In the same building [that houses the Tomb of David] was a memorial to the Nazi victims, called the Hall of Horrors. Tee first wanted to see it, then decided against it because of me—and then suddenly wanted to go. I was quite indifferent to whether I saw it or not, but went willingly. It was quite an experience, and of an entirely unexpected nature. They had there an exhibition of the desecration of the Torahs. . . . Tee was most affected by the soap made of Jewish fat, marked as such in German. Then there were the urns of ashes collected at the camps, and finally a black memorial with big black marble slabs each inscribed with one of the concentration camp names, and candles burning on each for some of its dead. There was one for Theresienstadt, next to that from Auschwitz. When I told the guide that my parents had been there, his voice turned into one of lament. He lit two candles, one for each of my parents and said the prayer for the dead. That really got both of us. It was the first time that I had a prayer said for my parents. And when the candles were placed on the tablet, it was as if there was a burial ground for my parents—the only tangible memory in the world of their departure. And that it will be forever. I arranged for yearly prayers for them, and the burning candles on Mt. Zion on the plaque of Theresienstadt will remain a memorial for them. That I didn't expect when I went up the slope of Mt. Zion. But that is Jerusalem, the City of Miracles.[2]

As Dreikurs's success grew in Israel, it filled him with great joy. He would say to Tee, "How could this happen to me? It's so wonderful." Tee, knowing that his mother was a devout Jew and early Zionist, teased gently, "It's not happening to you, it's happening to your mother." This amused him, Tee reflected. "He liked the idea. When he published the Hebrew version of *Social Equality*, he rededicated it to the memory of his mother. It was his own idea. It pleased him that he found a way to express his tie with her, with Jewishness, and with Israel."[3]

The excitement of their first arrival in Israel in 1960 filled the air and was intoxicating. He wrote home:

I know that you all are most eager to hear from us what our impressions of Israel are. To be frank, I too am eager to know what they are, and to find out by listening to what I am dictating. (Tee, too is eagerly awaiting what I will say, just as much as I am).

There can be no doubt that our experience here is different from any we had anywhere else. This country is different from any other; just what it is that is different, that is the question. Tee maintains it is my Jewish unconscious which made me respond strongly to this country, as part of my Jewish heritage. She feels that way herself. I don't know whether that is true for me too. I remember the elation which we both felt when we visited Haiti and for the first time saw a state entirely run by Negroes. We have never seen anything like that before and it made a deep impression on us. Something similar occurs here. . . . Here are all Jews, one people in all different disguises, forms and shapes, from the couple next door who look Chinese and were dressed like East Indians, to . . . the elegant models at the swank Hollywoodian Accadia Hotel in Herzliah, [and] to the maid and cleaning women at our hotel and in private homes, with their dark skin and utterly uncultured appearance, mostly from North Africa. We sat one evening at one of the many sidewalk cafes in the main street of Tel Aviv. The population in the cafes seems to be a very adequate reflection of the people of the country. . . . It seems as if the essence of the national perfume has been distilled in the sidewalk cafes. . . . The people sitting here in the cafes in Tel Aviv, . . . do not look too different from those in Paris, except that they are more informal and uninhibited both in appearance and behavior than any crowd we have ever seen. And you never see so many mixed types of culture, appearance, [and] color. . . . But one thing they all have in common, and that makes them different from any group anywhere else. They are the noisiest bunch I have ever seen. . . . Even what you see shouts . . . at you—the traffic, the hustle and bustle, the narrow squeeze through and squeeze by on streets and sidewalks. . . . The whole country, as far as we have seen . . . seems to shout, "look what we have done," or "what we are doing," or "what we intend to do." Everything is unfinished, but in the process of rapid completion. . . . Everything is somewhat stark, jolting, grasping, uneven. Next to the most fashionable house is the earth wounded with all kinds of rubble and ditches. Nobody bothers to straighten out the unevenness because it will be straightened out by new buildings and new farms. . . .

And what about the people themselves? The expressions of opinions which we encountered did not permit any conclusion. We are
baffled. I am convinced that we will be equally confused by contradictory opinions when we leave the country. These contradictions
seem almost to be a part of the shouting pattern of Israel. . . . It
seems to me that any integrated picture of Israel would be difficult to
form unless the contradictions and differences of opinion are as such
the best expression of what Israel is, a real Democracy, where each
one is free to think and feel as he chooses and makes considerable use
of this freedom.[4]

The trip to Israel was, of course, as much for professional purposes as
for any other. Dr. Esther Tauber, an Israeli who studied Individual Psychology at the Adler Institute in New York, first met Dreikurs in 1957 at a
meeting of the national society there. Before returning to Israel, she visited Chicago at his invitation to see the action-oriented work he was
doing, which fascinated her. They reached an agreement to include Israel
in his international training itinerary, with her as the contact for arrangements. When she arrived back in Israel, she initiated efforts for the translation of *Psychology in the Classroom* into Hebrew. His first visit, which
lasted four weeks, included a general course in Adlerian psychology and
psychotherapy for psychologists and doctors; a child guidance demonstration forum for the staff of the Israeli Social Service Department; a course
for the Probation Department with demonstrations in group work with
delinquent youths; a series of lectures for the Teachers' Association; and
public lectures for Hebrew University in Jerusalem, Bar Ilan University
and the Neuro-Psychiatric Society in Tel Aviv, and for the Medical Association in Haifa. In addition, he was introduced to leading figures in the
field of education with whom he argued for the urgency and significance
of new approaches to child rearing and education.

At that time, Israeli professional training in psychology, counseling,
psychotherapy, and social work was dominated by psychoanalytic
thought. There was a small group of older Adlerian therapists, many of
whom had migrated in the Hitler era to what was then Palestine. The
president of the small Israel Individual Psychology Association was Dr.
Wera Mahler, who had studied Adlerian psychology in Berlin, where she
was also a student of Kurt Lewin. She was a professor at Tel Aviv University and at the Teachers' College, but most of this group of older Adlerians were in private practice. For years, they met once a month for a

lecture or discussion, but that was all. There was little or no training in Adlerian methods. As in Europe, Adlerian psychology in Israel would have become extinct in another decade or so if the status quo were maintained. That status quo Dreikurs was determined to change, and he succeeded beyond even his optimistic expectations.

Starting nearly from scratch, for only a handful of Israelis knew of Dreikurs at all at that time, he quickly began to make an impact. "My talks to the public and to psychiatrists seem to have gained for me considerable respect, and my classes are much larger than anyone would have expected. Whenever I express an opinion it seems to fall on fertile ground. . . . I am the first adherent of any one school—except the Freudians—who was able to give courses and to train people."[5]

He sensed the pervasiveness of the Freudian influence, but detected a dissatisfaction among Israeli professionals. Commenting on his lectures to the Neuro-psychiatric Society of Israel, he wrote:

I was advised that the Psychiatrists are mostly Freudian oriented and would take me apart. I was careful and tried to take my sails out of their wind. And I succeeded. . . . Many psychologists and psychiatrists came there to size me up—and decided afterwards to study with me. The course for psychotherapists grew to over fifty. It includes . . . for the first time in my . . . experience, a goodly number of Freudians who are fascinated with a new approach. . . . The whole of Tel Aviv is talking about me. I knew that I could stir up interest and enthusiasm, as I did in Oregon, Jamaica, Delaware, and to a small extent in Athens. But I did not expect that it would go so fast in Israel. The field of psychology has been monopolized by the Psychoanalysts as it is in the States in psychiatry. I was even told I should feel at home here because of the strong American influence in this field. . . . The Universities seem dubious or hopeless. Everything is affected by American standards and procedures which are emulated. Psychology is primarily experimental, psychiatry is dominated by a small group of orthodox analysts. . . . The Psychoanalytic influence is waning here, and people are looking for more practical and effective approaches. Their concern with practical necessities is overwhelming and characteristic for this country. This makes them more open minded for heretofore untried ideas. . . . I started a fire, that I am sure. How much heat it will give and how long it will keep burning, that nobody knows.[6]

Reactions to Dreikurs were, as usual, indicative of his tremendous impact but often negative initially. Judith Eloul, a clinical psychologist working with the school system, attended his first lectures in Tel Aviv. "I didn't like him—he was aggressive and offended people, was my first reaction to him," she reflected. "I had gone to these lectures with Mica Katz, and we discussed him and both thought him a terrible person. After he left, I settled back into my work. We had some very difficult children with whom we were getting no results. After a while, I was so frustrated, I decided to try some of the ideas that 'bad' man suggested. 'What can I lose if I try them?' I thought. And I was sure that what he said wouldn't work anyhow. When I did try them, they worked. I was amazed. When he came back the next year, I made every effort to join his classes. I was ready to learn."[7] She and her colleague Mica Katz would become members of the first "intensive group" that trained under Dreikurs.

Achi Yotam, a rugged-looking young man, also encountered Dreikurs during that first visit. His experience was of a different quality. "I was a social worker for the city of Tel Aviv at that time, and had a young woman social worker, Hannah Tirosh, under my supervision. She happened to attend one of Dreikurs's sessions, and the next morning at work she said, 'You must go and hear this man.' 'Why?' I asked. 'Because you have something in common with him.' What she meant by that remark was my rebellion toward my strictly psychoanalytic training. I had a hard time adjusting to psychoanalytic ideas, I resisted them and even got into problems while in school. . . . I didn't know about Adler, didn't know an alternative approach even existed."

The first time Yotam saw Dreikurs do a demonstration, he was astounded. After interviewing the mother and before he even saw the child, Dreikurs told the audience what he expected would take place and the answers he expected the child would give. Yotam recalled:

> It all sounded very strange to me, but the amazing thing was that when the child came in, everything [Dreikurs] described would happen did. It seemed so strange, that I thought he had a certain suggestive power, that he used a subtle kind of hypnosis. Afterward, I told my young woman friend that it was an interesting evening, but I didn't think I could learn anything from him because he had extrasensory perception. It was a nice show, but what could he teach me? Hannah Tirosh disagreed.
>
> I wasn't too interested, but every day at the office, she kept nagging

me to come again. I did several times, and on each occasion, I had this same impression, and I began to tease Hannah for being so impressed with this man. Finally, one day, he failed. He interviewed a small boy, and it didn't go well, and he got harsh with the boy at a certain point, and the boy ran off crying. . . . The psychiatrist who brought the child for the demonstration got very upset and felt her patient had been mistreated.

"Who do you think you are?" she ranted at Dreikurs. "What gives you the right to treat a child like that?" And at that point, he got mad, and he started to scream right back at her. She became furious, and I thought she was going to hit him. I thought, we are going to have a terrible fight. At that point Tee Dreikurs stepped into the picture and asked them both to sit down, and she calmly tried to explain to both of them what had gone wrong. He sat there, his head resting on his hand, and collected himself. He then said to the group, "I want to thank Mrs. Dreikurs. You see I am still learning, too."

At that point something happened to the audience. Some were so disappointed that the "magic" of Dreikurs had failed that they were ready to leave. I felt differently. I mean, the interpretation I had of him changed. For the first time I saw him as a skilled human being who is not perfect, and I realized that these are skills, not magic, not ESP. If that is so, I concluded, then I am ready to study and work with him. I talked to him. He told me his visit was about to end, but he suggested I join with some other students who are forming a group and study with them.[8]

Yotam did join this small group of psychologists, psychiatrists, and social workers who wanted to study Dreikurs's ideas after he left Israel for Chicago. It included among others, Drs. Tauber and Mahler, as well as Judith Eloul, Mica Katz, and another young woman, Nira Kefir, who, like Eloul and Katz, had strongly opposed Dreikurs's ideas when she first encountered them.

"The group that gathered thought Dreikurs had a lot to offer; he stimulated our appetites to learn," Yotam said. "But we didn't get very far on our own. We didn't know enough, and we didn't have any material in Hebrew. We knew we would have to get him back again."

Dreikurs returned to Israel a second time in November of 1961 and stayed for four months. Again he held demonstrations and conducted courses for a variety of professionals working in the schools and state agencies. He taught at the University of Tel Aviv, and the University of Jerusalem, and trained probation officers in Tel Aviv. By the end of this stay he had had a considerable impact—but the students, whether teachers or social workers or psychologists, were still beginners. True they had learned new principles, a different approach to handling certain situations that worked, and had become enthusiastic. But Individual Psychology is deceptive. In theory it looks and sounds simple, but in practice, and especially in the consistent integration of theory with practice, there is unexpected subtlety and complexity. As a prominent physicist once remarked, "Physics is simple but subtle."[9] That also applies to Individual Psychology. Its basic tenets are few and remarkably easy to grasp in the larger sense. Turning them into a workable pattern of functioning reveals their complexity. It takes both training and experience to become a truly skilled practitioner of the principles. But the training of skilled practitioners was not Dreikurs's only aim. He also considered it imperative to train people who would in turn train others. For many neophyte students of Individual Psychology, there is an awesome gap between trying a new idea in a classroom with children or in the counseling of a family in private and demonstrating the principles and techniques in an open forum setting as Dreikurs did. It was a chasm few could imagine bridging.

The more years that passed and the older Dreikurs got, the more anxious he was to find, inspire, train, and encourage such individuals to carry on the work of teaching as well as practicing. By the end of this second visit, there was already a small group of genuinely enthusiastic students, eager to learn and dedicated, but mostly unable to see themselves performing the larger role Dreikurs had envisioned for them. Dreikurs considered this core group of more advanced students "the most important aspect" of his work in Israel.

His experiences in Oregon and even more so those in Israel led Dreikurs to approach his teaching on a new tack. Previously he would start his lectures with the theory of Adlerian psychology, then he would give demonstrations and describe practical applications. But too much time was lost in theoretical arguments. So he decided to conduct all introductory courses on a practical level, discussing only cases and problems. "I present my theoretical assumption as a working hypothesis which is not open for question since it is my personal choice, and serves merely to explain my practical approaches."[10] The student accepted this proposition readily, and the precious time spent arguing over theoretical issues that could not be proved anyway was now available for learning practical methods. His advanced training courses then became forums for examining theoretical issues. This made his efforts more efficient and diminished the sidetracking effect of people who were in fundamental disagreement with him on theoretical grounds. Now they learned the methods first, and if they worked, they were more open to a genuine discussion of the theoretical issues.

In Israel, Tee began to take an increasingly important role in all his efforts, in part because she was able to learn the Hebrew language easily, while he made little headway with it. Tee's growing contribution pleased him immensely:

> Tee is taking an active part in my classes, but [not quite as] we intended. She described her function best while we drove yesterday to the hospital—about half an hour out of Tel Aviv—to the early morning class. She was . . . sleepy, so she said she can fall asleep during my talk until she hears my voice getting louder. Then it will be time for her to move into action. And that she is doing consistently and very effectively, indeed. Whenever I get into a tangle with somebody, or something gets out of hand . . . she speaks up and takes the side of the one opposing me. But she does it so skillfully that it does not sound provocative or impertinent. And everybody loves her for it. It is most important for me because a few unpleasant situations can destroy the effectiveness of the whole session. . . . She always takes me off the hook. . . . Many times she brings new . . . points into the discussion.[11]

By the time this second visit ended, Dreikurs had discovered that Israeli youth and family life were experiencing much the same kind of disruptive rebelliousness as in the United States. Only it took on its own Israeli flavor and intensity:

> Of our attitude toward Israel, we see it with entirely different eyes than last year. I worked . . . with children . . . from all walks of life, the children of the Ministers and the financial leaders as well as those of the illiterate immigrants from the African States. I know that the problems of children seem almost insolvable. The function of the social worker for youth seems to be primarily . . . slowing down the process of the child being thrown out—from the family, from one school after the other, from a Kibbutz. . . . The social worker tries to

keep the child a little longer where he is—that's all she can do in many cases. Teachers particularly are unwilling to put up with the increasing number of misbehaving and highly disturbing children. Even the most devoted and typically Jewish parents want to have the child removed from the family [when] they feel they cannot control the child and he needs control for his own benefit. Each professional group blames the other for the difficulty and none knows what to do. If you can understand the youngsters then you can see in them the same spark of independence, guts and heroism which characterizes Israeli youth in general. These kids are not abnormal, but merely moving in the wrong direction. They are heroes without a cause. Unfortunately, the psychoanalytic influence and the prevalent social philosophies see only the abuse of children, their being rejected or neglected, and nobody sees to what extent they are spoiled and raised with the conviction that they have the right to get whatever they want—and primarily sympathy, thrill, and excitement. . . . A major change in the whole society in regard to children is mandatory, and I have accepted the challenge to move toward it."[12]

The "Intensives"

The following October (1962), Rudolf and Tee returned to Israel for an extended stay of seven months. The goal was to provide intensive, in-depth training for the core group of advanced students. It was a total-immersion experience. Tee recalled:

The students—psychologists, school counselors, teachers, social workers—all had full time jobs. Yet, most of them spent another thirty hours a week with us. They followed Dr. D. wherever he taught, demonstrated or lectured. Many hours were spent in our apartment—it was like Grand Central Station—two adjoining rooms which could separate by a sliding door, a small office, a kitchen and two verandahs. All were filled, either with those waiting for a private session, or a group study session. The refrigerator door opened and shut so often that the hinges had to be repaired at one time. Students came between other activities and had no time to eat. They checked and replenished food and I was a human coffee and tea dispenser. It was sheer joy to share their exuberance and enthusiasm, their youth and energy and the thought of a promise of such a marvelous group to carry on the work in Israel.[13]

"Everyday, we had sessions, sometimes from morning until late at night," Achi Yotam explained,

> We worked out all our life styles. He divided us into groups of four and we worked on each other's life styles, then we met in the larger group and with Dr. D. to compare notes, and he summarized the life styles. It had a tremendous effect on all of us—on our learning, in our private lives, in our relations as a group. We were transformed from a collection of individuals to a solid group that was interested in each other.
>
> He was so energetic! We often worked from morning until 11:30 or midnight. We'd all be exhausted, dying to go to sleep. And he would say, "Let's go for a walk by the sea," or "let's have some fun." "Dr. D., it's midnight," we would exclaim. "So, what," he replied. "What will you do all night?" "Sleep!" we proclaimed. "That's a waste of time!"

"The next morning at 7:00, he would call," Judith Eloul added. " 'What's new,' he would say, to launch the new day. We did group therapy, group demonstration, life styles. We all had some cases to work on, and we did double interviews with him."

Yotam and Eloul and Kefir and Tirosh regularly translated for Dreikurs when he gave his numerous lectures and demonstrations around Israel. "We translated his talks sentence by sentence, and he liked it very much. It was like team work or as he said, like playing duo pianos, which he loved. As time went by," Yotam remembered, "we got to the stage where we knew his material by heart, and we could finish his sentences before he did. When he finished the sentence, he would thus be repeating what I had already said. He'd wait, looking for me to finish. 'I already said it,' I explained, which always brought a big laugh."

Most of the "intensives," as they came to be known, were married and had families that often felt neglected or left out of the exuberance that characterized the feelings of this group. Eloul laughed, "My family used to tell me, 'The ceiling drips with Adler, the floors echo Dreikurs!' " So Dreikurs invited the "opposition," the spouses of the group members, to gather for a social event and lost no opportunity to try to involve them in a variety of projects, to utilize their professional skills in behalf of the large effort. It usually worked. One husband, when he first met Dreikurs, had a violent discussion with him, fell for Tee, and later confided, "He is extreme, but when one has to put an idea across, one has to believe that it is a universal panacea."[14] But in relaxed, thoughtful discussions, Dreikurs was not fanatical. He would explain that what he had to offer was the best available knowledge he had, but that knowledge expands, and in time, people will have better theories and techniques. He was always ready to accept new ideas and integrate them into his work if they were compatible with his theoretical views.

An experience with the intensive group demonstrated once again that with a purposive approach to behavior and the concept of the life style, one can, on occasion, effect a remarkable change in someone's conception of himself, and thereafter his behavior. The "intensives" wanted Dreikurs to demonstrate how he worked with groups. "Sure," he said, "present me with a group of patients, and we'll do it." So, someone brought in seven people in their late teens or early twenties—all stutterers. "It was a terrible trick to play on him," Tee recalled. "There was the problem of translation, plus the fact that they could not express themselves, and they stuttered all over the place. Hardly a suitable circumstance under which to demonstrate group processes."

But Dreikurs was game, and it turned out to be an interesting session. By the end of the evening, two of them had stopped stuttering altogether after he did some disclosures and talked generally about why people stutter. But there was one member of the group, Yaacov, who seemed feebleminded because every time a question was directed to him, he would answer with some statement that had nothing to do with what was going on. He seemed pathetic. But Dreikurs had a hunch and suggested very briefly that his inability to speak and his behavior were designed to keep everybody occupied with him and yet make no demands upon him. Later that evening, the intensive trainees evaluated the session with Dreikurs, and everyone agreed that it was a waste of time to have brought Yaacov, who did not get anything out of the session and was probably retarded. Dreikurs told them, "I think you are wrong."

The group of stutterers returned for a follow-up session and Dreikurs began it as he traditionally began every follow-up counseling session, by asking, "What do you remember from the last session?" They each remembered something, but Yaacov remembered everything Dreikurs said to him and repeated it almost verbatim. While he still stuttered, he had much improved in that regard and talked about going back to school, which he had quit some time earlier.

Following that, Yaacov saw Judith Eloul for additional counseling, but did not see Dreikurs again until a day or two before he and Tee were ready to leave Israel and return home. When the doorbell of their apartment rang, Dreikurs answered it but did not recognize the young man, and he could not understand his Hebrew, so he called Tee. "It was Yaacov," she later recalled, "but I hardly recognized him either, because his appearance had changed so dramatically. Instead of the disheveled, unkempt lad, he was neatly dressed, with a clean fresh shirt and his hair brushed back. He brought a book and a bouquet of flowers and told me that he came to say *shalom* before we left Israel, and then he departed. Inside the lovely book on Jerusalem was an inscription: 'Thank you, Professor, for helping me to understand that I can be like all other human beings.—Yaacov.'"

Late in March of 1963, just before Dreikurs left Israel, a farewell party was held. He told those dear new friends, the "intensives," that very few of his students had ever been as well trained as they, except his co-workers in Chicago. Achi Yotam never forgot Dreikurs's remarks that day. "You have all worked very hard these months, and it was a great effort for me too. And I want to tell you that if, after I leave, you don't start an institute and start teaching others what you have learned, I will consider the time I worked here as a waste."

"His absolute demand to start an institute was a shock to us," Yotam remembered,

> We were not prepared, as he had never mentioned it before, and we never thought about this possibility. We saw ourselves as beginners, and the idea of us running an institute was like picking up and going to the moon. Some people resented the idea and reacted immediately: "How can we do that, we don't know enough?" "You will learn by doing," he countered firmly. "You will never know what you can do until you do it. I don't care how you do it. I don't care how many difficulties—financial, technical, or whatever you might encounter. And I don't want to argue with you about it." But that was not all. He wanted our answer that night.
>
> We ended up giving him a commitment that we would do it. But we did it out of our personal feelings for him. He didn't convince us that we were capable. We surely felt we were not. We were so close to him, we loved him to such an extent that we couldn't say no.
>
> And sure enough, after he left, we did start the Alfred Adler Institute of Tel Aviv in the spring of 1963. The Department of Education

of Tel Aviv made a room available twice a week, and the institute began with a course for parents.

"We felt very inadequate," Eloul commented, "so we taught in pairs. At the time, I ran into personal opposition. I was well regarded by my colleagues, but they would typically say, 'Why do you mix with all this nonsense? You will ruin your career.' But we persisted, and now [1973] we are well accepted and our work is in high demand."

Dreikurs returned to Israel again in 1964/1965 for five months. This time he trained a second group of thirteen "intensives," in addition to eight courses he taught at universities in Tel Aviv or Jerusalem or for various government agencies. The institute was still small and generally unknown. Dreikurs made it a point that whatever he did was done in the name of the institute. When he was invited to give workshops or lectures, he would say, "I work for the Adler Institute, and you will have to make any arrangements for my services through them." Thus, he helped to make a name for the institute.

In the early years, the institute struggled to get off the ground. "We were good psychologists and good theoreticians, but we had our shortcomings because we were overworked," Eloul maintained. "We didn't write enough, and we were poor administrators." Whenever Dreikurs heard that the institute was having financial difficulties in those early years, he would send $500 or $1,000 or $1,500, whatever was needed. "He was most giving, very considerate about buying presents, sharing whatever he had, giving money away," Yotam observed.

ENCOUNTER AT EIN HOD

Rudolf Dreikurs, Jacob Moreno, and Fritz Perls were audacious pioneers in American psychiatry. All had the bold courage to risk demonstrating in open forums the way they did therapy. In no other applied professional discipline was there so much lack of information, so little opportunity to see and to learn, with all one's senses operating, the problems, skills, and insights that are essential to effective psychotherapy. This hampered the development of the field for decades. Dreikurs was a foremost pioneer in openly demonstrating what he did in therapy and counseling. Beginning in 1939, he did thousands of demonstrations—with families, children, adults, and groups in Chicago and throughout the

United States, Canada, the Caribbean, Brazil, Europe, and Israel. He knew the tremendous risks involved, the mistakes that would inevitably be made that would leave him wide open for attack and ridicule. Fritz Perls, the father of Gestalt Therapy, also pioneered in this way with demonstrations of his therapeutic approach. He borrowed the "hot seat" technique of Moreno and demonstrated it to a small number of students in the 1950s. But his methods were widely and publicly demonstrated beginning only in 1964, at the Esalen Institute in California, the spiritual center of the encounter movement.

There is considerable theoretical compatibility between the Adlerian and gestalt therapies. Both emphasize holism in their approach to understanding the individual, and both are based upon a similar model of man—one that emphasizes creativity, choice, self-determination, and the individual's responsibility for all his acts. Both are essentially existential in outlook, and Dreikurs recognized that both approaches were moving in the same direction. In a sense, Dreikurs's discovery, the "recognition reflex," is a gestalt phenomenon—a sudden insight or solution of a problem by recognition of its unitary pattern.[15]

For all their similarities, no two men were less alike in personality and general outlook. This was vividly revealed in an explosive encounter between them that took place in Israel in late 1962, shortly before Perls returned to the United States, where he became the famed "compleat guru" of the encounter movement.[16]

Eva Kirschner, an Israeli psychotherapist who became a student and close friend of Dr. D., described what took place the day she took him and Tee for an excursion into the Israeli countryside:

> We stopped at Ein-Hod, a village of artists on the slope of the Carmel Range. We had lunch there and were joined by a friend of mine, painter Ziporah Rubens, and a guest of hers, Dr. Fritz Perls, . . . the father of Gestalt Therapy. He was then in the midst of a crisis, about to abandon psychology and trying to cure his depression by traveling around the world. . . .
>
> The moment one saw the two of them together, it was clear that they must fight. Perls was a lean, demonic figure, a lone wolf set against the world and seeing in every attempt at friendship a threat to his independence. Dreikurs was rotund and convivial, insatiable in his curiosity for new people and new intimacies.
>
> They had a monumental exchange of venom, purely on a personal

basis, but which, of course, touched upon psychology, which left us all speechless. Perls sarcastically asked Dr. D. whether he still worked with his rubbish and announced that he is through with it. Dr. D., with exquisite politeness, smiling like a Cheshire Cat, said that not only does he go on but is extremely successful in his work and highly satisfied with it. Dr. D. was not too happy about the whole incident. He was ruthless to Perls to the point of cruelty, and it seemed to me at the time that there must have been a previous history of mutual dislike between the two. . . . [Or perhaps] two prophets in one small village were one too many. . . .

Dreikurs was loath to destroy. Whatever changes he wanted to achieve, he did so within the existing framework. Though he was a passionate fighter, what he fought for was never extreme: it was humanistic, balanced, and civilized. One of his outstanding contributions . . . was to teach that one has to fight to the bitter end for the gentle principles of democracy. Perls wanted to destroy and do away with the world as it is today. . . . Freud was his "unfinished business," because he could not do away with him completely.[17]

Dreikurs gave a brief account of the incident in his letters back to the United States: "In he came to the restaurant where we were sitting. 'What are *you* doing here?' was our mutual approach. He is the psychiatrist who developed Gestalt psychotherapy, who lost interest in the world. . . . He wants to find himself in learning to paint. You can imagine how I reacted to that. We had a free-for-all—two extremes meeting and clashing with the others watching in excitement. America in Israel—it was comical if it had not been so tragic. Two men coming from the same background, the same cultural atmosphere, and the same activity to . . . Israel, and finding here . . . opposite fulfillment."[18]

Did Dreikurs have an impact on Perls? No one can say, but shortly afterward, Perls ended his wandering search and returned to the United States, but as he put it, "still dragging my dismay with my profession as a heavy burden on my hunched shoulders. There was a meeting of the American Academy of Psychotherapy with three events that stand out. . . . The third was an outburst of despair I had during a group session. The outburst was for real. Violent sobbing, not minding the presence of strangers, *de profundis*. This outburst did it. Afterwards I was able to reassess my position and was willing to take up my profession again."[19]

THE MOMENTUM BUILDS

When Dreikurs departed Israel in the spring of 1963, he did not return directly to Chicago as he usually did. Instead, he and Tee headed east to complete an around-the-world tour. They spent several days in India, where Dr. D., of course, lost no time creating controversy and excitement over his ideas in a variety of lectures before the Indians and some of the Americans living there. He left in his wake a group of interested people who have continued to study his ideas and books. He also lectured briefly in Australia while visiting his daughter, Eva, and her family there.

Upon returning to Chicago, he felt some intestinal discomfort and went for a physical exam. A lesion in the lower bowel was discovered, cancer was suspected, and surgery was ordered. Dreikurs's reaction was:

Since the diagnosis was highly probable—although I couldn't believe it—and nobody could predict the outcome, it began to be a hellish nightmare particularly for Tee. I was stunned. I was functioning alright—but like a puppet, mechanically. Something happened to me. I must say, I was not afraid at any moment; but I looked at my own body as a rather strange object. Frankly the idea of having a cancer did not fit my concept of myself. . . .

The first four days after the operation were tough on me. . . . It took two days for the pathological examinations to be finished. And then the whole spook was over, thank God. It turned out that the tumor was probably quite old; I probably had it already in Israel. But my immunity against the cancer cells had held out. Even the glandular nodules in the immediate proximity and the tissues around it were completely free. There was a process of intense inflammation in the area where my body fought off the intrusion of the cancer cell, of the tumor in it. It restored my faith in my own body. . . .

The [upshot] of [it] all is that I had a cancer and that I am perfectly well again. Everything was removed and there is no danger for any recurrence. It seems to me that in order to get the second breath in life one has to overcome at least a coronary or a cancer. I feel like a newborn, certainly like having a new lease on life. And I am sure I will make the best use of it.[20]

In the aftermath of this bout with cancer, and though it is impossible to imagine how he would squeeze more into his life, Dreikurs's activities and plans only further increased, both in the United States and abroad. When he returned to Israel the following year, he took on a new group for in-depth training, the "second intensive," which in succeeding years added to a solid group of trained counselors, psychologists, and social workers. They formed the backbone of the institute's steady progress and have demonstrated outstanding service to their small nation, which is beset by more than the ordinary share of serious social problems. These include immigrant absorption from primitive cultures; refugees from the Soviet countries; the tragedies of war; as well as all the problems of a modern Western nation whose traditions in family life and education are experiencing serious breakdowns.

Always Dreikurs was moving to spread the knowledge he had acquired over forty years of professional work. In Israel he found a more receptive audience than in the United States. The Israelis, he found, were much like Americans in terms of equality and democratic functioning, and in some areas, such as in the kibbutz heritage and the professional roles of women, they were even ahead of the United States. Moreover, the Israelis are practical people, and Dreikurs's ideas had great appeal to many, not only for their effectiveness but also ideologically. Consequently, Dreikurs accomplished things in Israel that never materialized in the United States or that developed only after they were first tried out in Israel. All of these developments centered around what Dreikurs considered to be the necessary adjunct to his theory of social equality. It was a technology of human relationships, a series of principles of human interaction, democratic leadership, and conflict solving that were appropriate to the new democratic era that was rapidly spreading throughout the United States, Canada, Israel, and Europe. As Dreikurs's impact grew with each succeeding visit to Israel, he was able to embark on new avenues of work, advising the military and applying his ideas there and to labor-management relations, government administration, and even to a limited, yet highly significant degree, international relations.

A TECHNOLOGY OF HUMAN RELATIONS

A major breakthrough for testing his ideas about democratic functioning—his new "technology of human relations"—came in the mid-

1960s and from a most unexpected segment of the community—the military. Its inception followed a discussion Dreikurs had in Beersheba late in 1962 with Dr. Ginton Shelef, then with the Israeli Defense Ministry. It was just after the Cuban Missile Crisis and the ensuing power struggle between the United States and the Soviet Union. Dreikurs told Shelef that he had predicted the outcome of the crisis on the basis that nations interact with each other very much as individuals do, and that group dynamics were applicable to nations and other large groups and were not limited to small groups. At the Defense Ministry, Shelef had to deal with rapidly deteriorating relations between labor and management. His attempts to improve the situation were unsuccessful. He therefore was curious to learn more about Dreikurs's ideas.

"I was a chemical engineer," Shelef related, "and had never studied anything in psychology—not even as an amateur. As an engineer, I was willing to try most things and willing to experiment with his ideas regarding human relationships." So Shelef attended Dreikurs's course for school administrators that was held in Tel Aviv, as the only student without a background in either the social or the behavioral sciences. He was fascinated by what Dreikurs did with young children in the demonstrations. "He proved to me that what he was trying to do worked. But," he also noted, "the administrators and teachers could not believe or accept what he said. They were mostly 'blocked.' They were not even critical—they just sat there proving to themselves that nothing can be done with children, which they had concluded long before." By contrast, Shelef immediately put the ideas into practice, first with his family and then with his business associates and found that they "really worked." As Dreikurs told him, "You don't have to understand theory, you can learn the technique, just as is the case in engineering. Any scientist, or doctor, or engineer does not always understand everything he does. If he knows it works, and that it is a good technique, he doesn't care why it works."[21]

Following this experience, Shelef arranged a three-lecture seminar for industrial leaders sponsored by the Defense Ministry. Shelef was surprised that Dreikurs wanted to do a demonstration of family counseling before a group of industrialists and managers. Dreikurs explained that the principles are the same whether applied in disturbed relationships in a family or in school or in industry. And since most people who attended the seminar had children of their own, they could see more quickly the issues involved and the possible application in a work setting. He pointed out that when you strip away the veneer, the issues involved are the

same: whether I am the boss, and he is *my* laborer; I am the father, and
he is *my* child; or I am the husband, and she is *my* wife. The nature of the
conflict in all these situations is identical.

> Generally, it is a question of who wins and loses. As long as labor
> mediators only deal with "rights"—who is right and who is wrong—
> one will not be able to solve anything. Because solving one conflict
> will only lead to another conflict. We have to learn to deal not with
> the logical but the psychological reason for the conflict. Why is the
> worker demanding so much, what is labor fighting for? There is a
> need for improvement in wages, conditions, and so on, but in con-
> flicts, we go about the solution in the wrong way, trying to impose
> our ideas upon each other. . . . If we treat each other with contempt,
> with threats, with all kinds of hostility, we can never create the
> willingness to settle a problem in an amicable way. . . . We have to
> get together and get behind the logical objects of the conflict to what
> really bothers us—power, retaliation, revenge.[22]

The lecture series was successful, and the upshot was that Dreikurs
became an advisor and consultant to the Air Force Training School at
Haifa under the sponsorship of Col. Yaacov Shalmon, a strapping military man who became an enthusiastic booster of Dreikurs's ideas. Youths
go there for military preparatory and technical training prior to entering
the service. It was run with strict military regimen but was failing in its
mission. Many students quit or were nearly failing academically. Dreikurs
trained the staff in the principles of democratic leadership. The whole
school was shifted to a democratic structure, without punishment and
with participation in decision making. Academic achievement improved,
and discipline improved with it, all in an atmosphere that boosted the
morale and sense of purpose of the students and teachers. In succeeding
years, Dreikurs gave frequent seminars and lectures for high-ranking
Israeli military figures in the principles of democratic leadership. These
were will received and became integrated into the thinking of what is, by
all accounts, the most egalitarian army in the world. This pleased Dreikurs immensely. He exclaimed, "If democratic leadership can work successfully in a military institution, then it can work anywhere."[23]

THE MOVEMENT

With the steady growth of parent study groups both in the United States and Israel, Dreikurs began to think more and more in terms of a "movement." This was not a cultist notion, but something precise and meaningful—"an integration of well-defined problems and tasks directed toward a definite goal."[24] He envisioned a widespread grass roots organization linking professional and lay people in a concerted effort to introduce the principles of democratic human relationships at all levels of the community. It was a staggering idea—unrealistic in many ways. Yet few people were as committed to realism as Dreikurs. It was just another example of his insistence that one had to start putting ideas into practice—somewhere, and *now*—in whatever way one could.

The movement Dreikurs envisioned first began to take shape in the late 1960s in Israel. Spearheading the new organization, the Association for the Betterment of Human Relations, was Alex Omri, director of the Institute for Training and Productivity in the Building Trades and a lieutenant colonel in the army reserve. A practical and effective leader in the industry, he was captivated with the potentiality of Dreikurs's ideas. He remarked that in the course of his career, "I had participated in many courses on Human Relationships, but none, until Dreikurs's seminar, touched me as much, mainly because it was based on a very important value—equality." Since its beginning in 1968, the association, which is comprised of people from all walks of life and works in conjunction with the Alfred Adler Institute, has devoted itself to disseminating the ideas of a "new democratic tradition." "I'm in a very practical business," Omri continued, "and if I didn't see results from all this, I wouldn't spend five minutes on it."[25]

The association's activities have included forums, study groups, the establishment of a Manager's Counseling Center, and meetings with specific community groups—teachers, parents, managers, administrators, and the military.

During Dreikurs's last extensive visit to Israel in 1969, the Civil Service Commission of Israel sponsored a series of lectures given by Dreikurs before the top leadership in industry and labor. It was the first time he had been able to reach into the higher echelons of governmental and industrial leadership in a significant way. Recalling the impact of those lectures, Omri commented that some adopted the new approaches Dreikurs introduced, while others were skeptical, but he did convey the idea that equality had implications in daily conduct that can be implemented and practiced. In consequence, Dreikurs was invited to work with the directors of the Civil Service Commission in a more intensive training seminar. It was a convincing experience. "It was not therapy, it was human relations, and a very intensive effort with the directors," Omri said.[26]

A direct result of this work was Dreikurs's formulation of his *Four Principles of Conflict Resolution*, which he considered an essential part of a new "technology of human relations."[27] Conflicts exist and are indeed inevitable wherever people live and work together. In the past, such conflicts were resolved by the person or group in power, and the subordinate had to accept the terms of that solution. Such resolutions are based on a superiority-inferiority model of relations. This no longer works, because nobody is willing to accept imposition and defeat in today's democratic atmosphere, and every victory is short-lived. In a democratic atmosphere, successful conflict resolution can only take place when the equal value and dignity of each party is taken into consideration. The four steps he considered necessary to such successful conflict resolution are:

Step 1: Mutual Respect. Each party must grant the other the legitimacy of his stand. The guideline is neither to fight nor to give in. Fighting violates respect for the other party; giving in violates respect for oneself. Refusing to yield to undue demands is powerful if it is done in quiet firmness and not in an atmosphere of heated arguments where all accuse each other and no one really listens. Most hostilities result from deep discouragement, where one gives up hope of reaching a satisfactory and fair conclusion. Often the very first sign of understanding and respect for the opponent will melt his opposition. Encouragement of ourselves and our opponent is essential to the process.

Step 2: Pinpointing the Issue. Most conflicts arise over the consequences, but not the causes, of what is wrong. In every conflict—whether it is a labor dispute, a disagreement between spouses, or a child who refuses to do what he should—the factual situation is not the real issue. One must look for the goal behind the conflict and pinpoint the underlying psychological issue. The real issue at stake usually centers on feelings of resentment, humiliation, hurt, or defeat. Put another way, the issue revolves around "Who is right?" or "Who has the power to decide?" or "Who counts?"

Attitude is essential to successful conflict resolution. As Dreikurs pointed out, "When you like someone you will be inclined to do what he wants even if he has no "right" to demand it, and when you dislike somebody, you may not do what he wants although you may know he is right."[28]

Step 3: Mutual Agreement. The guideline here is "change yourself and thereby change the other." Dreikurs contended it is a mistaken notion to assume that conflict and fighting mean a breakdown in communication or a lack of cooperation. You can't fight with someone unless you indicate to him that you want to fight, and get his consent and cooperation to go along with it. Compromises and what are often mistakenly called "mutual agreements" are ineffective—and immoral—when they are obtained under duress or through pressure and imposition. Agreements obtained through force only plant the seeds for future conflicts, each preparing the stage for the next round of disagreement.

To break this vicious circle, one can decide what he will do. Everyone has the power to decide what kind of relationship he will develop, regardless of what the other party does. One needs to ask, "What can I do?" rather than demand what the other party should do. When one decides what he can do, then new, constructive actions, are possible.

Step 4: Shared Responsibility. The issue today is participation in decision making. "You simply cannot make any decision for anyone else, not even your child," Dreikurs often remarked. Shared responsibility requires democratic leadership, which can and must be taught in our homes, schools, and government institutions. Such leadership can enable people to come together to listen to each other, to recognize the reality of their common problem, and to share in deciding the outcome. In the right atmosphere even enemies can participate in deciding the question "What are we going to do about *our* problem?"

Dreikurs maintained that these four principles of conflict solving can be applied by everyone without too much training—assuming the individual will attempt them with an attitude of good will and a willingness to abandon beliefs held from past experiences. He regarded these principles as part of a new "technology of human relations" and not just as isolated techniques. Every nation, whether past or present, has a "technology" of relationships—a set of beliefs and values with a corresponding system of techniques or transactions for the conduct of human affairs. As we emerge from the autocratic past with its technology of superior and inferior relationships, a new technology must be developed that fits the democratic requirement of respect and equality.

A SMALL BEGINNING

Only after Dreikus's death did one of his farsighted plans become reality. The idea came to him following the Six Day War in 1967. He then began pushing for the immediate establishment of a dialogue between the Israelis and the Arabs who lived on the west bank of the Jordan River, now occupied by Israel and under its jurisdiction. Moshe Dayan had been thinking along the same lines, but official Israeli policy regarding the fate of the occupied territory was not clear, and Dreikurs's friends and even Tee thought his ideas were premature. Dreikurs felt that a genuine dialogue using Adlerian principles would alleviate the suspicions that the Israelis and Arabs harbored toward each other. He argued for the proposal for months, and it was only Tee's threat to return to Chicago and the persuasiveness of his army friends that forced him to abandon the idea, at least temporarily.

The first attempt to implement his plan came in December 1972, when a one-day seminar for Arab principals and teachers of East Jerusalem was held. It was conducted under the auspices of the Jerusalem municipality, in cooperation with the Ministry of Education and the Alfred Adler Institute.

In addition, Alex Omri instituted study groups with Arab mothers, and commented: "Their problems were just like those of Jewish mothers—how to get the children to study, relationships between husband and wife. The problems are there—even though in the traditional, autocratic Arab society, they have been submerged."

Achi Yotam approached the Arab community by working with the teachers:

> It is kind of difficult to work with families—especially Moslem families—because the wife is not allowed to come to a public place and they have to overcome strong religious beliefs in order . . . to attend. [The] fathers are very autocratic and believe in autocracy. We decided the best place to break through was the teacher. I must say that the work with the teachers was very fruitful. . . . Some of them did very interesting things to create a democratic atmosphere in their classrooms. If we have a chance with the Arabs, it is through the Arab teachers. But they too think it is too early to do family counseling with the traditional Arab family. . . .
>
> We see now the first generation to rebel against the autocratic

scheme of the traditional Arab society that has prevailed for hundreds of years. But these people are still young and they do not have families of their own. . . . I can foresee that the youngsters that are now 16, 18, and 20 will be different when they marry.[29]

Omri emphasized in discussions with the Arab students that the common goal for all Israelis is to create a genuine democratic society. If the Arab population would participate in the process of creating such a democracy, then both Arab and Jewish culture could coexist in mutual respect and harmony.

Nothing would have given Dreikurs greater satisfaction than to have been an active participant in that small beginning.

Notes for Chapter 21

1. Rudolf Dreikurs, "Science and Your Emotions," Speech given February 9, 1949, at the Third Unitarian Church, Chicago, Dreikurs Papers.

2. Dreikurs, Report no. 6, January 8, 1961. Dreikurs Papers.

3. Sadie "Tee" Dreikurs, personal communication, September 1974. Additional quotes from Tee Dreikurs, unless otherwise specified, are from this communication.

4. Dreikurs, Report no. 8, October 27, 1960, Dreikurs Papers.

5. Ibid.

6. Dreikurs, Report no. 10, October 31, 1960, Dreikurs Papers.

7. Judith Eloul, personal communication, July 1973. Additional quotes from Eloul are from this communication.

8. Achi Yotam, personal communication, July 1973. Additional quotes from Yotam, unless otherwise specified, are from this communication.

9. Quote attributed to Ehrenfest in Victor F. Weisskopf, *Physics in the Twentieth Century* (Cambridge, Mass.: M.I.T. Press, 1972), p. 3.

10. Dreikurs, Report no. 1, November 21, 1961, Dreikurs Papers.

11. Dreikurs, Report no. 12, December 12, 1961, Dreikurs Papers.

12. Dreikurs, Report no. 8, February 2, 1962, Dreikurs Papers.

13. Sadie "Tee" Dreikurs, "My Life with Rudolf Dreikurs."

14. Eva Kirschner, "My Personal Memories of Professor Dreikurs in Israel." Typescript, July 5, 1973, p. 4.

15. Heinz L. Ansbacher to Dreikurs, June 2, 1967, Dreikurs Papers. In this letter, Ansbacher enthusiastically pointed out the significance of Dreikurs's concept of the recognition reflex and noted its intrinsic relationship to the "aha!" experience, first described by Karl Bühler. "The recognition reflex," he wrote, embodies the "flashlike expression which accompanies the joyful experience of a sudden insight into, and solution of a problem . . . which is defined by the therapist and which the counselee accepts with astonishment about the excellent fit of the interpretation. . . . The recognition reflex shows that Adlerian therapy provides a sudden, insightful learning in accordance with its general kinship to Gestalt psychology."

16. Walt Anderson, "Fritz Perls Revisited," *Human Behavior* 2 (1973): 23.

17. Eva Kirschner, personal communication, August 1973.

18. Dreikurs, Report no. 12, January 9, 1963, Dreikurs Papers.

19. Frederick S. Perls, *In and Out the Garbage Pail* (New York: Bantam Books, 1972), p. 135.

20. Dreikurs, Report, October 10, 1963, Dreikurs Papers.

21. Ginton Shelef, from an interview conducted by Eva Kirschner, June 1973.

22. Dreikurs, *Human Patterns in a Changing Society*, p. 19.

23. Hannah Tirosh, personal communication, June 1977. Dreikurs frequently cited Kurt Lewin's famous Iowa Boy's Clubs experiments in 1939 and Lewin's book, *Resolving Social Conflicts* (New York: Harper & Bros., 1948), for inspiring his own thinking regarding democratic leadership. See: Rudolf Dreikurs, Bernice Bronia Grunwald, and Floy C. Pepper, *Maintaining Sanity in the Classroom* (New York: Harper & Row, 1971), pp. 176–178.

24. Dreikurs, "Early Experiments in Social Psychiatry," p. 143.

25. *Jerusalem Post*, December 29, 1972.

26. Alex Omri, from an interview conducted by Eva Kirschner, June 1973. Additional quotes from Omri are from this interview.

27. Rudolf Dreikurs, "Technology of Conflict Resolution," *Journal of Individual Psychology* 28 (1972): 203–206. "Toward a Technology of Human Relationship," pp. 127–136.

28. Dreikurs, Report no. 9, January 27, 1970, Dreikurs Papers.

29. Harold V. McAbee, "Adlerians at Work in Israel—An Interview with Achi Yotam," *Individual Psychologist* 13, no. 2 (1976): 6–15.

22

Last Years and Legacy

Cathedrals were not built by saints. The splendor of mankind is not always accomplished by glorious folk, but by
faithful ones. . . . What does leadership consist of? Surely
it is to have a vision of the future and the courage to walk
on it.

Henry Kissinger
1974

At the age of seventy, Dreikurs retired from the Chicago Medical School
and from an active role with his associates in private practice:

I never enjoyed myself so much as now when I am finally retired. I
became Emeritus Professor of the Chicago Medical School, which
is—I am told—a special honor, since most University Professors just
retire. While I was not very active at the Chicago Medical School for
a long time, as Professor Emeritus I will never be retired, but always
a consultant in the department of psychiatry. Imagine that, if you
know what difficulties I had at the School when the Psychoanalysts
took over. Now suddenly everybody wants to get on the bandwagon
and join me. A new experience in my life, indeed. And now when I
also retired from my office, I am completely free of any responsibility
and can do whatever I want.[1]

That same year, 1967, his longtime friends and colleagues feted him
with a marvelous birthday party at the Pick Congress Hotel in Chicago.
Messages of appreciation and goodwill from all parts of the United States
and from Canada, England, Germany, Switzerland, Denmark, Greece,
and Israel were read at the gathering. They characterize the immense
scope of his accomplishments during a career that spanned five decades.

His achievements were all the more remarkable because they were
accomplished in the face of continual opposition that few could have

withstood, let alone surmounted. So Dreikurs had every reason to be proud of his record and could easily have retired to California's sunny clime, there leisurely to write books and pursue all his neglected hobbies.

He could also devote more time to his beloved family. He felt great satisfaction that Eric and Eva had chosen psychology as their professions, for it reflected their regard for their father's work. Neither chose to follow exactly the same path he had taken. Eric, with the touch of the rebel like his father, adopted a differing ideological stance early in his career and settled in California, where he is in private practice as a clinical psychologist. In the latter years of his father's life, he moved closer to his father's theoretical position, and they collaborated in writing. His daughter, Eva Dreikurs Ferguson, currently professor of psychology at Southern Illinois University in Edwardsville, studied and worked with her father and became a close colleague. Her interests are oriented more toward academic and research psychology. "I owe both of them a great deal for helping me in my work,"[2] Dreikurs acknowledged. A loving and proud grandfather, he dedicated his last book to his four grandchildren.

But Dreikurs was not ready to retire. There were still obstacles to be surmounted, and a vision to be pursued. He was particularly dissatisfied with the state of the American Society of Adlerian Psychology (ASAP), which he, more than anyone else, had created and nurtured. Over the years, the split had grown between the conservative Adlerians centered in New York under the leadership of Drs. Alexandra and Kurt Adler and the activist group that had developed under his leadership. For years the meetings and policies of ASAP were controlled by the New York branch, which outnumbered Dreikurs and his colleagues. That group generally rejected his repeated efforts to transform what had become a rather erudite professional organization into an action-oriented, broadly based one. The membership had remained consistently low.

The tide began to turn, especially after 1967, as growing numbers of Dreikurs's students and colleagues joined the society. That year, Dreikurs was asked for the first time to demonstrate his method of family counseling at the annual meeting. In all the years that Dreikurs had actively been teaching by demonstration, most of the older and eastern Adlerian colleagues had never witnessed him in action. Heinz L. Ansbacher wrote to Dreikurs afterwards that it was a great experience that provided him with an opportunity to "learn what cannot be learned otherwise. . . . We think that demonstrations and workshops should be conducted at all future meetings."[3]

Ansbacher's new enthusiasm for Dreikurs's approach led to an invitation to conduct a summer course for teachers at the University of Vermont the following summer. The course he taught there in 1968 was video-taped and made available for national distribution through the Public Broadcast System stations and the public schools. The response to the course was enthusiastic, and Dreikurs returned to Vermont for the next three summers, where each year another television series was produced.[4] The film series is noteworthy because it offers an opportunity to see Dreikurs demonstrating his techniques and training others to attempt them under his supervision. It captures his technique of making guesses that he knew would sometimes be wrong, but that he also knew would more quickly establish the real situation through the feedback he received than would the endless fact gathering—"factophilia," as he disparagingly called it.

After 1968, the annual meetings of ASAP devoted much of the program to workshops and demonstrations that attracted a growing number of curious non-Adlerian professionals, who were impressed with what they witnessed and took back new ideas to their campuses or practices. A spurt of growth and a new vitality within the organization followed.

Reflecting on the longstanding difficulties between the New York and Chicago groups, there emerges what one might call a classic case of sibling rivalry. At a time when Adlerian psychology's survival as a viable school of thought was being threatened and when there was no effective leadership, Dreikurs moved with determination to fill the vacuum. He raised the Adlerian banner and carried it proudly and defiantly through all those years of attack and rebuff. He worked with great dedication to make ASAP the unified voice of Adlerian psychology. Yet with his assumption of a forceful leadership role, Dreikurs evoked a rivalrous relationship with the Adler family, who by name, loyalty, training, and belief felt themselves the rightful spokesmen and heirs to Adler's legacy.

The antagonisms of earlier years have diminished, and Kurt Adler recently acknowledged: "The main trend today seems to veer toward prevention. Adlerian psychology . . . has always been in the forefront in this area. Many years ago in Vienna, Adler adopted the motto 'teach the teachers.' . . . In this country, however, Dreikurs demonstrated that the parents themselves could be trained, and the tremendous impetus he gave . . . has already made an enormous impact, occupying the major efforts of many Adlerian groups and Societies."[5]

The last five years of Dreikurs's life were the most event-filled and rewarding of all. He traveled all over the United States, to Canada, to Jamaica, and back and forth to Europe and Israel. Everywhere, he gave lectures, demonstrations, seminars, and workshops and promoted his ideas with tireless zeal. The opposition he had always faced had faded. People were ready to hear what he had to say, anxious to learn new ideas. Professionals were less entrenched in their thinking. The impact was tangible. Study groups for parents proliferated. Professional training was sought in order to promote wider adaptation of Adlerian approaches in education and in the mental health fields. By 1976, Adlerian training institutes were functioning in Chicago; New York; Minneapolis; Toronto; San Francisco; Dayton, Ohio; and Bowie, Maryland (the Baltimore–Washington area). Training was also available through university courses in every region of the United States and Canada.

Adlerian psychology could at last come out of the closet. When professionals discovered that their work would be respected, they were willing to identify with Adlerian psychology. Though still relatively few in number, the effectiveness of these professionals in training people to work in schools, hospitals, and with families, delinquents, or individuals in therapy, has enabled them to assume an influential role among their colleagues.

The movement Dreikurs envisioned was beginning to gain momentum, but it was diffused across the nation and into Canada and was without centralized direction. It just happened. People wanted to share what they had learned with their friends and neighbors, with their children's teachers, and with anyone else who would listen. To overcome the ingrained pessimism that "nothing works with children" as well as the label of "cultism," which arose because of their great enthusiasm, their approach to others was: "Try it—experiment—find out for yourself if the ideas work or not."

In 1967, Dreikurs wrote to a close colleague, "Your main job now is to train people. And demonstration is the best training device, and could and should be done in public. I am even going beyond the requirement that that public should be primarily professionals. It is time we draw the lay public into our movement. As a matter of fact, I am trying to develop a new group of 'professional lay people.' They will have to play a larger part, not only to change the values of our society, but our institutions as well, schools, youth bureaus, etc."[6] Pioneering programs in paraprofessional training were subsequently begun in Wilmington, Delaware; and Washington, D.C.

Dreikurs always functioned with two goals in mind. One was to gain wider recognition of the long-neglected but highly relevant system of psychology originated by Alfred Adler. The other was to assure the continued development of this coherent and comprehensive system through well-trained professionals who would carry on his commitment to train others. Early in his career in America he had discovered the drawbacks to eclecticism: "Many scientists try to integrate Individual Psychology with other existing psychological theories. They believe that they can take one part of Adler's ideas and link it with some part of another school. What they actually establish thereby is not eclecticism which prides itself on taking the good parts from each school and discarding the bad. They create only new theories, often with more shortcomings and onesidedness than they attributed to the original schools."[7]

That explains why he labored so to train skilled transmitters of Individual Psychology. That also explains his great interest in a "movement." "Without a movement, we cannot spread," he wrote. "We need to motivate our students to identify themselves with a movement. Otherwise they learn from us what they can and go afterwards their own way and soon lose their identity and ability to train other Adlerians."[8]

Early in 1971, after a stimulating and rewarding trip to Hawaii, Dreikurs returned to Chicago. Not feeling well, he entered the hospital for tests that indicated surgery for prostate cancer. After several operations and hospitalizations, he emerged an ill, weakened shadow of his former self. He was seventy-four years old and had enjoyed good health and limitless energy throughout a long and hectic life. He had recovered rapidly from his earlier bout with cancer and again upon suffering a mild heart attack after his seventieth birthday. For someone as active as he, who still had so much to do and who had such great faith in his ability to rally in the face of adversity, it was a terrible blow. For the first time, he experienced depression and the awareness of impending death. He was not afraid of dying, but he would not accept it without a fight, just as he had fought all other obstacles in his life. He did not know if he could win this battle, but his basic optimism resurfaced time and again.

"He did not know how to be sick gracefully," Harold Mosak remarked. "As much in pain, uncomfortable, and sometimes depressed as he was, he did not lose his sense of humor. One Sunday I received a call to come and see him. . . . He was depressed and behaved like every depressed patient. He knew all the patients' tricks very well. I decided that to get him out of this depression I had better do what he taught me, that is, get the patient angry. So I set out to provoke him, and I got him real angry. He flared at me. But right in the middle, he stopped, smiled, shook his finger at me, and said, 'Harold, I taught you too good!' "[9]

Ill as he was in his last remaining year, plagued by persistent pain, frequent hospitalizations, and the awareness of his waning energy, he was more concerned about Tee's emotional pain than his own physical suffering. He continued to work, to make plans, and to write as he always had. In the summer of 1971, he "met his obligations"—conducting a week-long workshop at a university, completing his fourth and last television program at the University of Vermont, and returning to Bad Kissingen (West Germany) and Israel to lead the International Adlerian Summer School, as he always had since he initiated it in 1962.

In public, the casual observer would not have been aware of the extent of his difficulties. But for Tee and those close to him it was a torturous time. "His will to carry on was a source of unbelievable wonder," Tee reflected. "I had witnessed his courage all through our marriage, I had experienced his dedication to the task at hand, but this last period was something of a miracle."

In Germany and Israel, the other faculty members for the summer school made a pact: They would not be dependent on his contribution and would be ready to step in as substitutes at the last minute. To their amazement it was never necessary. "Before leaving for his assignments it appeared that he would not have the strength to get out of bed, but after a few minutes at the beginning of this task when he looked too feeble to talk, one could witness the adrenalin flowing—his appearance changed miraculously, and his brilliant performance would ensue."[10]

That summer, in one of his last statements, Dreikurs reflected on the meaning of his life's work:

> It is clear that at first Individual Psychology was not recognized or given full value because it appeared too superficial in comparison, for instance, to Psychoanalysis. But the Law of Parsimony has again discovered the advantages of simplicity. It states that where an observation allows several explanations, it is probable that the simpler explanation has a better chance of being correct. Complicated explanations usually cover up lack of understanding. . . . Psychoanalysis developed a wonderful theory but in practice it has little to offer to parents, teachers, educators, management, etc.
>
> Such new methods as Behavior Therapy, an outgrowth of Skinner's

work, also wants to bring about a change in behavior through simple methods. Such a manipulation of clients runs a danger, however, of leading to a general model of man that flies in the face of all the principles of democratic living. Skinner believes that man does not have his fate in his hands, that man needs someone to manipulate him. In this he plays into the hands of a potential dictator who has no great respect for people. That some of his methods often appear similar to ours is a risky comparison because his model of man is distorted and extraordinarily dangerous.

We need practical recommendations based upon a sound philosophy. Among those, the Rational Emotive Therapy of Ellis, like ours, captures the same basic model of man, but he pays no attention to social needs. Glasser's Reality Therapy recognizes social needs but pays little attention to motivation.

So it is this combination of a simple method with a sound basic philosophy which somehow sets [Adlerian psychology] apart and which probably in the next few decades will give our school special recognition. . . . The development of democratic living demands a feeling of equality, a necessity to live together as equals, to find new methods, to find dignity for all instead of the competition for power or superiority and the deadly rivalry which characterizes our present state of civilization. The methods we apply and demonstrate make possible an effective, democratic living and equality. I am of the opinion that in our work we not only treat and educate but we also influence the historical direction our society will take.[11]

Two months before he died, Rudolf Dreikurs was "especially honored" by the Chicago Medical School at a conference devoted to Adlerian techniques. While he "enjoyed international acclaim," Mosak noted, "he was a prophet without honor in his own city for most of his professional career."[12] That the Chicago Medical School, which had opposed him so completely twenty-five years earlier, should honor him was one of the crowning moments in his life.

Introducing Dreikurs that afternoon, Dean Leroy P. Levitt, who had been a medical student under Dreikurs, stated:

Little did I think that someday I would be standing here at such a symposium on Adlerian techniques and also honoring Professor Dreikurs. When I . . . participated in his classes . . . as a student, most of us had little interest in psychiatric methods. . . . But I clearly remember the energy and fervor with which Dr. Dreikurs worked at his task, and I was deeply impressed by this. . . . My training was immersed in the classical Freudian concept of psychoanalysis. But here I stand to honor, to give homage, to both Adlerian methods and to Dr. Dreikurs. Now there is adaptation for you. . . . My feelings about the mystique and the original seductiveness of certain ideas in psychoanalysis have indeed changed. . . . Adler was a prophet as regards our current social problems which have to do with ecology, racism and the liberation of women. . . . Adler was the original community psychiatrist, and Dr. Dreikurs' widespread activities in our city and elsewhere took him where no other psychiatrist had deigned to go . . . and that was to the people.[13]

That afternoon, his body ravaged and weakened by his losing battle with cancer, Rudolf Dreikurs drew upon his indomitable courage and unfailing faith to deliver two lectures and conduct two counseling demonstrations. It was his last public testament.

Two months later, on May 25, 1972, he died.

THE LEGACY

In the course of his long and rich career, Rudolf Dreikurs profoundly touched the lives of hundreds of thousands of people in the United States and abroad. His understanding of life's meaning and challenges and his disclosures of our self-created obstacles enabled him to offer concrete steps for effecting change. His genuine belief that everyone who wants to *can* change was vigorously conveyed through direct counseling and therapy, myriad demonstrations and lectures, and prolific writings. He encouraged us to move beyond the myopic limitations of self-interest and the anomie and despair that often accompany such isolated life styles. He guided us toward a larger vision—beyond ourselves—to understand, respect, cooperate with, and in turn, encourage others.

For thirty-five years following his move to America, his goal was to see Adler's psychology restored as a viable, actively practiced, and dynamic school of thought. His success in the face of the powerful opposition of Freudianism and a vapid eclecticism is testament not only to his persistence but also his integrity, his optimism, and the wisdom of his ideas. His was a total commitment, made possible by a personal life that was intricately interwoven with his professional endeavors.

Dreikurs enlarged and clarified Adler's brilliant concepts into a coherent system that was comprehensive yet specific and capable of practical application. Adlerian psychology, he often reiterated, is a psychology of use, not possession. It teaches that what counts is not the qualities and talents we possess but what use we make of them. Dreikurs remained true to that dictum. The knowledge he acquired from long years of experience was not hoarded but shared with all who would listen. He especially sought to share this knowledge with parents and teachers, who are the molders of the next generation. He eschewed the notion that a little knowledge is dangerous, countering that it is far less damaging than the injury perpetrated by individuals upon one another due to mistaken ideas and adherence to outdated myths.

Everything he achieved—whether in psychiatry, psychology, or education—started under humble and unpromising conditions. His vision of what could and must be accomplished often seemed unrealistic. Though his goals were far-reaching and meant modifying entrenched traditions in child rearing and education, Dreikurs was never stymied by the enormity of the task. He began with whoever was willing to work with him—a few distraught mothers searching for guidance or several teachers, demoralized and ready to quit public education. Whether he worked with six people or six hundred made no difference, for he approached each situation with total dedication and enthusiasm. He built his programs upon solid theoretical foundations and demonstrated how they could be applied in everyday life, until eventually the ideas took root and began to grow.

Dreikurs was one of those rare teachers of mankind who, in a dispassionate world, regard their fellow beings passionately. He inspired others through his faith in them and by illuminating a path through the hazy forest of self-defeating ideas. He acted as if he knew the answers to perplexing and complex problems, but he understood, in a scientific and historical sense, that there is no absolute knowledge. Nonetheless, we are continually required to judge and act upon the immediate situation that confronts us. And we must act with our existing knowledge, believing that it is true, or we accomplish nothing.

With courage and the unobscured vision of a pioneer, Dreikurs hewed new paths in psychiatry, psychotherapy, and counseling and glimpsed what was just looming on the horizon of our evolving social experience.

His work was a beginning, a rich legacy for his colleagues and students to continue to enlarge and refine.

Dreikurs dedicated his life to the proposition that all men, women, and children are truly equal in worth and dignity and that only in a condition of social equality will we experience harmony, peace, and human actualization in the grandest sense. In light of his goals and profound contributions, his very human weaknesses and idiosyncrasies pale.

The man of imperfections has come and gone. The world is a better place for his journey through it.

Notes for Chapter 22

1. Dreikurs, to his friends, September 2, 1968, Dreikurs Papers.

2. Dreikurs, "Guiding, Teaching, and Demonstrating," p. 157.

3. Heinz L. Ansbacher to Dreikurs, June 2, 1967, Dreikurs Papers. See also Krawiac, *The Psychologists*, pp. 34–35.

4. Study guidebooks are available for the four video-taped courses. They are: *Dynamics of Classroom Behavior* (Lincoln, Nebr.: Great Plains National Education Television Library, University of Nebraska, 1969); *Understanding Your Children*, ed. James A. and Neysa M. Peterson (Winooski, Vt.: Vermont Educational Television Network, 1969); *Motivating Children to Learn*, coauthored by Bernice Grunwald (Winooski, Vt.: Vermont Educational Television Network, 1970); *Counseling the Adolescent*, ed. James A. and Neysa M. Peterson (Winooski, Vt.: Vermont Educational Television Network, 1971). The video tapes from these series are available for rent or sale through the Great Plains National Educational Television Library, University of Nebraska, Lincoln, Nebraska.

5. Kurt A. Adler, "New Trends & Adlerian Psychology," *Individual Psychologist* 12 (1975): 78.

6. Dreikurs to W. L. Pew, November 23, 1967, Dreikurs Papers.

7. Dreikurs, "Present Position of Individual Psychology," p. 14.

8. Dreikurs to Pew, June 25, 1966, Dreikurs Papers.

9. "In Memory of Rudolf Dreikurs, 1897–1972," *Journal of Individual Psychology* 29 (1973): 18.

10. Sadie "Tee" Dreikurs, "My Life with Rudolf Dreikurs."

11. Dreikurs, "Rudolf Dreikurs: 1897–1972," in *Psychotherapie in Selbstdarstellungen*, pp. 121–122.

12. "In Memory of Rudolf Dreikurs, 1897–1972," p. 18.

13. Leroy P. Levitt, "Introduction," *Journal of Individual Psychology* 28 (1972): 123–124.

Rudolf Dreikurs Bibliography

1925

"Die Aufgabe der Modernen Geistenkrankenfürsorge." [The Tasks of a Modern Mental Health Service.] *Oesterreichische Blätter für Krankenpflege und Fürsorge* 2: 52–58.

"Die soziale Fürsorge in die Psychiatrie." [Social Welfare in Psychiatry.] *Jahrbuch für Psychiatrie und Neurologie* 44: 247–266.

[With O. Sperling.] "Über die Kombination von Schlafmitteln mit Koffein." [The Combination of Sleeping Pills with Caffein.] *Wiener Medizinische Wochenschrift* 49.

1926

"Einige Probleme der Epileptikerfürsorge." [Some Problems of Service for Epileptics.] *Wiener Klinische Wochenschrift* 39: 602–605.

"Über den gegenwärtigen Stand und die Probleme der Geisteskrankenfürsorge." [The Present State and Problems of Mental Health Services.] *Wiener Klinische Wochenschrift* 39: 869–872.

"Was soll mit unserer epileptischen Kindern geschehen?" [What Is to Happen with Our Epileptic Children?] *Zeitschrift für Heilpädagogik* 18.

1927

"Koffein und vegetatives System." [Caffein and the Vegetative System.] *Wiener Klinische Wochenschrift* 40.

[With Emil Mettauschek.] "Über Coffetylin." [On Caffetyline.] *Wiener Klinische Wochenschrift* 40.

"Über psychische Hygiene." [On Mental Hygiene.] *Zeitschrift für Soziale Hygiene: "Volksgesundheit"* 11.

1928

"Die Entwicklung der psychischen Hygiene in Wien, unter besonderer Berücksichtigung der Alkoholiker und Psychopathen- (Selbstmörder-) Fürsorge." [The Development of Mental Hygiene in Vienna, with Special Consideration to Treatment of Alcoholics and Psychopaths (Suicides).] *Allgemeine Zeitschrift für Psychiatrie* 88: 469–489.

"Koffein und vegetatives System." [Caffein and the Vegetative System.] *Deutsches Zeitschrift für Nervenheilkund* 107: 184–190.

"Psychische Hygiene, ihre Bedeutung und ihre Methoden." [Mental Hygiene, Its Importance and Methods.] *Arbeiterschutz* 24.

"Von der Geisteskrankenfürsorge über die soziale Psychiatrie zur psychischen Hygiene." [From Mental Health Service to Social Psychiatry and Mental Hygiene.] *Allgemeine Zeitschrift für Psychiatrie* 88: 567–573.

1929

"Der gegenwärtige Stand der psychischen Hygiene in Wien." [The Present State of Mental Hygiene in Vienna.] *Zeitschrift für Soziale Hygiene: "Volksgesundheit"* 3: 211–221.

[With Emil Mattauschek.] "Über die Verschlimmerung von alten Neurosen bei Kreigsbeschädigten aus sozialen Gründen (soziale Verschlimmerung)." [The Aggravation of Old Neuroses in War Invalids Because of Social Factors (Social Aggravation).] *Zentralblatt für die gesamte Neurologie und Psychiatrie* 119: 679–700.

1930

"Die Bedeutung der Sport- und Kampfspiele." [The Importance of Sports and Competitive Games.] *Volkssport* 2: 1–3.

"Die Frauensport im Alterum." [Women and Sports in Antiquity.] *Volkssport* 2.

"Zur Frage der Selbsterkenntnis." [On the Question of Self-Knowledge.] *Internationale Zeitschrift für Individualpsychologie* 8: 361–369. (Translation: English, 1937.)

"Zur Frage der Selbstmordprophylaxe." [On the Question of Suicide Prevention.] *Allgemeine Zeitschrift für Psychiatrie* 93: 98–114.

1931

[Review of] "Alfred Adler, *Das Problem der Homosexualität.*" *Internationale Zeitschrift für Individualpsychologie* 9: 62–63.

[Review of] "Erwin Wexberg, *Einführung in die Psychologie des Geschlechtslebens.*" *Internationale Zeitschrift für Individualpsychologie* 9: 63.

Seelische Impotenz. [Psychic Impotence.] Leipzig: Hirzel.

"Soziale Not und Spitalsaufenthalt." [Social Distress and Hospitalization.] *Oesterreichische Blätter für Krankenpflege und Fürsorge* 7: 49–54.

"Zum Problem der Neurasthenie." [On the Question of Neurasthenia.] *Internationale Zeitschrift für Individualpsychologie* 9: 16–25. (Translation: English, 1936.)

1932

"Einige wirksame Faktoren in der Psychotherapie." [Several Effective Factors in Psychotherapy.] *Internationale Zeitschrift für Individualpsychologie* 10: 161–176. (Translation: English, 1936.)

"Frigidity." *Individual Psychology Medical Pamphlets* [London], no. 3, pp. 13–18.

Das Nervöse Symptom. [The Nervous Symptom.] Vienna: Moritz Perls.

[Review of] "Georg Klatt, *Psychologie des Alkoholismus.*" *Internationale Zeitschrift für Individualpsychologie* 10: 153–154.

"Über Liebeswahl." [The Choice of a Mate.] *Internationale Zeitschrift für Individualpsychologie* 10: 339–353. (Translation: English, 1935.)

"Über Rauschucht und ihre individualpsychologische Behandlung." [Drug Addiction and Its Individual Psychological Treatment.] *Biol. Heilkunst* 13.

1933

Einführung in die Individualpsychologie. [Introduction to Individual Psychology.] Foreword by Alfred Adler. Leipzig: Hirzel. (Translations: Czech, 1937; English, 1935, 1950; Dutch, 193?; Greek, 196?; Italian, 1968; revised German ed., 1969; French, 1971.)

"Die 'Grenzen' der Leistungsfähigkeit." [The "Limits" of Efficiency.] *Lebenserfolgen* 29: 80–87.

"Die Individualpsychologie und ihre Kritiker." [Individual Psychology and Its Critics.] *Internationale Zeitschrift für Individualpsychologie* 11: 102–107. (Translation: English, 1934.)

"Die unrichtige Wahl in der Liebe." [The Wrong Choice in Love.] *Lebenserfolgen* 29: 257–262, 278–281.
"Was ist in Wirklichkeit die Neurose?" [What Really Is Neurosis?] *Internationale Zeitschrift für Individualpsychologie* 11: 193–201.
"Woher stammen die Konflikte in der Liebe?" [Where Do Conflicts in Love Come From?] *Lebenserfolgen* 29: 118–121, 154–156.

1934
"Die Bedeutung des Gemeinschaftgefühles für die moralische Erziehung." [The Importance of Community Feeling for Moral Education.] *Résumés du Congres d'education morale, Cracovicie, 1934.* pp. 25–28. Also in Zbiorowa, P., ed., *Sily Moralne: Wspolne Wszystkim Ludziom, Ich zredla I Rezwoj Przez Whychowanie.* Kraków: Sklad Glowny, pp. 221–230.
"Die Erziehungsberatung in Wien." [Child Guidance in Vienna.] *Sozialärztlich Rundschau* 9.
"Die Individualpsychologie des praktischen Arztes." [The Individual Psychology of the General Practitioner.] *Medizinische Klinik,* pp. 10–11.
"Ein Fall van Platzangst." [A Case of Agoraphobia.] *Internationale Zeitschrift für Individualpsychologie* 12: 92–96.
"Individual Psychology and Its Critics." *Individual Psychology Medical Pamphlets* [London], no. 12, pp. 53–57.
"Zur Kasuistik der funktionellen Magen-Darmstörungen." [On the Casuistry of Functional Stomach-Intestinal Problems.] *Internationale Zeitschrift für Individualpsychologie* 12: 11–15. (Translation: English, 1935.)

1935
"A Case of Functional Disturbance of the Digestive System." *International Journal of Individual Psychology* 1, no. 1: 57–62. Reprinted in *Psychodynamics,* 1967.
"The Choice of a Mate." *International Journal of Individual Psychology* 1, no. 4: 99–112.
"Die Finalität in Menschlichen Seelenleben." [Finality in the Human Emotional Life.] *Action et Pensee* 11: 73–79, 100–110.
An Introduction to Individual Psychology. Translated by Edna G. Fenning. London: Kegan, Paul, Trench, Trubner.

1936
"Certain Factors Effective in Psychotherapy." *International Journal of Individual Psychology* 2: 39–54.
Hoe voed ik mijn kind op? Techniek van een opvoeding zonder dwang. [How Shall I Raise My Child? The Technique of Education Without Coercion.] Utrecht: Bijleveld, 1936. Translated by Peter H. Ronge. Reprinted 1948.
"The Problem of Neurasthenia." *International Journal of Individual Psychology* 2, no. 3: 14–34. Reprinted in *Psychodynamics,* 1967.

1937
"In Memoriam, Alfred Adler." *Psychotherpeutische Praxis* 3: 208–209.
"An Introduction to Individual Psychology." *International Journal of Individual Psychology* 3: 320–349.
"On Knowing Oneself." *International Journal of Individual Psychology* 3: 13–23.
Uvod do Individualni Psychologie. [Introduction to Individual Psychology.] Prague: Cesklovensk Graficke Unie.

1940

"The Child in the Group." *Camping Magazine*, December, pp. 7–9.
"The Importance of Group Life." *Camping Magazine*, November, pp. 3–4, 27.
[Editor.] *Individual Psychology Newsletter*, 1940–41; *Individual Psychology Bulletin*, 1941–49, *American Journal of Individual Psychology*, 1950–1956.
[Review of] "C. A. Adler, 'The Anti-Babel: An Attempt to Clarify Some Controversial Points in 'Guidance.'" *Individual Psychology Newsletter* 1, no. 3: 2–3.

1941

"Dear Friends." *Individual Psychology Bulletin* 2, no. 1: 11.
"The Leader in the Group." *Camping Magazine*, January, p. 7.
"The Present Position of Individual Psychology." *Individual Psychology Bulletin* 2: 13–17.

1942

"The Changing Scope of Psychiatry." *Chicago Medical School Quarterly* 2: 7, 8, 38. (Translation: Portuguese, 1946.)
"Dear Friends." *Individual Psychology Bulletin* 2, no. 2: 1; no. 3: 1; no. 4: 1.
"The Educational Implications of the 'Four Freedoms.'" *Individual Psychology Bulletin* 2: 68–71.
"In Memoriam—Alfred Adler." *Individual Psychology Bulletin* 2: 76–77.
"Organizing Distribution of Knowledge." *Individual Psychology Bulletin* 2: 38–40.
[Review of] "N. E. Shoobs and G. Goldberg, *Corrective Treatment for Unadjusted Children*." *Individual Psychology Bulletin* 2: 73–75.

1943

"Neurosis, a Challenge to Medicine." *Chicago Medical School Quarterly* 4, no. 2: 4–6, 30–32. (Translation: Portuguese, 1946.) Reprinted in *Psychodynamics*, 1967.
"Our Child Guidance Clinics in Chicago." *Individual Psychology Bulletin* 3: 14–19. Reprinted in "Child Guidance," 1957.
[Review of] "*Bulletin of the Menninger Clinic*, 1943." *Individual Psychology Bulletin* 3: 92–96.

1944

"Clinical Child Guidance." *Mental Health Bulletin* 22, no. 4: 1–4.
"Editorial." *Individual Psychology Bulletin* 4: 31.
"The Jewish Family." *New Currents* 2: 28–31.
"The Meaning of Dreams." *Chicago Medical School Quarterly* 5, no. 3: 4–6, 25–26. Reprinted in *Psychodynamics*, 1967.
"The Technique of Psychotherapy." *Chicago Medical School Quarterly* 5, no. 1: 4–7, 35; and 5, no. 2: 7–9, 25–27. Reprinted in *Psychodynamics*, 1967.

1945

Manual of Child Guidance. Chicago: Chicago Medical School.
"Psychological Differentiation of Psychopathological Disorders." *Individual Psychology Bulletin* 4: 35–48. Reprinted in *Psychodynamics*, 1967.

1946

The Challenge of Marriage. New York: Duell, Sloan & Pearce. (Translations: Italian, 1947; Portuguese, 1949; Dutch, 1961; Hebrew, 1968; German, 1968.)

"The Confusion of Sex." *Chicago Medical School Quarterly* 7: 11–14, 32–34.
"How to Choose a Partner." *Ladies Home Journal*, October, p. 30. "Getting Along in Marriage," November, p. 28; "How to Get Along with Children," December, p. 40.
"Individual Psychology in Brazil." *Individual Psychology Bulletin* 5, no. 3: 91–93.
"Neurose: Um desafio à medicina." [Neurosis, a Challenge to Medicine.] *Revista Brasileira de Medicina* 3: 557–562.
"Orientação de Criança: A Situação dos Pais." *Revista Brasileira de Medicina* 3, no. 5: 363.
"Os Novos desígnios da psiquiatria." [The Changing Scope of Psychiatry.] *Revista Brasileira de Medicina* 3: 647–649.
"A Significação dos Sonhos." [The Meaning of Dreams.] *Revista Brasileira de Medicina* 3: 895–898.
"Técnica psicoterápica." [The Technique of Psychotherapy.] *Revista Brasileira de Medicina* 3: 706.
"The Training of Organic Symptoms." In *Archives of the 1st Inter-American Congress of Medicine, Rio de Janeiro.*

1947

"A Child with a Compulsive Neurosis." *Individual Psychology Bulletin* 6: 137–141. Reprinted in "Child Guidance," 1957.
"Falling in Love with Trouble." *Science Digest* 21: 38–42.
"Ferdinand Birnbaum: A Biographical Sketch." *Individual Psychology Bulletin* 6: 157–161.
"The Four Goals of the Maladjusted Child." *Nervous Child* 6: 321–328.
"The Last Ten Years." *Individual Psychology Bulletin* 6: 1–3.
La Sfida al Matrimonio. [The Challenge of Marriage.] Translated by Guiseppi Mannelli. Florence: Nerbini.

1948

The Challenge of Parenthood. New York: Duell, Sloan & Pearce. Reprinted in abridged edition as *The Challenge of Child Training: A Parent's Guide,* 1972; and *Coping with Children's Misbehavior: A Parent's Guide,* 1972.
[Review of] "Rose H. Alshuler and La Berta W. Hattwick, *Painting and Personality: A Study of Young Children.*" *College Art Journal* 8: 155–157.
"The Socio-psychological Dynamics of Physical Disability: A Review of the Adlerian Concept." *Journal of Social Issues* 4: 39–54. Reprinted in *Psychodynamics,* 1967.

1949

"Counseling for Family Adjustment." *Individual Psychology Bulletin* 7: 119–137. Reprinted in *Psychodynamics,* 1967.
"Editorial Comment." *Individual Psychology Bulletin* 7: 3–4.
Psicologia do Casamento. [The Challenge of Marriage.] Translated by O. Rocha and Maria Alzira Perestrello. Rio de Janeiro: Editora Civilizacao Brasileira.
"Psychotherapy Through Child Guidance." *Nervous Child* 8: 311–328. Reprinted in "Child Guidance," 1957.
"Report on the Community Child Guidance Centers of Chicago." *Individual Psychology Bulletin* 7: 35–37.
"Ten Premises for a Humanist Philosophy of Life." *Humanist* 9: 1.

1950

"Community Child Guidance Centers of Chicago: Report of the Medical Director." *Individual Psychology Bulletin* 8: 163–166.

Cultural Upheaval and Modern Family Life. Chicago: Community Child Guidance Centers.
"Editorial Comment." *Individual Psychology Bulletin* 8: 1.
Fundamentals of Adlerian Psychology. Rev. ed. New York: Greenberg.
"Guilt Feelings as an Excuse." *Individual Psychology Bulletin* 8: 12–21. Reprinted in *Psychodynamics,* 1967.
"Humanism—A Philosophy for Daily Living." *Humanist* 10: 25, 73–74, 121–122, 167, 215–216.
"The Immediate Purpose of Children's Mis-behavior, Its Recognition and Correction." *Internationale Zeitschrift für Individualpsychologie* 19: 70–87.
"Psychotherapie de Groupe." [Group Psychotherapy.] *Bulletin de Centre de Psychologie Adlerienne* 2: 3–14.
"Religion Without the Supernatural." *Progressive World,* 9: 388–395.
"Techniques and Dynamics of Multiple Psychotherapy." *Psychiatric Quarterly* 24: 788–799. Reprinted in "Group Psychotherapy and Group Approaches," 1960.

1951

"Causality Versus Indeterminism." *Individual Psychology Bulletin* 9: 108–117.
"Editorial Comment." *Individual Psychology Bulletin* 9: 94–95.
"Family Group Therapy in the Chicago Community Child Guidance Centers." *Mental Hygiene* 35: 291–301.
"The Four Goals of the Disturbed Child." *Sauvegarde de l'Enfance* 12: 104–114.
"The Function of Emotions." *Christ. Register* 130: 11–14, 24. Reprinted in *Psychodynamics,* 1967.
"How Does Humor Affect Our Lives?" *Northwestern Reviewing Stand.* 17.
"The International Picture of Individual Psychology." *Individual Psychology Bulletin* 9: 1–3.
"Understanding the Child: A Manual for Teachers." Mimeographed. Chicago: Alfred Adler Institute.
"Understanding the Exceptional Child." *Music Therapy* 1: 41–46. Reprinted in "Child Guidance," 1957.
"The Unique Social Climate Experienced in Group Psychotherapy." *Group Psychotherapy* 3: 292–299. Reprinted in "Group Psychotherapy and Group Approaches," 1960.

1952

Character Education and Spiritual Values in an Anxious Age. Boston: Beacon Press. (Translation: Hebrew, 1966.) Reprinted 1971.
"Group Psychotherapy: A General Review and Response." In *Proceedings of the 1st International Congress of Psychiatry, Paris.* 1950, Pt. 5. *Actualities Scientifiques et Industrielles,* no. 1172. Paris: Hermann & Cie, pp. 223–239, 301–302. Reprinted in "Group Psychotherapy and Group Approaches," 1960.
[With B. H. Shulman and H. H. Mosak.] "Patient-Therapist Relationship in Multiple Psychotherapy. I. Its Advantages to the Therapist. II. Its Advantages to the Patient." *Psychiatric Quarterly* 26: 219, 227, 509–516. Reprinted in "Group Psychotherapy and Group Approaches," 1960.
"The Program of the Journal: An Editorial." *American Journal of Individual Psychology* 10: 1–3.

1953

"Adler's Contribution to Medicine, Psychology, and Education." *American Journal of Individual Psychology* 10: 83–86.
"The Dynamics of Music Therapy." *Music Therapy* 3: 15–23.

"How Equal Can We Get?" *Torch*, January.
"The Programme of Humanism." In *Proceedings of the 1st International Congress of Humanism and Ethical Culture, Amsterdam*, 1952. Utrecht: Humanitische Verbond, pp. 106–111.

1954

"Clinical Interpretation of Music Therapy." *Music Therapy* 4: 79–84.
"Emotional Predisposition to Reading Difficulties." *Archives of Pediatrics* 71: 339–353.
"Psychiatric Concepts of Music Therapy for Children." *Music Therapy* 4: 81–84. Reprinted in "Child Guidance," 1957.
"The Psychodynamics of Disability—A Group Therapy Approach." *American Archives of Rehabilitation Therapy* 2: 4–8. Reprinted in "Group Psychotherapy and Group Approaches," 1960.
"The Psychological Interview in Medicine." *American Journal of Individual Psychology* 10: 99–122. Reprinted 1963. Also reprinted in *Psychodynamics*, 1967.
[Review of] "Sigmund Freud, *The Origins of Psychoanalysis: Letters, Drafts and Notes to Wilhelm Fliess, 1887–1902.*" *Science* 120, no. 3116: 453.
[With Raymond J. Corsini.] "Twenty Years of Group Psychotherapy." *American Journal of Psychiatry* 110: 567–575. Reprinted in "Group Psychotherapy and Group Approaches," 1960.

1955

"Adlerian Analysis of Interaction." *Group Psychotherapy* 8: 298–307. Reprinted 1959. Also reprinted in "Group Psychotherapy and Group Approaches," 1960.
"The Adlerian Approach in the Changing Scope of Psychiatry: Collected Papers on Psychodynamics and Counseling." Mimeographed. Chicago: Alfred Adler Institute.
"Group Psychotherapy and the Third Revolution in Psychiatry." *International Journal of Social Psychiatry* 1: 23–32. Reprinted in "Group Psychotherapy and Group Approaches," 1960.
"Individual Psychology." In *Present-day Psychology*, edited by A. A. Roback. New York: Philosophical Library, pp. 711–731.
[With Dorothy B. Crocker.] "Music Therapy with Psychotic Children." *Music Therapy* 5: 62–73. Reprinted in "Child Guidance," 1957; and "Music Therapy," 1960.
"The Psychological Approach in the Classroom." *American Teacher* 39: 9–12. Reprinted in "Child Guidance," 1957.
"The Religion of Democracy." *Humanist* 15: 210.
"Tele and Inter-personal Therapy: Appraisal of Moreno's Concept from the Adlerian Point of View." *Group Psychotherapy* 8: 185–191. Reprinted in "Group Psychotherapy and Group Approaches," 1960.

1956

"Adlerian Psychotherapy." In *Progress in Psychotherapy*, edited by Frieda Fromm-Reichmann and Jacob L. Moreno. New York: Grune & Stratton. Reprinted in *Psychodynamics*, 1967, pp. 111–118.
"The Contribution of Group Psychotherapy to Psychiatry." *Group Psychotherapy* 9: 115–125.
"Editorial." *American Journal of Individual Psychology* 12: 177–179.
"Freud and Adler." *Guide to Psychiatric and Psychological Literature* 2: 8–9.
"Goals in Psychotherapy." *American Journal of Psychoanalysis* 16: 18–23. Reprinted in *Psychodynamics*, 1967.
"A New Adlerian Contribution to Education." *American Journal of Individual Psychology* 12: 69.

1957

"Child Guidance and Education: Collected Papers." Mimeographed. Eugene, Ore: University of Oregon Press.

["Comments on Moreno's Code of Ethics of Group Psychotherapists."] *Group Psychotherapy* 10: 226–229.

"The Cultural Implications of Group Psychotherapy." *Zeitschrift für Diagnostische Psychologie und Persönlichkeitsforschung* 5: 186–197. Also in *Gruppen Psychotherapie*, edited by H. Hiltman et al., Bern and Stuttgart: Huber, 1957. Reprinted in "Group Psychotherapy and Group Approaches," 1960.

"Group Psychotherapy from the Point of View of Adlerian Psychology." *International Journal of Group Psychotherapy* 7: 363–375. Reprinted in "Group Psychotherapy and Group Approaches," 1960. Also reprinted in 1963, 1969.

"Perspectives of Delinquency Prevention." *Journal of Correctional Psychology* 2: 1–9.

"Psychiatric Considerations of Music Therapy." *Music Therapy* 7: 31–36.

"The Psychological and Philosophical Significance of Rhythm." *Bulletin of the National Association of Music Therapists* 6: 7. Reprinted in "Psychological Significance," 1961.

Psychology in the Classroom. New York: Harper & Row. Also, London: Staples Library. Reprinted 1968. (Translations: Danish, 1969; German, 1967; Greek, 1968; Hebrew, 1962; Italian, 1961.)

"Psychotherapy as Correction of Faulty Social Values." *Journal of Individual Psychology* 13: 150–158. Reprinted in *Psychodynamics*, 1967.

[With J. Dennis Freund.] "Value of Funkenstein Test in Predicting Psychosurgery." *Diseases of the Nervous System* 18: 134–138.

1958

"Die Anfänge der Gruppenpsychotherapie in Wien." [The Origin of Group Psychotherapy in Vienna.] *Wiener Medizinische Wochenschrift* 108: 845–848.

"The Cultural Implications of Reward and Punishment." *International Journal of Social Psychiatry* 4: 171–178.

"Group Dynamics in the Classroom." In *Proceedings of the 13th Congress of the International Association of Applied Psychology, Rome 1958.* Rome: Ferri. Reprinted in "Group Psychotherapy and Group Approaches," 1960.

"Die Individualpsychologie Alfred Adler." [The Individual Psychology of Alfred Adler.] In *Die Psychotherapie in der Gegenwart*, edited by E. Stern. Zurich: Rascher, pp. 68–88.

"Minor Psychotherapy." *Transactions of the Academy of Psychosomatic Medicine* 5: 253–260. Reprinted in *Psychodynamics*, 1967.

"Musiktherapie mit Psychotischen Kindern." [Music Therapy with Psychotic Children.] In *Musik in der Medizin*, edited by H. R. Teirich. Stuttgart: Gustav Fischer, pp. 68–76. Reprinted 1969.

Organic or Functional Disorder: A Diagnostic Aid. Chicago: Abbott Labs, 1958.

"Raising Children in a Democracy." *Humanist* 18: 77–83.

"A Reliable Differential Diagnosis of Psychological or Somatic Disturbances." *International Record of Medicine* 171: 238–242. Reprinted in *Psychodynamics*, 1967.

1959

"Adlerian Analysis of Interaction." In *Essays in Individual Psychology*, edited by Kurt A. Adler and Danica Deutsch. New York: Grove Press, pp. 75–87.

[With Raymond Corsini, Raymond Lowe, and Manford Sonstegard.] *Adlerian Family Counseling: A Manual for Counseling Centers.* Eugene, Ore.: University of Oregon Press.

"Basic Principles in Dealing with Children." In *Adlerian Family Counseling: A Manual for Counseling Centers*, edited by Rudolf Dreikurs, Raymond Corsini, Raymond Lowe, and Manford Sonstegard. Eugene, Ore.: University of Oregon Press, pp. 23–31.

["Comments on Twelve Incidents."] In *Critical Incidents in Psychotherapy*, edited by S. W. Stendal and Raymond Corsini, Englewood Cliffs, N.J.: Prentice-Hall.

"Communication Within the Family." *Central States Speech Journal* 11: 11–19. Reprinted in "Group Psychotherapy and Group Approaches," 1960; and *Psychodynamics*, 1967.

"Do Teachers Understand Children?" *School and Society* 87: 88–90. Reprinted 1968.

"Early Experiments with Group Psychotherapy." *American Journal of Psychotherapy* 13: 882–891. Reprinted in "Group Psychotherapy and Group Approaches," 1960. Reprinted 1963, 1969.

"Fundamental Principles of Child Guidance." In *Adlerian Family Counseling: A Manual for Counseling Centers*, edited by Rudolf Dreikurs, Raymond Corsini, Raymond Lowe, and Manford Sonstegard. Eugene, Ore.: University of Oregon Press, pp. 17–21.

"A Humanist View of Sex." *Humanist* 19: 84–92.

"The Impact of the Group for Music Therapy and Music Education." *Music Therapy* 9: 93–106.

"A Record of a Family Counseling Session." In *Adlerian Family Counseling: A Manual for Counseling Centers*, edited by Rudolf Dreikurs, Raymond Corsini, Raymond Lowe, and Manford Sonstegard. Eugene, Ore.: University of Oregon Press, pp. 109–153.

[Review of] "Lawrence E. Cole and William F. Bruce, *Educational Psychology*." *Journal of Individual Psychology* 15: 241–242.

"What Is Psychotherapy? The Adlerian Viewpoint." *Annals of Psychotherapy* 1: 16–21.

1960

"Are Psychological Schools of Thought Outdated?" *Journal of Individual Psychology* 16: 3–10.

[With John M. Shlien and Harold H. Mosak.] "A Comparison of Client-Centered and Adlerian Psychotherapy." *Counseling Center Discussion Papers* 6, no. 8. Also, *American Psychologist* 15: 415 [abstract].

"Coping with the Child's Problem in the Classroom." In *Professional School Psychology*, edited by Monroe G. Gottsegen and Gloria B. Gottsegen. New York: Grune & Stratton, pp. 162–176.

"The Current Dilemma in Psychotherapy." *Journal of Existential Psychology* 1: 188–206.

"Group Psychotherapy and Group Approaches: Collected Papers." Mimeographed. Chicago: Alfred Adler Institute.

"Music Therapy with Psychotic Children." *Psychiatric Quarterly* 34: 722–734.

[Review of] "J. Neumann, *Der Nervöse Charakter und Seine Heilung*." *Journal of Individual Psychology* 16: 94–96.

"The White House Conference on Children and Youth, 1960; A Critique: Triumph of Institutionalism." *Humanist* 20: 281–287.

1961

"The Adlerian Approach." *Annals of Psychotherapy* 2: 40–43.

"The Adlerian Approach to Psychodynamics." In *Contemporary Psychotherapies*, edited by Morris I. Stein. New York: Free Press of Glencoe, pp. 60–79.

"The Adlerian Approach to Therapy." In *Contemporary Psychotherapies*,, edited by Morris I. Stein. New York: Free Press of Glencoe, pp. 80–94.

"Adult-Child Relationships: A Workshop in Group Discussion with Adolescents." Mimeographed. Eugene, Ore.: University of Oregon Press. Reprinted 1967.

"Early Experiments in Social Psychiatry." *International Journal of Social Psychiatry* 7: 141–147.
"L'Education des Parents et le Travail de Groupe." In *6th Congres Internationale de Sante Mentale, Paris, Informational Socials*, no. 12, pp. 32–33.
Equality: the Challenge of Our Times. Chicago: Alfred Adler Institute. (Translation: Hebrew, 1967.) Reprinted as *Social Equality: The Challenge of Today*, 1971.
Het Huwelijkeen Uitdaging. [The Challenge of Marriage.] Translated by M. Muller-Metz. Utrecht: Bijleveld.
Prevention and Correction of Juvenile Delinquency. Saint Louis: Metropolitan Youth Commission. Reprinted 1962.
Psicologia in Classe: Manuale Practico per i Maestri. [Psychology in the Classroom: A Practical Manual for Teachers.] Translated by Corinna Ranchitti. Florence: Editrice Universitaria.
"The Psychological and Philosophical Significance of Rhythm." *Bulletin of the National Association of Music Teachers* 10: 8–17.
"Rationale of Counseling." In *Proceedings of the Delta Workshop on Counseling Minority Youth, June 14–16, 1961.* Portland, Ore.: Oregon State System of Higher Education.
"The Religion of the Future." In *Reconstruction in Religion: A Humanist Symposium*, edited by A. E. Kuenzli. Boston: Beacon Press, pp. 3–20.
"The War Between the Generations: Juvenile Delinquency Stumps the Experts." *Humanist* 21: 15–24.

1962

"Can You Be Sure the Disease Is Functional?" *Consultant* [Smith, Kline French] 2: 34–36.
"Discussion on: Frigidity and Postpartum Frigidity; Differential Diagnosis." In *Psychosomatic Obstetrics, Gynecology and Endocrinology*, edited by William S. Kroger. Springfield, Ill.: Charles C. Thomas, pp. 415–417, 455–459.
[With John M. Shlien and Harold H. Mosak.] "Effect of Time Limits: A Comparison of Two Psychotherapies." *Journal of Counseling Psychology* 9: 31–34.
"The Interpersonal Relationship in Hypnosis; Some Fallacies in Current Thinking About Hypnosis." *Psychiatry* 25: 219–226.
"Living Together in a Family." *Family Life* 22, no. 5: 1–5.
Prevention and Correction of Juvenile Delinquency. Chicago: Alfred Adler Institute.
Psikhologia Bakita. [Psychology in the Classroom.] Tel Aviv: Ostar Hamoreh.

1963

[With Don Dinkmeyer.] *Encouraging Children to Learn: The Encouragement Process.* Englewood Cliffs, N.J.: Prentice-Hall. (Translations: German, 1970; Portuguese, 1972; Spanish, 1968).
"Group Psychotherapy from the Point of View of Adlerian Psychology." In *Group Psychotherapy and Group Function*, edited by M. Rosenbaum and M. Berger. New York: Basic Books, pp. 168–179.
"Individual Psychology: The Adlerian Point of View." In *Concepts of Personality*, edited by J. M. Wepman and R. W. Heine. Chicago: Aldine, pp. 234–256.
"Psychodynamic Diagnosis in Psychiatry." *American Journal of Psychiatry* 119: 1045–1048. Reprinted in *Psychodynamics*, 1967.
"The Psychological Interview in Medicine." *Indian Journal of Psychiatry* 5: 59–71, 134–139.
"Psychological Uncertainty Principle." *Proceedings of the 5th International Congress of Psychotherapy, Vienna, August 1961. Part 2. Topical Problems of Psychotherapy.* Vol. 4. New York: S. Karger, pp. 23–31.
"Die Rolle der Gruppe in der Erziehung." [The Role of the Group in Education.] In

Sozialerziehung und Gruppenunterricht, International Gesehen, edited by Ernst Meyer. Stuttgart: Ernst Klett, pp. 16–35.
"The Significance of 4 Goals." *Oregon Society of Individual Psychology Newsletter* 4: 12–13.

1964

[With Margaret Goldman.] *The ABC's of Guiding the Child.* Chicago: Community Child Guidance Centers.
"The Changing Scope of Psychiatry." *Medical Digest. III. Psychiatry* [Bombay] 32, no. 7: 333–353.
[With Vicki Soltz.] *To Pedi* [Children: The Challenge.] Translated by Juliet Cavadas. (Translations: French, 1972; German, 1966; Greek, 1964; Hebrew, 1967; Italian, 1969.)
"Impact of Equality." *Humanist* 24: 143–146.
[With Vicki Soltz.] *To Pedi* [Children: The Challenge.] Translated by Juliet Cavadas. Athens: Tachydromos.

1965

"Aphorism." *Voices* 1: 24.
"Civilization and Szasz's Discontents: [Review of] Thomas S. Szasz, *The Ethics of Psychoanalysis.*" *Humanist* 25: 274.
"Educating for Self-Government: A Survey of Four Experimental Schools." *Humanist* 25: 8–12.
"The Educational Revolution or a New Deal for Youth." *Tantalus* [Texas Technological College] 2: 1–2.
"Karl Nowotny, 1895–1965." *Journal of Individual Psychology* 21: 234.
"Models of Man." *Humanist* 25: 259–260.
"Music Therapy." In *Conflict in the Classroom: The Education of Emotionally Disturbed Children,* edited by Nicholas J. Long, William C. Morse, and Ruth G. Neuman. Belmont, Calif.: Wadsworth Pub. Co., pp. 199–202.
[With Vicki Soltz.] *Your Child and Discipline: A Briefing for Parents.* Washington, D.C.: National Education Association. Also in *NEA Journal* 54: 32–47.
"Youth: There Is a War Between the Generations." *Humanist* 25: 233.

1966

"Alte und Neue Erziehungsmethoden." (Gesendet am 4. Juni 1965.) [Old and New Educational Methods (Broadcast 4 June 1965).] In *Die Nachlese: Publikationen des Deutschschweizerischen Radios.*
"The Development of the Child's Potential." In *Explorations in Human Potentialities,* edited by Herbert A. Otto. Springfield, Ill.: Charles C. Thomas, pp. 223–239.
"The Holistic Approach: Two Points on a Line." In *Education, Guidance and Psychodynamics: Proceedings of the Conference of the Individual Psychology Association of Chicago, St. Joseph's Hospital, November 13, 1965.* Chicago: Alfred Adler Institute.
Itsub Ha-ofi v'hakniyat orchim b'iday shel charada. [Character Education and Spiritual Values in an Anxious Age.] Translated by Aaron Ben-Nahum. Tel Aviv: Alfred Adler Institute.
[With Vicki Soltz.] *Kindern Fordern uns Heraus.* [Children: The Challenge.] Translated by Erik Blumenthal. Stuttgart: Ernst Klett.
"The Scientific Revolution." *Humanist* 26: 8–13. Reprinted 1969.
[With Manfred Sonstegard.] "A Specific Approach to Practicum Supervision." *Counselor Education and Supervision* 6: 18–25.

[With Harold Mosak.] "The Tasks of Life. I. Adler's Three Tasks." *Individual Psychologist* 4: 18–22.

1967

Adult-Child Relations: A Workshop in Group Discussion with Adolescents. Chicago: Alfred Adler Institute.

"Goals of Psychotherapy." In *The Goals of Psychotherapy,* edited by Alvin R. Mahrer. New York: Appleton-Century Crofts, pp. 221–237.

"Guiding, Teaching, and Demonstrating: An Adlerian Autobiography." *Journal of Individual Psychology* 23: 145–157.

"Hesitant Therapist." *Voices* 3: 17.

[With Harold Mosak.] "The Life Tasks. III. The Fifth Life Task." *Individual Psychologist* 5: 16–22.

Psychodynamics, Psychotherapy, and Counseling: Collected Papers. Chicago: Alfred Adler Institute.

Psychologie im Klassenzimmer. [*Psychology in the Classroom.*] Translated by Erik Blumenthal. Stuttgart: Ernst Klett.

"Regine Seidler (1895–1967)." *Journal of Individual Psychology* 23: 137.

"Rudolf Dreikurs Bibliography: 1925–1967." *Journal of Individual Psychology* 23: 158–166.

Shivuyon: Ha-etgar. [Equality: The Challenge.] Translated by Aaron Ben-Nahum. Tel Aviv: Joshua Chachik.

[With Harold Mosak.] "The Tasks of Life. II. The Fourth Life Task." *Individual Psychologist* 4: 51–56.

[With Manford Sonstegard.] *The Teleoanalytic Approach to Group Counseling.* Chicago: Alfred Adler Institute.

[With Vicki Soltz.] *Yeladim: Ha-etgar.* [Children: The Challenge.] Translated by Ofra Burla-Adar. Tel Aviv: Joshua Chachik.

1968

[With Manford Sonstegard.] "The Adlerian or Teleoanalytic Group Counseling Approach." In *Basic Approaches to Group Psychotherapy and Group Counseling,* edited by George M. Gazda. Springfield, Ill.: Charles C. Thomas, pp. 197–232.

"Adler's Contributions to Contemporary Psychology." *Individual Psychologist* 5: 15–21.

[With Don Dinkmeyer.] *Cómo Estimular al Niño: El Processo de Estimulo.* [Encouraging Children to Learn: The Encouragement Process.] Translated by J. A. Baca. Valencia, Spain: S. A. Alcoy.

"Determinants of Changing Attitudes of Marital Partners Toward Each Other." In *The Marriage Relationship: Psychoanalytic Perspectives,* edited by Salo Rosenbaum and Ian Alger. New York: Basic Books, pp. 83–102.

"The Developing Self in Human Potentialities." In *Human Potentialities: The Challenge and the Promise,* edited by Herbert A. Otto. Saint Louis: Green, pp. 80–92.

"Do Teachers Understand Children?" In *Guidance and Counseling in the Elementary School: Readings in Theory and Practice,* edited by Don Dinkmeyer. New York: Holt, Rinehart & Winston, pp. 180–183.

Die Ehe, Eine Herausforderung. [The Challenge of Marriage.] Translated by Erik A. Blumenthal. Stuttgart: Ernst Klett.

"How the Psychiatrist Can Assist the Attorney in Rehabilitating Broken Marriages." In *Therapeutic Family Law: A Complete Guide to Marital Reconciliations,* edited by N. C. Kohut. Chicago: Family Law Publications, pp. 207–218.

"Introduction." In *Piano: Guided Sight-Reading,* by Leonard Deutsch. Chicago: Alfred Adler Institute, pp. xiv–xv.

I Psikhologia Stin. [Psychology in the Classroom.] Translated by Juliet Cavadas. Athens: Kedros.

Lineamenti Della Psicologia di Adler. [Fundamentals of Adlerian Psychology.] Translated by Giordano Falzoni. Rome: La Nuova Italia.
[With Loren Grey.] *Logical Consequences: A New Approach to Discipline.* New York: Meredith. Reprinted 1970 as *A Parent's Guide to Child Discipline.*
Nisooin: Ha-etgar. [The Challenge of Marriage.] Translated by R. Algad. Tel Aviv: Joshua Chachik.
Psychology in the Classroom. 2d ed. New York: Harper & Row.
[With Manford Sonstegard.] "Rationale of Group Counseling." In *Guidance and Counseling in the Elementary School: Readings in Theory and Practice,* edited by Don Dinkmeyer. New York: Holt, Rinehart & Winston, pp. 278–287.
"Zwischen Verwöhnung und Strenge." [Between Spoiling and Discipline.] In *Kinder in ihrer Welt, Kinder in unserer Welt,* edited by R. Hörl. Hamburg: Furche Verlag.

1969
"Adler's Contribution to Individual Psychology." *Individual Psychologist* 6: 15–21.
[With Vicki Soltz.] *I Bambini: Una Sfida.* [Children: The Challenge.] Translated by Isolda Gentili. Milan: Ferro Edizioni.
"Die Bedeutung des Gruppenunterrichts." [The Importance of Group Instruction.] In *Didaktische Studien,* edited by Ernst Meyer. Stuttgart: Ernst Klett, pp. 95–103.
"Can We Find Peace in the War Between the Generations? What Role Can Our Education Systems Play?" In "War Between the Generations: An Attempt at Reconciliation. Proceedings of the American Society of Adlerian Psychology Conference, Minneapolis, November 1968." Mimeographed. Minneapolis: Alfred Adler Society of Minnesota.
"Dialog in der Familie." [Dialog in the family.] In *Kontexte.* Vol. 5. Edited by Hans J. Schulz. Stuttgart: Kreuz Verlag, pp. 51–57.
Dynamics of Classroom Behavior: Teacher's Guide to an In-Service Educational TV Series. Lincoln, Nebr.: Great Plains National Educational Television Library.
"Early Experiments in Group Psychotherapy." In *Group Therapy Today: Styles, Methods, and Techniques,* edited by Hendrik M. Ruitenbeck. New York: Atherton, pp. 18–26.
"Group Psychotherapy from the Point of View of Adlerian Psychology." In *Group Therapy Today: Styles, Methods, and Techniques,* edited by Hendrik M. Ruitenbeck. New York; Atherton, pp. 37–48.
Grundbegriffe der Individualpsychologie. [Fundamentals of Individual Psychology.] Stuttgart: Ernst Klett.
"Irvin Neufeld, M.D., 1903–1969: Orthopedist and Individual Psychologist." *Journal of Individual Psychology* 25: 226–230.
"Kinderpsychotherapie durch Erziehungsberatung." [Child Psychotherapy Through Educational Counseling.] In *Handbuch der Kinderpsychotherapie.* Vol. 1. Edited by G. Biermann. Munich: Ernst Reinhart, pp. 95–107.
"Learning to Live Together in a Democracy." *Canadian Counsellor* 3: 4–9.
"Musiktherapie mit Psychotischen Kindern." [Music Therapy with Psychotic Children.] In *Handbuch der Kinderpsychotherapie.* Vol. 1. Edited by G. Biermann. Munich: Ernst Reinhart, pp. 499–507.
Psykologi i Klassevaerelset. [Psychology in the Classroom.] Translated by Jesper Nielsen. Copenhagen: Hans Reitzel Forlag.
"The Scientific Revolution." In *Foundations of Guidance and Counseling: Multidisciplinary Readings,* edited by C. E. Smith and O. G. Mink. New York: Lippincott, pp. 59–69.
"Social Interest: The Basis of Normalcy." *Counseling Psychologist* 1: 45–48.
Understanding Your Children: Study Guidebook. Edited by James A. Peterson and Neysa M. Peterson. Winooski, Vt.: Vermont Educational Television Network.

1970

"The Courage to Be Imperfect." In *Articles of Supplementary Reading for Parents.* Chicago: Alfred Adler Institute, pp. 17–25.

Eklogi Dreikurs. [Dreikurs Sayings.] Edited and translated by Juliet Cavadas. Athens: Kedros.

[With Don Dinkmeyer.] *Ermutigung als Lernhife.* [Encouragement as a Learning Aid.] Translated by Rosemarie Hagen. Stuttgart: Ernst Klett.

[With Vicki Soltz.] *Happy Children: The Challenge for Parents.* London: Souvenir Press. (British ed. of *Children: The Challenge.*)

The Human Element in Urban Renewal. Tel Aviv: Urban Renewal Authority, Israel Ministry of Housing.

Human Patterns in a Changing Society. Jerusalem: Israel Civil Service Commission.

"The Influence of Individual Psychology on the International Scene." *Individual Psychologist* 7: 29–37.

"Introduction." In *The Education of Children*, by Alfred Adler. Chicago: Henry Regnery, Gateway Edition, pp. v–x.

[With Bernice Grunwald.] *Motivating Children to Learn.* Winooski, Vt.: Vermont Educational Television Network.

[With Marvin Chernoff.] "Parents and Teachers: Friends or Enemies?" *Education* 91: 147–154.

[With Loren Grey.] *A Parent's Guide to Child Discipline.* New York: Hawthorn Books. (Translation: Danish, 1971.)

"The Potential of the White House Conference on Children and Youth." *National Committee on Children and Youth Reporter* 1: 1–2.

"Psychotherapie: Überwindung falscher gesellschaftlicher Normen." [Psychotherapy: Overcoming Wrong Social Standards.] In *Die Wirklichkeit und das Böse*, edited by U. Derbolowsky and E. Stephan. Hamburg: Hans Christian Verlag, pp. 247–257.

"The War Between the Generations." *British Journal of Social Psychiatry* 4: 31–39.

"The White House Conference on Children and Youth—Another Triumph of Institutionalism?" *Humanist* 30: 6–7.

1971

Character Education and Spiritual Values in an Anxious Age. Chicago: Alfred Adler Institute.

Counseling the Adolescent. Edited by James A. Peterson and Neysa M. Peterson. Winooski, Vt.: Vermont Educational Television Network.

"The Delinquent in the Community." *Individual Psychologist* 8: 7–14.

[With Loren Grey.] *Demokrati og Opdragelse: En Vejledning for Foraeldre.* [Democracy and Discipline: A Guide for Parents.] (Danish ed. of *A Parent's Guide to Child Discipline.*) Translated by Nina Lautrup-Larsen. Copenhagen: Hans Reitzel.

"Epilogue." In *Techniques for Behavior Change: Applications of Adlerian Theory*, edited by Arthur Nikelly. Springfield, Ill.: Charles C. Thomas, pp. 217–219.

"Foreword." In *Teach Your Baby*, by Genevieve Painter. New York: Simon & Schuster, pp. 7–9.

"Individual Psychology: The Adlerian Point of View." In *Perspectives on Personality: A Comparative Approach*, edited by Salvatore R. Maddi. Boston: Little, Brown, pp. 260–272.

[With Thomas W. Allen.] "An Interview with Rudolf Dreikurs." *Counseling Psychologist* 3: 49–54.

[With Bernice Bronia Grunwald and Floy Pepper.] *Maintaining Sanity in the Classroom: Illustrated Teaching Techniques.* New York: Harper & Row.

[With Miriam Pew, W. L. Pew, and Vicki Soltz Statton.] *Manual for Life Style Assessment: Part 1.* Minneapolis: Hennepin County Court Services.

La Psychologie Adlerienne. [Adlerian Psychology.] Paris: Blood & Gay.
Social Equality: The Challenge of Today. Chicago: Henry Regnery.

1972

"The ABC's of Guiding the Child." *Prime Areas* [Brit. Col. Primary Teachers Association] 15: 1–2.
"Am I an Adlerian?" *Individual Psychologist* 9: 35–37.
The Challenge of Child Training: A Parent's Guide. New York: Hawthorn Books.
"Comments." In *Critical Incidents in School Counseling,* edited by Vincent F. Calia and Raymond J. Corsini. Englewood Cliffs, N.J.: Prentice-Hall, pp. 95–97, 160–161, 172–174, 213–214, 226–228, 283–285.
[With Loren Grey.] *Como Lograr la Disciplina en el Niño y en el Adolescente: Guia Practica para Padres y Maestros.* [How to Accomplish Discipline with the Child and the Adolescent: A Practical Guide for Parents and Teachers.] Buenos Aires: Editorial Paidos.
"Conflict Solving." *Alberta Counsellor* 2: 13–22.
Coping with Children's Misbehavior: A Parent's Guide. New York: Hawthorn Books.
"Counseling a Boy." *Journal of Individual Psychology* 28: 223–231.
[With Vicki Soltz.] *Le Defi de l'Enfant.* [The Challenge of the Child.] Translated by Yves Leschallier de l'Isle. Paris: Laffont.
[With Pearl Cassel.] *Discipline Without Tears.* Toronto: Alfred Adler Institute of Ontario. Also, New York: Hawthorn Books.
"Dreikurs Sayings." *Individual Psychologist* 9: 38–45.
"Education at the Crossroads." *Individual Psychologist* 11: 56–62.
[With Don Dinkmeyer.] *Encorajando Criancas a Apprender.* [Encouraging Children to Learn.] Translated by T. Ebeli and Y. Salles. São Paulo: Edicoes Melhoramentos.
"Equality: The Life-Style of Tomorrow." *Futurist* 6: 153–155.
"Family Counseling." *Journal of Individual Psychology* 28: 207–222.
[How to Get Along With Oneself: Selected Papers.] Edited and translated by Juliet Cavadas. Athens: Kedros.
"The Individual Psychological Approach." In *Handbook of Child Psychoanalysis,* edited by Benjamin B. Wolman. New York: Van Nostrand Reinhold, pp. 415–459.
"Margaret Goldman, 1920–1971." *Journal of Individual Psychology* 28: 113–114.
[With Bernice Grunwald and Floy Pepper.] "Never Underestimate the Power of Children." *Intellectual Digest,* July 1972, pp. 54–56.
"The Realization of Equality in the Home." *Individual Psychologist* 9: 46–55.
Soziale Gleichwertigkeit: Die Forderung unserer Zeit. [Social Equality: The Demand of Our Time.] Stuttgart: Ernst Klett.
"Technology of Conflict Resolution." *Journal of Individual Psychology* 28: 203–206.
"Toward a Technology of Human Relationship." *Journal of Individual Psychology* 28: 127–136.

1973

[With Manford Sonstegard.] "The Adlerian Approach to Group Counseling of Children." In *Counseling Children in Groups: A Forum,* edited by Merle M. Ohlsen. New York: Holt, Rinehart & Winston, pp. 47–77.
[With Harold H. Mosak.] "Adlerian Psychotherapy." In *Current Psychotherapies,* edited by Raymond Corsini. Itasco, Ill.: Peacock, pp. 35–83.
[With Erik Blumenthal.] *Eltern und Kinder: Freunde oder Feinde?* [Parents and Children: Friends or Enemies?] Stuttgart: Ernst Klett.
"The Private Logic." In *Alfred Adler: His Influence on Psychology Today,* edited by Harold H. Mosak. Park Ridge, N.J.: Noyes Press, pp. 19–31.

"Rudolf Dreikurs: 1897–1972." In *Psychotherapie in Selbstdarstellungen,* edited by Ludwig J. Pongratz. Bern, Switzerland: Hans Huber, pp. 107–128.

1974

[With Shirley Gould and Raymond J. Corsini.] *Family Council: The Dreikurs Technique for Putting an End to War Between Parents and Children (and Between Children and Children).* Chicago: Henry Regnery.

1977

"Holistic Medicine and the Function of Neurosis," *Journal of Individual Psychology* 33: 171–192.

Undated

Alfred Adler's Individualpsychologie. Translated by Pieter H. Ronge and A. C. Pabbruwe. Rotterdam: J. M. Bredee's Uitevers, 193?.

Eisagoge eis ten Atomiken Psychologian. [Greek edition of *Fundamentals of Adlerian Psychology.*] Translated by Juliet Cavadas. Athens: Ekdotikos Oiskos M. S. Saribaxebane, 196?.

Audiovisual Materials

Counseling Demonstration with Pre-adolescents. Cincinnati: Sound Seminars. 46 min. tape.

Equality: The Challenge of Our Time. Cincinnati: Sound Seminars. 54 min. tape.

The Family Power Struggle: Counseling Session with Parents. Cincinnati: Sound Seminars. 46 min. tape.

Masculinity: The Male's Dilemma. Cincinnati: Sound Seminars. 58 min. tape.

A Mother with Two Sons: Two Counseling Sessions. 2 tapes. Cincinnati: Sound Seminars. 58 min. & 58 min.

The Predicament of Motherhood. Cincinnati: Sound Seminars. 45 min. tape.

The Underachiever: Counseling Parents of Five Children. Cincinnati: Sound Seminars. 57 min. tape.

Understanding the Difficult Child. Cincinnati: Sound Seminars. 46 min. tape.

Your Child and Discipline. Washington, D.C.: National Education Association. Color filmstrip and 15 min. 33⅓ rpm record.

Video Tapes

Counseling the Adolescent. Ten 30-min. programs. University of Vermont, June 1971.

Dynamics of Classroom Behavior. Twelve 30-min. programs. University of Vermont and the Vermont Educational Television Network, 1968.

[With Bernice Grunwald.] *Motivating Children to Learn.* Fifteen 30-min. programs. University of Vermont and the Vermont Educational Television Network, 1970.

All of the above are available through the Great Plains National Educational Television Library, University of Nebraska, Lincoln, Nebr. 68508.

Understanding Your Children. Twenty-six 60-min. programs, produced at the University of Vermont with the Vermont Educational Television Network, 1969. Available through Eastern Educational Television Network, Newton Upper Falls, Mass.

Index